'Nobler imaginings and mightier struggles'
Octavia Hill, social activism and the remaking of British society

For Hugh, Bertie, Charlie and Harry
and
Julie, Reuben and Toby
with our thanks

'Nobler imaginings and mightier struggles'
Octavia Hill, social activism and the remaking of British society

Edited by
Elizabeth Baigent and Ben Cowell

LONDON
INSTITUTE OF HISTORICAL RESEARCH

Published by
UNIVERSITY OF LONDON
SCHOOL OF ADVANCED STUDY
INSTITUTE OF HISTORICAL RESEARCH
Senate House, Malet Street, London WC1E 7HU

All papers © their respective authors 2016
All rights reserved

ISBN 978 1 909646 00 1

Contents

Acknowledgements	vii
About the contributors	ix
Abbreviations	xiii
List of illustrations	xv
Foreword *Dame Helen Ghosh, director general, National Trust*	xix

I. 'The habit of seeing and sorting out problems': Octavia Hill's life and afterlife — **1**

1. Octavia Hill: 'the most misunderstood … Victorian reformer'
   Elizabeth Baigent — 3

2. Octavia Hill: lessons in campaigning
   Gillian Darley — 27

II. 'Beauty is for all': art in the life and work of Octavia Hill — **45**

3. Octavia Hill: the practice of sympathy and the art of housing
   William Whyte — 47

4. Octavia Hill's Red Cross Hall and its murals to heroic self-sacrifice
   John Price — 65

5. 'The poor, as well as the rich, need something more than meat and drink': the vision of the Kyrle Society
   Robert Whelan — 91

6. Octavia Hill: the reluctant sitter
   Elizabeth Heath — 119

III. 'The value of abundant good air': Octavia Hill and the meanings of nature — **139**

7. Octavia Hill, nature and open space: crowning success or campaigning 'utterly without result'
   Elizabeth Baigent — 141

8. Octavia Hill and the English landscape — 163
   Paul Readman

IV. 'A common inheritance from generation to generation': Octavia Hill and preservation — 185

9. 'To every landless man, woman and child in England': Octavia Hill and the preservation movement — 187
   Astrid Swenson

10. Octavia Hill and the National Trust — 209
    Melanie Hall

V. 'The loving zeal of individuals which cannot be legislated for by Parliament': Octavia Hill's vision in historical context — 241

11. At home in the metropolis: gender and ideals of social service — 243
    Jane Garnett

12. Octavia Hill, Beatrice Webb, and the Royal Commission on the Poor Laws, 1905–9: a mid Victorian in an Edwardian world — 255
    Lawrence Goldman

VI. Hill's legacy — 275

13. 'Some dreadful buildings in Southwark': a tour of nineteenth-century social housing — 277
    William Whyte

14. For the benefit of the nation: politics and the early National Trust — 295
    Ben Cowell

Index — 317

Acknowledgements

This volume comes out of a conference of the same title which was held at the National Trust's Sutton House, London, on 27 and 28 September 2012. We should like to thank all of those who were involved in it: the staff of Sutton House, particularly Christopher Cleeve and Robyn Finney for their generous hospitality and home-made cakes (which are still fondly remembered); Octavia Housing, particularly chief executive Grahame Hindes for facilitating the generous sponsorship of the conference, and staff members Hannah Thompson and Rachel Harrison who helped with its administration and the tour of housing sites with which it ended; Jessica Hindes of Royal Holloway, University of London, for her invaluable and self-effacing help with the conference's planning and execution; the opening speaker, Dame Fiona Reynolds, director general of the National Trust, for setting the scene so aptly; the session chairs – Dr. Peter Funnell of the National Portrait Gallery, Professor Charles Watkins, of the University of Nottingham, Loyd Grossman of The Heritage Alliance, Samuel Jones of Tate, and Jessica Hindes – for ably introducing our speakers and guiding our discussion; the participants for lively questions and pleasant conversations; and all the speakers, including those whose papers became chapters in this volume, but also our graduate student speakers whose papers greatly added to the conference's first day.

The process of translating the conference papers into a book has had to fit around many busy schedules, and it is a pleasure to thank the publishers, particularly Jane Winters, professor of digital history and head of publications at the Institute of Historical Research (IHR), University of London, and all the contributors for seeing the project through to the end.

The book has benefited greatly from its illustrations, made possible by a grant from the Scouloudi Foundation, in association with the IHR, for which we are most grateful. We hope the images and maps increase readers' use and enjoyment of the volume. The institutions and individuals who have made their images available to us are credited alongside the relevant illustration, but are warmly thanked here, particularly where they did so at no or a reduced cost. Giles Darkes's expert help with cartography is warmly acknowledged.

Many institutions have helped the contributors and editors of this book: the National Trust has supported the project in a number of ways, including as partner in the conference and as the custodian of the archives on which several contributors depended (archival staff Janette Harley and Iain Shaw deserve particular thanks). The Octavia Hill Birthplace Museum Trust, Wisbech, under its director Peter Clayton has been a supportive presence, while Patricia McGuire, archivist, King's College, Cambridge, has given generous assistance to various authors. Other institutions and individuals are named separately in the chapter footnotes.

Finally, thanks must go to our families (Hugh, Bertie, Charlie and Harry, Julie, Reuben and Toby) for their patience: their knowledge of the little lady in the mushroom hat, as C. R. Ashbee memorably called Octavia Hill, is probably more extensive than they'd bargained for. This book is dedicated to them.

Elizabeth Baigent, Oxford, and Ben Cowell, Newport, Essex.

About the contributors

Elizabeth Baigent is reader in the history of geography at the University of Oxford. She publishes widely on the history of travel, exploration and cartography. She became interested in the early conservation movement while research director of the *Oxford Dictionary of National Biography* and her work on Hill and other conservationists such as Sir Robert Hunter and Edward North Buxton stems from this time.

Ben Cowell is regional director for the National Trust in the east of England. He is also deputy chairman of The Heritage Alliance, and worked formerly for English Heritage and the Department for Culture, Media and Sport. He has published widely on aspects of history and heritage, including a short biography of Sir Robert Hunter, co-founder of the National Trust.

Gillian Darley is a writer and biographer. Her biography of Octavia Hill was first published in 1990 and the revised edition, retitled *Octavia Hill: Social Reformer and Founder of the National Trust* came out in 2010. Gillian is a trustee of the Society for the Protection of Ancient Buildings (SPAB) and from 2008 to 2015 was its nominee to the National Trust council. She is president of the Twentieth Century Society.

Jane Garnett is fellow and tutor in history at Wadham College, Oxford. From 1994 to 2004 she was consultant editor for women on the *Oxford Dictionary of National Biography*. She has published widely on the intellectual, cultural and religious history of the nineteenth, twentieth and twenty-first centuries, and on gender and visual culture over wider periods. Recent publications include (with Gervase Rosser), *Spectacular Miracles: Transforming Images in Italy from the Renaissance to the Present* (2013) and (co-edited with Alana Harris), *Rescripting Religion in the City: Migration and Religious Identity in the Modern Metropolis* (2013).

Lawrence Goldman is director of the Institute of Historical Research at the School of Advanced Study, University of London, where he is also professor of history. From 2004 to 2014 he was editor of the *Oxford Dictionary of National Biography*, and he has published extensively on nineteenth-century Britain, including *Science, Reform, and Politics in Nineteenth Century Britain: the Social Science Association 1857–86* (2002), and most recently *The Life of R. H. Tawney: Socialism and History* (2013).

Melanie Hall is associate professor and director of museum studies, in the History of Art and Architecture Department at Boston University, USA, having previously worked on the listed buildings resurvey for English Heritage. She writes on material culture and the preservation of landscapes and buildings at the turn of the twentieth century, and recently edited *Towards World Heritage: International Origins of the Preservation Movement 1879–1930* (2011). She was for many years a volunteer expert lecturer for the National Trust and is completing a history of its origins.

Elizabeth Heath is assistant curator (research) at the National Portrait Gallery, London (NPG), working part-time on the later Victorian portraits catalogue for which she has undertaken research into portraits of Octavia Hill. She is a third-year collaborative PhD student, based at the NPG and the University of Sussex, and her research investigates the professional practice of Sir George Scharf, the gallery's first secretary and director (1857–95).

John Price is a lecturer in modern British history at Goldsmiths, University of London. His research interests include constructions of civilian heroism, the history of social movements and popular protest, and the history of London. His recent publications include *Everyday Heroism: Victorian Constructions of the Heroic Civilian* (2014) and *Heroes of Postman's Park: Heroic Self-Sacrifice in Victorian London* (2015).

Paul Readman is professor of modern British history at King's College London. He is the author of *Land and Nation in England: Patriotism, National Identity, and the Politics of Land 1880–1914* (2008), and has co-edited two other volumes including *Borderlands in World History, 1700–1914* (2014). His present research focuses on historical pageants and the place of the past in modern Britain, funded by the Arts and Humanities Research Council, and on meanings of landscape in England between c.1750 and c.1950.

Astrid Swenson is senior lecturer in European history at Brunel University. She obtained her PhD from Cambridge University and was a research fellow at the Institute for Human Science,s Vienna, the Cambridge Victorian Studies Group, and Darwin College, Cambridge. Her publications include *The Rise of Heritage: Preserving the Past in France, Germany and England* (2013) and (co-edited with Peter Mandler) *From Plunder to Preservation: Britain and the Heritage of Empire* (2013).

Robert Whelan was editorial director of the independent think-tank Civitas until his retirement in 2015. His books include *Helping the Poor: Friendly Visiting, Dole Charities, and Dole Queues*; *Octavia Hill and the Social Housing Debate* and *Octavia Hill's Letters to Fellow-workers 1871–1911*.

Notes on contributors

William Whyte is professor of social and architectural history and a fellow of St. John's College, Oxford. He is the author of *Oxford Jackson* (2006) and *Redbrick: a Social and Architectural History of Britain's Civic Universities* (2015), and editor or co-editor of several other volumes, including *George Gilbert Scott: an Architect and his Influence* (2014). He is currently completing a book on nineteenth-century church buildings, which grew out of his 2014 Hensley Henson lectures.

Abbreviations

AHRC	Arts and Humanities Research Council
BWD	Beatrice Webb's Diary <http://digital.library.lse.ac.uk/collections/webb>
COS	Charity Organization Society
CPS	Commons Preservation Society
CWAC	City of Westminster Archives Centre, London
KCC	King's College, Cambridge library
KSAR	Kyrle Society Annual Reports
LCC	London County Council
LFW	*Octavia Hill's Letters to Fellow Workers 1872–1911, together with an Account of the Walmer Street Industrial Experiment*, ed. R. Whelan, with A. Hoole Anderson, I. Ginsberg, L. Probert, G. Tucker, S. Wheeler and E. Wilson, and a foreword by J. Lewis (2005)
NT	National Trust
NTA	National Trust archive, Swindon
NYPL	New York Public Library
ODNB	*Oxford Dictionary of National Biography*, ed. H. C. G. Matthew, B. H. Harrison and L. Goldman, online edn.
OHBMT	Octavia Hill Birthplace Museum Trust, Wisbech
RCPL	Royal Commission on the Poor Laws and Relief of Distress
SPAB	Society for the Preservation of Ancient Buildings, London
TNA	The National Archives of the UK, Kew

List of illustrations

Figure		
1.1	Octavia Hill's gravestone, Crockham Hill churchyard.	8
1.2	Tomb effigy to Octavia Hill, Crockham Hill Church.	9
1.3	Memorial bench to Octavia Hill.	10
1.4	View from memorial bench.	10
1.5	Octavia Hill memorial window, Crockham Hill Church.	15
1.7	Memorial stone to Octavia Hill, Westminster Abbey, installed in 2012.	19
1.6	Blue plaque to Octavia Hill at 2 Garbutt Place, Marylebone, London.	19
1.8	Octavia Hill Woodlands, Toys Hill, Kent, part of the National Trust's Octavia Hill Centenary Trail.	20
2.1	Undated photograph of Wisbech taken from North Brink looking towards Octavia Hill's birthplace on the right.	28
2.2	Margaret Gillies' on-the-spot sketches of women and children at work in the mines.	32
2.3	Paradise Place, now Garbutt Place. Sketch by Karel Kirby-Turner, 1956.	37
2.4	Miranda Hill.	38
2.5	Alfriston Clergy House before restoration.	41
2.6	Back-to-back houses at Derry Street, Camden. Photograph by Henry Dixon and Son, 1897.	43
2.7	Derry Street, Camden. Photograph by Henry Dixon and Son, 1897. These houses, owned by Mr. and Mrs. Flight, exemplified the problems that Hill described to the commissioners in 1884.	43
4.1	The interior of the Red Cross Hall, Southwark (*English Illustrated Magazine*, June 1893).	73
4.2	Illustration of Walter Crane's mural, 'Alice Ayres', erected in the Red Cross Hall in 1890 (*English Illustrated Magazine*, June 1893).	74
4.3	The Union Street Fire, Borough, 1885 (unreferenced newspaper cutting, Southwark Local History Library).	75
4.4	Illustration showing part of the planned panel layout for the mural project in the Red Cross Hall (*English Illustrated Magazine*, June 1893).	77

4.5	Walter Crane, *Study for 'Alice Ayres' for the Red Cross Hall, Southwark, c.*1889.	79
4.6	Enlarged detail from Walter Crane, *Study for 'Alice Ayres' for the Red Cross Hall, Southwark, c.*1889.	80
4.7	Enlarged detail from Walter Crane, *Study for 'Alice Ayres' for the Red Cross Hall, Southwark, c.*1889.	81
4.8	Illustration of the Walter Crane mural, 'Jamieson', erected in the Red Cross Hall in 1892 (*English Illustrated Magazine*, June 1893).	83
5.1	Cover of the Kyrle Society Annual Report for 1897.	94
5.2	The verse by George Herbert in mosaic on St. John's church, Waterloo.	102
5.3	Drury Lane burial ground.	104
5.4	The mosaic of *The Sower* is the only one of the original Red Cross garden ornaments to remain on the site.	106
5.5	The prince and princess of Wales opening Vauxhall Park on 7 July 1890 (engraving from *The Illustrated London News*, 12 July 1890).	110
5.6	Bas-relief of St. Christopher, erected on St. Christopher's Buildings, St. Christopher's Place, by the Kyrle Society in 1879.	114
6.1	Octavia Hill, by John Singer Sargent, oil on canvas, 1898.	122
6.2	Octavia Hill, possibly by a Barton family member, pencil, *c.*1864.	132
6.3	Octavia Hill, by Edward Clifford, pencil, 1877.	135
8.1	Churchyard Bottom Wood (later Queen's Wood), Highgate.	168
8.2	West Wickham Common, Kent.	171
8.3	A footpath through bluebells in April at Mariners Hill, near Crockham Hill, Kent.	172
9.1	National Trust Executive Committee Meeting on 15 April 1912. Watercolour by Thomas Matthews Rooke (1924).	188
9.2	Reverse of watercolour of National Trust Executive Committee Meeting on 15 April 1912.	189
10.1	Alfriston Clergy House after restoration, photograph by C. R. Ashbee, *c.*1898.	230
10.2	Long Crendon Courthouse, Buckinghamshire.	232

10.3	Stone bench to Caroline Southwood Hill, on Mariners Hill, Kent.	380
12.1	Beatrice Webb.	257
13.1	Map of Southwark, based on the Ordnance Survey of 1894–96.	278
13.2	Modern-day map of Southwark.	279
14.1	Robert Hunter (undated).	299
14.2	Canon Hardwicke Rawnsley (undated).	299
14.3	Sayes Court (undated).	305

Table

5.1	Receipts to the four branches of the Kyrle Society, in pounds, selected years.	103

Acknowledgements for figures

Figures 1.1, 1.2, 1.3, 1.4, 1.5, 5.1, 5.2, 5.3, 5.5 are the chapter authors' own images. Figure 1.6 © Historic England. Figures 1.7, 2.3 8.3, 10.1, 14.1, 14.2 ©National Trust. Figure 2.1 ©National Trust/Sue James. Figure 2.4 © Westminster City Archives. Figures 2.5 and 2.6 courtesy of Camden Local Studies and Archives Centre. Figure 2.7 courtesy of The Octavia Hill Birthplace Museum Trust, Wisbech. Figure 4.3 courtesy of Southwark Local History Library. Figures 4.5, 4.6 and 4.7 reproduced with kind permission of the Royal Borough of Kensington and Chelsea Library and Arts Service. Figures 6.1 and 6.2 © National Portrait Gallery, London. Figure 6.3 © Collection of the Guild of St George, Sheffield Galleries & Museums Trust. Figure 8.1 courtesy of Friends of Queen's Wood. Figures 8.2 and 10.2 © David Anstiss/Creative Commons. Figures 9.1 and 9.2 courtesy of Andrew Oliver. Figure 10.1, King's College Cambridge (ref. CRA/1 vol. 5, 1898–9, 9/128). Figure 12.1 © London School of Economics. Figure 14.3 © Lewisham Local History and Archives.

Foreword

Dame Helen Ghosh, director general, National Trust

I am often asked for my view on how 'the spirit of the National Trust' might be best summarised. I long ago learned that there is no single 'spirit' and that almost all our millions of members and visitors would have their own view of what the trust represents and where we should focus our efforts.

As a historian by background, my response to the question is usually to reach to the past, to look at what our founders hoped we would achieve, or to trace the history of the issues we have championed. In 2012 the National Trust was pleased to mark the centenary of the death of one of our founders, Octavia Hill. Our extensive celebrations, enjoyed by no one more than my predecessor Fiona Reynolds, for whom Octavia Hill was a particular source of inspiration, culminated in a memorial's being installed in Westminster Abbey – the national pantheon.

As well as enjoying the public celebrations, the trust welcomed the chance to take a more critical and academic look at Octavia Hill and her life's work. This collection of papers given at a conference at Sutton House, Hackney, in September 2012 is the result. Hill, the best known of the trust's three founders, emerges from these pages as a woman of her time and background. Her devout faith and strong sense of social purpose led her to a set of beliefs about individual responsibility (the 'deserving' and 'undeserving' poor), the role of women and of government that many find surprising or indeed inimical now. But her tireless work to preserve and create beauty in nature and in the arts, to give people access to this beauty, and to trust them to appreciate it, remain inspiring. These are values which the trust holds to today – and of course the work of our many volunteers today follows the example of Hill and her 'fellow-workers', underpins our achievements, and brings a range of diverse people in touch with the trust through the bond of personal knowledge which Hill valued so highly.

The many facets of discussion in the book, which ranges across subjects as varied as the history of art, conservation, charity, women and religion, together give a far more rounded picture of Hill than has hitherto been possible. The chapters enable us to see the founding of the trust not just in terms of how it subsequently developed, but in the context of contemporary politics and culture in this country and abroad. The book is a good example of the value of academics working in partnership with organisations such as the National Trust. Researchers working in the humanities can throw light on issues of considerable significance to the world today, while entities like the National Trust can help to bring the benefits of scholarship to a wider audience. Collections such as this help us to use the past to guide action in the present and the future.

But it is of course not only in connection with the National Trust that the book can be read. Hill was active in an astonishing range of societies, campaigns, and schemes, and, reading about them, readers will I hope come away with a richer understanding of Octavia Hill and the various endeavours to which she devoted her life.

I. 'The habit of seeing and sorting out problems': Octavia Hill's life and afterlife

1. Octavia Hill: 'the most misunderstood ... Victorian reformer'*

Elizabeth Baigent

Octavia Hill (1838–1912) was in her lifetime, if not a household name, an acknowledged authority on a range of social problems and their solution. Her advice was sought on urban housing and its management, urban poverty, effective charity and poor people's lack of access to open space, while her views influenced public policy in Britain and private social initiatives in several countries.[1] Although most familiar to her contemporaries as a manager of housing for poor Londoners – something which she undertook as an individual, working with a fluctuating band of female volunteer 'fellow-workers', and not under the auspices of any institution – she was also widely known as a member of an impressive tally of important bodies.

Hill was sometimes a founder member and often the only prominent female member of these institutions, some of which are still active today. They included the Commons Preservation Society (founded 1865, active today as the Open Spaces Society, Hill joined by 1875);[2] the Kyrle Society (Hill was one of two founders in 1875/6, some regional branches active today);[3] the National Trust (founded 1895, active today, Hill was one of three founders);[4] the Army Cadet Force (various origins, including Hill's Southwark Cadet Company, formed in 1889, active today);[5] the Charity Organization Society (COS, founded as the Association for the Prevention

---

* A. S. Wohl, *The Eternal Slum: Housing and Social Policy in Victorian London* (1977), p. 179. I should like to thank the contributors to this volume for comments on this chapter.

[1] E.g., through her service on the Royal Commission for the Poor Laws, as Goldman elaborates in this volume. The Octavia Hill Verein in Berlin and the Octavia Hill Association in Philadelphia are two of the best known institutions to have adopted her ideas (Wohl, *Eternal Slum*, p. 181).

[2] G. Darley, *Octavia Hill* (1990), p. 168.

[3] E.g., the Bristol Kyrle Society, founded 1905, active from 1943 to the present as the Bristol Civic Society (V. Waite, *Bristol Civic Society (Incorporating the Bristol Kyrle Society): the First Sixty Years 1905–1965* (Bristol, 1965), reprinted in *Bristol Building and Design Centre Journal* (May 1965), reproduced at <http://www.bristolcivicsociety.org.uk/about-us/past-achievements> [accessed March and May 2014]).

[4] G. Murphy, *Founders of the National Trust* (1987).

[5] <https://armycadets.com/about-us/our-history/> [accessed 2 March 2014].

of Pauperisation and Crime in 1868, active today as Family Action, Hill was a founder member);[6] the Ladies' National Association for the Diffusion of Sanitary Knowledge, better known as the Ladies' Sanitary Association (active from at least 1857 to 1880 as a series of autonomous local branches, Hill present at the foundation and active afterwards);[7] and the Women's University Settlement (founded 1887, active today as Blackfriars Settlement, Hill closely involved from its inception).[8] This selection shows Hill fully embracing the voluntarism which dominated ideas of social activism in her youth and middle life.

Through individual and institutional action – and without ever having specifically intended it – Hill became a prominent actor in the large and influential 'feminine public sphere' which helped to define contemporary civil society and the nineteenth-century middle-class woman.[9] Conservative enough to think men's and women's gifts and responsibilities complementary rather than identical, and to oppose women's suffrage, Hill nonetheless had a very wide understanding of what women's roles were. She often played a leading part in the societies she joined, as the list above shows, while her numerous essays in periodicals and collections such as *The Homes of the London Poor* (1875) and *Our Common Land* (1877), her many letters to the press, and her public speaking (her essay 'Open spaces', for example, was originally a lecture to the National Health Society) show that she had a very catholic view of women's public roles.[10] Indeed, she thought involvement in public life a duty, not an option, for women. When a man she met in 1866 'defined a woman's duties ... He patronizingly enumerated little offices she might fulfil ... "Oh, certainly", I said, "if the real, solemn, large

[6] Darley, *Hill*, p. 113; M. Rooff, *A Hundred Years of Family Welfare* (1972); <http://www.family-action.org.uk/section.aspx?id=1155> [accessed 2 March 2014]; H. Barnett, *Canon Barnett: his Life, Work, and Friends* (2 vols., 1918), i. 28.

[7] B. Raynes Parker, 'The Ladies' Sanitary Association', *English Woman's Journal*, 14 Apr. 1858, p. 32; F. Prochaska, *Women and Philanthropy in Nineteenth-Century England* (Oxford, 1980); [Ladies' Sanitary Association], *The Black Hole in Our Own Bed Rooms* (c.1860); A. S. Wohl, *Endangered Lives: Public Health in Victorian Britain* (1983); L. Goldman, *Science, Reform, and Politics in Victorian Britain: the Social Science Association, 1857–1886* (Cambridge, 2002); A. Hepplewhite, '"The public vocation of women": lectures to ladies on sanitary reform in England, 1855–1870' (unpublished Simon Fraser University MA dissertation, 1996), esp. pp. 16–17.

[8] B. Judge, *Octavia Hill and the Women's University Settlement* (Wisbech, 1996); <http://www.blackfriars-settlement.org.uk/history> [accessed 2 March 2014].

[9] M. Smitley, *The Feminine Public Sphere: Middle-Class Women in Civic Life in Scotland, c.1870–1914* (Manchester, 2009); M. J. Peterson, *Family, Love, and Work in the Lives of Victorian Gentlewomen* (Bloomington, Ind., 1989).

[10] O. Hill, 'Open spaces', pp. 105–51, in O. Hill, *Our Common Land and Other Short Essays* (1877), from a lecture on 9 May 1877.

business of life does not demand too much of her thought and strength"'.[11] Though her housing work relied on volunteer labour (notably hers), she did not oppose paid work for women: rather the reverse, having always earned her own living, and coming from a family of women who did the same.[12] She is credited with having started professional housing management (something which she appeared to acknowledge as she began to train more housing managers than she had immediate need for in the houses under her control) and professional occupational therapy, and even as an early influence on accounting.[13] Thus, though she never articulated women's social advancement as part of 'the real, solemn, large business of life', such advancement unquestionably happened as she and women under her direction joined the numerous others attending to that business.[14]

Though Hill was part of the progressive shaping of a public sphere for women, by the time she reached old age, the principles of voluntarism and strict circumscription of public welfare provision which underpinned her work were in retreat before central state measures, including the Old Age Pension Act of 1908, and municipal welfare work, especially in housing and particularly as undertaken by the London County Council (formed in 1889), as Lawrence Goldman illustrates in this volume. Fearing that her reputation was narrowing around her apparently unbending adherence to an outdated ideology, her family and friends began even before her death to fashion a softer, more attractive reputation for posterity, one shaped more by personal qualities than by a rigid ideology. To mark her sixtieth birthday they commissioned a portrait from John Singer Sargent (1898, see Figure 6.1), as Elizabeth Heath discusses in detail in this volume. Sargent was by no means an obvious choice, and he presented a soft, reposeful and even tentatively glamorous view of his sitter, who freely admitted that she lacked such qualities. She wrote: 'my pity and sympathy were always with Martha

---

[11] Hill to Mary Harris, 5 Nov 1866 (cited on p. 94 of *Octavia Hill: Early Ideals, from Letters*, ed. E. S. Maurice (1928)).

[12] This is particularly emphasized in Darley, *Hill*.

[13] M. Brion, *Women in the Housing Service* (1995); A. A. Wilcock, *Elizabeth Casson OBE, MD, DPM, 1881–1954: Founder of the First School of Occupational Therapy in the UK, Dorset House, Bristol, 1st January 1930* (2004); A. A. Wilcock, *Occupation for Health* (2 vols., 2001–2); S. P. Walker, 'Octavia Hill: property manager and accountant', in *Women and their Money, 1700–1950: Essays on Women and Finance*, ed. A. Laurence, J. Maltby and J. Rutterford (2009), pp. 165–77.

[14] T. Adam, *Buying Respectability: Philanthropy and Urban Society in Transnational Perspective, 1840s to 1930s* (Bloomington, Ind., 2009) considers how Hill's influence spread to North America and the rest of Europe, particularly Germany. He argues that such 'cultural transfers' helped social elites to consolidate their position, but does not adduce any evidence that this was Hill's motive.

[the biblical woman who did all the housework while her sister Mary sat and listened to Jesus], and I have felt it hard to believe that hers was not the better part ... At any rate Martha's part must be mine, so I must see what can be made of it. Certainly the resolution to make pauses for quiet thought is a most difficult duty.'[15] Sargent's Hill appears to be pausing for just such quiet thought and finding it by no means difficult or unwonted.

After her death, relatives and sympathizers continued to craft a Hill who was more reflective and gentle Mary than busy and vigorous Martha. Obituaries and letters of appreciation appeared in the general British and US press, and in the specialist press (for example, *Charities Organization Review*, xxxii (1912); *The Friend*, 30 August 1912).[16] A sympathetic *Times* obituary on 15 August was followed the same day by an 'appreciation', an article the day afterwards on her 'teaching', and then a letter by Robert Hunter on 17 August drawing attention to her open space work and her many friendships.[17] These were not anodyne (the obituary, for example, admitted that her housing work had been eclipsed in scale by model and municipal housing schemes, and the article on her 'teaching' attributed her 'completely successful' housing projects to an iron rule over her tenants), but they were kind enough that Hill's friend and disciple Henrietta Barnett wrote: 'when I read obituary notices of her, crediting her with the commonplace virtues of kindness and unselfishness and gentleness, it annoyed me because those were not her virtues ... [She was] strong-willed ... often dictatorial in manner ... and she dealt out disapprobation and often scorn to those who fell below her standards for them'.[18] Hill frankly confessed the traits which Barnett observed and knew her shortcomings: 'Oh it is easy to work early and later, to keep accounts, and manage house-keeping, etc., but the gentle voice, the loving word, the ministry, the true tender spirit, these are great gifts, and will endure when the others have perished. The first are the works of strength, the others of goodness'.[19]

Hill's works of strength, though admired by Barnett, proved a minority taste. Canon Rawnsley in his memorial address dwelt instead on Hill's 'queenliness' – something which Jane Garnett examines in greater depth in this volume;[20] while the book-length memoirs about Hill which soon

---

[15] Hill to Mary Harris, 14 Jan. 1866 (cited in Maurice, *Hill*, p. 92).
[16] E.g. *Morning Post*, 15 Aug. 1912; *Boston Transcript*, 31 Aug. 1912, n. 124, in G. W. Liebmann, *Six Lost Leaders: Prophets of Civil Society* (Lanham, Md., 2001); 'Death of Miss Octavia Hill', *The Times*, 15 Aug. 1912, p. 7; R. Hunter, 'Miss Octavia Hill and open spaces', *The Times*, 17 Aug. 1912, p. 8.
[17] 'Octavia Hill and her teaching', *The Times*, 16 Aug. 1912, p. 5.
[18] Barnett, *Canon Barnett*, i. 30–1, and see Peterson, *Family, Love, and Work*.
[19] Maurice, *Hill*, p. 40.
[20] 'Deaths', *The Times*, 22 Aug. 1912, p. 7.

appeared emphasized the goodness that she aspired to, rather than the strength that came naturally to her. They included the rapidly published *Life of Octavia Hill* (1913), edited by Charles Edmund Maurice, Hill's brother-in-law and son of her spiritual mentor F. D. Maurice, and *Octavia Hill: Early Ideals* (1928), edited by her sister, Emily Southwood Maurice. These were complemented by Henrietta Barnett's extensive coverage in her memoir of *Canon Barnett: his Life, Work and Friends*;[21] the memoir in the *Dictionary of National Biography* (1927) by Helen Bosanquet, fellow member of the COS; *Octavia Hill* (1942) by Enid Moberly Bell, educationalist, feminist and, like Hill, committed Anglican; *Octavia Hill: Pioneer of the National Trust and Housing Reformer* (1956) by Hill's relation William Thomson Hill; *Octavia Hill* by Elizabeth E. M. White (1957) in the Cassell series commemorating 'Women of devotion and courage'; and *Pioneer Women: Hannah More, Mary Carpenter, Octavia Hill, Agnes Jones* by Margaret E. Tabor for the Society for Promoting Christian Knowledge in 1927. Just as Hill was unusually ready to go into print in her lifetime, so she was unusually widely memorialized after her death, overcoming even the uncommonly fierce competition for a place in the *Dictionary of National Biography*, a rather slim volume which recorded deaths in the decade her life came to an end. The memorials carefully cultivated her memory, helped by family affection, shared ideology and the fact that many of the authors were women, who have proved far more sympathetic to Hill than have men. The most effective memoirs carefully select letters to show Hill at her most attractive: those written as a young woman reveal her youthful idealism, high aspirations, ardour, search for a vocation and candour about her shortcomings.

Complementing these early commemorations in print were early physical memorials – an important one being by a woman – which similarly emphasized her gentler points: her spiritual nature, aesthetic sensibilities, generosity and sense of service. Hill left the Sargent portrait to the National Portrait Gallery, where it hung from 1915, securing an early place in the public's visual memory for her softened image. Shortly after Hill's death 'a commission was given to a gifted American sculptress, Miss Abbott, to make a recumbent figure of Miss Hill, in the belief that she would produce a more entirely satisfactory record of her spiritual power than is shown in Sargent's otherwise fine portrait'. The effigy was to be placed in Holy Trinity church, Crockham Hill, Kent, which Hill attended when at Larksfield, her retirement home, and in the graveyard of which she was buried under a simple gravestone with her sister Miranda and Harriet Yorke, the companion of her later years (see Figure 1.1). After delays due to Miss

---

[21] Barnett, *Canon Barnett*.

'Nobler imaginings and mightier struggles'

Figure 1.1. Octavia Hill's gravestone, Crockham Hill churchyard.

Abbott's failing health, the effigy was finally installed in December 1928. It portrays a recumbent Hill in flowing garb, the allusion to a knightly crusader tomb retrospectively hallowing her endeavours as a crusade against evil, 'fully confirm[ing]' the hope that Hill's spiritual qualities would be permanently memorialized (see Figure 1.2), and hinting at the 'nobility' of which she believed all capable.[22] Close to the church, the National Trust erected a stone memorial seat to Hill at Ide Hill, Kent (see Figure 1.3). With the inscriptions 'This land was given in memory of Octavia Hill 1915' and

[22] Miss Margaret J. Shaen to the editor, 1928, *The Spectator*, 21 July 1928, p. 20; <http://www.crockhamhillchurch.org/#!history/c1xu8> [accessed 26 Feb. 2014].

Octavia Hill: 'the most misunderstood ... Victorian reformer'

Figure 1.2. Tomb effigy to Octavia Hill, Crockham Hill Church.

'To the honoured memory of Octavia Hill who loving nature with a great love secured this view for the enjoyment of those who came after her', this monument emphasizes Hill's delight in views from uplands and her sense that such views could and should be widely shared (see Figure 1.4).[23] The beauty of the bench's situation contributes to the portrayal of the softer Hill, as does the walk along the River Wandle at Mitcham which was given in 1913 to the National Trust as a memorial to Hill.[24]

---

[23] The trust's landholdings at nearby Toys Hill were based around Hill's original gift of 1898 (<http://www.nationaltrust.org.uk/article-1356403422022/> [accessed 26 Feb. 2014]; <http://www.nationaltrust.org.uk/article-1356403422022/> [accessed 26 Feb. 2014]; <http://www.nationaltrust.org.uk/cs/Satellite?blobcol=urldata&blobheader=application%2Fpdf&blobheadername1=Content-Disposition&blobheadername2=MDT-Type&blobheadername3=Content-Type&blobheadervalue1=inline%3B+filename%3D%252Ftmp%252Ftrail_1356403423866%252Co.pdf&blobheadervalue2=abinary%3B+charset%3DUTF-8&blobheadervalue3=application%2Fpdf&blobkey=id&blobtable=MungoBlobs&blobwhere=1349112993534&ssbinary=true> [accessed 26 Feb. 2014]) (see Figures 1.3 and 1.8).

[24] 'Riverside walks and gardens', *The Times*, 26 Dec. 1913, p. 4.

Figure 1.3. Memorial bench to Octavia Hill.

Figure 1.4. View from memorial bench.

An 'unshakeable belief in the moral superiority of the middle and upper classes': Hill's fall from grace[25]

Despite her early pre-eminence, the cultivation of an attractive memory by her family and friends, and the remarkable success of the institutions which she helped to found, Hill fell from public favour in the UK during the twentieth century. Her opposition to women's suffrage and the welfare state, and her support for the COS, which came to epitomize middle-class busybodies from charities interfering in the lives of the poor people they professed to help, made her unattractive and alien to modern sensibilities. Moreover, her Christianity, when combined with her apparently wholehearted embrace of laissez-faire, made her, her projects and her writings seem hypocritical, pietistic and moralistic. Her fiercest critics were mostly men, among them left-leaning historians who worked on urban poverty. Gareth Stedman Jones, in *Outcast London* (1971) and *Languages of Class* (1983), was a biting critic. *Outcast London*'s Hill showed some insight into poor people's lives, for example petitioning George Peabody to allow single rooms to be rented by those who could not afford more (p. 204). Hill also demonstrated some foresight into how shallow some proposed solutions were, presciently warning, for example, of the dangers of reproducing inner London problems in outer suburbs (p. 323). On the whole, though, Stedman Jones considers Hill to have had a 'narrow imaginative range' (p. 196); her housing schemes to have been at best a 'palliative' (ch. 9) and at worst the ideological bulwark against the only real solution to the housing problem – municipal housing (p. 229). Hill's insistence that the rent be paid punctually showed 'unbending disregard' of the London economy's seasonality, for all her vaunted personal knowledge of her tenants (p. 265). Stedman Jones highlights Hill's belief that money given to the poor disappeared in drink (p. 300), while her management of the 'destructive classes' instilled bourgeois morals in them – and turned a tidy profit for bourgeois investors (p. 193).[26]

John Springhill's *Youth, Empire, and Society: British Youth Movements 1883–1940* (1977) made Hill's army cadet work look less than unique and ideologically reactionary, while Anthony Wohl's measured but critical accounts of her work in housing and public health, beginning in 1971 with 'Octavia Hill and the homes of the London poor', described her housing method as 'despotism', albeit 'benevolent'. He concluded that the final result of her work was negative: by proving that her system could never

---

[25] 'Octavia Hill', in *Founders of the Welfare State: a Series from New Society*, ed. P. Barker (1984), pp. 31–6, at p. 32.

[26] The *Five Per Cent Philanthropy* in John Nelson Tarn's 1973 book of that title.

solve the problem of housing for the poor she opened the door to municipal and state systems.[27] Peter Malpass, meanwhile, acknowledged her in 1984 as one of the *Founders of the Welfare State*, but accused her of having an 'unshakeable belief in the moral superiority of the middle and upper classes'.[28] Hill was not always recognizable in the straw woman whom critics attacked. Paul Spicker, commendably alert to the dignity of and respect due to poor people, appeared in a 1985 polemic to criticize Hill for disregarding their rights, when in fact she could be remarkably sensitive, and required her fellow workers to be similarly thoughtful.[29] 'I had rather be a table than a Ragged School child', she once memorably wrote, recoiling as Spicker did from condescending charity.[30] Much of the criticism levelled against Hill was gendered: in particular, she was criticized for the scale of her work, as if its being small scale marked her out as someone who could not see beyond the end of her nose, lacking the (masculine) detached gaze which could take in the general situation. Hill, the woman who aimed to lead housing reform by example, is myopic, whereas men who led by example – George Cadbury or Titus Salt, say – are visionary.

Though Hill's reputation waned in the UK, a fairly consistently kinder history was being told in the USA where she was fêted as an exemplar of the voluntarism and philanthropy which Americans admire.[31] Her influence in the USA was exerted through individual American women who had trained or worked with her and not least by the Octavia Hill Association, based in Philadelphia and influential in other cities, which linked her name squarely with housing reform. The Philadelphia association's historian, Fullerton Leonard Waldo, was sympathetic in *Good Housing that Pays: a Study of the Aims and the Accomplishment of the Octavia Hill Association, 1896–1917* (1917), while John F. Sutherland, in 'The origins of Philadelphia's Octavia Hill Association: social reform in the contented city' (1975), presented a picture of 'middle-class rigidity … alleviated by compassion'[32] (p. 34) within the association's housing management. His depiction was also of an organization which pioneered slum investigation and moved into

---

[27] 'Octavia Hill and the homes of the London poor', *Journal of British Studies*, x (1971), 105–31; Wohl, *Eternal Slum* (1977), ch. 7; Wohl, *Endangered Lives*.

[28] Barker, 'Octavia Hill', pp. 31–6, at p. 32.

[29] 'Legacy of Octavia Hill', *Housing* (June 1985), pp. 39–40. He has been a critic of Hill since his doctoral thesis, published as *Stigma and Social Welfare* (1984). See Brion, ch. 2 for more on his criticism.

[30] Hill to Mary Harris, 28 June 1856 (Maurice, *Hill*, p. 28).

[31] Anthony Wohl, though active in the USA, was a Briton by birth and education (see Hall and Swenson's chapter for more about her influence in the USA).

[32] 'The origins of Philadelphia's Octavia Hill Association: social reform in the contented city', *The Pennsylvania Magazine of History and Biography*, xcix (1975), p. 34.

politics to force through city-wide improvements in housing, underpinned by legislation.[33] Though far more moderate than later neoliberal US works, Sutherland ends by pointing to the continued relevance of Hill's personal system in the face of statist failures. Another favourable view came from Robert Bremner, the US historian of welfare and philanthropy, who in 1965 declared Hill to have wielded 'An iron scepter twined with roses', loved by and personally known to her tenants.[34]

Hill, sympathy and her 'poorer friends':[35] revisionism, celebration of Hill and reappraisal of Hill's context

In the late twentieth and early twenty-first centuries there have been several re-examinations of Hill's life and work from inside academic history and in the wider sphere of public affairs. In academia the intellectual and ideological context for this re-appraisal was the new attention to the role of women in the nineteenth century. While criticism of Hill in the 1970s and 1980s had been voiced largely by men, women historians led the re-examination of the social reformer. Early re-appraisals included Gillian Darley's *Octavia Hill: a Life* (1990), which, though far from anodyne, found much to commend in Hill's life and work. Robert Whelan from Civitas, an independent think tank, edited Hill's essays and letters on the social housing debate (1998) and her *Letters to Fellow Workers* (published by Kyrle Books, 2005), bringing Hill's own words to, and interpreting her doctrines of self-help for, a modern audience.[36] These works, together with Darley's *Oxford Dictionary of National Biography* memoir (2004), her revised biography *Octavia Hill* (2010) and a largely appreciative episode of *In Our Time* (BBC Radio 4, April 2011), chaired by a sympathetic Melvyn Bragg, drew renewed attention to the aspects of her work that are most acceptable to modern sensibilities. The revised 2010 edition of Darley's biography, for example, flags her acceptable roles (*Social Reformer and Founder of the National Trust*) in its subtitle. These works also pointed to the continuing relevance of

---

[33] *The Pennsylvania Magazine of History and Biography*, xcix (1975), 20–44.
[34] '"An iron scepter twined with roses": the Octavia Hill system of housing management', *Social Service Review*, xxxix (1965), 222–31.
[35] O. Hill, *Homes of the London Poor* (1875), p. 24.
[36] *Octavia Hill and the Social Housing Debate: Essays and Letters by Octavia Hill*, ed. R. Whelan (1998); *Octavia Hill's Letters to Fellow Workers 1872–1911, together with an Account of the Walmer Street Industrial Experiment*, ed. R. Whelan, with A. Hoole Anderson, I. Ginsberg, L. Probert, G. Tucker, S. Wheeler and E. Wilson, and a foreword by J. Lewis (2005) (hereafter individual 'letters to fellow-workers' [Hill used a hyphen] will be cited as Hill, *LFW*, 18xx). For more information about Civitas, see <http://www.civitas.org.uk/about.php> [accessed 6 March 2014].

Hill's work and the longevity of the institutions which she helped to found. As those institutions celebrated anniversaries, several issued publications that proclaimed Hill's achievements along with their own: for example, the Rowe Housing Trust with *Octavia Hill and Rowe Housing Trust* (1986); the Octavia Hill Housing Trust with *The Work of the Century: the Origins and Growth of the Octavia Hill Housing Trust in Notting Hill* (1998);[37] and the National Trust with a Hill memorial window for Holy Trinity church, Crockham Hill, Kent (1995) (see Figure 1.5), as well as Graham Murphy's *Founders of the National Trust* (1987).[38]

Besides being the subject of biographical treatments, Hill and her work feature in more general scholarship on nineteenth-century society, particularly social work and women's role in it. This scholarship has helped to uncover the extent and variety of women's social work, and provided more sensitive and nuanced portraits of its aims and methods, the constraints it came up against, and the opportunities it afforded women. By revealing women's social work as typical of the age and to some extent definitive of it, this research has tempered the exceptionalist comment of some earlier works about Hill.[39] In this vein, Jane Lewis in *Women and Social Action in Victorian and Edwardian England* (1991) took seriously the sense of duty which motivated Hill and other women to undertake voluntary social work, while in 'Social facts, social theory and social change: the ideas of Booth in relation to those of Beatrice Webb, Octavia Hill, and Helen Bosanquet' (1995) she carefully placed Hill's ideas in the context of contemporary debates.[40] Ruth Livesey, in 'Reading for character: women social reformers and narratives of the urban poor in late Victorian and Edwardian London', analysed how poor Londoners were described and placed in a wider narrative by Hill and others of the COS, on the one hand, and sensationalist journalists or novelists, on the other.[41] Diana Maltz's

---

[37] By P. Malpass, who also wrote 'Continuity and change in philanthropic housing organisations: the Octavia Hill Housing Trust and the Guinness Trust', *London Journal*, xxiv (1999), 38–57. Malpass is professor at the University of the West of England and writes for academic and professional audiences.

[38] The gift of the Orpington and Chislehurst National Trust Centre <http://www.crockhamhillchurch.org/#!history/c1xu8> [accessed 26 Feb. 2014].

[39] Typically such works challenged stereotypes, e.g. being titled *Public Lives: Women, Family and Society in Victorian Britain* (E. Gordon and G. Nair, 2003), though this has less about voluntary work than about women's social roles; or Smitley, *The Feminine Public Sphere: Middle-Class Women and Civic Life in Scotland* (Manchester, 2009). Peterson, in *Family, Love, and Work*, shows how enduring was the stereotype of women as absent from the world of work (p. 132).

[40] In *Retrieved Riches: Social Investigation in Britain, 1840–1914*, ed. D. Englander and R. O'Day (Aldershot, 1995), pp. 49–67.

[41] R. Livesey, 'Reading for character: women social reformers and narratives of the urban poor in late Victorian and Edwardian London', *Journal of Victorian Culture*, ix (2004), 43–68.

Octavia Hill: 'the most misunderstood ... Victorian reformer'

Figure 1.5. Octavia Hill memorial window, Crockham Hill Church.

British Aestheticism and the Urban Working Classes, 1870–1900: Beauty for the People (2006), though highly critical of Hill's work and the 'fantasy' which underpinned it, usefully set her approach in the context of a wider 'missionary aestheticism' – the attempt to improve the lot of poor people through art and beauty. The great bulk of the renewed attention to Hill concerned her housing reforms. Two of the few studies to consider her contribution to preservation of open spaces were Barbara T. Gates's *Kindred Nature: Victorian and Edwardian Women Embrace the Living World* (1998) and James H. Winter's *Secure from Rash Assault: Sustaining the Victorian Environment* (1999) – their American place of publication a witness to the fact that environmental history was far more highly developed in the USA than in the UK at this period. Winter in particular credits Hill with some quite advanced ecological views.[42]

Several recent examinations of nineteenth-century social work shared a postmodern willingness to engage with its affective and specifically religious sides. Frank Prochaska's *Women and Philanthropy in Nineteenth-Century England* (1980) took seriously the religious motives of women such as Hill: half of its empirical coverage was devoted to women who worked under 'the power of the cross'. Prochaska continued his sensitive examination in *Christianity and Social Service in Modern Britain: the Disinherited Spirit* (2006), again taking at face value the religious motives of early activists, however alien their outlook and perspectives to a modernist view. Against this background, Nancy Boyd gave explicit consideration to *Josephine Butler, Octavia Hill, Florence Nightingale* as 'social activists whose lives and vocations were shaped and directed by their theology'.[43] Sharing their world view, she presented very kind portraits of these *Three Victorian Women who Changed their World* (1982) and, in the case of Hill, thought that her religion had made her sympathetic, non-judgemental and broad-minded for her time, and caused her to give priority to 'mercy' rather than insist on 'law and order'.[44] Victoria N. Morgan and Clare Williams took the analysis further in *Shaping Belief: Culture, Politics, and Religion in Nineteenth-Century Writing* (2008) in which they considered the link between writing and religious belief in various authors including Hill. These sophisticated treatments of religion were a welcome change

---

[42] E.g., pp. 181–2 and 188, which report her arguments for the preservation of untidy and unfashionable natural landscapes.

[43] N. Boyd, *Josephine Butler, Octavia Hill, Florence Nightingale: Three Victorian Women who Changed their World* (1982), p. xv.

[44] Boyd, *Josephine Butler, Octavia Hill, Florence Nightingale*, p. 155. A similar comparison of Hill and Nightingale had been made in *The Times* very shortly after her death ('Octavia Hill and her teaching', *The Times*, 16 Aug. 1912, p. 5).

from some earlier assessments.[45] They ran in parallel with more explicitly Christian memorials to Hill. Richard Symonds, a member of the Society of Friends, pointed out in 1988 that of the *Alternative Saints: the Post-Reformation British People Commemorated by the Church of England* in 1980 only one, Josephine Butler, was female. The reason for this was, according to the (female) chair of the responsible committee, that 'behaviour which was held to imply sanctity in men only appeared as insanity when engaged in by women'.[46] In 1993, in *Far Above Rubies: the Women Uncommemorated by the Church of England*, Hill was first among those women whom Symonds claimed to have 'excited others to sanctity' (the Church of England's criterion for inclusion in its calendar), and thus to be worthy of commemoration as one of the 'Saints and Heroes of the Christian Church in the Anglican Communion'.[47] Hill's inclusion in 2000 as one of those 'Saints and Heroes' was another instance of her epitomizing wider issues of gender.[48]

At much the same time, from outside church and academy, came a number of frankly admiring texts, some overtly neoliberal, and others reflecting a more general loss of confidence in modernist, large-scale responses to urban problems. In 1997 a collection of Hill's writings was reissued for an American audience under James Payne's editorship. Entitled *The Befriending Leader: Social Assistance Without Dependency*, its political stance was clear. George W. Liebmann's *Six Lost Leaders: Prophets of Civil Society* (2001) praised just those aspects of Hill's work which Stedman Jones thought had stood in the way of social progress. Hill ('one small woman without the advantage of birth') personifies the ideology of self-help which she preached, and which the author admires and thinks vindicated by experiments with statist alternatives. The same ideology in the UK led the Institute for Economic Affairs ('the UK's original free-market think-tank') to publish *Octavia Hill and the Social Housing Debate* under Robert Whelan's editorship in 1998.[49] Meanwhile, from a US planning perspective, Samantha G. Driscoll's 2011 thesis 'Practical preservation in Philadelphia: the Octavia Hill Association 1896–1912' applauded Hill and the association for preserving existing buildings rather than advocating

---

[45] E.g., Spicker, *Stigma*, pp. 9–10, and 'Legacy'.

[46] Cited in *Far Above Rubies: the Women Uncommemorated by the Church of England*, ed. R. Symonds (1993), pp. vii, 2.

[47] She is remembered as a 'social reformer' on the anniversary of her death <http://www.churchofengland.org/prayer-worship/worship/texts/the-calendar/holydays.aspx> [accessed 28 Feb. 2014].

[48] Symonds, *Far Above Rubies*, p. 5.

[49] <http://www.iea.org.uk/about> [accessed 27 Feb. 2014].

modernist comprehensive clearance and rebuilding whose aesthetic and social consequences she regrets.[50]

These positive views from outside the academy were matched by publications about Hill in professional presses speaking to professional audiences. Thus housing managers could read of Hill's influence or system in pieces by Janet M. Upcott, who had been trained by Hill and wrote regularly for the housing management press, for example 'The management of municipal housing estates on Octavia Hill lines', published by the Association of Women House Property Managers in 1928; while the association's later incarnation, the Society of Women Housing Managers, published and republished *Housing Estate Management: Being an Account of the Development Work Initiated by Octavia Hill* (1938, 1946 and 1950). Marion Brion, a sometime housing manager, began her 1995 review of *Women in the Housing Service* with a thoughtful chapter devoted to Hill and her legacy.[51] Other professional views included Peter H. Mann's 'Octavia Hill: an appraisal' for the *Town Planning Review* (1952);[52] Ann A. Wilcock's *Occupation for Health* for the College of Occupational Therapists (2001–2);[53] Daphne Spain's 'Octavia Hill's philosophy of housing reform: from British roots to American soil' for the *Journal of Planning History* (2006);[54] and Stephen Walker's rediscovery of her influence on accounting for the Routledge International Studies in Business History series (2009).[55]

Although such publications have appeared with remarkable regularity over the century since Hill's death, their authors often claim Hill's contribution to have been forgotten, at least in their particular professional constituency. They also generally find it remarkable that a woman of her time should have achieved so much, the popular stereotype of the Victorian middle-class women in her private sphere having been little disrupted by academic studies showing women active in the public sphere. Professional studies are on the whole positive about Hill. Wilcock, for example, thinks Hill 'not widely known', but 'a gem of the nineteenth century' and 'the once missing link between nineteenth[-]century social activists and the development of occupational therapy in England' and

---

[50] S. G. Driscoll, 'Practical preservation in Philadelphia: the Octavia Hill Association 1896–1912' (unpublished University of Pennsylvania MA dissertation, 2011) <http://repository.upenn.edu/cgi/viewcontent.cgi?article=1166&context=hp_theses> [accessed 27 Feb. 2014].

[51] There are many other examples cited in M. Brion, *Women in the Housing Service* (1995).

[52] *Town Planning Review*, xxiii (1952), 223–37.

[53] A. A. Wilcock, *Occupation for Health* (2 vols., 2001–2).

[54] D. Spain, 'Octavia Hill's philosophy of housing reform: from British roots to American soil', *Journal of Planning History*, v (2006), 106–25.

[55] Walker, 'Octavia Hill'.

Octavia Hill: 'the most misunderstood ... Victorian reformer'

Figure 1.6. Blue plaque to Octavia Hill at 2 Garbutt Place, Marylebone, London.

Figure 1.7. Memorial stone to Octavia Hill, Westminster Abbey, installed in 2012.

Figure 1.8. Octavia Hill Woodlands, Toys Hill, Kent, part of the National Trust's Octavia Hill Centenary Trail.

the USA.[56] Brion's measured assessment readily credits Hill with starting housing management as a profession and making it a respected site of women's activity and expertise, and begins a tentative analysis of Hill's reputation in the light of women housing managers' continuing struggle for acceptance on an equal footing with men.

As well as being the subject of sustained attention in various presses, Hill continued to be commemorated more widely. One of the most important organizations involved in this was the Octavia Hill Society, formed in 1992 and based at Hill's birthplace in Wisbech, Cambridgeshire.[57] Bearing a blue plaque, erected by the Wisbech Society and Preservation Trust to Hill as 'One of the founders of the National Trust', the museum houses displays, organizes lectures and sermons, and publishes a series of booklets which bring Hill's life and work to a popular audience.[58] The first in the booklet series was Betty

---

[56] Wilcock, *Occupation for Health*, i. 381, 386. The seemingly inevitable Sargent portrait appears on p. 381.

[57] <http://www.octaviahill.org/octavia-hill-society/> [accessed 3 March 2014].

[58] <http://www.wisbech-society.co.uk/blueplaques.html> [accessed 2 March 2014]. The work of Peter Clayton in the society is of particular note.

Judge's *Octavia Hill and the Women's University Settlement* (1996), after a 1994 lecture of the same title; subsequent ones keep Hill in the regional and to some extent the national consciousness. The London Borough of Southwark erected a blue plaque ('Voted by the People') on Red Cross Hall to celebrate the fact that 'Octavia Hill, social reformer, established this garden, hall and cottages, and pioneered Army Cadets 1887–90', while in 1991 English Heritage unveiled a blue plaque at 2 Garbutt Place (previously Paradise Place), Marylebone, London, stating that 'Octavia Hill, housing reformer, co-founder of the National Trust began her work here' (see Figure 1.6).[59]

The centenary of Hill's death (2012) triggered a flurry of interest in her life and work, fostered particularly by societies in which she had been active. These included events by the National Trust (helped by the personal interest of the trust's first woman director general, Dame Fiona Reynolds), Hill's Birthplace Trust at Wisbech, and Octavia Housing, the social housing body which manages houses previously under Hill's charge. This interest was, unsurprisingly, celebratory and manifested itself in various ways. The National Trust and Birthplace Trust collaborated on a commemorative booklet and Centenary Green at Wisbech, while Octavia Housing produced its own brochure.[60] Combining the postmodern revival of interest in spiritual matters with the established church's continuing role as a site of commemoration, religious events and monuments in sacred places featured prominently. There were two nationally focused centenary services in October 2012 (one organized by the Birthplace Trust at Southwark Cathedral, the site of her memorial service in 1912, and the other by the National Trust at Westminster Abbey).[61] At the latter service a memorial stone was dedicated to her as 'Social reformer and a founder of the National Trust' (see Figure 1.7). Prominently placed in the centre of the nave, the stone accomplished what she had resisted: commemoration in the national pantheon.

The National Trust created two centenary trails in Kent, taking in the site of the 1915 memorial bench mentioned above, the beauty of the landscape conducive to a sympathetic popular view of her work (see Figure 1.4).[62] It

---

[59] <http://openplaques.org/plaques/510> [accessed 26 Feb. 2014]; <http://openplaques.org/plaques/1152> [accessed 26 Feb. 2014].

[60] P. Clayton, *Octavia Hill: Social Reformer and Co-Founder of the National Trust*, ed. G. Knappett, with a foreword by Dame Fiona Reynolds, (2012); Jenny Rossiter, *Nobler and Better Things: Octavia Hill's Life and Work* (2012) <http://www.octaviahill.org/octavia-hill-society/> [accessed 2 March 2014].

[61] 'News in brief', *The Times*, 17 Aug. 1912, p. 6.

[62] <http://www.nationaltrust.org.uk/cs/Satellite?blobcol=urldata&blobheader=application%2Fpdf&blobheadername1=Content-Disposition&blobheadername2=MDT-Type&blobheadername3=Content-Type&blobheadervalue1=inline%3B+filename%3D%252Ft

'Nobler imaginings and mightier struggles'

also set up Octavia Hill awards for volunteers active in the trust or the wider community in saving open space or promoting broader or imaginative use of such areas.[63] A centenary collection of essays from Demos, 'Britain's leading cross-party think-tank', entitled *'To the Utmost of her Power: the Enduring Relevance of Octavia Hill* (2012), saw prominent authors from fields such as housing and open space argue that Hill's ideas could speak to contemporary civil society. Tellingly, however, the editor Samuel Jones admitted that Hill was unknown to most of the contributors before they became involved in the project.[64] Her 'enduring relevance' was then created post hoc in one of Hill's periodic rediscoveries, and it would be more accurate to say that the authors identified Hill as a prominent advocate of voluntarism and self-help, which were as controversial in the era of prime minister David Cameron's 'big society' as they had been at the end of Hill's life.[65] Jones's editorship led, among other things, to his involvement in a BBC Radio 4 programme to mark the centenary of Hill's death, led by Tristram Hunt, Labour MP (13 August 2012), and to various lectures, including one on 13 September 2012 at the National Portrait Gallery, where the prominence of Sargent's portrait of Hill marks her continuing place in the national memory.[66] Hunt's article on Hill on the National Trust website pointed to her 'radical vision' as he joined those questioning whether she really was reactionary.[67]

Though welcome in many ways, centenary celebrations threatened to reinvigorate the exceptionalism which characterized earlier treatments of Hill – and much of the exceptionalist praise, like the earlier criticism, was gendered. There had been hints of this earlier in 1995, the National Trust's centenary year, when, for example, Hill alone among the founders

---

mp%252Ftrail_1356403423866%252C0.pdf&blobheadervalue2=abinary%3B+charset%3DUTF-8&blobheadervalue3=application%2Fpdf&blobkey=id&blobtable=MungoBlobs&blobwhere=1349112993534&ssbinary=true> and <http://www.nationaltrust.org.uk/article-1356403422022/> [accessed 26 Feb. 2014]. There is also a National Trust Octavia Hill Wisbech Heritage Walk which uses her name to attract interest to a trail around sites largely unconnected to her (<http://www.nationaltrust.org.uk/article-1356403129760/> [accessed 2 March 2014]).

[63] <http://www.nationaltrust.org.uk/get-involved/competitions-and-offers/octavia-hill-awards/> [accessed 28 Feb. 2014].

[64] <http://www.demos.co.uk> [accessed 28 Feb. 2014]; S. Jones, personal communication, Oct. 2012.

[65] Accusations that the 'big society' called on voluntary and/or charitable activity to plug gaps in shrinking state provision were widespread (see, e.g., <http://www.cass.city.ac.uk/research-and-faculty/centres/cass-centre-for-charity-effectiveness/resources/thought-pieces?a=37264> [accessed 28 Feb. 2014]).

[66] <http://www.bbc.co.uk/programmes/b01lswvg> [accessed 28 Feb. 2014]; personal knowledge, Sept. 2012.

[67] <http://www.nationaltrust.org.uk/article-1356393664070/> [accessed 29 March 2014].

had a rose named after her.⁶⁸ The centenary of the death of Robert Hunter (1844–1913), who was much more important than Hill in establishing the National Trust on a firm and enduring footing, and active in many other preservation societies, passed with scant celebration at the National Trust or more widely.⁶⁹ Ben Cowell's short if attractive memoir of Hunter was not an official publication, notwithstanding Cowell's employment by the trust;⁷⁰ Hunter has no place in Westminster Abbey or in the Church of England's calendar, notwithstanding his national role and firm faith, or on the National Portrait Gallery's walls, and the 2013 conference 'Heritage past, present and future', co-organized by the Arts and Humanities Research Council (AHRC), English Heritage, The National Trust and the Society of Antiquaries of London, marked the centenary of the Ancient Monuments Consolidation and Amendment Act of 1913 rather than of Hunter's death.⁷¹ Ironically, Hill, smiling out through her Sargent portrait, threatened to become the celebrity face of Victorian open space activism.

As part of the Hill centenary programme, and to complement wholeheartedly celebratory events, Elizabeth Baigent of the University of Oxford and Ben Cowell of the National Trust, with generous sponsorship by Octavia Housing, organized an academic conference on Hill. Entitled '"Nobler imaginings and mightier struggles": Octavia Hill and the remaking of British society', the conference aimed to re-assess Hill and her work critically and to examine how various academic, professional and popular portrayals of Hill did or did not intersect. The centenary was the immediate prompt for the conference, but it was set against a century of claims that Hill had been forgotten and misunderstood. Hill's regular rediscovery/reinvention in professional presses has been noted, and Anthony Wohl's 1977 claim, in the title of this essay, that Hill was the 'most misunderstood … Victorian reformer' echoes that made in the days immediately following Hill's death that 'the real lessons' of her life and work had been 'obscured by misapprehension [and] constantly neglected and [were] in danger of being forgotten'.⁷² The conference was also set against at least a century

---

⁶⁸ By Harkness, UK (<http://www.rosefile.com/RosePages/RosePageNo.php?866> [accessed 9 May 2014]).

⁶⁹ L. W. Chubb, 'Hunter, Sir Robert (1844–1913)', rev. G. Murphy, *Oxford Dictionary of National Biography* (Oxford, 2004; online edn., Oct. 2007) [accessed 20 Feb. 2014] (hereafter '*ODNB*').

⁷⁰ B. Cowell, *Sir Robert Hunter: Co-founder and 'Inventor' of the National Trust* (Stroud, 2013).

⁷¹ 16–17 Sept. 2013 at the Society of Antiquaries, Burlington House; personal knowledge Sept. 2013; Heritage Past, Present and Future conference <http://www.youtube.com/playlist?list=PLGOCpw7BaRwXsx8SbPhfYCLlU7GkmHH65> [accessed 28 Feb. 2012].

⁷² 'Octavia Hill and her teaching', *The Times*, 16 Aug. 1912, p. 5.

of conflicting claims about Hill, prompted by changing political and economic ideologies and buttressed by the abundance of primary sources by and about her. Her working life extended into six decades, and her words range from private letters of youth, to polished public speeches or articles of middle age, to the unprepared comments of old age.

With an oeuvre of this size and variety, Hill can be portrayed justifiably as a reactionary (citing, for example, her chilling rejection of state involvement in poverty relief in a memorandum to fellow members of the Royal Commission on the Poor Law who had recommended some small reforms, or her view that the army cadets would catch 'the young lad before he gets in with a gang of loafers').[73] But she can also come across as a sensitive and remarkably modern spirit, as the comment about the Ragged School child above shows. Hill's was not a simple journey from an idealist and imaginative youth to a narrower old age. She, like most of us, held seemingly contradictory views throughout her life: the elderly Hill, for example, still ardently resisted state intervention in housing, but had come round to thinking that municipal authorities should supply open spaces in towns, while private efforts should concentrate on wilder spots.[74]

The conference, then, was prompted by a recognition of Hill's complexity and of how a reappraisal was timely, based on careful reading of works by her and those who knew her, as well as sensitivity to the context in which she worked and a resistance of exceptionalism. It was appropriate, given the nature and scope of Hill's work, that contributors came from important British institutions such as the *Oxford Dictionary of National Biography* (Goldman), the National Portrait Gallery (Heath), and the universities of Oxford (Garnett, Whyte, Baigent) and London (Readman), and that their perspectives were complemented by others from continental Europe (Swenson) and the USA (Hall), places where Hill and her followers were active. It was also fitting, given Hill's views on the importance of the individual, that independent scholars were represented (Darley, Whelan).

The conference papers, which form the basis of the chapters in this volume, without making exaggerated claims to have uncovered the 'real' Hill, confronted aspects of her work, such as her artistic activity and her views on women's roles, which proved problematic to earlier attempts to rescue her memory, and set those questions at the heart of a new appraisal of her work. Thus her involvement in the fine arts was characterized not as a dilettante interest or an aberration from a life of social activism, but as

---

[73] 'Miss Octavia Hill and the "Majority Report"', *The Times*, 20 Aug. 1912, p. 7; <https://armycadets.com/about-us/our-history/> [accessed 2 March 2014]; letter from Major L. W. Bennett, 'Deaths', *The Times*, 20 Aug. 1912, p. 7.

[74] R. Hunter, letter to *The Times*, 17 Aug. 1912; and see the chapter by Baigent.

springing from the same emotional and ideological root as did her 'human work' (Whyte, ch. 3). Her understanding of gender roles was not dismissed as at best mildly embarrassing and at worst hopelessly reactionary, but was theorized in the context of the writings of John Ruskin, Walter Pater and F.D. Maurice, and of wider contemporary social critiques (Garnett, ch. 11). Her Christianity and theological understanding of nature and society were not dismissed as embarrassing or of only personal relevance, but as a key to understanding her activism in several areas (Garnett, Baigent, ch. 7). Her apparent devotion to laissez faire was tempered by more radical and democratic readings of her texts and analyses of her work (Readman, ch. 8; Baigent).

As well as these theoretical insights, the conference illuminated aspects of her work by considering new empirical evidence. It considered accounts of the very various, sometimes irreconcilable, agendas of those active in the early National Trust including some episodes unlikely to feature prominently in its official histories (Hall); discussion of the politics and ideologies of preservation in an international context (Swenson); links between nature, the open space movement and patriotism (Readman);[75] the elusive Kyrle Society (Whelan, ch. 5); and the murals in the Red Cross Hall, one of her most important artistic projects which is often referred to but not analysed in detail (Price). Attention was also paid to the way in which Hill has been memorialized (Heath) – something which this introduction also discusses. Memorialization ranged from cartoons and portraits produced in her lifetime (Heath), to a fascinating group portrait for which the subjects never sat as a group and which has coloured our understanding of institutional working (Swenson), to the legacy of her housing projects in art and the landscape at large (Price, ch. 4; Whyte, ch. 13). Topping and tailing the conference and this collection are an account of Hill's early years and the formative experiences which shaped her alertness to social questions and her methods of tackling them (Darley), and a retrospect showing how ideas about reform and welfare had changed by the time of her death and how this has coloured her reputation (Goldman, ch. 12).

Taken together the chapters corroborate the suggestion made above, that a sympathetic view of her motives and intentions is justified (Baigent, Readman), but also that, at least by the end of her life, the view of her as rigidly unsympathetic was well supported (Goldman). Cowell's chapter (14) serves as a coda to the volume, but not a conclusion. Inasmuch as there is a

---

[75] This theme has received less attention in Britain than in Germany, for obvious ideological reasons, or than in the USA, for reasons connected with the early emergence there of the environmental history field.

conclusion, this historiographic preamble serves as it. Since the aim of the introduction, the conference and this volume has not been to identify the 'real Hill', a conclusion would simply point to her complexity, something that the introduction has already established and that the individual chapters amply exemplify. The book, then, is offered to those interested in women's history, environmental history, social history, art history, and the history of ideas and of religion. Its aim is to present Hill as worthy of study in her own right and, inevitably and perhaps little as she would have liked it, as emblematic of the women of her time. It invites readers to make their own judgement on Hill on the basis of what they read and, in the company of William Whyte whose conference tour notes form chapter 13 here, follow the example of conference participants and get out into the streets of Southwark to see for themselves what she (and her contemporaries) achieved – something of which Hill would surely have approved.

2. Octavia Hill: lessons in campaigning

Gillian Darley

The centenary of Octavia Hill's death in 2012 offered a reminder of the breadth and scale of her achievements. It also prompted me, her most recent biographer, to consider again how she conducted herself during a lifetime of strategic campaigning, in person, in print and by example.[1] Octavia Hill was a woman who surmounted obscurity, poverty and disadvantage to become a formidable campaigner for her work, and to shape attitudes within late Victorian society. Hill mastered the means of disseminating knowledge of her ideas and her practice, giving them a reach far beyond the relatively limited scale within which she effected them in her lifetime. This chapter is concerned with that process. It gives a brief account of Hill's life, partly so that those unfamiliar with it may set in context the detailed arguments of subsequent chapters, but largely to explore how she campaigned for the particular projects which absorbed her energies at successive stages of her life. It asks what she considered to be the most effective methods of spreading her convictions and sharing her experience, and how, when and from whom she had learned these skills, the key to the efficacy of her many causes and projects.

Earliest years: the need for practicality and the benefits of the printed word

The focus falls initially on Hill's family and the turbulent years of her early childhood. She was born in Wisbech in Cambridgeshire, where her father, James Hill (d. 1871), was a corn merchant and banker in comfortable circumstances (see Figure 2.1). The family business was based in Peterborough and Wisbech in a prosperous agricultural region of fertile alluvial fen soils. The river Nene linked the two towns with each other and Wisbech to the sea, making the town a leading port with considerable business across the North Sea. Despite the wave of urban bank failures in the 1820s, trade in agricultural commodities in richer farming areas such as East Anglia continued to support a healthy private banking business, and

---

[1] G. Darley, *Octavia Hill: a Life* (1990), 2nd revd. edn. as *Octavia Hill: Social Reformer and Founder of the National Trust* (2010); G. Darley, 'Hill, Octavia', *ODNB*. Unless otherwise specified, all information and citations below come from the 2010 biography.

Figure 2.1. Undated photograph of Wisbech taken from North Brink looking towards Octavia Hill's birthplace on the right.

the Hill brothers' corn and banking enterprise continued through the 1830s. Despite his privileged background, James Hill was acutely aware of his moral responsibilities. In an unpublished memoir written many years later, his wife Caroline Southwood Hill remembered his saying 'every shower of rain makes me a thousand pounds richer … one hates that it should be by the People's food becoming dearer'.[2] Hill was a Unitarian and an idealist. He stood as a radical Liberal in the town elections in 1819 (the year after he had moved to Wisbech) in the aftermath of the Ely and Littleport riots of 1816 which had been prompted by high unemployment and grain prices. His reformist ambitions continued to be directed at local disaffected, politicized agricultural workers. These men and women and their families were the first to feel the economic and employment repercussions of a succession of exceptionally bad harvests and the strictures of the New Poor Law Act of 1834. James Hill's immersion and personal investment in the principles of Owenite socialism took practical form in polemical journalism (in 1836 he became the co-publisher and editor of the Wisbech paper *The Star in the East*);[3] the establishment in 1837 of an infant school in the town;[4] and his

---

[2] Cited in Darley, *Hill*, p. 17.
[3] Darley, *Hill*, pp. 19–21.
[4] The premises built in 1837 survive as a community arts centre and theatre.

involvement in William Hodson's Utopian colony, Manea Fen, set up in 1838 on Hodson's land in the marshes south of Wisbech.[5]

Octavia's mother was Caroline Southwood Smith (1809–1902), an early and able advocate of the advanced, child-centred educational ideas of Johann Heinrich Pestalozzi, on which she published articles in leading national journals.[6] These publications brought her to the attention of Hill whose first and second wives had died, leaving him in sole care of their six small children. Hill invited Caroline Southwood Smith to leave her teaching position in Wimbledon to come to Wisbech as his children's governess. That invitation soon turned to one of marriage. They married in 1835, and Miranda, their first daughter, was born on 1 January 1836, followed by Gertrude (1837) and Octavia (1838) (so named because she was Hill's eighth daughter) in August 1838. Two more sisters, Emily (1840) and Florence (1843), followed. Caroline Hill was an advocate of working motherhood and James Hill's school in Wisbech offered her an ideal opportunity to put her radical Pestalozzian educational theories to the test, and was in many respects the proving ground of her as a teacher. She continued to report on her findings in print, notably in her husband's radical newspaper for which she wrote under the pseudonym 'C'.[7]

Almost immediately after Octavia Hill's birth her family was brought to the brink of poverty by a series of crop failures in the 1830s which fatally undermined the Hills' financial position. Like many comparable enterprises, the Hill brothers' business failed and James and Thomas Hill were declared bankrupt in March 1840. The family's financial problems were exacerbated by James Hill's idealistic profligacy. Robert Owen's ideas had once closely reflected Unitarian principles transposed on to a secular platform, but the Owenite movement was veering towards millenarianism, and took Hill and fellow-minded men with it. The Manea Fen scheme proved unsustainable and his various financial woes brought on the collapse of James Hill's mental health.[8] From her childhood Octavia Hill learnt two lessons which later characterized her working methods. The first was the danger of radical idealism and disregard for the consequences of untested actions when taken to an extreme – politically or personally. Oblivious to risk, in particular financial risk, James Hill jeopardized his efforts and failed those he intended to help. Many of Octavia Hill's concerns and practices in her working life, from accurate accounting to the absolute clarification

---

[5] W. H. G. Armytage, *Manea Fen: an Experiment in Communitarian Agrarianism 1838–40* (Manchester, 1956); *Utopian Studies*, xxiii (2012), 504–31.

[6] K. Gleadle, 'Hill, Caroline Southwood', *ODNB*.

[7] Darley, *Hill*, p. 266.

[8] Darley, *Hill*, p. 24.

of purposes and beneficiaries of charity and her adherence to the principles of the Charity Organization Society, were founded on her early experience. While accusations that she was intransigent in the distribution of charity were sometimes justified, this early experience makes them comprehensible and should temper criticism.

The second lesson Hill drew from her early life was the beneficial power of the polemical printed word. She saw how strong but unorthodox views could be spread among a growing network of sympathetic readers.

Thomas Southwood Smith and the power of first-hand observation

In 1840 Caroline Hill and her large family of small children left Wisbech and spent the next years moving between Essex, Yorkshire and the vicinity of London. After James Hill's nervous breakdown, medical advice persuaded Caroline, against her strong inclinations, to leave him permanently.[9] The role of father to the family was assumed by Caroline's father, Thomas Southwood Smith (1788–1861), a leading doctor.[10] Despite his high professional standing, Southwood Smith had extremely limited means but he unhesitatingly shouldered responsibility for his daughter's family. He adopted the second daughter, Gertrude (who later married Charles Lewes, son of George Eliot's partner, George Henry Lewes), and supported the others as best he could. Southwood Smith practised as a physician in the East End of London, the more important of his posts being physician to the London Fever Hospital and, from 1848, the only medically qualified member of the General Board of Health. He was steeped in his experience of severe material deprivation and disease: he had observed cholera epidemics at first hand and struggled to understand the causes, as well as to treat the symptoms, of that and other waves of fever that ravaged the poorest areas of London. In addition, he was appointed to the Royal Commission on the Employment of Children (Mines) which reported in 1842–3. Octavia Hill was brought up in a household immersed in his leading part in effecting a broad swathe of reformist measures (including public health, housing, employment), and the wide range of articles and books he published. He introduced her to a life of unstinting work on behalf of others less fortunate than himself. But, in marked contrast to her father, he sought practical solutions to the problems he encountered.

---

[9] Darley, *Hill*, pp. 24–5 discusses the advice behind and the reporting of this separation.

[10] R. K. Webb, 'Smith, Thomas Southwood', *ODNB*; J. R. Guy, *Compassion and the Art of the Possible: Dr. Southwood Smith as Social Reformer and Public Health Pioneer*, Octavia Hill Memorial Lecture (Wisbech, 1993; 2nd edn. 1996).

As one of the four commissioners investigating children's employment in mines, alongside the economist Thomas Tooke and two experienced factory inspectors, Southwood Smith visited mines in West Yorkshire and Leicestershire to gather evidence. He engaged his artist companion Margaret Gillies (1803–87) to provide illustrations, especially of Scottish mines, to accompany the account.[11] The first report appeared in May 1842 with twenty-six illustrations by Gillies (possibly drawn on the spot) which showed small children – many of them girls – at work underground. She drew them dragging trucks along the rails as if they were pit ponies, or clambering up and down ladders or steep inclines within the mine shafts, with their backs heavily laden with coal, as dislodged material rained down on them (see Figure 2.2). These images had, and still have, an immediacy and impact that no verbatim interview could have produced – however shocking the experience or frank the prose.[12] It was the first government blue book to provide visual evidence for its audience and its contents and style were immediately and spectacularly effective. Action to ameliorate conditions was swiftly taken and in August 1842, Ashley's Mines and Collieries Bill was passed, ensuring that no women or boys under ten were employed underground. Few nineteenth-century campaigns for humanitarian reform were as fast and effective as this and some of its success stemmed from the fact that, as well as being well informed, clearly conveyed and efficiently focused, the commission's report had also been visually arresting. That a woman, one within her own family circle and to whom she was particularly close, could have been a pioneer of such effective visual polemic, must have impressed Octavia and her sisters greatly.

The Highgate circle: well-qualified women and the female public sphere

Southwood Smith was estranged from his wife and lived with Margaret Gillies and her sister Mary in Highgate. Margaret was only six years older than Caroline Hill, despite being effectively her stepmother. Octavia and her sisters called Margaret by the pet name 'Dawie', and even in the 1870s the two 'aunts' remained central figures in the lives of Octavia's small nieces. Southwood Smith lived with the Gillies sisters as part of the Highgate circle of Unitarian radicals which included the Leigh Hunts, the Howitts, R. H. Horne, and many individuals whose personal lives ran counter to mid

---

[11] C. Yeldham, *Margaret Gillies RWS, Unitarian Painter of Mind and Emotion 1803–1887*, (Lewiston/Queenston/Lampeter, 1997), pp. 47–50.

[12] The conclusions are summarized on the National Museum of Wales website <http://www.museumwales.ac.uk/2191> [accessed 7 Feb. 2015].

'Nobler imaginings and mightier struggles'

Figure 2.2. Margaret Gillies' on-the-spot sketches of women and children at work in the mines.

Victorian social and religious norms. Several couples lived together outside marriage, feminism was implicitly or explicitly a guiding principle for many, and political action and radical thought were highly prized. It was in this society that Octavia Hill learned or at least sensed that she and her sex were capable of achieving anything they embarked on, whatever the apparent constraints. This sense was reinforced by her mother's continuing to publish to support her children, and to maintain her engagement with new educational ideas described, for example, in *Memoranda of Observations and Experiments in Education* (1845), a collection of her articles on education, and, posthumously, *Notes on Education for Mothers* (1906), the latter edited by Octavia Hill as a tribute to her mother.

In her teens Hill took part in direct action in progressive causes, helping Barbara Leigh Smith (later Bodichon) to canvass and collect signatures in support of the Married Women's Property Act. A family friend, Anna Mary Howitt, recalled that Octavia, 'looking so bright and happy', had sent home the group of Ragged School children that she had been accompanying in Highgate fields and went to the Howitts' house to help paste up the signature sheets – some 3,000 from London alone – that were to be presented to parliament.[13]

In 1852 Octavia began to work alongside her mother at the Ladies' Cooperative Guild for unskilled women who had fallen into material distress. Although the guild was not financially successful, it was important for early feminist activists as a strategy for helping women to earn an independent living.[14] At the guild Octavia was forced into an adult role well before she was mature enough to handle the pressure. Initially reading to the women and helping with practical matters such as the stores and accounts, she quickly became the salaried manager of the toymakers – twenty or more girls who were employed to make doll's house furniture. The nearly destitute children laboriously created tiny miniatures of the kind of furniture that filled the comfortable town houses in the terraces and streets within a short distance of their grim yards and courts. The contrast could hardly have been starker. Hill had learned from Southwood Smith's example that close observation at first hand was the only way to gather accurate information about the lives of the poorest people. Thus, if her toymakers were absent from the guild workshop for any length of time, Octavia visited them at home and so found herself penetrating the dank, overcrowded courts of Holborn, shocking in their lack of privacy, amenities or security of tenure.[15]

---

[13] Darley, *Hill*, p. 54.

[14] Gleadle, 'Hill'.

[15] For housing conditions and the role of the slum landlord, see S. W. Job, *Cat's Meat Square: Housing and Public Health in South St. Pancras 1810–1910* (2012).

These visits, when she was an impressionable teenager, were the foundation of Hill's work, revealing to her the misery of poor people's lives, and a conviction that they must be encouraged and allowed to take responsibility for their surroundings – much as the Ladies' Guild was attempting to do by offering mothers secure paid work. Here lay the roots of Hill's life work in housing and social reform.

At the same time Hill was, at least peripherally, caught up in a groundswell of action, often by women for women, focused on the desperate need for educational opportunities for girls, the potential for independent working lives for young women, and moves towards securing the franchise and property rights. The methods and objectives of a group of forceful reforming women, whose ideas and activities gathered momentum, and who polished their strategies and gained increasingly wide support in enlightened circles in the early 1860s, were part of Hill's family's world as she considered her own future work. Hill was an acquaintance of Elizabeth Garrett, later Elizabeth Garrett Anderson, and had a close if turbulent friendship with Sophia Jex-Blake, two of the pioneers who spearheaded the move of women into the salaried medical profession and whose circle was involved in a variety of education reforms for women and girls which aimed to increase their employment opportunities and hence independence.[16] Her acquaintance and friendship with some of these leading women showed Octavia Hill what could be done with a strong sense of purpose, personal drive, a good cause, and organization and fellowship to reinforce these characteristics.

Christian Socialism: the unity of faith and social action, and the power of oratory

Caroline Southwood Hill's (paid) work for the Ladies' Guild drew her family into the circles around the Christian Socialists, a group of committed men of intellectual, theological and literary renown, who exemplified the potential for integrating social action and faith. Among them were Frederick Denison Maurice, teacher and theologian, Charles Kingsley, and the author Thomas Hughes, whose sister Jeanie (Nassau Senior) later became one of Hill's closest friends and supporters. Ties to this circle were strengthened by Hill's education at Queen's College, Harley Street, which proved an important step in her working and intellectual life. Her mother's example showed her that, for women, becoming a governess was one of few avenues for paid work, so that teaching and attainment of educational qualifications were important steps for Hill. Queen's College had been established in 1848 as a foundation of the Governesses' Benevolent Institution. Inspired

---

[16] E. Crawford, *The Garretts and their Circle* (2002).

by Maurice and having Arthur Stanley, dean of Westminster, as its first principal, it offered daytime classes to girls over twelve and evening courses for governesses. The latter left with certificates of proficiency, though these qualifications were not recognized nationally. Competition was discouraged, and pupils were neither rewarded nor punished.[17] In 1853 the college received its royal charter and, by the time Emily Hill, Octavia's younger sister and later F. D. Maurice's daughter-in-law, won a scholarship to study there in the late 1850s, Maurice was teaching English literature and modern history, while Charles Kingsley was professor of English literature and composition. Soon afterwards Sophia Jex-Blake became a mathematics tutor there. Octavia Hill received her certificate from Queen's College in March 1864 and shortly afterwards began teaching at the Working Women's College, an offshoot of Maurice's Working Men's College.

Octavia and her sisters became regular visitors to the Lincoln's Inn chapel where Maurice preached. Hill found Maurice's sermons intellectually and spiritually persuasive, and these evenings also demonstrated to her the power of public address. Maurice's preaching exemplified the direct appeal of the spoken word, but also the further, and enduring, reach of a published text. His sermons were published, first in 1873 followed by six volumes of the Lincoln's Inn sermons in 1891, so that his reputation as a thinker grew, even though some of his views excited controversy among theologians and led to his being dismissed from his position at King's College London.

This early exposure to persuasive public speaking taught Octavia Hill to take to that platform herself to persuade an audience of the rightness of a cause and to contribute funds and solid support. Her eagerness and ability to confront a large hall of unfamiliar people, and a sometimes unfriendly or at least sceptical audience, was in later years to become one of her greatest assets. She was a highly effective public speaker, using her sonorous, musical voice and very small stature to great effect. But she also followed Maurice, and indeed her parents and grandfather, in continually working to ensure her words were never thrown away, but were published to reach a wider audience.

The Christian Socialist emphasis on the divine family with God the father at its head accurately reflected Hill's insistence on the family's central role in society, something she incorporated into her housing and social work.[18]

---

[17] <http://www.british-history.ac.uk/report.aspx?compid=22141> [accessed 7 Feb. 2015].
[18] D. Young, *F. D. Maurice and Unitarianism* (Oxford, 1992), esp. ch. 7, where Young discusses the Unitarian roots of Maurice's 'commitment to the person of God as Father'.

John Ruskin: art, social action and the dangers of the printed word

Through the Ladies' Guild, Hill came into contact with the most important figure in her life's work: John Ruskin. She had already read and admired his *Modern Painters* when she first met him in late 1853.[19] By 1855 the guild was foundering as the items produced proved unsaleable, and Ruskin was generous with his support for it and Hill herself. He commissioned a piece from the guild and, when it was obvious that its days were numbered (it closed in 1856), he offered Hill employment as a copyist helping to prepare material for *Modern Painters*, each volume of which was illustrated with a selection of plates after the masters. By early 1860 Hill told a friend that she was copying a Turner (it appears in volume five). After her first visit to Denmark Hill, Ruskin's family home, she wrote, 'well-used, this friendship (?), so happily begun, may be a long and growing one'.[20]

Ruskin provided an instantaneous solution to one of Hill's self-imposed rules: that all social work should be voluntary. Her ten years as his paid copyist provided her with an income to add to anything she might earn from teaching, and allowed her to formulate her ideas about the kind of work she could best carry out. Once her choice was made and shared with Ruskin, he used some of the large inheritance from his father to invest in a row of rundown cottages in Marylebone, Paradise Place (now Garbutt Place), to provide a test bed for Hill's theories of housing and social reform (see Figure 2.3). From 1865 onwards Hill's formidable energies were directed to her work on improving existing housing stock and, in so doing, offering self-reliance and confidence to all but her most intransigent tenants.

Octavia Hill's aesthetic discipleship of Ruskin influenced other areas of her work. She was always passionate about the power of colour to enliven the monotonous urban scene, which was in winter frequently fog- or smog-bound, in summer drab and dirty. 'All bright colour exhilarates and gives a sense of gladness', she told the Kyrle Society, which Miranda Hill and she had founded in 1876 to bring the arts and beauty into working lives (see Figure 2.4).[21] Elsewhere she wrote of her own memories, in her customary vivid fashion: 'Till you stay a little in the colourless, forlorn desolation of the houses in the worst courts, till you have lived among the monotonous, dirty tints of the poor districts of London, you little know what the colours of your curtain, carpets, and wall-papers are to you'. She asked her readers to

---

[19] E. Jackson, 'Ladies' Guild furniture' <http://www.dollshousespastandpresent.com/issue8feb2011p3.htm> [accessed 7 Feb. 2015].

[20] Cited in Darley, *Hill*, p. 47.

[21] This and other quotations in this section from O. Hill, 'Colour, space, and music for the people', *Nineteenth Century*, xv (1884), 741–52.

Figure 2.3. Paradise Place, now Garbutt Place.
Sketch by Karel Kirby-Turner, 1956.

imagine the simple, yet exhilarating effect of 'a geranium in the window, a coloured print on the wall or a gay quilt on the bed'.

Her relationship with Ruskin very publicly soured in an episode which taught Octavia Hill the two-edged power of the published word. Hill's early life had shown her the benefits of publication, and she put this lesson into practice as soon as her housing work began, publishing her observations and experiences in widely read journals, beginning with 'Cottage property in London', which appeared in the *Fortnightly Review* in November 1866.

Figure 2.4. Miranda Hill.

Complementing her publications were her Letters to fellow-workers, which were printed for private circulation. The letters were a detailed record of her work, property by property, with accounts and lists of donors and supporters. The first such report was for a single scheme and made a strong case to the parish of St. Mary's, Bryanston Square, for a new project: the Walmer Street Industrial Experiment. It was produced in 1870, and another followed the next year.[22] In 1872 Hill launched a fuller account of her housing schemes and other projects, such as a children's playground and a summary of recent activities and plans for new ventures and properties, together with an account of donations (and donors' names). She produced such a letter

[22] Hill, *LFW*, p. xxxiii.

every year but one – even when she was out of the country, recuperating from nervous exhaustion – until 1911, the year before her death. She insisted they remain unpublished, arguing that this enabled her to be frank about failures, as well as celebrating success since she wrote for friends.[23] But her ability to mount campaigns, especially ones involving fundraising, was greatly enhanced by these letters circulated to the like-minded.

On 1 January 1871 Ruskin began publishing his own newsletter, a monthly pamphlet with the resounding title *Fors Clavigera* and subtitled *Letters to the Workmen and Labourers of Great Britain*. It was in *Fors* during 1877 that Ruskin, who by then had no compunction about the repercussions of anything he wrote or published, launched a cruel attack on Octavia Hill and her failure to endorse his scheme at the St. George's Guild. He was essentially correct in identifying the causes of her unwillingness; she was worried about his fragile state of mind, the cost of the venture, and its financial implications for the housing schemes that she had transformed and now managed on his behalf. Ruskin's first biographer, W. G. Collingwood, declared that, 'To read *Fors* is like being out in a thunderstorm', and the episode brought Hill to nervous collapse.[24] When she had recovered, after a long respite period far away from her responsibilities, Ruskin informed her vindictively that he wished to sell Paradise Place and a similar property, Freshwater Place. In 1881 Hill managed to buy the former but was unable to raise the funds to purchase both. Her lawyer William Shaen, who with his family had become close friends with Hill, stepped in to buy Freshwater Place, to ensure continuity of management.

This painful episode brought home to Hill the dangers of publication, and underlay her discrimination between matter for publication and that for private circulation. Thus she continued to write thoughtful pieces for leading periodicals, including the *Nineteenth Century*, *Macmillan's Magazine* and the *Fortnightly Review*, and periodically to put these together as book publications, beginning with *Homes of the London Poor* (1875). However, she continued to insist that her Letters to fellow-workers remain unpublished.

Civil society and government: the power of wider engagement

After her difficulties in the mid 1870s Octavia Hill's work revealed a far more focused, sophisticated grasp of the institutions of civil society, and an insistence that women should play a leading, forthright role there. She had

---

[23] Hill, *LFW*, pp. xxxi–ii.
[24] W. G. Collingwood, *The Life of John Ruskin* (1911), cited in T. Hilton, *John Ruskin: the Later Years* (2000), p. 189.

learned that many Christian Socialists had little sympathy for a wider role for women (as Thomas Hughes put it in 1873, 'the State wants men who are brave, truthful, generous; the State wants women who are pure, simple, gentle').[25] Hill considered that it was at the local level, as Poor Law guardians and members of Local Government Boards, that energetic and experienced women had important parts to play. Ironically, this was a view she held with increasing conviction while her resistance to municipal intervention, the widening of the franchise to women, and the introduction of universal benefits for the elderly hardened.

Although print was paramount, another of Hill's key strategies was to form alliances with campaigning bodies and like-minded individuals. One of her first campaigns (1875) was to oppose the development of the part of Hampstead Heath known as Swiss Cottage Fields. She had played in these fields as a child, and continued to take tenant groups up to them. Hill appealed for money to buy the land but ultimately failed.[26] Robert Hunter recalled how that setback deeply affected her tactics: 'in all subsequent projects of the kind with which she was connected, a definite option of purchase for a specific time was obtained before public support was solicited'.[27] It also persuaded her there was a need to form alliances and she joined the committee of the Commons Preservation Society (CPS) which had been founded in 1865. Hill was eager to lend weight to the CPS's efforts to safeguard open space around London, in the face of its seemingly unchecked expansion. In a paper of 1888 she calibrated the imbalance between open space to the west and that east of London, and used her evidence to argue for rapid adjustment, as well as what might be regarded as a prototype green belt.[28] She also enlisted the help of the Society for the Protection of Ancient Buildings (founded by William Morris in 1877) for some of the earliest National Trust properties such as Alfriston Clergy House (see Figure 2.5). She encountered Canon Hardwicke Rawnsley as an activist in the campaign around Thirlmere in the Lake District. The Kyrle Society, nominally headed by Miranda Hill but significantly dependent on Octavia, brought together many people in a mesh of small committees, all with the objective of bringing beauty into the lives of the poor. The National Trust drew on all these initiatives and all these people. One of Octavia Hill's most effective strategies was to knit her networks together – the lists of supporters for miscellaneous campaigns often featured the same names. Once Hill had identified people likely to be sympathetic or

[25] E. R. Norman, *The Victorian Christian Socialists* (Cambridge, 2002), p. 88.
[26] O. Hill, 'Space for the people', *Macmillan's Magazine*, xxxii (1875), 328–30.
[27] Darley, *Hill*, p. 166.
[28] O. Hill, 'More air for London', *Nineteenth Century*, xxiii (1888), 181–8.

Figure 2.5. Alfriston Clergy House before restoration.

helpful to one of her causes, she kept them in her sights, approaching them – usually directly, with a brief letter – and requesting their support for a particular initiative or campaign.

From her grandfather Hill had also learned another route to achieving her objectives: the political approach. She published *Homes of the London Poor* (1875) to coincide with the Artisan Dwellings Bill's consideration by the House of Commons, and demonstrated her skilful grasp of this sphere by straddling the divide between government and opposition, the better to campaign in support of an enabling bill which 'will put it in our power collectively to clear the foul places away if we wish'.[29] She was knowledgeable on legislation (and foresaw the traps ahead) and sensitive to party political differences and modes of operation.

Although she increasingly operated on a wider public stage, Hill never held a paid public position or public office. In 1872 James Stansfield, president of the Local Government Board, offered her a salaried post in Whitehall as government inspector with particular responsibility for children within the workhouse system, reporting on 'Poor Law subjects as he sees that women's work is needed' and in particular 'to go thoroughly into all the ins and ours of Boarding-out [of Poor Law children]'. Had she accepted, she would have

[29] Hill, 'Introduction' to Hill, *Homes of the London Poor*.

been the first woman civil servant. Tempted as she was by the security and the value of the role, Hill turned it down in order to pursue her housing work and 'the gradual extension of the system'.[30] In the end, Hill's close and trusted friend and colleague Jeanie Nassau Senior was appointed instead.[31] In 1884 Sir Charles Dilke's intention to invite her to be a commissioner on the Royal Commission on Housing for the Working Classes was vetoed by the home secretary, Sir William Harcourt, who was unable to countenance a woman's taking such a role. Had she been appointed she would have been the first female royal commissioner. Despite this, Hill's evidence to the commission proved influential. Her contributions were widely reported in the press, as she described urban poverty and living conditions and analysed the part played by landlords in the iniquitous situation.[32] Her views profoundly influenced the consequent Housing of the Working Classes Act of 1885, which though admittedly imperfect, laid the foundations for further housing legislation. As she explained to the commissioners in 1884, it was the regular, personal contact between the tenants and those who collected rents that was best able to reach feckless tenants and reverse the houses' deteriorating fabric. She considered the fact that her management also proved financially profitable to be further proof of the effectiveness of her ideas. She told the commissioners about the approach she took to the building stock: 'When we buy these old houses we do nothing to them but the drains and the water supply and put the roofs to rights and everything else of every sort and kind is added in proportion to the tenant's own care'.[33] The lack of harassment by the landowner, and opportunities for others in the tenant's family (work for their children on the building, educational opportunities, excursions to the countryside and improving entertainment), were combined in Hill's 'system', and she adduced the evidence of improved conditions and tenants to prove her point.

Hill spoke not just about her system, but about the strategies employed by slum landlords who held sway over vast swathes of lucrative property, spent nothing on maintenance, and remained indifferent to the levels of subletting that were the only means by which rents could be paid. As Hill told the commission members, she had endeavoured to buy properties from certain notorious individuals such as 'that man Flight' (a 'house farmer' who was said to have owned around 18,000 properties in the poorest areas of London, including Derry Street in Camden, see Figures 2.6 and 2.7) but always without

---

[30] S. Oldfield, *Jeanie, an 'Army of One': Mrs Nassau Senior 1828–1877. The First Woman in Whitehall* (Brighton, 2008), pp. 174–5.

[31] Oldfield, *Jeanie*.

[32] <http://archive.org/stream/housingofworking00londrich/housingofworking00lond rich_djvu.txt> [accessed 7 Feb. 2015].

[33] Royal Commission on the Housing of the Working Classes 8866.

Figure 2.6. Back-to-back houses at Derry Street, Camden. Photograph by Henry Dixon and Son, 1897.

Figure 2.7. Derry Street, Camden. Photograph by Henry Dixon and Son, 1897. These houses, owned by Mr. and Mrs. Flight, exemplified the problems that Hill described to the commissioners in 1884.

'Nobler imaginings and mightier struggles'

success. Thomas Flight and, after his death in 1877 his widow Mathilda, often acquired houses in their clerks' names, in order to sublet them without being identified in the rate books. With a vast additional business in money lending, the Flights often advanced the mortgages on the properties too.[34] The reach and tactics of such slum housing entrepreneurs – and there were many of them – and the state of their properties, as Figures 2.6 and 2.7 exemplify, make it obvious that Hill's piecemeal, time-consuming approach, based entirely on personal influence, could never effect change of the necessary scale, and she knew this; in answer to a questioner on the commission, she replied 'Such work may be small, it may be large, it may be capable of growth or it may not; but I know of no other way'.[35]

Conclusion: a campaigner for a change of heart

Octavia Hill was adamant that public opinion had to be shifted and enlightened if necessary advances in living conditions for the poor were to be achieved. Prejudices had to be challenged and the clear light of good example thrown into dark corners. Her methods of campaigning – in person, in print or on the platform – were of her time, and showed her ready to take advantage of contemporary developments such as the growth of the periodical press and of women's voluntary activity; yet, in choosing and using each, she drew on a rich store of personal experience and memory. She attempted to use each to best effect to further her causes, continuing with those methods she considered had proved successful (detailed first-hand investigation, for example, remained the bedrock of all her work) and adopting new ones as times changed and earlier methods proved inadequate (the wider engagement in civic society and the government machinery which characterized her later campaigns, for example). Characteristically, however, she emphasized (influenced by F. D. Maurice in this) that her aim in her campaigning methods and her detailed management in her housing and open space projects was not to lay down a 'system, not an association, not dead formulas … but [to awaken] the quick eye to see, the true soul to measure, the large hope to grasp the mighty issues of the new and better days to come'.[36]

---

[34] Job, *Cat's Meat Square*, pp. 36–7.
[35] Royal Commission on the Housing of the Working Classes 8865.
[36] Darley, *Hill*, p. 322, speech given on the presentation of the John Singer Sargent portrait to Octavia Hill, 1 Dec. 1898, at Grosvenor House; see also the chapter by Heath in this volume.

II. 'Beauty is for all': art in the life and work of Octavia Hill

3. Octavia Hill: the practice of sympathy and the art of housing

William Whyte

Ruskin's prophecy about Octavia's Hill future work is now well known, but it nonetheless bears repetition. Meeting her at his home in January 1858, he made this observation on her drawings: 'If you devote yourself to human expression, I know how it will be, you will watch it more and more, and there will be an end of art for you. You will say "*Hang* drawing!! I must go and help people"'. Of course, Hill was quick to deny it – 'I told him it would not be so' – and, of course, Ruskin was right.[1] Only a year later, she attended the inauguration of the Ladies' Sanitary Association, where she heard another idol – Charles Kingsley – make a call for educated women to take charge of working-class housing. A few years afterwards, in 1864, Ruskin's financial support enabled her to do just that: apparently fulfilling his prediction and bringing to a close her life as a putative artist. It was something she self-evidently found hard to accept, writing: 'I know it will seem all right in time, perhaps better than ever, but it feels so sad now. For ten years and a half I have worked for him, and been so proud of my work, and now it is all over'.[2] The rest of her life would indeed be devoted to helping people.

One way of understanding what happened to Octavia Hill in the years between 1858 and 1864 is to see it in precisely the terms apparently dictated by Ruskin: a change from art to social work; from paintings to people. In some respects, this was also the way that Hill herself subsequently accounted for her ostensibly dramatic change of tack from what she called 'artistic work' to what she termed 'human work'.[3] And it is not hard to see why this narrative should appeal. Ruskin employed Hill for just over a decade to undertake the most painstaking 'artistic work', which saw her spending four, five or six hours a day copying in great detail paintings by Turner and the Italian masters in pencil and in watercolour. All this does seem a long way from her pioneering 'human work' in housing and social reform, and it is little wonder that her biographers likewise have tended to reproduce this

---

[1] Quoted in *Octavia Hill: Early Ideals, from Letters*, ed. E. S. Maurice (1928), p. 131.
[2] Maurice, *Hill*, p. 163.
[3] E. M. Bell, *Octavia Hill: a Biography* (2nd edn., 1942), p. 38.

sharp dichotomy between useful social work and useless artistic toil in their own analyses, with Enid Moberly Bell's 1942 account just the most striking example. 'While Ruskin was giving her the work to which she attached so much importance', she wrote, '[F. D.] Maurice was giving her the work she could do so admirably'. She added, 'It is impossible not to grudge the time and energy Octavia gave to Ruskin's work, to this meticulous copying which wore her out to no useful purpose'.[4]

Where historians have perceived some continuity, it has tended to be in the more obviously aesthetic sides of Octavia Hill's work. It is not hard to see, for example, how her involvement in the Kyrle Society, with its attempt to make art accessible to all, and her efforts to preserve the natural environment, owed much to a sort of romantic, artistic idealism. 'Ruskin's values', observes Robert Hewison in an essay on Octavia Hill and Ruskinian values, 'live on in those of the National Trust'.[5] Hill's interest in what she described as 'the beauty side' of housing is also a good Ruskinian practice, as was her employment of the architect Elijah Hoole for more than forty years – most notably at Red Cross and White Cross cottages in Southwark and at her own home in Kent.[6] Hoole was another true believer, an Arts and Crafts architect who wrote on Ruskin and embodied many of Ruskin's precepts within his own work.[7] That the hall Hoole built for Red Cross cottages was to be ornamented with heroic paintings by the eminently Ruskinian Walter Crane seems only to complete an all-too-obvious picture.[8]

Moreover, as Robert Whelan has also noted, there is a deeper sense in which Hill's underlying philosophy always owed much to a wider Victorian debate about the impact of the environment on people's behaviour.[9] She never escaped the associationist psychology which similarly shaped Ruskin and a whole generation of Victorian thinkers, and which taught her that bad surroundings helped to make bad people, while an attractive environment helped to ennoble.[10] The 'poor of London', she famously observed, 'need

---

[4] Bell, *Hill*, p. 40.

[5] R. Hewison, '"You are doing some of the work that I ought to do": Octavia Hill and Ruskinian values', in '*To the utmost of her power...': the Enduring Relevance of Octavia Hill*, ed. S. Jones (2012), p. 62.

[6] Quoted in G. Darley, *Octavia Hill: Social Reformer and Founder of the National Trust* (1990; 2010), p. 293.

[7] E. Hoole, 'A summary of Mr Ruskin's earlier architectural criticism', *Transactions of the Royal Institute of British Architects*, xx (1869–70), 91–103. For Hoole's distinctive views on Ruskin, see B. Harrison, *Architects and the 'Building World' from Chambers to Ruskin: Constructing Authority* (Cambridge, 2003), pp. 257–8.

[8] For a contemporary – and very Ruskinian – account, see Mrs. R. Barrington, 'The Red Cross Hall', *English Illustrated Magazine*, cxvii (1893), 609–18.

[9] *Octavia Hill and the Social Housing Debate*, ed. R. Whelan (1998).

[10] G. L. Hersey, *High Victorian Gothic: a Study in Associationism* (Baltimore, Md., 1972).

joy and beauty in their lives'.[11] The image of St. Christopher affixed to the wall at Barrett's Court; the Walter Crane murals in Red Cross Hall; the creepers and flowers in so many of her developments: all these can be seen – and indeed have been viewed – as legacies of her early artistic training, and especially her contact with Ruskin.[12] Indeed, her appeal in 1873 to raise funds for an inscription to be installed at Freshwater Place, one of the earliest of her housing schemes, was articulated in frankly Ruskinian terms. His words, she observed, 'no doubt taught me to care for permanent decoration, which should endear houses to men'.[13]

Yet to observe that Octavia Hill never quite stopped being a Ruskinian – even after his notorious attack on her in 1877; to note that she considered 'colour, space, and music' as issues just as important in housing the poor as sanitation and regular rent collection is to tell us very little, and certainly hardly anything that can be considered new.[14] Hill was just one of many who wished to bring art to the people and to expose the poor to beauty.[15] As early as the 1840s, Kingsley similarly asserted that 'Picture-galleries should be the workman's paradise … to which he goes to refresh his eyes and heart with beautiful shapes and sweet colouring, when they are wearied with dull bricks and mortar'.[16] Nor was she unusual in stressing the significance of the environment for behaviour. Indeed, this was a commonplace of the period. For the Victorian educationalist Edward Thring, for example, environment was everything: 'The mere force of fine surroundings', he argued, was transformative; '*Whatever men say or think, the almighty wall is, after all, the supreme and final arbiter*'.[17] In comparison, Hill's relatively small-scale forays into architecture, ornament and gardening can seem at worst commonplace and even at best hardly worth further elaboration.[18]

---

[11] O. Hill, *Homes of the London Poor* (1883), p. 29.

[12] Although for an alternative view, see R. H. Bremner, '"An iron scepter twined with roses": the Octavia Hill system of housing management', *Social Service Review*, xxxix (1965).

[13] *The Life of Octavia Hill as Told in her Letters*, ed. C. E. Maurice (1913), p. 295.

[14] D. Maltz, 'Beauty at home or not? Octavia Hill and the aesthetics of tenement reform', in *Homes and Homelessness in the Victorian Imagination*, ed. M. Baumgarten and H. M. Daleski (New York, 1998), pp. 187–211; reprinted as ch. 2, in D. Maltz, *British Aestheticism and the Urban Working Classes, 1870–1900: Beauty for the People* (Basingstoke, 2005).

[15] G. Waterfield, 'Art for the people', in *Art for the People: Culture in the Slums of Late-Victorian London*, ed. G. Waterfield (exhibition catalogue, 1994).

[16] Quoted in M. Bright, *Cities Built to Music: Aesthetic Theories of the Victorian Gothic Revival* (Columbus, Ohio, 1984), p. 217.

[17] Quoted in W. Whyte, 'Building a public school community, 1860–1910', *History of Education*, xxxii (2003), 601–26.

[18] Although, for a firm defence of the importance of Hill's small-scale projects, see A. Anderson and E. Darling, 'The Hill sisters: cultural philanthropy and the embellishment of lives in late-nineteenth-century England', in *Women and the Making of Built Space in England, 1870–1900*, ed. E. Darling and L. Whitworth (Aldershot, 2007).

'Nobler imaginings and mightier struggles'

This chapter, however, will suggest that more remains to be said about Octavia Hill and art. It will contend, moreover, that Octavia Hill's change of direction did not represent a radical caesura; indeed, that her approach to social work was not just generally but very particularly shaped by her understanding of art. More than this, I shall argue that until now, historians have been mistaken in seeing Hill's decade-long programme of copying great masters as a dead end or somehow irrelevant to her later social work.[19] By paying proper attention to this most important, time-consuming – indeed, all-consuming – part of her life, I will seek to demonstrate that her art was always intended to be social work, just as her social work was a form of art.

That Octavia Hill possessed an elevated idea of the artist's vocation is undeniable. Writing to her sister Gertrude, Hill, aged only thirteen, celebrated the genius of the great Renaissance masters in terms which arguably even exceeded Ruskin's encomia. 'Think of Raphael and Michael [sic] Angelo!', she observed:

> To think that every grand feeling they had could preserve for centuries! Oh what an influence they must have! Think of the thousands of great thoughts they must have created in people's minds; the millions of sorrow [sic] that one great picture (one truly great picture) would calm and comfort.[20]

This was the vocation to which Octavia Hill felt called: art for art's sake, it most certainly was not.

There are two elements to Hill's account of the artist's work that require further exploration. In the first place, it is worth noting that, for her – as for most of her contemporaries – art was a means of communication; it was, in many respects, a literal language. In 1842, ten years before Octavia Hill addressed her own calling, for example, the engraver G. R. Lewis made exactly the same point, claiming that 'art can be made a vehicle of communication as well as [can] letter press'.[21] Similar impulses self-evidently shaped the contemporary development of Pre-Raphaelite painting, where everything, from the subject of the picture to the text on the frame, was intended to communicate a message.[22] Sending her friend Mary Harris a picture in 1857, Octavia Hill wrote:

---

[19] See, e.g., Darley, *Octavia Hill*, p. 71; S. Eagles, *After Ruskin: the Social and Political Legacies of a Victorian Prophet, 1870–1920* (Oxford, 2011), p. 118.

[20] Maurice, *Life of Octavia Hill*, p. 27.

[21] Quoted in W. Whyte, 'Sacred space as sacred text: church and chapel architecture in Victorian Britain', in *Sacred Text–Sacred Space: Architectural, Spiritual, and Literary Convergences in England and Wales*, ed. J. Sterrett and P. Thomas (Leiden, 2011), p. 255.

[22] K. Flint, 'Reading the *Awakening Conscience* rightly', in *Pre-Raphaelites Re-viewed*, ed. M. Pointon, (Manchester and New York, 1989); P. Mitchell and L. Roberts, 'Burne-Jones's picture frames', *Burlington Magazine*, cxlii (2000), 362–70; K. D. Rowe, 'Painted sermons: explanatory rhetoric and William Holman Hunt's inscribed frames' (unpublished Bowling Green State University PhD thesis, 2005).

You will not know all that is connected with every line ... but you will know that there is much ... fancy how all the little flowers clustering round the stem speak of union and support, which could not be known by the separate flowers, think how every line of beauty spoke of a love greater than any earthly one. Look then at the Virginian creeper, and its companion, all of London growth, telling of the smoky and dusty earth, where they struggled to live in glorious beauty, and could only live in solitary sorrow, but with strength of heart which bore a message to the other inhabitants of London.[23]

Nor did this symbolic – strictly speaking, this typological – approach to visual analysis ever leave her.[24] Writing to Ruskin she observed that throughout her life 'all that I longed to say has come to me in visible forms, pictures or symbols'.[25] More than thirty years later, in 1890, she said something similar to the young Sydney Cockerell. 'Remember', she wrote, 'there is a Truth of *things*, as well as of *words*. Our words are indeed feeble exponents of the Truth'.[26] Art, then, was not just one vehicle of communication for Octavia Hill, it was – and remained – the supreme vehicle, a language more compelling and more vital than mere text.

It is here that the second of Octavia Hill's beliefs about art comes into play. For Hill, as for Ruskin and many mid Victorians, great art could evoke a profound emotional response.[27] J. M. W. Turner, in particular, was seen as almost uniquely capable of 'leading the viewer to contemplate elevating poetic and philosophical thought' through his paintings.[28] But all art was measured against the same criteria. Qualities of form or style or even the accuracy of representation were not as important as the psychological effect that art could produce.[29] Paintings, therefore, were not just narratives and art was not merely a means of communicating a story. Precisely because it was a language which directly engaged the emotions, art was considered a uniquely potent means of teaching. In a famous phrase, Ruskin declared that:

---

[23] Maurice, *Octavia Hill*, pp. 50–1.
[24] See H. L. Sussman, *Fact into Figure: Typology in Carlyle, Ruskin, and the Pre-Raphaelite Brotherhood* (Columbus, Ohio, 1979); and G. P. Landow, *Victorian Types, Victorian Shadows: Biblical Typology in Victorian Literature, Art, and Thought* (Boston, Mass., 1980).
[25] Maurice, *Hill*, p. 141.
[26] Maurice, *Life of Octavia Hill*, p. 509.
[27] H. Roberts, '"Trains of fascinating and of endless imagery": associationist art criticism before 1850', *Victorian Periodicals Newsletter*, x (1997), 91–105.
[28] H. E. Roberts, 'Art reviewing in early-nineteenth-century art periodicals', *Victorian Periodicals Newsletter*, vi (1973), 19.
[29] C. Arscott, 'Sentimentality in Victorian paintings', in Waterfield, *Art for the people*, p. 65.

> The greatest thing a human soul ever does in this world is to see something, and tell what it saw in a plain way. Hundreds of people can talk for one who can think, but thousands can think for one who can see. To see clearly is poetry, prophecy, and religion, — all in one.[30]

For Hill, this was an insight of real – indeed, of religious – importance.[31] In an undated letter to Ruskin, she observed of her artistic work: 'I think to arrange beautiful colour, to show what I believe God's works are the symbols of, and to tell a little about the good and suffering I have seen, these are the only desires I have about it all'.[32]

This combination of assumptions justified the peculiar artistic education to which John Ruskin subjected his pupils. They were learning a language – one that many believed to be 'untranslatable', and one intended to speak to – to teach – the heart.[33] By copying great art exactly, Octavia Hill was engaged in a process of training her visual acuity and learning how to reveal the truth that she had witnessed. The advice Ruskin offered to the children's book illustrator Kate Greenaway might equally have applied to Hill. 'You should', he wrote in 1883, 'resolve on a summer's work of utter veracity – drawing – no matter what, *but* as it *is* … I want your exquisite feeling given to teach – not merely to amuse'.[34] It was an arduous process, to which Octavia Hill submitted apparently willingly – if not always uncomplainingly, writing of a visit to view Turner's *Fighting Téméraire*:

> If I could impart to anyone my own perception of the picture, could only let them have an opportunity of looking at it for as long as I did, I should have done something worth living for. That union of truth with the ideal is perfect, solemn, glorious, awful and mighty. It will I trust never fade from my memory.[35]

Her copying would ensure that the memory never did fade – and, more than this, that she was able to offer others the experience she herself had enjoyed.

Now, it must be said that not everyone accepted this analysis. Increasingly, towards the end of the nineteenth century, there were those – like the artist James McNeill Whistler – who rejected the notion that art

---

[30] J. Ruskin, *Modern Painters*, iii (1856), 250.

[31] For an analysis of Ruskin's own dependence on biblical texts for this notion, see also J. Drury, 'Ruskin's way: *tout à fait comme un oiseau*', in *History, Religion, and Culture: British Intellectual History, 1750–1950*, ed. S. Collini, R. Whatmore and B. Young (Cambridge, 2000).

[32] Maurice, *Hill*, p. 127.

[33] K. Flint, *The Victorians and the Visual Imagination* (Cambridge, 2000), p. 203.

[34] M. H. Spielman and G. S. Layard, *The Life and Work of Kate Greenaway* (1905; 1986), p. 115.

[35] Maurice, *Life of Octavia Hill*, p. 64.

was reducible to a sort of language; although even he had to admit that 'the vast majority of English folk cannot and will not consider a picture as a picture, apart from any story which it may be supposed to tell'.[36] Others, more sympathetic to Ruskin and to Hill, also expressed their own doubts about the capacity of art to convey ethical truths.[37] So it was, for example, that despite his involvement in the Kyrle Society, Lord Leighton opposed the murals intended for the Red Cross Hall on the ground that paintings were inherently incapable of expressing the acts of heroism they were intended to depict.[38] Octavia Hill evidently had her own doubts about the decision to train as an artist instead of concentrating on more direct ways of ameliorating social conditions, writing to Ruskin, 'I have puzzled people because I have set myself so resolutely to become a painter, and yet have cared for people so much'.[39]

Nevertheless, the way in which Hill addressed these doubts is telling, for she went on to suggest that caring for people and training as an artist were two aspects of the same endeavour:

> If I did *not* care for them, would not all that is not selfish in my artistic plans be lost? ... If I did not care that little boys in the backstreets should have some pleasure, the earnest faces of the little children, who stretched their heads out of the attic windows into sunlight on the first spring day that they might see the little lark and hear his song, [it] would have no interest for me.[40]

The breathless, deathless lyricism of this passage is noteworthy. It speaks of Hill's emotional commitment to her art and of her attempts, which are frequently repeated in her writing, to convey her argument synecdochically: using 'little boys in the backstreets' and 'little children' stretching 'their heads out of the attic windows into sunlight on the first spring day' to stand for society – and especially 'the poor' – as a whole. More than anything else, it illuminates an important and easily overlooked aspect of Hill's thinking. Art, just like social work, is in this analysis the practice of empathy – or, more precisely, of sympathy. In all sorts of ways, this is the key to both Octavia Hill the artist and the social reformer.

That the notion of sympathy was important to Hill is clear. It was personally significant: central to her sense of self. 'Why is entering into other people's feelings, even sad, so restful?' she wrote in 1859. 'Is it not

---

[36] Flint, *Victorians and Visual Imagination*, p. 197.
[37] Arscott, 'Sentimentality in Victorian paintings', p. 65.
[38] Mrs. R. Barrington, *Leighton and John Kyrle: 'The Man of Ross'* (Edinburgh, 1903), p. 21.
[39] Maurice, *Hill*, p. 127.
[40] Maurice, *Hill*, p. 127.

'Nobler imaginings and mightier struggles'

because we are meant to bear one another's burdens?'[41] Sympathy was also an ideal that she publicly affirmed. The term occurs again and again in her writing:[42] sometimes applied to the poor;[43] sometimes applied 'to those who are trying to serve them'.[44] Occasionally 'sympathy' is contrasted with 'action';[45] but more usually, a 'thoughtful sympathy',[46] a 'real human sympathy',[47] or 'an awakened English sympathy'[48] is shown almost as an active agent in its own right – 'an underlying current of sympathy',[49] or even 'a wave of right hearty sympathy' sweeping all before it.[50] Little wonder that Octavia Hill proudly recorded Ruskin's praise of her own 'infinite sympathy'.[51]

As Lars Spuybroek has recently argued, sympathy lay at the heart of Ruskin's message. Sympathy was not empathy, nor merely feeling sorry for someone; it was a powerful force that mediated the relationship between people and between people and things. It is, as Spuybroek puts it, 'the very stuff relations are made of':

> To Ruskin, a painting is not a *sign* of sympathy between us and some tree or old house; it is itself that sympathy, yes, between us and the tree, between us and the painting, between the painter and the tree, and between the painting and the tree … Art is the original method of multiplying sympathy, the privileged form of distributing it among as many of us as possible.[52]

It was this highly precise Ruskinian conception that so attracted Octavia Hill.

Indeed, to a great extent, it was this idea that drew Hill to Ruskin himself. Hearing him talk about geology, for example, she confessed herself unable to follow his scientific arguments; but she went on to marvel

> how he told us of the cracks and fissures, the weakness of the mountains filled with stronger substances, like mighty veins becoming bands of union to all parts of the mountain, of how each atom of that gigantic mass is purifying itself

---

[41] Maurice, *Life of Octavia Hill*, p. 168.
[42] See, e.g., Hill, *Homes of the London Poor*, pp. 19, 20, 55, 66, 77, 89, 105, 112, 114, 118, 155.
[43] Hill, *LFW*, 1887, p. 227.
[44] Hill, *LFW*, 1874, p. 40..
[45] Hill, *LFW*, 1979, p. 114.
[46] Hill, *LFW*, 1891, p. 301.
[47] Maurice, *Life of Octavia Hill*, p. 534.
[48] Hill, *LFW*, 1882, p. 156.
[49] Hill, *Homes of the London Poor*, p. 19.
[50] Maurice, *Life of Octavia Hill*, p. 502.
[51] Maurice, *Hill*, p. 156.
[52] L. Spuybroek, *The Sympathy of Things: Ruskin and the Ecology of Design* (Rotterdam, 2012), p. 229.

daily, through the ages, of the mighty because incessant, movement of those apparently changeless hills; of the sympathy they seem to show men.[53]

Nor was this appreciation confined only to those moments when Hill was baffled by Ruskin's subject matter. A lecture on architecture in 1869 left her disappointed because, although it was 'powerful, interesting, and full of great thoughtful views of life and art', it did not touch 'on those deep questions of feeling where he is greatest of all'.[54]

Ruskin's account of sympathy was attractive, not least because it helped to make sense of Hill's own ideas and impulses. She experienced exactly the sort of charged relationship with apparently inanimate objects that he sought to articulate, with plants occupying an especially important part in her emotional life. For Hill, a bramble was never simply a bramble: it was 'so full of signs, as well as beauties'; it was also a type, carrying 'like all thorned plants, the mark of sorrow'.[55] Similar typologies were also evoked by objects like her lamp: 'a guard throwing light, before which dark deeds quail … a type of much of the character of the way we have to work'.[56] But these encounters with things were never just about typology. They were always freighted with sympathetic significance, with Hill going so far as to describe herself as 'oppressed with a sense of injustice' when planting a Virginia creeper in one of her tenements: she could not rid herself of the guilt that it was exposed 'to so different a fate from its companions'.[57] Her attitudes to architecture were infused by similar sorts of ideas, seeing ornamentation, for example, as not simply decorative but somehow inherently capable of embodying 'generosity' – an insight which, as she acknowledged, she owed directly to Ruskin.[58]

Octavia Hill's artistic work was all of a piece with this, with her copying more than just an exercise in draughtsmanship. For one thing, she clearly saw it as a training in true acuity more generally: 'the only fit preparation for perception of truth in picture or in life'. For another, it evidently operated in her mind as a means of articulating sympathy: sympathy for Ruskin, whom she believed would obtain 'real comfort' from her work; sympathy for the paintings themselves, 'which don't change when we change, nor depend for their power or beauty on our thoughts about them'; as well as sympathy for those who would come to see and learn from her work.[59] In

[53] Maurice, *Hill*, p. 160.
[54] Maurice, *Hill*, p. 177.
[55] Maurice, *Hill*, p. 55.
[56] Maurice, *Life of Octavia Hill*, p. 276.
[57] Maurice, *Hill*, p. 193.
[58] Hill, *LFW*, 1879, p. 121.
[59] Maurice, *Life of Octavia Hill*, pp. 144–6.

this scheme, right perception would always lead to true sympathy. Small wonder Ruskin warned that studying human expression would lead her away from art towards housing.

As a result, Hill's move from apprentice illustrator to energetic social reformer represented not so much the rejection of her artistic education as the fulfilment of it. Assuming that art could communicate and would move the emotions, she was determined 'to develop the love of beauty among my tenants', not just for its own sake, but because of what she believed it would achieve.[60] Hence, for example, the Walter Crane murals in the Red Cross Hall, which she celebrated for 'the teaching' they offered their viewers.[61] Hence, too, the apparently quixotic decision to install an inscription on the wall of St. John's Church, Waterloo, with a quotation from George Herbert picked out in gold and blue tiles: 'All may have,/ if they dare try, a glorious life or grave'. Hill wrote, 'I liked to think of the words being there':

> I believed the words might go home to many a man as he hurries along the crowded thoroughfare near, if he caught sight of them between the trees, their colour attracting his notice, perhaps, first, in its contrast with the dreary dinginess all around. I liked to think some busy man might renounce a profitable bargain, or might even dream, for a minute or two, of renouncing it, for the sake of some good deed. Or I have sometimes liked to fancy a working man from among the men who sit in that public garden, might be reminded, as he read the words, that though his life was out of men's sight and seemed occupied with little things, seemed perhaps somewhat broken and wasted, there was the possibility of nobleness in it, if bravely and unselfishly carried on. But to whatever heart it might or might not go, the words seemed fit to be spoken to each one of the multitude, hurrying in and out, or pausing there, and worthy to be set, with some care, in lovely colour, to last for years.[62]

And it was not just representational art or public inscriptions that were expected to instruct. The houses Hill built were similarly intended to convey ideas and evoke emotions. Writing of her visit to the Tyrol, she evinced her admiration for the 'beauty and simplicity' of the architecture and determined that she too would 'make the houses of the poor beautiful'. But what she admired was more than the aesthetic qualities of these buildings; it was also their expressive function, the way in which peasant domesticity was symbolized by 'home-like oriel windows' and 'home-like irregularity' of form. Built in London, she went on, similar houses 'would be a delight to

---

[60] Hill, *Homes of the London Poor*, p. 29.
[61] Hill, *LFW*, 1892, p. 320.
[62] Hill, *LFW*, 1883, p. 174.

all who passed down the street in proportion as they grew to like what was home-like, quaint and pretty'.[63]

Hill, of course, had no confidence that people – much less her people – would grow to like what was 'home-like, quaint and pretty' on their own. As she put it: 'I am sure that the power of enjoying things that are lovely and quiet is one of which the poor stand in need, that it wants cultivation, which means in this case sympathy with the germs of it which are innate, and a little food to nourish it, and occasional quiet to let it assert itself.'[64] The regular flower shows, the annual May Day celebrations, the musical performances and country visits that Hill organized: all these formed part of a programme of aesthetic education. Her building projects and opposition to large-scale housing developments: these too, were driven by her belief in 'the utter impossibility in the block building of getting any kind of individual taste developed'.[65] Hill's hope was that her tenants would come to see the world – to see it, to understand it, and to respond to it emotionally – in the way that she did. Thus, for instance, the introduction of climbing plants into the laughably misnamed Paradise Place was articulated in these terms: 'The women have cared so much for the idea, and I think it may be a permanent joy for them, and give them a sense of progress to watch the creepers climb higher on the walls'.[66] For Hill, even plants were potentially parables – if only people would learn to read them aright.

This was not, though, the 'fantasy' of 'pastoral domesticity' or 'the garden as a panacea for all social and psychological ills' that Diana Maltz has discerned – and condemned – in Octavia Hill's thought. *Pace* Maltz, Hill never 'allowed aesthetic taste to overcome reason'.[67] Far less is it evidence that Hill (in Marion Brion's words) was 'a doer and not a theorist'.[68] As Jane Lewis has noted, for all her condemnation of 'windy talk', Hill 'nevertheless worked to a firm set of principles'.[69] Believing that 'the two improvements of people and dwellings must go hand in hand', she offered a graduated programme of training.[70] For the artisans and workers, 'oppressed', as she saw it, by the 'ugliness' around them, there was to be art and gardening, and the sorts of 'rather pretty'

---

[63] Hill, *LFW*, 1879, pp. 121–2.
[64] Maurice, *Life of Octavia Hill*, p. 270.
[65] Hill, *LFW*, 1886, p. 202.
[66] Maurice, *Octavia Hill*, p. 193.
[67] Maltz, 'Beauty at home or not?', pp. 198–9.
[68] M. Brion, *Women in the Housing Service* (1995), p. 12.
[69] J. Lewis, 'Social facts, social theory, and social change: the ideas of Booth in relation to those of Beatrice Webb, Octavia Hill, and Helen Bosanquet', in *Retrieved Riches: Social Investigation in Britain, 1840–1914*, ed. D. Englander and R. O'Day (Aldershot, 1995), p. 49.
[70] *Royal Commission on the Housing of the Working Classes* (Parl. Papers 1884–5 [C 4402]), Q 9172.

cottages designed by Elijah Hoole.[71] For those she unselfconsciously described as 'the destructive and the criminal classes', there would be less elaborate, less easily damaged developments.[72] But all Hill's tenants were exposed to a similar experience as she sought to train them to treat their homes, their gardens, their children with the 'love and care' which she believed she was lavishing on them.[73] This was a training in sympathy.

Nor was it just the poor that required such training. Octavia Hill was well aware that her 'fellow-workers' also needed to preserve – and develop – their own sympathetic gifts. As she put it: 'harshness, suspicion, and hopelessness … creep over those dealing habitually with a very low class in a bad big town. It needs a highly educated person to preserve gentleness, faith or height of standard'.[74] Naturally, she did not mean by this an academic education – after all, she scarcely possessed that herself. Rather, Hill's notion of an education was one based on her own experiences, and it was that which she sought to inculcate in those who followed her example. Again, in this respect, the sympathy of things was just as important as a sympathy towards people: indeed, the two bled into one another. Writing in December 1879, for instance, Hill observed that the work she offered:

> Implied a share in the people's pain … bringing, I know you have all felt by this time, something of the same quiet sense of indestructible connection, a solemn blessing in fulfilment of simple duty. It has brought you also, I feel sure, a real attachment to your people. You know they are yours; they know it; and as the years go on this sense of attachment will deepen and grow.

Eventually, she went on, 'Even the places – those ugly London courts – will be to you so dear; for you will remember how and where you made them lighter, cleaner, better: the rooms, the yards, the streets will be associated with the faces that brighten when they see you, and with victories over evil which you helped to achieve'.[75] Nearly two decades later, in 1895, Octavia Hill returned to these themes, reflecting, after a successful 'Playground Festival' on 'Ruskin's passage about Association and how places become enriched by the life that has been passed within them'.[76]

---

[71] O. Hill, *Colour, Space, and Music for the People* (repr. from *Nineteenth Century*; London, 1884), p. 5; *Royal Commission on the Housing of the Working Classes*, Q8967. See also S. M. Gaskell, 'Gardens for the working class: Victorian practical pleasures', *Victorian Studies*, xxiii (1980).

[72] *Royal Commission on the Housing of the Working Classes*, Q 8864.

[73] Hill, *Homes of the London Poor*, p. 19.

[74] Maurice, *Hill*, p. 205.

[75] Hill, *LFW*, 1879, p. 115.

[76] Maurice, *Hill*, p. 535.

That Hill's collaborators wholly embraced these attitudes is hard to prove – although it is telling that Ellen Chase's account of *Tenant Friends in Old Deptford*, a text which differs from Hill in many of its conclusions, nonetheless articulates similar ideas about the power of surroundings and the need for beauty.[77] Famously, too, Samuel Barnett observed that 'It is not the poverty that is such a weight upon everybody in the East End, it is the ugliness'.[78] More significant still is the fact that observers of Octavia Hill's work revealingly identified a ruling tendency among her fellow workers. Encountering one of Hill's most devoted supporters, the indefatigable Emma Cons, the young Beatrice Webb observed that she 'spoke to her people with that peculiar mixture of sympathy and authority which characterizes the modern class of *governing women* ... Unlike the learned women, the emotional part of their nature is fully developed, their sympathy kept almost painfully alive'.[79] Hill could not have hoped for more.

In many respects, however, Octavia Hill's most remarkable efforts were directed not at her tenants nor at her fellow workers, but towards those who provided the financial support for her work. As Enid Moberly Bell observed, she was always 'as much concerned about the spiritual development of the rich as of the poor'.[80] Indeed, even before she renounced any explicitly artistic ambitions, Hill expressed herself horrified at what she described as 'the frightful want of feeling in all classes'.[81] Intriguingly, in the same conversation with Ruskin during which he prophesied that she would abandon art, he also offered a predication about the future development of painting and architecture more generally, hoping that artists would soon come to depict the 'pathos' of everyday life and a 'nobler view' of human expression. Hill happily recorded that, 'He thinks Pre-Raphaelites will turn their attention to it, and so will architectural workmen'.[82] Nonetheless, excepting Ford Madox Brown's magnum opus, *Work* (1852–63), such a development did not occur.[83] Nor, of course, did Hill come to paint these themes herself. But it is not such an imaginative leap to see that in both her words and her work more widely she took up Ruskin's challenge and, in so doing, sought to represent the poor to the rich. It is worth considering both these themes.

---

[77] E. Chase, *Tenant Friends in Old Deptford* (1929), pp. 11, 15.
[78] Quoted in Bell, *Octavia Hill*, p. 151.
[79] *The Diary of Beatrice Webb*, ed. N. and J. Mackenzie (4 vols., Cambridge, 1982), i. 136.
[80] E.g., see Bell, *Octavia Hill*, pp. 278–9.
[81] Maurice, *Life of Octavia Hill*, p. 203.
[82] Maurice, *Hill*, p. 130.
[83] For a good recent analysis, see T. Barringer, J. Rosenfeld and A. Smith, *Pre-Raphaelites: Victorian Avant-Garde* (exhibition catalogue, 2012), pp. 130–1.

'Nobler imaginings and mightier struggles'

Beyond the reflection that Octavia Hill's writing was made 'increasingly prolix and ornamented with purple passages' under Ruskin's influence, surprisingly little has been made of her prose style.[84] Yet, as Marion Brion has noted, her wider reputation was based as much on what she wrote as what she actually did.[85] Hers was an approach which made much use of anecdote and still more of metaphor to evoke the world that she sought to reform. Just as in her art, small details stood in for the wider whole. Her depictions of a future garden at Henry Place in Southwark, for instance, were consequently as crowded as any Victorian narrative painting. It would be, she wrote, a place

> where, in time to come, the trees may grow, and crocuses flower, and where men may sit and smoke on summer evenings, and women, weary of the noise indoors may just cross that road with their work and breathe cooler air; a playground where children too small to go to park or gymnasium, may run about freely.[86]

So too, Hill's description of Kent and Surrey – an account of such minute exactitude that it almost descends into self-parody. They were, she declared, 'the play places of our wearied Londoners – not of the rough who robs the bank of its primrose roots, but of the doctor and his wife, of the young student, of the clergymen's convalescent child, of the busy merchant'.[87]

These texts are worth reflecting on not merely because they do indeed reveal the apparently inescapable influence of Ruskin's writing on Hill. They also, of course, bear out the truth of her own claim to a strong visual imagination: one that could envisage crocuses growing in 'the most unpromising piece of ground'; one that could conjure up visions of convalescent children being healed by a holiday in the Home Counties.[88] Above all, Hill's prose shows her seeking to evoke sympathy. This was true even of her depictions of degradation, which similarly sought to establish sympathetic connections between the haves and have nots:

> There is a court I know well, a great blank, high, bare black wall, which rises within a few feet of the back windows of a number of rooms inhabited by the poor. I have shown it to many ladies and gentlemen, and have said how cheerless it made the rooms. Some feel it, and seem to realise what sitting opposite to it day after day would be. Some say it isn't so *very* dark, and almost seem to add 'Can you show us nothing worse?' Then I never do.[89]

---

[84] Darley, *Octavia Hill*, p. 69.
[85] Brion, *Women in the Housing Sphere*, p. 11.
[86] Hill, *LFW*, 1886, p. 204.
[87] Hill, *LFW*, p. 352.
[88] The comment is Lord Ducie's (see Hill, *LFW*, 1886, p. 205n).
[89] Hill, *Colour, Space, and Music*, p. 5.

Here was Hill, no longer painting, but still seeking an emotional response from the things and people she was portraying; a response born of sympathy, of a shared sense of humanity – and a response which demanded action from those who experienced it.

The same was true of Octavia Hill's work more generally. As Anne Hoole Anderson has noted, the Red Cross Hall's heroic murals were never intended for Hill's tenants alone; they were also, as she puts it, 'a lesson for the "well-to-do-classes", that the poor were capable of nobility'.[90] The architecture Hill commissioned from Elijah Hoole served a comparable purpose, with the Red Cross cottages in particular evidently intended to affect visitors as much as they were meant to mould their inhabitants. In part inspired, as Hill made clear, by the pleasant peasant homes of the Tyrol, they also drew on the fashionable Arts and Crafts motifs that had recently become so popular with the progressive middle classes.[91] Similar, self-consciously vernacular artisans' houses were, for example, erected only a few years before by the improving T. G. Jackson, whose gabled, bay-windowed, irregularly-roofed Lime Tree Walk in Sevenoaks (1878–82) was likewise the product of alarm at what he termed 'the mischievous sorting out of classes into … two hostile camps'.[92] Leafy Sevenoaks was, of course, a very different world from urban Southwark, but both sets of developments shared a similar architectural inspiration. Tile-hung, rendered and artfully picturesque, Hoole's and Jackson's work breathed the spirit of the so-called 'Surrey style', with all its Arcadian evocations of a lost, more coherent community.[93] What could be more appropriate for Hill, whose self-declared ambition was to create an environment where 'poor and rich may be friends as in a country parish'?[94]

Far from representing a 'hopelessly myopic', much less an 'irrational' response to social problems,[95] Octavia Hill's small-scale building schemes are best understood as an ideal type, not unlike the model village of Saltaire

---

[90] A. Hoole Anderson, 'Bringing beauty home to the people: the Kyrle Society, 1877–1917', in Hill, *LFW*, pp. 703–33, esp. p. 726.

[91] See M. Girouard, *Sweetness and Light: the 'Queen Anne' Movement, 1860–1900* (Oxford, 1977); D. E. B. Weiner, *Architecture and Social Reform in Late-Victorian London* (Manchester and New York, 1994).

[92] Quoted in W. Whyte, *Oxford Jackson: Architecture, Education, Status, and Style, 1835–1924* (Oxford, 2006), p. 206.

[93] R. Gradidge, *The Surrey Style* (Godalming, 1991).

[94] Hill, *LFW*, 1881, p. 148.

[95] A. S. Wohl, 'Octavia Hill and the housing of the London poor', *Journal of British Studies*, x (1971), 125, 130. Interestingly, Maltz also condemns Hill for her 'myopic view of tenement reform' in *British Aestheticism*, p. 58.

'Nobler imaginings and mightier struggles'

which she visited towards the start of her career in housing.[96] More than this, they were in a very real sense works of art – and never more so than when they formed the backdrop for the social events which she hoped would draw together both benefactors and recipients of help. The flower shows and maypole dancing may now appear simply 'ludicrous', but they were in fact deliberate attempts to use spectacle in the service of sympathy.[97] Framed by their homely houses – each one made distinct and different through the use of artisan ornament and solid brick buttressing; placed within an attractive, ornamental garden; displaying the fruit and flowers that they themselves had grown: in those moments the tenants of Red Cross cottages were portrayed as the worthy recipients of support and the happy consequences of Hill's efforts. From the balcony which overlooked the garden, Octavia Hill and her supporters were thus presented with an image of harmony and social improvement: the poor no longer distant, unknown or a threat but the focus of real human affection. She cherished 'the friendly greetings of poor and rich' which these events encouraged.[98]

Such assumptions were not, of course, unproblematic. Indeed, Octavia Hill's belief in the power of sympathy was double-edged. Just as she insisted on the emotional pull of the inanimate, so it was all too easy for her to fall into the trap of depicting her tenants as things too. The subjects of her charity were thus often treated as objects. In Ruth Livesey's words, Hill's approach ensured that the poor were 'never full actors in the making of place'; any agency was always hers rather than theirs.[99] Nevertheless, these attitudes do represent real continuity, because the 'human work' she undertook was so obviously impelled by the same motivations and underwritten by the same assumptions as the 'artistic work' she had apparently abandoned. Certainly, this is all a long way from the sort of caesura previously depicted, much less Gareth Stedman Jones's notion of Octavia Hill as someone whose work represented 'the application of moral force to political economy'.[100] For this committed Ruskinian, nothing could be further from the truth.[101]

Indeed, that Octavia Hill remained fundamentally true to a single vocation is something that she herself increasingly came to accept. Writing to 'a Friend who is giving up art for business' in 1889, she observed:

---

[96] M. Hardman, *Ruskin and Bradford: an Experiment in Cultural History* (Manchester and New York, 1986), pp. 4–5.
[97] Wohl, 'Octavia Hill', p. 124.
[98] Hill, *LFW*, 1905, p. 523.
[99] R. Livesey, 'Women rent collectors and the rewriting of space, class, and gender in East London, 1870–1900', in *Women and the Making of Built Space*, p. 94.
[100] G. Stedman Jones, *Outcast London* (1971; Harmondsworth, 1976), p. 196.
[101] See also her comments on Mill in Maurice, *Hill*, p. 100.

> I remember so well a somewhat similar trial in my own early life, and how I seemed to have to turn away from my ideal; and, by unexpected ways, I found, years afterwards, that just the sacrifice I had to make brought me, by ways that I did not know, to that ideal.[102]

Not through her painting, nor solely through her work for the poor, but above all in her work representing the poor to those she hoped would help them, Octavia Hill did indeed remain true to a single ideal. In her art, as in her later endeavours, she sought more than anything else to evoke human sympathy and by evoking this sympathy she hoped to change the world. Just as she wrote to Ruskin, she always intended to 'preach a Gospel to the people by hand or brush'.[103]

---

[102] Maurice, *Life of Octavia Hill*, p. 485.
[103] Maurice, *Hill*, p. 128.

4. Octavia Hill's Red Cross Hall and its murals to heroic self-sacrifice

John Price

At a meeting on 25 November 1886 the ecclesiastical commissioners of England agreed a 999-year lease, at a rent of a farthing a year, on a third of an acre plot of land in the south London borough of Southwark.[1] The site of a derelict paper factory, the plot was sandwiched between White Cross Street and Red Cross Street opposite the Stanhope and Mowbray Buildings, a large housing development that had been built in 1884–5 by the Victorian Dwellings Association and the Metropolitan Industrial Dwellings Association.[2] The one condition attached to the lease was that the plot must include a garden and playground to serve the families living in the nearby dwellings, and other poor residents of Southwark. That was unproblematic as the lessee was a firm believer in the necessity of recreational open spaces in poor urban areas. She was Miss Octavia Hill.

Hill's passionate interest in open spaces and fresh air was shared by her sister Miranda and in 1876 the two formed the Kyrle Society with the aim of 'bringing beauty home to the people'.[3] Those involved with the society included the journalist and illustrator George Sala, artists such as Edward Burne-Jones, George Frederic Watts, Frederic Leighton, Walter Crane and, importantly for the story told in this chapter, Emilie (Mrs. Russell) Barrington.[4] Octavia acted as treasurer, although it is clear from the work of the society that her role was more central than that title implied, as Robert Whelan explores in this volume.[5] Among the society's founding aims, established at its first public meeting and reported in *The Spectator* in January 1881, were to 'decorate, by mural paintings, pictures, gifts of flowers, &c., workmen's clubs, schools, and mission-rooms, used for social

---

[1] Hill, *LFW*, 1886, pp. 203–4; Bankside Open Spaces Trust, Southwark, *Red Cross Gardens: Landscape Restoration Management Plan* (2001). Some material in this chapter was previously published in J. Price, *Everyday Heroism: Victorian Constructions of the Heroic Civilian* (2014).

[2] Hill, *LFW*, 1884 and 1885, p. 188.

[3] Hill, *LFW*, 1876; A. Hoole Anderson, 'Bringing beauty home to the people: the Kyrle Society, 1877–1917', in Hill, *LFW*, pp. 703–33.

[4] Anderson, 'Bringing beauty home'.

[5] G. Darley, *Octavia Hill* (1990), p. 179.

or religious gatherings' and also to 'secur[e] ... open-air spaces in poor neighbourhoods to be laid out as public gardens'.[6] When Hill persuaded the ecclesiastical commissioners to lease her the derelict paper factory, these two aims encompassed her vision for the scheme and the society became the organizational and financial body which furthered its development.

Hill had planned to canvass the wider Kyrle membership and the public at large for donations towards the garden but after Julia Reynolds-Moreton, Lady Ducie, gave £1,000 to meet that need, Hill instead appealed for funds to purchase the plot of land next to the garden, formerly a hop warehouse, which she persuaded the commissioners to set aside for her.[7] Her plan, as outlined in her letter to *The Times* of 14 March 1887, was to build six workers' cottages and a community hall which would act as a 'parish parlour' – part library and part reading room.[8] The £2,000 Hill estimated she needed for the hall's construction was given by Henry Cowper, former MP for Hertford, while the £1,300 required for the six cottages was donated by Lady Jane Dundas.[9] Work soon began and by December 1887 Hill excitedly informed her friends and patrons that 'the walls of my hall begin to rise, and three of my cottages are getting their roofs on'.[10]

The Red Cross Hall and Gardens were opened on 2 June 1888.[11] The cottages had been completed earlier in the year and were, according to Hill, forming comfortable homes for families. The hall and cottages were designed by Elijah Hoole and had echoes of the Gothic as well as being inspired by Hill's visits to the Tyrol.[12] *The Times* described the scene thus: 'beyond the garden the eye rests, not on tall warehouses or mean and grimy dwelling houses, but on gables and red bricks, lattice windows and brightly painted paintwork', while *The Graphic* reported that Hill had created 'a cheerful little oasis' in otherwise grimy Southwark.[13] The gardens provided the open space and glimpse of natural beauty so desired by Hill, while the hall provided warm, dry, communal space for residents and was the perfect setting for the plays, readings, music recitals, art exhibitions and other educational entertainments championed by Hill, acting by herself and through the Kyrle Society. Furthermore the interior of the hall was to

---

[6] *The Spectator*, 29 Jan. 1881; H. L. Malchow, 'Public gardens and social action in late Victorian London', *Victorian Studies*, xxix (1985), 108.

[7] Robert Hunter, later co-founder with Hill of the National Trust, supplied the goldfish for the ornamental pond (Hill, *LFW*, 1886, pp. 203–6).

[8] *The Times*, 14 March 1887.

[9] Hill, *LFW*, 1887, pp. 221–9.

[10] Hill, *LFW*, 1887, p. 222.

[11] Bankside Open Spaces Trust, *Red Cross Gardens: Landscape Restoration Management Plan*.

[12] Hill, *LFW*, 1887, p. 223, n. 12.

[13] *The Times*, 2 June 1888; *The Graphic*, 30 June 1888.

contain a unique scheme of decoration intended to 'bring beauty home to the people' and thereby to uplift their behaviour.

It is this 'noble scheme of pictorial decoration', as Hill described it, which this chapter considers.[14] A series of murals depicting acts of civilian heroism, it shows the influence Hill commanded through her extended network of liberal and philanthropic artists and writers, who, following Matthew Arnold, believed that the newly enfranchised working classes must be culturally and spiritually educated if they were fully to participate in modern society and politics.[15] Hill largely left the details of the mural scheme to others within the wider network, but it echoed many of the sentiments she voiced in her public speeches and Letters to fellow-workers. Indeed, the whole Red Cross project was, in many respects, the 'perfect example' of Hill's and the Kyrle Society's holistic approach to environment, and the decorative scheme for the hall was the epitome of her aspirations to bring beauty to the people as much for its moral as for its aesthetic qualities.[16] Hill believed that 'man ceases to be man if he lives only for creature comforts; there is no one so forlorn or degraded', and this, a restating of the biblical injunction that man should not live by bread alone, underpinned her intentions for the hall murals and other examples of public art, as well as her plans to bring colour into private homes and to bring poor people into natural open spaces.[17]

As William Whyte shows in his chapter, evoking humanity and sympathy through art and beauty were central to Hill's social work and to her belief that such things affected human character and development. A question common to several essays in this volume is whether Hill was radical or reactionary, and a close reading of the decorative scheme for the Red Cross Hall may help this debate. Another recurrent theme is the 'nobility' which Hill ascribed to people, ideals and practical projects, and the Red Cross decorative scheme, enthusiastically labelled 'noble' by Hill, provides a further illustration of the meanings she intended to convey with the word. Famous for her close management of all her projects and people, and known to place a high value on the exemplary power of the Red Cross development, Hill shared many, though not all, of the social, cultural and political views of those in her network to whom she entrusted the decoration of her hall. Consequently, the more we understand them and their motivations, the more we understand Hill and hers.

---

[14] Hill, *LFW*, 1892, p. 320.

[15] M. Arnold, *Culture and Anarchy* (1869); for a case study of such ideas, see H. E. Meller, *Leisure and the Changing City, 1870–1914* (1976).

[16] Quotation from Anderson, 'Bringing beauty home', p. 716.

[17] O. Hill, 'The Kyrle Society', *Charity Organisation Review*, July–Dec. 1905, p. 315.

Mrs. Barrington and a 'suggestion for the Kyrle Society'

The first two characters we encounter in Hill's network are biographer, novelist and artist Emilie Isabel Barrington (née Wilson) and artist George Frederic Watts. Barrington met Watts through her association with Rossetti and the Little Holland House circle, and their relationship was strengthened when she persuaded her husband, Russell Barrington, to buy a house next to Watts's studio on Melbury Road.[18] Barrington, like Hill, was committed to improving the lot of the poor through art and was a prime mover in the Kyrle Society since its inception (as well as being one of Hill's portraitists, as Heath discusses in this volume).[19] In late September 1887, Watts wrote to *The Times* to call attention to 'heroism in every-day life', that is, events in which 'ordinary' members of the public lost their life while attempting to save others.[20] Less than a month later Barrington wrote to *The Spectator* with 'A suggestion for the Kyrle Society'. She reproduced Watts's letter and suggested that 'there has never arisen a better opportunity for carrying out such an idea as is afforded by the opening of the People's Palace'.[21] The palace, opened in 1887, was an impressive public hall on the Mile End Road between Stepney and Bow, modelled on the 'Palace of Delight' in Walter Besant's novel *All Sorts and Conditions of Men* (1882) and 'conceived as a grand center of learning, culture and recreation for the East End Poor'.[22] After outlining at some length her opinions on the nature of heroism and heroes, Barrington concluded by suggesting that 'if any art could be created which would recall such emotions, the Kyrle Society would have found a work to do worthy of all possible labour and skill. The "if", doubtless, is a very big one'.[23]

One artist who believed the 'if' to be not only big but virtually insurmountable was another member of Hill's extended network and a supporter of the Kyrle Society, Frederic Leighton. Barrington sent Leighton copies of her *Spectator* letter and Watts's letter to *The Times* to seek his opinion on the project and he was not reticent in expressing it. Although

---

[18] R Mitchell, 'Barrington, Emilie Isabel (1841–1933)', *ODNB*; M. Westwater, *The Wilson Sisters: a Biographical Study of Upper Middle-Class Victorian Life* (Cleveland, Ohio, 1984).

[19] Mitchell, 'Barrington, Emilie Isabel (1841–1933)'.

[20] *The Times*, 5 Sept. 1887; J. Price, *Postman's Park: G. F. Watts's Memorial to Heroic Self-Sacrifice* (Compton, Calif., 2008).

[21] *The Spectator*, 24 Sept. 1887.

[22] S. Joyce, 'Castles in the air: the People's Palace, cultural reformism, and the East End working class', *Victorian Studies*, xxxix (1996), 513–38, quotation at p. 515; D. Weiner, 'The People's Palace: an image for East End London in the 1880s', in *Metropolis London: Histories and Representations since 1800*, ed. D. Feldman and G. Stedman Jones (1989), pp. 40–55.

[23] *The Spectator*, 24 Sept. 1887.

'not seeking to throw cold water or to be what is called a wet blanket', he felt he should remind her of the complexity of the problem.[24] Yes, he thought Watts's idea an excellent one, and he 'sympathize[d] warmly with the thought of keeping the memory of heroic deeds alive in our people'. He also, of course, wished to see good art spread among the masses. However, he was unsure 'how far the idea of purely and directly didactic painting … is compatible with the *adornment* of spaces with a view to training the eye of the people to a sense of *beauty*' and he wondered whether art could satisfactorily communicate the determination and perseverance required by these heroic individuals. He cited the case of the Southwark nursemaid Alice Ayres, described by Watts, as an example:

> her refusal to save herself, the successive journeys backward and forward, the spirit of self-sacrifice sustaining her throughout; that is the subject and it is not expressible in Art which requires one poignant moment. No one moment out of that drama could convey its meaning or its greatness.

Leighton concluded by asserting that, 'you may paint a picture (perhaps) of one moment in that drama, but you could not in a picture even hint at what makes it sublime'.

Leighton's discouragement did not, however, dampen Barrington's zeal. It was thirteen years before Watts was able to realise his desire to commemorate working-class heroism and construct his Memorial to Heroic Self-Sacrifice in Postman's Park, an open space in the city of London secured with the very active involvement of Hill, individually and collectively through the Kyrle Society. Unveiled in 1900, the memorial, described by Hill as 'very simple, very beautiful; and strangely peaceful', consisted of a wooden cloister sheltering a series of memorial tiles manufactured by William de Morgan.[25] Prior to that, though, Barrington pressed ahead with her own scheme and, in 1893, she was able to report that 'Miss Octavia Hill, Lady Wentworth [later Lovelace, a member of the Kyrle Society's general council], Mr Walter Crane, and the present writer decided they would propose to the Kyrle Society a scheme for decorating the Red Cross Hall with designs by Mr Walter Crane'.[26]

---

[24] All the quotations in this paragraph are from Leighton's letter to Barrington reprinted in A. Corkran, *Frederic Leighton* (1904), pp. 156–9.

[25] Hill, *LFW*, 1900, p. 457.

[26] E. (Mrs. Russell) Barrington, 'The Red Cross Hall', *The English Illustrated Magazine*, cxvii (1893), 610–18, quotation at p. 614.

Walter Crane and ideals in art

Walter Crane, decorative artist and art theorist, was a socially and artistically progressive figure and an important character in Hill's extended network and in the Kyrle Society.[27] Hill's admiration for his work and many of his sentiments led her to choose him to design and make the 'inscription in beautifully coloured tiles' at Freshwater Place, as she described in her 1873 Letter.[28] Barrington was also a friend and admirer of Crane who was, in turn, strongly associated with William and Mary Morris and the wider Arts and Crafts movement which connected him to Ruskin and Watts among others. Crane was further linked to Hill through his association with Hardwicke Rawnsley: in 1897 Crane visited the 'well equipped and housed Arts and Crafts School at Keswick, which owes much to the zeal of Canon and Mrs Rawnsley', and where local people learned practical craft skills, such as wood carving and metalwork.[29]

It is not clear exactly when Crane became involved with Barrington's plans for the Red Cross Hall, or indeed when the plans were first put forward, but a basic timetable of events can be assembled. In 1887, Barrington, Hill and Crane met to discuss the venture, then in *The Times* of March 1888 Barrington solicited donations, declaring the scheme was underway with Crane as its designer; and by 1892, Hill reported to her fellow workers that 'Mr Crane has all the sketches ready'.[30] It is unsurprising to find Crane at the heart of the project, given his links with Barrington, Hill and the Kyrle Society and many of its most influential supporters. However, other elements of this scheme made it especially attractive to him.

Crane believed art, and especially large-scale murals, to be a powerful tool for educating the public. He lamented that 'the modern world has grown too accustomed to the idea that art is a luxury to be passively enjoyed … to realise its active and stimulating powers, its moral and educative function, its positive and practical side'.[31] In fact, according to Crane, examples from ancient and medieval cities showed that 'patriotism and citizenship was [sic] stimulated by pictured parables of heroic deeds of local saints and heroes'.[32] Consequently, in his 1905 study *Ideals in Art* he argued

---

[27] M. O'Neill, *Walter Crane: the Arts and Crafts, Paintings, and Politics, 1875–1890* (New Haven, Conn., 2010).
[28] Hill, *LFW*, 1873, p. 19.
[29] W. Crane, *An Artist's Reminiscences* (1907), p. 449.
[30] E. Barrington, 'The Red Cross Hall', *English Illustrated Magazine*, x (1893), 610–18; *The Times*, 30 March 1888; Hill, *LFW*, 1892, p. 320.
[31] W. Crane, 'Art and character', in P. L. Parker, *Character and Life: a Symposium* (1912), pp. 107–50, quotation at p. 124.
[32] Crane, 'Art and character', p. 113.

that, 'if education was considered ... might we not, from the storehouse of history and folklore, picture our school and college walls with great and typical figures of heroes?'[33] Mural painting, he argued, could communicate didactic messages to wide and impressionable audiences, and Crane sought to exploit this unique element of large-scale public murals: the link between their message and their location.

As Clare Willsdon has argued, 'in public buildings, churches or schools, murals might offer a focus for ritual and remembrance, or provide propaganda and instruction'.[34] While moveable paintings or pictures in books could be viewed in a variety of places, murals were, by their nature, designed for a specific location, and place and subject might be particularly strongly linked: William Bell Scott's series of eight murals (1855–61) for Sir Walter and Lady Trevelyan of Wallington Hall, Northumberland, for example, depicted scenes from Northumbrian history, while Ford Maddox Brown's twelve murals for Manchester's Town Hall (1879–93) showed notable events in the city's history.[35] Crane was fully persuaded and claimed 'the true place for the decorative perpetuation of local history and legend is the Town Hall'.[36] He further believed that any public space – school, college or hospital – was suitable as long as the message was designed for the audience. As Morna O'Neill has concluded, 'as the "Drawing Room" of Southwark, the Red Cross Hall functioned as an open book for moral education, and the murals of Walter Crane depicting the everyday heroic deeds of the worker would provide the lessons'.[37] Since one of the first declared objectives of the Kyrle Society was to provide decorative murals, the Red Cross Hall scheme met many of the aspirations of Hill, Crane and the society.

Crane and the Red Cross Hall murals

Elijah Hoole designed the Red Cross Hall with a series of large mural spaces, eleven-and-a-half feet long by six feet wide, which, according to

---

[33] W. Crane, *Ideals in Art* (1905), p. 98.
[34] C. A. P. Willsdon, *Mural Painting in Britain 1840–1940: Image and Meaning* (Oxford, 2000), p. 1.
[35] P. Usherwood, 'William Bell Scott's iron and coal: northern readings', in *Pre-Raphaelite Painters and Patrons in the North East*, ed. J. Vickers (Newcastle, 1989), pp. 39–56; J. Treuherz, 'Ford Madox Brown and the Manchester murals', in *Art and Architecture in Victorian Manchester*, ed. J. G. Archer (Manchester, 1985), pp. 162–207; P. Barlow, 'Local disturbances: Ford Madox Brown and the problems of the Manchester murals', in *Re-Framing the Pre-Raphaelites: Historical and Theoretical Essays*, ed. E. Harding (Aldershot, 1996), pp. 81–97.
[36] W. Crane, 'Thoughts on house decoration', in *Ideals in Art*, p. 120.
[37] M. O'Neill, 'Everyday heroic deeds: Walter Crane and Octavia Hill at the Red Cross Hall', *The Acorn: Journal of the Octavia Hill Society*, ii (2003), 4–21, quotation at p. 11.

Hill, were left bare to accommodate decoratively painted plaster panels designed by Crane (see Figure 4.1). There were five spaces along one long side and four on the other. It was envisaged that Crane would design and create quarter-size versions of the murals to be scaled-up and painted on to plaster panels by other artists under his close supervision before being put up in the hall. Crane had advocated this method in an essay of 1893 on decorative painting and design: 'by a method of working in ordinary oil colours on a ground of fibrous plaster … much of the quality of fresco or tempera may be obtained, with the advantage that the plaster ground may be a movable panel'.[38] The *Pall Mall Gazette* of 8 October 1890 announced that Crane had completed all nine preparatory sketches and that work was getting underway on the first of the full-scale panels.[39] It also reported that the designs had been exhibited in 1890 by the Arts and Crafts Exhibition Society, whose founding president was Crane.

The facts about most of the deeds that the murals depict are hard to ascertain. Crane did not say who supplied him with the particulars of the acts, and Barrington makes no mention of the subject in any of her reports on the project. The series of five panels was to feature: 'An explosion in a mine', 'Rescue from drowning by a youth', 'Rescue from fire: a man holding a ladder while his arms are exposed to a dropping of melted lead', 'A Sister of Mercy holding back a dog from attacking her school-children' and 'The rescue of a boat's crew from the rocks'. On the opposite wall the planned panels were to depict: 'Rescue from a well', 'Alice Ayres', 'Jamieson' and 'The man who took the bull by the horns'.[40] Ultimately, only three designs – those depicting 'Alice Ayres', 'Jamieson' and 'Rescue from a well' – were translated into full-size versions and erected in the hall.

In its choice of subject matter, the project was somewhat radical. The models of heroism promoted by the establishment in the second half of the nineteenth century often relied on military examples to encourage citizenship and loyalty to crown, empire or nation-state.[41] As civilian heroism became more widely reported, it was recognized using existing establishment or ruling-class methods: decorations for civilian gallantry, for example, complemented those for military gallantry.[42] The people

---

[38] W. Crane, 'Of decorative painting and design', in *Arts and Crafts Essays*, ed. W. Morris (1893), pp. 39–51, quotation at p. 50.

[39] *Pall Mall Gazette*, 8 Oct. 1890. Crane produced the designs for all nine murals, but did not paint all the full-size panels.

[40] Barrington, pp. 610–18.

[41] J. Price, *Everyday Heroism: Victorian Constructions of the Heroic Civilian* (2014), pp. 64–5.

[42] Price, *Everyday Heroism*, ch. 1.

Octavia Hill's Red Cross Hall and its murals to heroic self-sacrifice

Figure 4.1. The interior of the Red Cross Hall, Southwark (*English Illustrated Magazine*, June 1893).

behind the Red Cross Hall scheme, by contrast, were among the reformers, philanthropists, artists and writers who championed civilian heroes, rather than simply accommodating them, and sought to commemorate them through alternative media such as art and architecture in which otherwise 'ordinary' people tended not to be represented as heroes.

The first design undertaken by Crane commemorated Alice Ayres, and the finished panel was erected in the hall in 1890 (see Figure 4.2). In it, Ayres stands on the ledge of an open window, wearing a long, flowing gown and holding a small child in her arms while another cowers behind her. In the foreground a fireman and a seaman have climbed a ladder to help her.

'Nobler imaginings and mightier struggles'

Figure 4.2. Illustration of Walter Crane's mural, 'Alice Ayres', erected in the Red Cross Hall in 1890 (*English Illustrated Magazine*, June 1893).

Octavia Hill's Red Cross Hall and its murals to heroic self-sacrifice

Figure 4.3. The Union Street Fire, Borough, 1885 (Southwark Local History Library, unreferenced newspaper cutting).

'Nobler imaginings and mightier struggles'

The fireman, depicted in vivid and well-crafted detail, holds his arms wide to receive Ayres and the child, while the seaman cradles a third child. An arm reaching up from below suggests that further helpers stand ready, and Ayres appears calm and collected as she waits to be drawn into the arms of her gallant rescuers.

Contemporary reports of the incident, however, suggest a very different story. Witnesses to the terrible fire at 194 Union Street, Borough, in 1885, described how Alice Ayres, clad in her nightdress and carrying a small, crying child, appeared suddenly at an upper-storey window. Having thrown a feather bed out of the window to cushion the child's fall, Ayres carefully let the small child drop (see Figure 4.3). Deaf to the cries of crowd who implored her to save herself, she disappeared back into the smoke, but reappeared with a second child whom she also let fall into the waiting arms of the crowd. Once more she disappeared and reappeared, clutching a third child whom she also dropped from the window to the people below. This time she heeded the calls to save herself but, apparently overcome by smoke and exhaustion, fell limply from the window, struck part of the shop front in her fall, and hit the pavement below. Her spine severely injured, she was conveyed to Guy's hospital where her condition deteriorated and she died two days later.[43]

There was no ladder, no fireman and no seaman, and Alice, although showing great presence of mind, certainly did not stand serenely on the window ledge and await her rescue. Perhaps Leighton's assertion was correct and Crane had been unable to capture the unfolding drama of the event in a single image or perhaps he felt that the moral lesson of heroism would be diluted if the panel dwelt too much on tragedy. Whatever the reason, Crane chose to create a symbolic image that allowed him to communicate the messages he considered important. The fireman and the seaman, both working-class archetypes, hint at the more typically understood heroism of their class and gender. As Morna O'Neill has highlighted, Crane disdained artists such as Frederick Brown and Henry Herbert La Thangue whose depictions of labourers offered only a negative image of oppression.[44] Crane's portrayal of the fire directs attention to the three children who were safely rescued and is silent about the tragic death of Alice and other family members. Furthermore, an examination of how the design evolved shows how Crane gradually moved away from factual accuracy the better to convey a highly idealised and symbolic message of exemplary heroism.

---

[43] *Southwark Recorder and Bermondsey and Rotherhithe Advertiser*, 2 May 1885; *South London Press*, 2 May 1885; *South London Observer*, 29 Apr. 1885.
[44] O'Neill, *Walter Crane*, pp. 107–8.

Octavia Hill's Red Cross Hall and its murals to heroic self-sacrifice

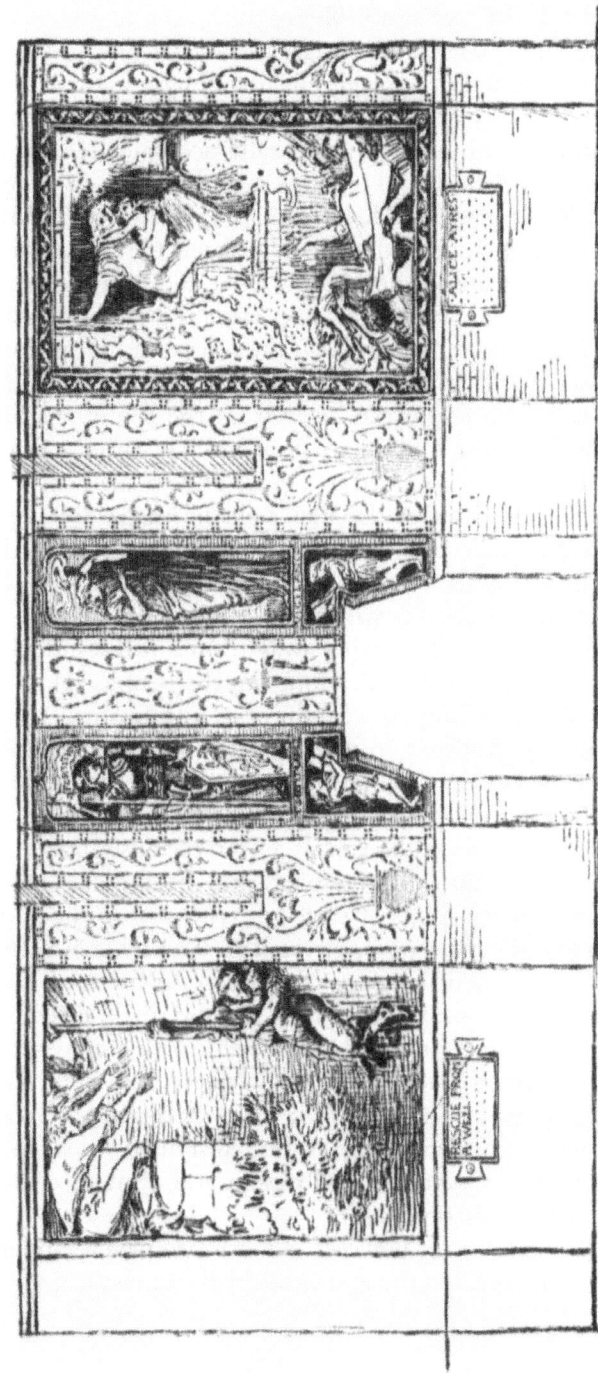

Figure 4.4. Illustration showing part of the planned panel layout for the mural project in the Red Cross Hall (*English Illustrated Magazine*, June 1893).

'Nobler imaginings and mightier struggles'

The evolution of the mural designs

Crane substantially changed the design at least twice before settling on the version that was erected in the hall. His first design, known only through a drawing reproduced by Mrs. Barrington in the *English Illustrated Magazine* of 1893, is undoubtedly the most factually accurate (see Figure 4.4, top right-hand corner). This design was also described by a *Times* reporter: 'Mr Walter Crane has represented her [Ayres] holding one child in her arms, and below another being lifted out of the sheet, the flames rising towards the window'.[45] Ayres sits on the window ledge and supports herself with an outstretched arm while waiting to drop the child she is carrying into the sheet below. This design closely follows the real events of the fire as reported by eyewitnesses, with no fireman, seaman or ladder. Given that the Red Cross Hall lay only a few streets away from the site of the fire, many of those who saw the mural would have been familiar with the facts of the case which were also to be expounded in a descriptive panel beneath the image. Despite this, it was felt that the first realistic image did not adequately communicate the desired message – whether Crane's, Hill's or Barrington's – and the artist set about altering the design.

Crane's second design, for which the original quarter-size preparatory sketch has survived, moved sharply away from a realistic depiction of the facts of the case (see Figure 4.5). Gone are the people below holding the sheets into which the children were dropped and, instead, a fireman on a ladder stretches out his arms to rescue Ayres and the child she is holding. At the foot of the ladder a young woman grasps another child, apparently already rescued from the flames (see Figure 4.6). Unlike the first design, in which Ayres and the child she carries are precariously poised, the second design invites the reading that heroism, on the fireman's part, will save the day. Even so, it still hints at tragedy. Ayres sits on the window ledge, apparently in her nightdress, supporting herself with her arm and she seems uncertain and concerned as she looks down to the fireman. The nakedness of the child she holds speaks of urgency and the small, disembodied arms, shown reaching upwards in the window next to her, suggest a third child desperate to be saved (see Figure 4.7). Maybe this was three year-old Elizabeth Chandler who later perished from the burns she received before she was dropped from the window. Although stylised when compared with the actual incident, Crane's second design still contained elements that hinted at the actual outcome.

Realistic elements were, however, almost completely absent from the design which was erected in the Red Cross Hall (see Figure 4.2). The fireman

---

[45] *The Times*, 6 June 1888.

Figure 4.5. Walter Crane, *Study for 'Alice Ayres'* for the Red Cross Hall, Southwark, c.1889.

Figure 4.6. Enlarged detail from Walter Crane, *Study for 'Alice Ayres' for the Red Cross Hall, Southwark*, c.1889.

remains, but the female figure at the foot of the ladder becomes a male seaman. No longer seated, Ayres is upright, her right foot apparently resting on the shop sign while she places her left knee on the window ledge, though this is difficult to see because her simple nightdress has become a classical robe. No longer holding on for safety, she instead wraps both arms around the child and appears calm, an almost serene smile playing on her lips. The disembodied arms of the third child have become a whole figure who stands beside Ayres in the window, uninjured and calmly awaiting its inevitable rescue. Ayres and the seaman look out from the picture to the imagined viewer, rather than realistically inwards at the other characters. All sense of urgency has gone as the children are clothed and, despite the flames that lick the window frame, the scene is not one of impending tragedy, but rather of calm and effective heroism – shared equally by the fireman, the seaman and, to a lesser extent, Ayres. Realism is gone and a study in heroism takes its place.

A similar story can be told of the second panel which was erected in the hall in 1892.[46] No preparatory sketches for this design appear to have survived, but an illustration of the final panel was reproduced in the *English*

[46] Crane, *An Artist's Reminiscences*, p. 359.

Octavia Hill's Red Cross Hall and its murals to heroic self-sacrifice

Figure 4.7. Enlarged detail from Walter Crane, *Study for 'Alice Ayres'* for the Red Cross Hall, Southwark, c.1889.

Illustrated Magazine in 1893 (see Figure 4.8). In the foreground of the panel two railwaymen work on the line while in the distance an express train bears down on them. Their fellow workers beside the track attempt in vain to alert the workmen and driver to the impending disaster. Crane's portrayal of this incident was, like that of the Ayres fire, highly stylized. The facts of the case were that around 8.15am on 8 July 1874 the Glasgow express came down the Glasgow and Paisley joint line and, not seeing the railwaymen at work on it, its driver continued at his usual speed.[47] Some of the men who were moving a sleeper saw the approaching train and ran in fear of their lives, dropping the sleeper on the line. This would have derailed the train had Alex Jamieson and his nephew Alexander not rushed to move it. Unable then to get themselves clear of the line, they were killed instantly as the express struck them.

In Crane's depiction there is no indication that the bystanding workmen had caused the problem which the Jamiesons died trying to correct. Instead, the two heroes are simply bent over the track, labouring hard, as the train approaches, while their fellow workers seem almost resigned to the heroes'

[47] *The Glasgow Herald*, 9 July 1874; *The Preston Guardian*, 11 July 1874.

fate. Crane was perhaps alluding to the 'heroism' displayed routinely by labouring men in the course of their working day: the Jamiesons are poised to lose their lives while labouring, the tools of their trade still in their hands and lying beside them on the track. The traditional workman's pipe, apparently dropped on the track by one of the Jamiesons (central bottom of Figure 4.8), may represent his discarding or sacrificing something personal for the good of others. These symbols perhaps allude to the idea of the 'nobility of labour', propounded by Thomas Carlyle and others and illustrated by contemporaries of Crane's such as Ford Madox Brown in *Work* (1852–65) and James Sharples in *The Forge* (1859).[48] One of the fellow workers waves a warning towards the train, but the other two appear to wave at the Jamiesons, perhaps in a gesture of farewell, or perhaps even to the viewer in an appeal to pity men working under such conditions. Whatever his intention, when Crane depicted the Paisley platelayers, as with the Ayres story, his aim was less to relay the facts of the matter and more to communicate exemplary and educative messages through an idealized image.

In 1894 the third full-size panel was erected in the hall, on the same wall and adjacent to the previous two, and it portrayed the rescue of a child from a well. Little is known of the actual incident from contemporary press reports, but Edwin Mead's pamphlet *Heroes of Peace* (1912) reported that the mural depicted George Eales, a fifty-eight-year-old labourer who in December 1887 at Drummer, near Basingstoke in Hampshire, had gone down a well to rescue a five-year-old child who had fallen in. Neither Crane's original design or sketches nor a satisfactory reproduction of the panel is known, so it is difficult to comment on its conception or development. Nevertheless it can be imagined that Crane would have favoured idealized symbolism over graphic realism with this as with the first two panels.

Although nine murals were proposed and initially designed by Crane, 'Rescue from a well' was the last panel erected in the hall. Despite an initial contribution of £35 by Mrs. Barrington in 1888 and a donation of £5 in 1892 from the Red Cross Hall committee, many of whom represented the local working men's club which used the hall, the money available was inadequate.[49] As Crane explained, 'the work had to be largely a labour of love, as very little money was available for such a purpose, and as other work had to be attended to … the scheme is still incomplete'.[50] Public support may have waned because of the long delay between the announcement of

---

[48] T. Carlyle, *Past and Present* (1843); T. Barringer, *Men at Work: Art and Labour in Victorian Britain* (2005).

[49] Hill, *LFW*, 1892, p. 319.

[50] This and the following quotation are from Crane, *An Artist's Reminiscences*, p. 360.

Octavia Hill's Red Cross Hall and its murals to heroic self-sacrifice

Figure 4.8. Illustration of the Walter Crane mural, 'Jamieson', erected in the Red Cross Hall in 1892 (*English Illustrated Magazine*, June 1893).

the project and the completion of the initial panels or the project's sporadic progress. Crane was also disillusioned after discovering that 'the hall is not all one could wish for such a work and I fear that the use of gas has injured the paintings'. It had indeed, and though Hill reported in 1911 that she was 'glad to say we have had electric lights installed, partly for the sake of better preserving the Walter Crane panels', the damage was done.[51] The project, begun with such high hopes, thus came to a sad end: six of nine panels unrealized and the other three, first damaged by smoke, and then apparently painted over when ownership of the Red Cross Hall changed in the 1930s.[52]

The Red Cross Hall project and Hill's associates

The decorative scheme at the Red Cross Hall gives a particularly valuable insight into the aims of Hill's associates who, as they formulated and undertook the project, made clear their views and objectives. They were motivated primarily by art and beautification, on the one hand, and moral and social education, on the other. Acts of everyday heroism were ideal vehicles for addressing both.

With her interests in art, her close involvement with the Kyrle Society and her association with artists such as Ruskin, Leighton and Watts, Mrs. Barrington was an enthusiast for beautifying spaces through public art. Writing to *The Times*, she described public murals as 'a treasure worthy of the best and healthiest times of art growth'.[53] Moreover, works of art and acts of heroism mutually reinforced one another. Down the years those who looked at the murals as works of art would also see 'a lasting testimony to the heroism of Englishmen and women who have displayed virtues [of] courage, fortitude and an unquestioning sense of duty', while those who came looking for educational or inspirational tales of heroism would also see first-rate and enduring works of art.[54]

Crane, as his involvement with the Kyrle Society and the Arts and Crafts movement attests, also claimed that art could improve lives, and the acts of everyday heroism at the heart of his murals provided an ideal subject. As he wrote, in 1897, about the decoration of public buildings, 'a people without art, collectively speaking, is inarticulate, and … after all, the highest, most vital art is the expression of character'.[55] Crane sought to create public art

[51] Hill, *LFW*, 1911, p. 658.
[52] O'Neill, *Walter Crane*, p. 227, n. 155; Southwark Local Studies Library, *Public Hall* file.
[53] *The Times*, 30 March 1888.
[54] *The Times*, 30 March 1888.
[55] W. Crane, 'Of the decoration of public buildings' (1897), p. 163.

which could intelligibly and articulately convey morality, humanity and exemplary character, but which was not dependent on either religious or capitalist symbols or conventions: as Greg Smith has argued, Crane sought a 'secular language of public art'.[56] In this, he took inspiration from Ford Madox Brown who, writing in 1893 on the completion of his Manchester Town Hall murals project, had asserted, 'I have noticed that subjects that interest infallibly all classes, educated or illiterate, are religious subjects. It is not a question of piety – but comes from the simple breadth of poetry and humanity usually involved in that class of subject'.[57]

In similar vein, Crane sought to communicate his didactic messages through secular imagery with a firm moral grounding. As Isobel Spencer has concluded, 'Crane believed that an artist's aim in depicting ordinary life should be to infuse it with improving factors like dignity, devotion and heroism'.[58] Not only did everyday heroism provide secular, yet universally appealing, subject matter, it also provided an honourable and noble subject worthy of the honourable and noble medium through which it was to be communicated. As a lifelong committed Christian, Hill would not necessarily have understood Crane's desire for a secular interpretation of religious themes. She did, though, believe in the presence of the divine in everyday objects and events, and she and the Kyrle Society consistently rejected religious exclusivity. At its first public meeting, reported in *The Spectator*, it was declared that the Kyrle Society was to meet its objectives 'without distinction of creed'.[59] Consequently, Crane's depictions of everyday heroism could be read by Hill and others using a non-sectarian Christian lexicon, just as readily as they could be read by those more receptive to a secular message.

Inspiration and moral instruction formed the second, and more important, motive behind the decorative project, as Barrington made clear in a letter to *The Spectator* in 1887. Her intention was 'to try and use such a record as a lever to raise the standard of good and excite admiration in many a nature which might otherwise remain unconscious and indifferent'.[60] In 1888 she claimed that 'no place is more worthy or more appropriate [than the Red Cross Hall] in which to commemorate the heroic deeds of the poor', and yet a year earlier she had made the same claim for the People's Palace

[56] G. Smith, 'Developing a public language of art', in *Walter Crane 1845–1915: Artist, Designer, and Socialist*, ed. G. Smith and S. Hyde (Manchester, 1989), pp. 13–23, quotation at p. 13.
[57] F. M. Brown, 'Of mural painting', in *Arts and Crafts Essays*, ed. W. Morris (1893), pp. 149–60, quotation at p. 158.
[58] I. Spencer, *Walter Crane* (1975), p. 133.
[59] *The Spectator*, 29 Jan. 1881.
[60] *The Spectator*, 24 Sept. 1887.

in Mile End.[61] The same reasoning, however, applied to both locations: in each, the murals would be seen primarily by working-class people. Such people were not only, according to Barrington, those most in need of moral and social education, but also those with whom 'the heroism displayed by people of their own way of living' would most resonate. Furthermore, this link between audience and subject was not lost on Crane.

Like all murals, those in the Red Cross Hall were intrinsically tied to their location: though created on moveable panels, they were not intended to be removed once installed and, in any case, were designed with the site in mind. Deeds of everyday heroism appealed to Crane because they were 'proof of the strength of the social bond and feeling of solidarity of the community when it is a question of life and death' – something which was closely related to his political beliefs.[62] In his early teens Crane was influenced by the polemicist and ardent Chartist William James Linton, to whom he was apprenticed as an engraver's draughtsman in 1859. In 1884 Crane declared himself a socialist, initially joining Henry Hyndman's Social Democratic Federation, but then following his close friend William Morris into the Socialist League and, in 1890, the Hammersmith Socialist Society.[63] Crane created designs and illustrations for a number of socialist and trade union organizations, many with different agendas, but always in support of ideals of liberty and equality. Crane believed that his art and designs could further his social and political ends, especially when communicated through an appropriate medium to a relevant audience, and this informed his approach to the Red Cross Hall murals. Crane's socialism – secular, theoretical and often connected with organized labour – was, of course, quite different from Hill's theologically informed Christian Socialism. However, the two conceptions shared ideas that Hill would have described as the 'nobility' of the poor and both recognized the importance of art and the power of example in the realization of that nobility.

In the Alice Ayres mural, Crane amended his original design, which depicted Ayres acting largely alone, to include a fireman and seaman, both working-class archetypes, as the heroes of the occasion. Likewise, in the Paisley railway accident mural, the heroic individuals are unmistakably identified as labouring men, their clothing, tools and activities marking them out from supervisors or foreman. Both designs, and their intended accompanying narrative plaques, refer to specific acts of individual heroism,

---

[61] *The Times*, 30 March 1888; *The Spectator*, 24 Sept. 1887.
[62] Crane, *An Artist's Reminiscences*, pp. 358–9.
[63] A. Crawford, 'Crane, Walter (1845–1915)', *ODNB*.

but Crane's designs also communicate a broader message which celebrated and championed the enduring, everyday heroism of labouring men or women who undertook their work diligently and responsibly, even when it cost them their lives. This possibility of nobility in the ordinary was a message with which Hill readily sympathized, and the possibility that art could both commemorate and stimulate such nobility (though at some levels merely fanciful as Maltz has argued) was central to Hill and her associates as they conceived and undertook the decoration of the Red Cross Hall.[64]

Crane recognized that Hill's 'parish parlour' was particularly fertile ground on which to cast his seeds of socialism. The nine panels could very easily have contained designs showing Nelson at Trafalgar, Wellington at Waterloo, Gordon at Khartoum, Florence Nightingale, Henry Havelock or Charles Napier, all of whom largely exemplified the establishment hero.[65] However, Crane, Barrington, Hill and the others in the same network adopted a more radical approach, believing working-class heroes provided more relevant, and therefore influential, examples for their largely working-class audience. Their argument was certainly not that these were lesser heroes for lesser audiences. In her 1892 Letter, Hill cited the funeral oration for the Paisley railwaymen at which the minister quoted lines from Tennyson's 'Ode on the death of the Duke of Wellington'. Similar valour, Hill implied, impelled both the national, military hero and the obscure, provincial railwayman and both deserved memorialization.[66] However, each memorial taught a specific lesson to a specific audience, and the Red Cross audience might find fellow feeling particularly with working-class heroes.

Such beliefs can be seen as homogenizing the working-classes and misunderstanding commonality as a product of social class rather than being based on a range of more nuanced factors. Nevertheless, evidence suggests that heroic acts undertaken by working-class people did speak uniquely to those who were similarly placed. The funeral of Alice Ayres,

---

[64] D. Maltz, *British Aestheticism and the Urban Working Classes, 1870–1900: Beauty for the People* (Basingstoke, 2005).

[65] G. Dawson, *Soldier Heroes: British Adventure, Empire, and the Imagining of Masculinities* (1994); J. M. Mackenzie, 'Heroic myths of empire', in *Popular Imperialism and the Military 1850–1950*, ed. J. M. Mackenzie (Manchester, 1992), pp. 109–38; I. Pears, 'The gentleman and the hero: Wellington and Napoleon in the nineteenth century', in *Myths of the English*, ed. R. Porter (Cambridge, 1992), pp. 216–36; M. Vicinus, 'What makes a heroine? Girls' biographies of Florence Nightingale', in *Florence Nightingale and her Era: a Collection of New Scholarship*, ed. V. L. Bullough, B. Bullough and M. P. Stanton (New York, 1980), pp. 96–107; J. H. Waller, *Gordon of Khartoum: the Saga of a Victorian Hero* (New York, 1988); A. Yarrington, *The Commemoration of the Hero 1800–1864* (1988).

[66] Hill, *LFW*, 1892, p. 319.

for example, was a very public affair and widely reported in national and local newspapers. One representative report described how 'amidst many local manifestations of sorrow ... the coffin was carried [through the streets from her parents' house] to the grave by 16 firemen, who relieved each other in sets of four'. On 10 May 1885 a memorial service for Alice was held at St. Saviour's church, Southwark, and 'long before the service commenced the church was crowded and many were obliged to turn away having been unable to find standing room'. The numbers in attendance and their class is evidenced by the collection at the service: although amounting to little more than £7, it consisted of around 950 coins.[67]

A potent image of working-class Southwark, and the effect of Ayres's heroism on it, was evoked by Laura Lane, who visited the area around Union Street where the fire took hold to speak to people about Alice for her book, *Heroes of Every-day Life* (1888). Lane was best known as an author of semi-didactic advice novels for girls, but she was also an interesting figure, who shared Hill's philanthropic spirit and a concern for the oppressed or overlooked.[68] As early as her mid twenties Lane was helping her sister run a charity school and collecting evidence about women in sweated labour on behalf of the feminist and trades unionist Clementina Black. Later in life, she wrote and edited publications for Hilma Molyneux Parkes's Women's Liberal League of New South Wales.[69] Lane's account of her visit to Southwark was littered with quotations apparently from working-class residents. Their praise for Ayres was unsurprising, but Lane also highlighted how moved people were by the incident: 'I have seen the cheeks and lips of strong men grow pale as ashes; I have heard rough voices falter; I have seen tears spring to hard eyes, as the story of Alice Ayres' magnificent daring was poured into my ears'. Even allowing for Lane's middle-class mediation and the influence of the popular contemporary genres of sensationalist and voyeuristic journalism and literature about working-class life, her account shows that local residents found Ayres's everyday heroism admirable but also profoundly moving.[70] Octavia Hill's own account of a gathering in the Red Cross Hall corroborates this:

> The other Sunday a gentleman recited a beautiful ballad about a heroic rescue from fire. The hall was hushed in breathless attention while the words re-echoed through it. As I passed down among the audience just afterwards I was twice

---

[67] *South London Chronicle and Southwark and Lambeth Ensign*, 16 May 1885.
[68] E.g., L. Lane, *'A Character': a Story for Girls* (1879); *My Sister's Keeper: a Story for Girls* (1879); *Ella's Mistake: a Tale* (1882).
[69] M. Bettison, 'Luffman, Lauretta Caroline Maria (1846–1929)', in *Australian Dictionary of Biography*, ed. M. Nolan, x (1986), 167.
[70] P. J. Keating, *The Working Classes in Victorian Fiction* (1971).

stopped. One man said 'did you see how every eye was turned to her' pointing to the Alice Ayres. A woman said 'I couldn't but think of Alice Ayres'. 'Did you know her?' I asked. 'Yes, I always dealt there' she said 'and I was glad when they put up the panel there'.[71]

Hill and her contemporaries had clearly reached their audience at the Red Cross Hall, who were touched by both the murals and their message, or, as Hill put it, 'the teaching which lies in the memory of deeds like this, and the help which beautiful and powerful art offers in districts like Southwark'.[72]

Conclusion

This chapter has located Octavia Hill at the centre of an influential, liberal-minded, radical network of social reformers who thought that the decorative arts could bring improving messages to working people. The decorative scheme for the Red Cross Hall is a valuable case study because it brings together various people in that network and shows the range of ideas that informed them and, by association, Hill. For Barrington, the scheme realized her beliefs that cultural and aspirational education was as valuable to working-class people as was alleviating material hardship. For Crane, it showed that art could communicate ideas about working-class people, and the nobility and class-consciousness of labour. For Watts, the subject matter of the murals was the key as it would ensure that the messages behind the images would reach their working-class target. For Hill, the scheme epitomized her views that poor people were as innately capable of nobility as rich people, and that such nobility could be glimpsed in their exceptional heroic actions, in the daily struggle of their everyday lives, and in their reactions to beauty – natural and artistic. Situating Hill within this network shows that she was closely associated with people who sought new approaches to the issues of the day, and thus hints at her radical rather than reactionary leanings. The murals may have gone but the hall, cottages and garden survive and bear witness to the wide and varied influences that coalesced around the remarkable figure of Octavia Hill.

---

[71] Hill, *LFW*, 1893, p. 344.
[72] Hill, *LFW*, 1892, p. 320.

5. 'The poor, as well as the rich, need something more than meat and drink':[1] the vision and work of the Kyrle Society

Robert Whelan

Throughout her life Octavia Hill insisted that:

> Men, women and children want more than food, shelter and warmth. They want, if their lives are to be full and good, space near their homes for exercise, quiet, good air, and sight of grass, trees and flowers; they want colour, which shall cheer them in the midst of smoke and fog; they want music, which shall contrast with the rattle of the motors and lift their hearts to praise and joy; they want suggestion of nobler and better things than those that surround them day by day.[2]

The Kyrle Society, the organization that she set up to further her aims, was strikingly successful, at least in the provision of art and nature, though whether the recipients were uplifted to praise and joy was, and remains, controversial. Yet it is now almost completely forgotten. This chapter examines hitherto unused sources to explore the work of the society and the reasons for its fall into obscurity.

The uses of art
In her conviction that everyone, including the poorest, could appreciate and should be able to enjoy art, Hill was part of a movement which dated at least to the report of the 1836 Select Committee 'appointed to enquire

---

[1] O. Hill, 'The Kyrle Society', *The Magazine of Art*, iii (1880), 210–12. I am indebted to Anne Anderson for her help with this chapter. Unless otherwise specified, the sources cited below are drawn from the author's collection, which in turn derives from the following archives and libraries: The Octavia Hill Birthplace Museum Trust, Wisbech; the Church of England Archive, Lambeth Palace Library; the Women's Library at the London School of Economics; Westminster City Archive; and the London Library. I extend warm thanks to the archivists and librarians of those institutions for their help over many years. Further details on the archival sources on which this chapter relies are provided in my earlier volumes *Octavia Hill and the Social Housing Debate* (1998), and O. Hill, *Octavia Hill's Letters to Fellow-Workers 1872–1911*, ed. R. Whelan (2005) (hereafter 'Hill, ed. Whelan').

[2] O. Hill, 'The Kyrle Society', *Charity Organisation Review*, v (1905), 314.

into the best means of extending a knowledge of the arts and the principles of design among the people (especially the manufacturing population of the country)'.[3] Although not its prime focus, the committee in passing considered whether exposure to art could improve the morals and manners of the poor. 'Do you not think', asked one member of a witness, 'that the institution of such places of instruction and such galleries of art would have the effect, not only of improving manufactures, but the moral and social conditions of the people?'[4]

Such views were part of wider debates on the societal roles of culture and art shaped by Matthew Arnold, John Ruskin and William Morris, and they gained considerable acceptance.[5] Practical action in consequence included the Sunday opening of museums and galleries, and late opening at the Royal Academy's summer exhibition in the evenings 'for the admission of the working classes'.[6] Art exhibitions for working people began in 1879 with a loan exhibition of paintings in the South London Working Men's College, followed by loan exhibitions organized by the Sunday Society in Aldersgate and Bishopsgate.[7] Samuel Barnett, rector of St. Jude's Whitechapel, organized annual loan exhibitions of paintings in his parish school from 1881 to 1898, and later on at his Whitechapel Art Gallery. The shows attracted support from wealthy owners, including Queen Victoria, who lent important canvases, and from tens of thousands of working-class viewers.[8] Barnett's exhibitions were renowned, yet, by the time his first exhibition opened in 1881, his old mentor Octavia Hill had been running her own vehicle for cultural philanthropy for fifteen years.

The foundation of the Kyrle Society

The Kyrle Society began life in October 1875 when Miranda Hill, Octavia's sister, read a paper to the girls in the school she ran with her sisters in their Marylebone home. It was called 'A suggestion to those who love beautiful things'. She spoke of the beauty of nature, and of how beautiful scenes

---

[3] F. Borzello, *Civilising Caliban: the Misuse of Art 1875–1980* (1987).
[4] Borzello, *Civilising Caliban*, p. 12.
[5] L. Dowling, *The Vulgarization of Art: the Victorians and Aesthetic Democracy* (Charlottesville, Va., 1996); H. Cunningham, *Leisure in the Industrial Revolution, 1780–1880* (1980); B. Harrison, *Drink and the Victorians: the Temperance Question in England 1815–1872* (1976), esp. chs. 14, 15; D. A. Reid, 'Playing and praying', in *The Cambridge Urban History of Britain*, iii: *1840–1950*, ed. M. Daunton (Cambridge, 2000), pp. 745–808; H. Meller, *Leisure and the Changing City 1870–1914* (1976).
[6] Borzello, p. 42.
[7] Borzello, pp. 45–6.
[8] Borzello, p. 69.

inspire spiritual reflection. From the beauty of nature, she moved to the beauty of art: 'Beautiful pictures, music, architecture, do more than merely delight us – I believe they make us better'. She spoke, controversially, of the importance of beautifying churches with works of art before going on to stress the metropolitan focus that characterized the Kyrle Society's work: 'There is no place where the need of beauty is felt so much as in our towns. "It is not the poverty that is such a weight upon everybody in the east end", says Mr Barnett [the vicar of St. Jude's, Whitechapel], "it is the ugliness"'. To address the problem, Miranda proposed 'a little society for the purpose of helping this great work of making beautiful places for the poor', to be called the Society for the Diffusion of Beauty, in imitation of the Society for the Diffusion of Christian Knowledge. 'I do not propose anything very formal,' she wrote, 'nor have I any ambitious projects'.[9] Her ideas were limited to bringing a few flowers back from visits to the country for poor people, gifts of evergreens and Virginia creepers for decorating communal rooms, making flags to hang in school halls 'where the poor people meet together', singing classes for the poor, and putting up some pictures in the Girls' Institute in Barrett's Court.[10]

It was scarcely a revolutionary programme, but Octavia Hill was so impressed by the paper that she arranged for Miranda to deliver it again to a meeting of the National Health Society, and then had it printed and circulated in December. 'Though it is only a week old', Octavia wrote to Florence Davenport Hill on 12 December 1875, 'it is meeting with the warmest response, so that I fancy we shall have to let it become something larger and more public'.[11] In her 1875 Letter to fellow-workers Octavia refers to 'my sister's small society, of which most of you will have heard',[12] and in the 1876 Letter we find the first mention of it as the 'Kyrle Society', as it had been formally constituted during that year.[13] Its name was the

[9] M. Hill, 'A suggestion to those who love beautiful things' (pamphlet, printed for circulation with the 1875 'Letter to fellow-workers'), Dec. 1875 (copy in author's collection from an original previously in possession of Emily Maurice, Octavia and Miranda's sister). A much-abbreviated version of the talk was included in KSAR (1910), pp. 7–8, marking Miranda's death. It omitted the final section, outlining Miranda's very modest practical suggestions, probably because they would have formed such a contrast with what the Kyrle Society had actually done.

[10] M. Hill, 'A suggestion'.

[11] Octavia Hill, letter to Florence Davenport Hill, 12 Dec. 1875, in *Life of Octavia Hill as Told in Her Letters*, ed. C. E. Maurice (1914), p. 340.

[12] 'Letter to my fellow-workers to which is added account of donations received for work among the poor during 1875', in Hill, *LFW*, 1875, p. 55.

[13] 'Letter accompanying the account of donations received for work amongst the poor during 1876', in Hill, *LFW*, 1876, p. 70. Some confusion existed among members as to the date of the foundation. Although Hill announces it in the letter for 1876, the Kyrle Society

'Nobler imaginings and mightier struggles'

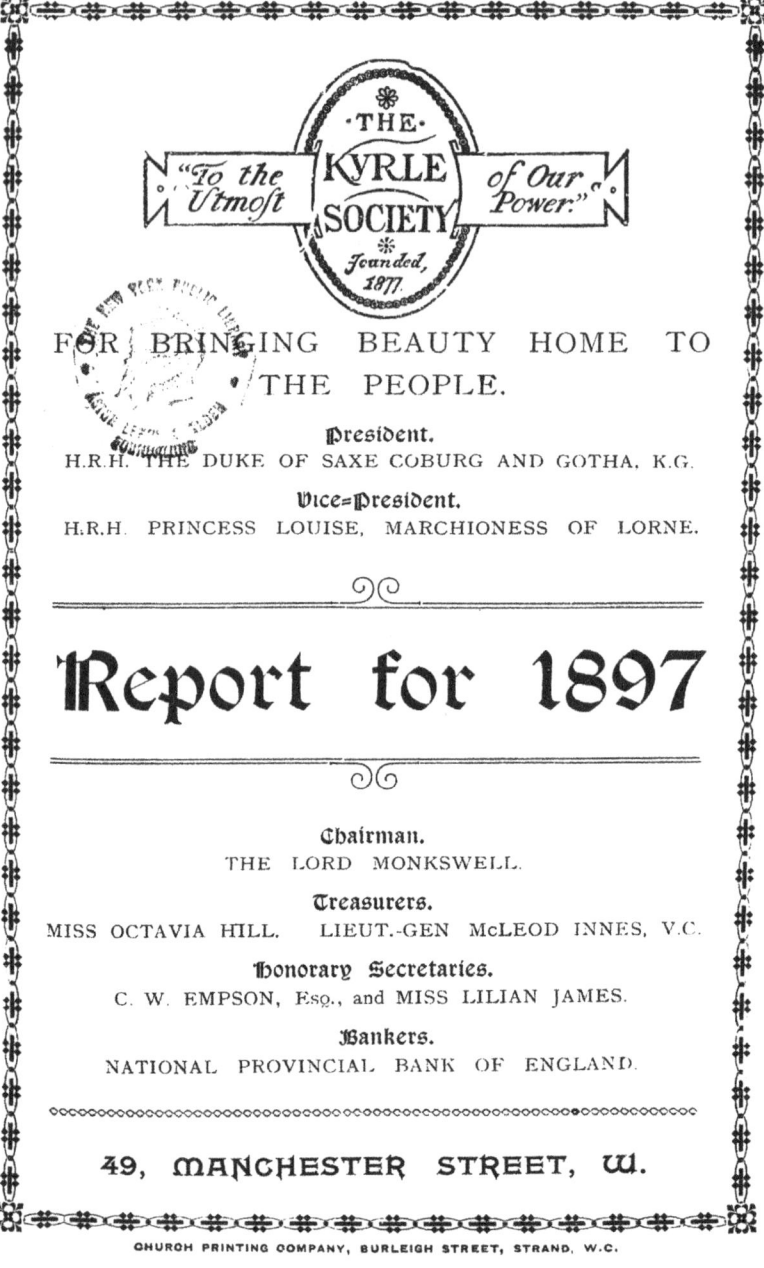

Figure 5.1. Cover of the Kyrle Society Annual Report for 1897.

'happy inspiration' of 'Mr Nattali [M. A. Nattali, London bookseller] ... one of the oldest members of the Society'.[14] John Kyrle (1637–1724), the 'Man of Ross', was celebrated by Alexander Pope in his *Epistle to Bathurst* on 'The use of riches', for having performed many acts of philanthropy in Ross-on-Wye despite having had only a modest income. Octavia always referred to the Kyrle Society as her sister's organization, of which she was treasurer (see Figure 5.1), but this was a polite fiction since the ability to run a campaigning organization was not one of Miranda's strengths.

The aims of the Kyrle Society

In March 1878 *The Academy* published an article describing the aims of the young society:

> Under the name of the Kyrle Society an association of ladies and gentlemen has lately been formed for the purpose of 'bringing the refining and cheering influences of natural and artistic beauty into the homes and neighbourhood of the poor'. These influences are undoubtedly felt to a greater extent than formerly among the middle classes of society, and it is a pleasant and unselfish aim to wish to extend their effects as far as possible, so that the taste for beautiful things shall become still wider spread. We therefore sympathise entirely with the Kyrle Society in its endeavour:
>
> 1. To decorate with mural and other paintings, carved brackets, &c., rooms used by the poor for social purposes, such as clubs, schoolrooms, and mission rooms.
> 2. To make gifts of pictures and flowers for the homes of the poor.
> 3. To lay out as gardens any available strips of waste ground, and to encourage the cultivation of plants.
> 4. To organise choirs of volunteer singers.
> 5. To co-operate as far as possible with the Commons Preservation Society in securing open-air spaces in poor neighbourhoods to be laid out as public gardens, and
> 6. To further any effort at abating the smoke nuisance in manufacturing districts.[15]

---

reports carried the date 1877 on their title pages until 1909, when it became 1876. Several of the annual reports state that 'The Kyrle Society owes its origin to a letter written in 1876 by Miss Miranda Hill ... in 1877 a Society was started', both dates being one year too late. In her speech at the Mansion House, in April 1895, Octavia Hill gave 1876 as the year of foundation (NYPL, KSAR (1912), p. 9).

[14] NYPL, KSAR (1911), p. 6.
[15] *The Academy*, 2 March 1878, p. 197.

'Nobler imaginings and mightier struggles'

These six aims were to be realized by four sub-committees or branches. The Decorative Branch aimed 'To decorate by mural paintings, pictures, stencil works, mottoes, and other means, workmen's clubs, hospital wards, parish rooms or any room used for social gatherings, without distinction of creed'. The Open Spaces Branch was 'To secure and assist in securing any open spaces in or near the metropolis, and to prevent spaces being illegally built upon. To co-operate with local societies for the preservation of commons, footpaths, village greens, and roadside strips. To render available as public gardens, disused burial grounds and other waste spaces, and to provide seats, plants, etc., for them'. The Literature Distribution Branch was 'To distribute books, magazines, and periodicals, as loans or gifts, to hospitals, infirmaries, workhouses, clubs, and libraries for the benefit of the poor'.[16] Finally, the Musical Branch was:

a. To organise a voluntary choir[17] of singers to perform oratorios[18] for the poor. These are frequently given in churches and halls, situated in poor neighbourhoods and districts of London, where good music could hardly otherwise be heard.

b. To give miscellaneous concerts in halls, schoolrooms, and other places, with a view to provide recreation and amusement in poor districts.

c. To provide bands to play at stated intervals in parks and public gardens during the summer months, so as to provide free open-air music for the poorer residents in London. In connection with this branch of the Society the Countess of Meath provides entertainments in workhouses and hospitals during the winter months.

---

[16] NYPL, KSAR (1889), pp. 6–7. There were additions as the years went by, e.g. the Open Spaces Branch provided gymnasia and playgrounds, as well as window-boxes and flower distribution, while the Musical Branch provided singing classes: 'There is probably no way in which music can be more closely or helpfully brought into the lives of the working people than by training them in the practice of part-singing or instrumental music amongst themselves' (NYPL, KSAR (1890), pp. 7, 25). In 1892 the Decorative Branch began to publish cheap pamphlets on art for working-class readers (NYPL, KSAR (1891), p. 10 and (1892), pp. 5–6).

[17] Kyrle Choir was founded in 1878 (NYPL, KSAR (1887), p. 24). A second Kyrle Choir was called for to meet the demand (NYPL, KSAR (1890), p. 10).

[18] 'Admission to these performances [oratorios] … is in all cases free … The requests for oratorios are, every term, too many for general compliance; the necessary selection is therefore made in favour of places hitherto unvisited, or of those at which it has been observed that the audiences are the largest and the most entirely drawn from the working classes or the very poor' (NYPL, KSAR (1877), p. 15).

The work of the four branches

The Kyrle Society's annual reports demonstrate the practical application of these principles. The anonymous author of one report leaves no doubt concerning the society's crusading mission:

> The key-note of the Kyrle Society is the influence for good which all beautiful, harmonious, and noble things exercise upon human beings brought into contact with them, and it seeks to bring such within the experience of all, and more particularly perhaps, of those less fortunate members of the community whose lives of hard toil and little recreation give them but few opportunities of enjoying the better influences of life ... Natural beauty, the beauty of trees and plants and flowers of distant view, of lake and river – these above all things help towards that *mens sana in corpore sano* which is the ambition of everyone for himself and others. But there is the beauty of Art as well as of Nature, and the Society has endeavoured to bring this also into the lives of the poorer classes. That the drunkard or the wife-beater will be reformed by the sight of a fine picture is not of course to be imagined; but there can be no doubt of the influence for good, especially upon the young, of beautiful things.[19]

This was not art for art's sake: the intention was to reform manners. 'Music in parks and gardens', according to the 1890 report, 'not only brightens the lives of the poor, but it is a really useful factor in their elevation ... It has been the first aim to raise the moral sense of the audience, but in so doing their taste is raised as well'.[20] The Musical Branch gave priority to oratorios, that is, sacred works: 'The *Messiah* and *Elijah* continue to prove the most attractive oratorios'.[21] The Literature Distribution Branch, 'believing as they must do that the dissemination of sound literature is a valuable factor in improving the condition of the poorer classes', was ever alert to the dangers posed to moral welfare of the young by sensational literature: 'The amount of pernicious and directly harmful reading which is in circulation is enormous, and the only antidote to the "penny dreadful" is good and wholesome literature'.[22] One of the activities of the Open Spaces Branch was the presentation of cut flowers and potted plants to the urban poor: 'your sub-committee was ... enabled to supply growing flowers to the various girls' clubs and homes, where they are a refining and civilising agency ... the girls themselves so appreciate [the plants and flowers] that they form a real attraction to the home, and are a civilizing influence'.[23]

---

[19] NYPL, KSAR (1910), pp. 5–6.
[20] NYPL, KSAR (1890), p. 18; NYPL, KSAR (1887), p. 18.
[21] NYPL, KSAR (1891), p. 18.
[22] NYPL, KSAR (1892), p. 25; NYPL, KSAR (1908), p. 13.
[23] NYPL, KSAR (1889), p. 20; NYPL, KSAR (1890), p. 21.

Quite how the flowers, oratorios and paintings were going to elevate the poor was left largely unexamined by Kyrle Society members, though they were no vaguer on this point than were other similarly minded reformers. Octavia Hill's writings make clear that the society's works might provide the occasion and, in the case of open spaces, the location for the accession of 'noble' thoughts or whispers of 'better things' which she characteristically understood in a Christian sense, though the Kyrle Society as an institution was not explicitly religious.[24]

In April 1895 Octavia Hill was invited to address a meeting at the Mansion House held in aid of the Kyrle Society. She looked back over thirty years of work, and admitted that there were now other organizations doing the work of the Open Spaces, Musical and Literature Distribution branches. However, she claimed that the Decorative Branch was *sui generis*: 'It stands almost by itself in London in supplying decoration in public rooms used by the poor'.[25] Its work is therefore of special significance in understanding the particular approach of the Kyrle to cultural philanthropy.

The Decorative Branch

The Decorative Branch provided paintings, murals, brackets, friezes and mottoes to hundreds of buildings used by the poor. Sometimes leading artists became directly involved, such as when G. F. Watts presented a chalk full-size copy of *Hope* to the Mission to Seamen in Poplar,[26] and when Walter Crane undertook to paint the second and third panels in the Red Cross Hall scheme.[27] Most of the projects, however, were carried out by volunteer amateur artists who either designed the schemes themselves or followed designs prepared by professional artists; copied old master paintings; or copied and enlarged book illustrations by leading contemporary artists. A copy of Giotto's *Death of St. Francis*, for example, was provided for the St. Francis Home for Working Boys, Marylebone, and copies of Flaxman's illustrations to *The Pilgrim's Progress* were given to the Castle Yard Institute, Blackfriars.[28] The favourite artist, by a very long way, was Walter Crane, 'who has always shown himself a true friend to the Kyrle Society'.[29] His

---

[24] E.g., O. Hill, 'Space for the people', in Hill, *Homes of the London Poor* (1875).

[25] The speech was reproduced in NYPL, KSAR (1912), marking Hill's death (at p. 10).

[26] NYPL, KSAR (1895), p. 7.

[27] Anne Anderson, 'Bringing beauty home to the people: the Kyrle Society 1877–1917', in Hill, *LFW*, pp. 703–33, this point at pp. 724–5. The first panel had been painted by Mrs Russell Barrington, working from Crane's designs, with only finishing touches applied by Crane himself.

[28] NYPL, KSAR (1908), p. 10; NYPL, KSAR (1892), p. 8.

[29] NYPL, KSAR (1899), pp. 9–10.

illustrations to *Aesop's Fables* were enlarged and copied in the Westminster Union workhouse in Poland Street;[30] the All Saints' mission hall in Grays;[31] the parish hall in St. Mark's, Walworth;[32] and the Holme Court Industrial School in Isleworth.[33] His designs for Earth, Air, Fire and Water were reproduced in the parish room of Holy Trinity, Lambeth,[34] and thirteen panels taken from his illustrations to *Flora's Feast* adorned the girls' school of the St. Patrick's Benevolent Society in Southwark.[35]

Other celebrated artists enlisted by the Decorative Branch included Arthur Rackham who, between 1910 and 1912, supervised the copying of a set of six designs, illustrating the Arthurian legend, for St. Luke's parish hall in Deptford: 'Measuring seven feet by five feet each, telling the story of King Arthur ... these pictures ... are the largest works yet undertaken by the Society ... they constitute, the Committee believes, a distinct advance in the work of the Society.'[36] In 1892 Charles Voysey presented designs for the billiard room of the Trinity College Mission in Camberwell, in which 'Crouching figures of boys playing marbles are skilfully introduced among scrollwork to form a narrow border above the dado, the walls being tinted a soft yellow, and the colouring is most cheerful and effective'.[37] The Decorative Branch often used designs in more than one place. This was the case with Crane's works, mentioned above, and other examples include Mrs. G. F. Watts's 1889 scheme for the infant schoolroom in Spitalfields based on the rhyme 'all for the lack of a horse-shoe nail', which scheme, fourteen years later, was applied to the church hall in Shadwell.[38] In 1899 the boys' school of the St. Patrick's Benevolent Society in Southwark was decorated with twelve oil panels representing 'the costumes, customs, and landscapes' of different nations. Two years later, they appeared in the Jewish Girls' Club in Bayswater.[39] A set of 'Water Baby' designs, installed

---

[30] NYPL, KSAR (1891) p. 9.

[31] NYPL, KSAR (1898), p. 9. 'Although this district is technically beyond the usual limits of the work of this Branch, the special appeal made on the ground that the population consists almost entirely of labourers in the London Docks could not be disregarded by the Committee'.

[32] NYPL, KSAR (1892), p. 8.

[33] NYPL, KSAR (1907), p. 10.

[34] NYPL, KSAR (1892), pp. 9–10.

[35] NYPL, KSAR (1899) 10. These panels were enlarged from the original book illustrations to five feet by three feet. 'The Society desires to express its thanks to Mr Crane and Messrs Cassell and co. for their courtesy in allowing it the use of these designs'.

[36] NYPL, KSAR (1910), p. 11; NYPL, KSAR (1911), p. 10; NYPL, KSAR (1912), p. 17.

[37] NYPL, KSAR (1892), p. 9.

[38] NYPL, KSAR (1906), p. 10.

[39] NYPL, KSAR (1899), pp. 9–10 and (1901), p. 8.

'Nobler imaginings and mightier struggles'

in the Victoria Hospital, Chelsea, was repeated in the children's ward of the Westminster hospital in 1909.[40]

The involvement of celebrity artists was gratifying to the Decorative Branch committee, but most of its work was carried out by amateurs. Given the aim of elevating the poor, there was inevitably a preference for didactic projects. The Seven Ages of Man, copied 'from Antonio di Federigo's outlines in Sienna cathedral', and the Eight Virtues, 'adapted from various Italian painters', uplifted visitors to the parish hall of St. Clement's, Fulham Palace Road, while reminding them of their mortality;[41] the hare and the tortoise who raced across Homerton parish hall exhorted parishioners to perseverance;[42] while Temperance, Fortitude, Industry and Charity watched over the decorous pleasures of visitors to Paddy's Goose, a temperance mission in a converted pub in Shadwell.[43] Some of the schemes were intended to inspire by example: portraits of famous men (Giuseppe Garibaldi, General Gordon, Thomas Carlyle) in the Working Men's Club in Kennington,[44] and famous women (Florence Nightingale, and the writers Georgina Craik and Charlotte Yonge) in the Club for Factory Girls in Aldersgate.[45] Some were patriotic or imperial. The dining room of the Lambeth Guardians' School was decorated with the four patron saints of Britain and Ireland, together with the arms of the eight principal colonies of the empire, and the Boys' Club in Bermondsey with views of the empire.[46] The Decorative Branch also believed in the uplifting power of mottoes and stencilled 'Live pure, speak true, right wrong' around a reading room in Bethnal Green,[47] and 'He that good thinketh, good will do' in the Malvern College Mission in Canning Town.[48] All the mottoes were stirring, some used a quasi-biblical language, and some were explicitly Christian. In her Letter of 1883 Hill describes the Kyrle Society's project to install a mosaic frieze containing a line of verse along the side wall of St. John's Church, Waterloo.[49] The intended text was 'Do noble things', from Charles Kingsley's 'A farewell' (1856), but the final choice, from stanza fifteen of George Herbert's poem 'The church porch', is: 'All may have, if they dare try, a glorious life or grave' – a more clearly religious message (see Figure 5.2):

[40] NYPL, KSAR (1909), p. 11.
[41] NYPL, KSAR (1889), p. 11.
[42] NYPL, KSAR (1887), p. 5.
[43] NYPL, KSAR (1889), pp. 12–13.
[44] NYPL, KSAR (1889), p. 13.
[45] NYPL, KSAR (1892), p. 10.
[46] NYPL, KSAR (1889), p. 15.
[47] NYPL, KSAR (1898), p. 9.
[48] NYPL, KSAR (1911), p. 13.
[49] D. Owen, *English Philanthropy 1660–1960* (Cambridge, Mass, 1965), p. 496, citing E. M. Bell, *Octavia Hill: a Biography* (1942), p. 152.

I liked to think of the words being there, they were to run the whole length of the blank outside wall of the church, which bounds the garden. I believed the words might go home to many a man as he hurries along the crowded thoroughfare near, if he caught sight of them between the trees, their colour attracting his notice, perhaps, first, in its contrast with the dreary dinginess all round. I liked to think some busy man might renounce a profitable bargain, or might even dream, for a minute, of renouncing it, for the sake of some good deed. Or I have sometimes liked to fancy a working man, from among the men who sit in that public garden, might be reminded, as he read the words, that though his life was out of men's sight and seemed occupied with little things, seemed perhaps somewhat broken and wasted, there was the possibility of nobleness in it, if bravely and unselfishly carried on. But to whatever heart it might or might not go, the words seemed fit to be spoken to each one of the multitude, hurrying in and out, or pausing there, and worthy to be set, with some care, in lovely colour, to last for years.[50]

Despite the occasional intrusion of militaristic themes (the celebration of Gordon and the display of arms mentioned above), the projects largely stressed loftier and more universal themes of virtues, great personal qualities and divine love. There were some explicitly British themes but they were generally not crudely nationalistic (Arthur and the British patron saints, for example, spoke more to universal virtues than to British supremacy). This stress on virtue rather than crude nationalism more generally distinguished the Kyrle Society from, for example, the Metropolitan Public Gardens Association which ostensibly shared some of the Kyrle's aims.[51]

Octavia Hill and the Open Spaces Branch

The Kyrle Society was chronically underfunded throughout its existence. Its annual reports form a depressing narrative of oratorios refused and decorative schemes postponed for want of basic materials like paint and canvas. In 1907 it was reported: 'It is very difficult to vary the appeal for funds which each year the Committee is forced to make. Demand outruns supply with unfailing regularity, and "more money" is the text upon which the Committee has to harp year in and year out'.[52] The author of the 1910 report tried to relieve the monotony with wit: 'An Annual Report without an appeal for funds would indeed be a rarity, and the Committee has no opportunity for making so startling an innovation'.[53] In contrast to the very

---

[50] Hill, *LFW*, 1883, p. 174.
[51] H. L. Malchow, 'Public gardens and social action in late Victorian London', *Victorian Studies*, xxix (1985), 97–124.
[52] E.g. NYPL, KSAR (1907), p. 5.
[53] NYPL, KSAR (1910), p. 13.

'Nobler imaginings and mightier struggles'

Figure 5.2. The verse by George Herbert in mosaic on St. John's church, Waterloo.

modest resources available for the other branches, the Open Spaces Branch, with which Octavia Hill had her greatest involvement, was much better funded. It was chaired by Robert Hunter, and Hill was listed as neither a committee member nor officer. However, her enthusiasm for the work and the strength of her personality meant that the Open Spaces Branch operated on a different scale from the other branches, as the receipts demonstrate.[54]

Table 5.1. Receipts to the four branches of the Kyrle Society, in pounds, selected years.

Year	Decorative	Open Spaces	Musical	Literature
1889	22	6,939	36	13
1890	61	425	78	17
1891	27	171	172	19
1892	37	1,058	67	15
1895	24	14	68	13
1897	26	623	63	7
1898	31	1,096	32	13
1901	21	21	27	13
1905	34	7	24	9
1906	41	17	25	13
1907	27	7	27	12
1911	30	442	35	18

Source: Kyrle Society Annual Reports, selected years
Note: all figures are in pounds rounded

The Open Spaces Branch swung into action as soon as the Kyrle Society was launched. On 1 May 1877 the burial ground in Drury Lane was opened to the public, having been planted by the society at a cost of £160 (see Figure 5.3). Problems arose on the opening day when crowds of people trampled on the flowers, and the vestry had to close it. Hill insisted that there had been no deliberate vandalism, but that the numbers of people in that densely populated area wanting to get in were simply too large. All that was needed was a bit of replanting plus careful supervision, possibly involving admission by ticket at peak times. She offered to manage the

---

[54] See Paul Readman's chapter for an account of the friction this generated with members of other committees.

'Nobler imaginings and mightier struggles'

Figure 5.3. Drury Lane burial ground.

garden for a year herself if the vestry had any doubts about it. It was soon open again.[55]

The Kyrle Society became involved with many more campaigns to preserve small open spaces in central London, especially after the passing in 1881 of the Metropolitan Open Spaces Act, for which Hill had campaigned.[56] The act permitted local authorities to receive parcels of land, including churchyards which could now be transferred directly from the vestry to the local authority, and deploy rate income to maintain them.[57] Over the next

[55] O. Hill, *Our Common Land* (1887), pp. 118–21. This section of her book represents a talk that Octavia gave to the National Health Society on 9 May 1877, eight days after the burial ground was opened.

[56] In 1887 The Kyrle Society joined the Metropolitan Public Gardens Association and the Commons Preservation Society to lobby the charity commissioners to allow the substantial funds of the City of London Parochial Charities to be spent on open spaces in London, particularly East London. The request was warmly received at a meeting on 14 Dec. 1887 and reported in *The Times* of 17 Dec.: 'A worthier object for the application of moneys dedicated to the benefit of London can scarcely be conceived' (NYPL, KSAR (1887), pp. 9–13).

[57] E. Crawford, *Enterprising Women: the Garretts and their Circle* (2002), p. 220.

few years the Kyrle Society campaigned to save Horsemonger Lane Gaol, the churchyards of All Saints', Mile End, St. Peter's, Bethnal Green, St. Nicholas, Deptford and the graveyard of St. George's, Hanover Square (all opened in 1883/4); the graveyard of St. George the Martyr in Bloomsbury (opened 1889); and the Poor's Land in Bethnal Green (opened 1895).

Towards the end of the 1880s, the Kyrle Society was responsible for laying out the garden of the Red Cross development in Southwark. Designed by Fanny Rollo Wilkinson, the first professional woman landscape gardener to act in this capacity for the Kyrle's Open Spaces sub-committee, this involved winding paths, flower beds, shrubs, a bandstand, a pond with a fountain and little bridge, and a covered playing area for children in wet weather.[58] The ornaments made clear the moral intentions of the donors and, unusually for the society, were wholly Christian. The mosaic of The Sower (i.e., a biblical allusion to Christ) (see Figure 5.4) was created by James Powell after a sketch by Lady Waterford. 'The panel, a circular one, has been executed at Messrs Powell's by the same workmen who did the mosaic at St. Paul's. It is not complete, and we are daily expecting that it will be fixed', wrote Hill excitedly in 1896. It was the gift of Miss Minet, who also presented a sundial inscribed with the words: 'As hour follows hour, God's mercies on us shower'. The mosaic of the Good Shepherd, the gift of Misses Lynch and Gregg, was the work of Antonio Salviati's Venice and Murano Glass and Mosaic Co., and was described by Hill nineteen years later as preserving 'its freshness and colour completely'. It has long since disappeared, but Hill's 1887 description makes clear the religious work it was intended to accomplish: 'The shepherd lays his hand quietly on the head of the lambs which feed around Him, and the words are those which tell of His love. Into that love we may enter; then neither life nor death can separate us from Him, nor storm nor change can shake our perfect peace'.[59]

Vauxhall Park

In 1887 the Kyrle Society took the leading role in the campaign to preserve eight acres in south London for what became Vauxhall Park. Henry Fawcett (d. 1884), the popular MP and postmaster general, wished the grounds of his house (No. 8, The Lawn, South Lambeth Road) to be laid out as a public garden. His widow, Millicent Fawcett, tried to carry out her

---

[58] Although Fanny Wilkinson is not named in any of the accounts, she was certainly the Kyrle Society's landscape gardener by 1887, and probably before that, so the design of the Red Cross Garden would have come within her remit (Crawford, *Enterprising Women*, p. 221).

[59] Hill, *LFW*, 1896, p. 391; *Charity Organisation Review*, Aug. 1888, p. 369; Red Cross Hall and Garden Report, 1906, pamphlet, author's collection; Hill, *LFW*, 1887, p. 231.

'Nobler imaginings and mightier struggles'

Figure 5.4. The mosaic of *The Sower* is the only one of the original Red Cross garden ornaments to remain on the site.

husband's wishes, but in 1886/7 the entire site of The Lawn, together with a large house next door called Carroun or Caron House, was acquired by speculative developer John Cobbledick, who planned to lay out several streets of houses there. In January 1887 Octavia Hill wrote to the Lambeth vestry proposing that the site be acquired as an open space for local people, and the letter was published in *The Times* on the thirty-first of that month. Her initiative led to a series of meetings during 1887, organized by Slingsby Tanner, honorary secretary of the Kyrle Society, Mark Beaufoy, MP for Kennington, and William Morris.[60] They asked 'all Working Men and Women' to come to these meetings and express their opinions about securing the land for a People's Park.[61] A campaign

---

[60] NYPL, KSAR (1887), p. 8.
[61] Flysheet, 1 July 1887, publicizing a public meeting in the grounds of Carron House at 6 pm on Saturday 16 July 1887, author's collection. A flyer produced by the Kyrle Society

was set up to purchase the land from Cobbledick, and during the course of 1888, Hill, as treasurer of the Kyrle, received £7,400 in donations.[62] However, much more was needed. On 21 January 1889, a meeting was held in Willis's Rooms, attended by HRH the Princess Louise, vice-president of the Kyrle Society, to raise more money.[63] On the platform with Princess Louise were Hill, Emma Cons, Millicent Fawcett, Mark Beaufoy and Lieut.-Gen. Keatinge, the society's chairman. Other members of the Vauxhall Park committee included Robert Hunter, George Shaw-Lefevre of the Commons Preservation Society, Walter Derham and F.D. Mocatta, a wealthy philanthropist. A letter was read out from the archbishop of Canterbury supporting the campaign 'to save The Lawn and Carroun House from the builder [because it] would greatly enhance the health of the neighbourhood, and secure to future generations of children a reasonable chance of growing up under favourable conditions of existence'.[64] The Lambeth vestry, the charity commissioners and the Metropolitan Board of Works each promised £12,750;[65] donations from the public amounted to £9,400. The purchase price of £43,500 was raised and ownership of the land passed to the Lambeth vestry in May 1889. The Kyrle Society accounts for 1889 show a total expenditure of £6,790 13s 5d on Vauxhall Park, including a contribution of £5,577 16s towards the purchase price, £1,174 14s for laying out the grounds,[66] and £38 3s 5d for miscellaneous expenses.[67] Donations to the appeal (which were listed under a separate heading in the society's accounts for 1889 and 1890) came to £6,707 9s 7d, including donations of £500 from the duke of Bedford and Henry Tate.[68] The accounts for 1890 show expenditure on Vauxhall Park of £1,148 8s 4d and donation income for the project of £176 9s 6d.[69]

The houses were all demolished, save Fawcett's. This was initially preserved as a memorial to his work for the poor, although there was never any clear idea of what should be done with it, and the Kyrle Society's tentative suggestion that 'if possible, it should be the home of a small museum or art collection',

---

in Jan. 1889 reported that: 'The working men of the locality have formed themselves into a Committee, collected subscriptions, organised meetings, and have shown the keenest desire to secure their garden' (author's collection).

[62] Hill, *LFW*, 1888, p. 241.
[63] NYPL, KSAR (1889), p. 17.
[64] Hill, *LFW*, p. 259n.
[65] NYPL, KSAR (1887), p. 8.
[66] In a letter to *The Daily Graphic* (7 July 1890) Hill put the full cost to the Kyrle Society of laying out the park at £2,000.
[67] NYPL, KSAR (1889), p. 31.
[68] NYPL, KSAR (1889), accounts, pp. 31, 34, 43.
[69] NYPL, KSAR (1890), accounts, pp. 32, 40.

which would neatly have united its aims of promoting natural and artistic beauty, came to nothing. In the absence of a clear purpose, the house was demolished by the Lambeth vestry in 1891, despite the society's protest in defence of 'a house of such personal, and it might almost be said, historical interest; but it is sorry to say that the vestry did not heed its wishes'.[70] The trend, which Melanie Hall describes in this volume, to consider buildings touched by association with great people or with the past as in some senses sacred had evidently not penetrated as far as Lambeth by this time. The Kyrle paid for laying out the park, again by Fanny Wilkinson.[71] The Lambeth vestry was far from enthusiastic about the prospect of taking on the expense of maintaining eight-and-a-half acres of open space, showing the typical reluctance of public bodies to spend ratepayers' money on acquiring and maintaining open spaces, a cause of severe problems for the open spaces movement towards the end of the nineteenth century. Hill's projects suffered from this reluctance as late as 1907 when the levying of a two-pence-in-the-pound rate to acquire Purley Beeches was so controversial that a poll of the whole parish was taken, and 40 per cent of the ratepayers voted against it.[72] The society lamented in 1887: 'Many vestries and local bodies appear slow to realise the benefit resulting from public gardens which, by affording the opportunity of rest and recreation in the open air, do something to mitigate the evils resulting from the over-crowded houses and unsanitary conditions in which so many of the poor are unfortunately obliged to live. As time goes on, however, and the advantages of existing gardens are better appreciated, it may be hoped that broader views will prevail'.[73] The Lambeth vestry had no such broader view and required a personal guarantee from the officers of the Kyrle Society that the work would be carried out in accordance with the plan deposited with them, and would not go over the budget of £2,000. Committee members were understandably reluctant to give such personal guarantees, and this restricted the scope of the work and 'the scheme suffered in consequence'.[74] The vestry was so concerned about park maintenance costs that Mark Beaufoy had to guarantee them for the first three years, as well as paying the interest on the £12,750 that the Metropolitan Board of Works had lent towards the purchase price. This sum was to be reimbursed by the

[70] NYPL, KSAR (1890), p. 17; NYPL, KSAR (1891), p. 16.
[71] Crawford, *Enterprising Women*, p. 221.
[72] Hill mentions Purley Beeches in her 1904 letter as one of 'three most important schemes for the acquisition of land' that were occupying the Kent and Surrey Committee of the Commons Preservation Society. The parish vote took place on 2 Feb. 1907 (Hill, *LFW*, 1904, p. 524 and n).
[73] NYPL, KSAR (1887), p. 5.
[74] NYPL, KSAR (1890), p. 18.

City Parochial Charities. Without his generosity the project would probably have failed, but the society took the view that Vauxhall Park should be passed from the vestry to the LCC as soon as possible to release Beaufoy from his 'exceptional expenses'.[75]

Fanny Wilkinson's informal and picturesque design consisted of two main paths meeting at a right angle at Fawcett House, together with other winding paths and banks of shrubs and flowers. Charles Harrison Townsend, a member of the Kyrle Society, designed the gates and railings, most of which have gone. When Fawcett's house was demolished in 1891, Sir Henry Doulton continued the park's purpose of commemorating the founder by donating a colossal terracotta statue of him by George Tinworth to be erected on the site.[76] Doulton accepted the £75 10s that had been raised by auctioning the contents of Fawcett House as full payment for a magnificent Doulton Ware fountain.

On 7 July 1890 Vauxhall Park was formally opened (see Figure 5.5) by the prince and princess of Wales at a ceremony, organized by the Kyrle Society and attended by the duke of Edinburgh, Princess Louise and the archbishop of Canterbury. 'A feature of the ceremony was the presence and co-operation of working men. The drives and paths in the Park were lined with the members of the various Friendly Societies of Lambeth, and an address, written by the working men's Committee, was presented to the Prince, who responded most graciously and cordially'.[77] Hill devoted most of the space allocated to Vauxhall Park in her 1890 Letter to the account of this ceremony, which was much more than a social occasion in her eyes: 'It was to me a very solemn scene, because all classes were so entirely gathered in, each to do what in them lay to accomplish the good work'.[78] The scene epitomized Hill's view of the fellowship which might transcend class and the possibility that working people might contribute to 'noble' projects, as Baigent discusses in this volume.

In retrospect, the laying out of Vauxhall Park can be seen as the high-water mark of the Kyrle Society. Although other organizations had been involved, the society had been the main driver throughout and its behind-the-scenes liaison among groups, funders, public bodies and commercial interests was critical to the success of the project. However, the 1890s was marked by developments in the open spaces movement, and in Hill's involvement with it, that saw the society reduced to relative insignificance.

---

[75] NYPL, KSAR (1990), p. 18.
[76] NYPL, KSAR (1892), p. 17.
[77] NYPL, KSAR (1890), p. 16.
[78] Hill, *LFW*, 1890, p. 287.

'Nobler imaginings and mightier struggles'

Figure 5.5. The prince and princess of Wales opening Vauxhall Park on 7 July 1890 (engraving from *The Illustrated London News*, 12 July 1890).

The vision and work of the Kyrle Society

The Kyrle Society was one of several organizations involved with preserving open spaces towards the end of the nineteenth century, but none could own and manage land. Land had to be handed over to public authorities: the vestries in the case of small plots; the LCC and the City Corporation in the case of larger ones. (The management of the Red Cross garden by a board of trustees was extremely unusual, and unique for a Kyrle project.) For Hill, whose attitude towards public bodies was always ambivalent, this was not ideal and throughout the 1880s she worked with Robert Hunter on a plan to start a new organization that would not only campaign to save open spaces, but would own and manage them. This resulted in the formation of the National Trust in 1894 and following that the trust ('with which the Kyrle Society is in active sympathy') became the main focus of Hill's and Hunter's open space efforts.[79] It operated on a larger scale and generally outside London. Instead of six acres in Bethnal Green or eight acres in Vauxhall, the trust acquired 108 acres in Derwentwater[80] and 700 acres in Ullswater.[81] The impact of this on the society was predictably damaging. Though it outlived both Miranda (d. 1910) and Octavia (d. 1912), and struggled on until 1917, it faded after Hill's attention wavered. In her 1894 Letter, in which Hill reports the founding of the National Trust, she also mentions that 'the Kyrle Society is in sore need of funds',[82] and this becomes the theme of the increasingly rare references to the society in subsequent letters. Its annual report for 1895 begins with the ominous observation that: 'The work of the Kyrle Society during the year has been of a quiet and uneventful nature. It has carried out no scheme of great importance'.[83] Hill had not given up on the Kyrle: in 1895 she wrote to *The Times* to report that the society's work was 'in danger of being seriously crippled for want of funds, and the amount needed is not large. An addition of £100 a year would make all the difference', she claimed, but the end was in sight and the society petered out.[84]

Why has the Kyrle Society been forgotten?

The Kyrle Society has effectively disappeared from the historical record. Frances Borzello makes no mention of it in *Civilising Caliban*, nor Linda Dowling in *The Vulgarisation of Art*, although both authors could have used

---

[79] NYPL, KSAR (1908), p. 22.
[80] Hill, *LFW*, 1901, p. 473.
[81] Hill, *LFW*, 1904, pp. 525–7.
[82] Hill, *LFW*, 1894, p. 359.
[83] NYPL, KSAR (1895), p. 5.
[84] O. Hill, 'A plea for the Kyrle Society', letter to the editor, *The Times*, 5 Feb. 1895.

'Nobler imaginings and mightier struggles'

it to demonstrate their theses.⁸⁵ The society's disappearance is the more surprising as it had an impressive record and attracted a distinguished cast of members. Its first three presidents were children of Queen Victoria – successively, Prince Leopold, the duke of Edinburgh and Princess Louise, who had been vice president from the start. The committee included, with dukes and countesses, leading artists such as William Morris and G. F. Watts. Walter Crane, C. F. Voysey and Charles Harrison Townsend were happy to associate themselves with it, and Hill exerted her impressive influence to bring together otherwise strange bedfellows: at its first public meeting in Kensington Town Hall in 1881, royalty (Prince Leopold and Princess Louise) worked alongside William Morris and Sir Frederic Leighton.⁸⁶

Several reasons might be suggested for the society's fall into obscurity. First, that it was founded and largely run by women; yet all of Hill's activities involved significant participation by women, and they were not in consequence taken less seriously. Second, that it left few records. There was an annual report, but no British library has a collection of them.⁸⁷ Hill's references to the Kyrle Society in her *Letters to fellow-workers* fade out after the 1890s. There are brief descriptions of its activities in the *Charity Organisation Review*, and occasional references in *The Times* and other periodicals. The lack of records is in keeping with its informal organization. It was a source of pride that it was 'Officered entirely by volunteers, whose constant devotion to their duties the Committee most gratefully recognises – the funds are burdened by no salaries or "personal expenses", so fruitful a source of waste in many cases'.⁸⁸ However such informality, compounded

---

⁸⁵ Borzello, *Civilising Caliban*; Dowling, *The Vulgarization of Art*. Critical commentary is provided in D. Maltz, *British Aestheticism and the Urban Working Classes, 1870–1900: Beauty for the People* (2005).

⁸⁶ *The Daily News*, 28 Jan. 1881; *The Standard*, 28 Jan. 1881, p. 3.

⁸⁷ NYPL has an incomplete set of reports from 1887 to 1912. These were small printed pamphlets (approximately 19cm x 12cm but with small variations from year to year) which normally ran to 32 pages, although some later ones ran over by four or eight pages. All contributions were anonymous and formal in style. They consisted of a front cover bearing the Kyrle motto 'To the Utmost of Our Power' and the legend 'For Bringing Beauty Home to the People' (the legend was dropped when the cover was redesigned by Audley Mackworth in 1909); contents; officers, and committees; an account of the remit of the four branches; introduction; summary of work accomplished during the society's existence; reports from the four branches of projects carried out during the year; list of provincial Kyrle Societies; accounts; list of donations; and subscriptions. The motto was devised by William Morris (W. Morris, 'Speech at the meeting of the Kyrle Society, 27 January 1881', cited in M. Morris, W. Morris and G. B. Shaw, *William Morris: Artist, Writer, Socialist* (2 vols, Oxford, 1936), i. 196.

⁸⁸ NYPL, KSAR (1892), p. 5. NYPL, KSAR (1905), pp. 5–6, thanked committee members for not claiming expenses. NYPL, KSAR (1911), p. 12, explained that 'those who contribute

by its lack of a headquarters (for many years its office address was Hill's home), prejudiced the keeping and preservation of historical records and made the writing of the society's history problematic.[89]

A third reason for the Kyrle Society's fall into obscurity was that it left no monuments. The Literature Distribution Branch's work was superseded by public libraries, despite the society's insistence that the opening of free libraries would not reduce the demand for private charitable efforts.[90] The Musical Branch started no enduring tradition that would have perpetuated its memory. The work of the Open Spaces Branch was swamped by the National Trust, but perhaps the cruellest fate befell the Decorative Branch's endeavours to 'bring beauty home to the people' by adorning hospital wards, workhouses and schools with works of art. It seems likely that no interior has survived. The buildings have been demolished or redecorated, the stirring legends and delicate flower paintings lost under institutional magnolia.[91] The mosaic of The Sower at the Red Cross garden is the only original garden ornament to survive, though not in its original location. At Vauxhall, the statue of Fawcett and the Doulton Ware fountain have disappeared, their present whereabouts unknown. Taken out of their contexts, the message of the works of art is diluted. Two of the society's decorative projects are known to exist *in situ*: the bas-relief sculpture of St. Christopher in St. Christopher's Court (see Figure 5.6) and the mosaic inscription of a line of George Herbert's verse that runs along the side of St. John's, Waterloo.

A final reason for its obscurity is that the Kyrle Society stayed in the background, facilitating but not claiming credit for co-operative projects. Its Open Spaces Branch, in particular, achieved its goals by co-ordinating the work of a number of organizations (several of which counted Hill as

---

to the Society's funds have the satisfaction of knowing that their money goes to the objects of the Society and not to the payment of heavy office costs. The old principle of volunteer help is still relied on'.

[89] From its inception until 1890 the Kyrle Society's address was Hill's home at 14 Nottingham Place in Marylebone for which a nominal rent was paid (NYPL, KSAR (1990), pp. 8–9). When the house was demolished the society moved to 49 Manchester Street, then, in 1900, to 2 Manchester Street, and, in 1909, to 192 Marylebone Road, the house next door to Hill ('Through the kindness of Miss Octavia Hill the Committee has been able to acquire new offices at a much lower rental' (NYPL, KSAR (1909), p. 6)).

[90] NYPL, KSAR (1891), p. 6.

[91] There is a tantalizing reference in 1895 to 'special photographs [that] have been taken of the decoration of some of the more important Institutions, forming an interesting record of the recent work of this Branch [Decorative] of the Society' (NYPL, KSAR (1895), p. 7). Copies of these images could be bought 'either separately or in sets'. The author would be glad to hear of any surviving copies.

Figure 5.6. Bas-relief of St. Christopher, erected on St. Christopher's Buildings, St. Christopher's Place, by the Kyrle Society in 1879.

a member). 'The work ... has been chiefly in co-operation with the other open space societies in movements having for their object the protection or acquisition of open spaces of considerable importance' and indeed 'The Kyrle Society desires to express its mature conviction that no more useful work can be done by the Open Spaces Branch than that of aiding other Societies in their efforts to secure important open spaces to the public'.[92] In her 1879 Letter Hill explains how Burnham Beeches was saved:

> I don't underestimate what others did. We all know the Corporation [of the City of London] paid the money, and the Commons Preservation Society helped greatly in the conduct of the matter, but neither one nor the other would have brought the thing to pass without the quiet, persevering labour of members of the sub-committee [of the Kyrle Society] I speak of, or the high, confident, sustained hope they had throughout, that however large the thing might look, there was a chance that *someone* would *give* this great gift to the people if once the way were made quite clear and the business done, and the scheme got into workable form.[93]

Unlike self-promoting nineteenth-century philanthropists such as William Booth or Thomas Barnardo, Hill disliked personal publicity,[94] and she carried this over to her work with the Kyrle Society. As the annual reports reminded their readers:

> The very unobtrusiveness of [the Kyrle Society's] work to a certain degree militates against its interests by preventing its existence from coming prominently before the general public ... quiet, unobtrusive work gives little opportunity for 'bold advertisement', and in an age where most goes to those who shout loudest, it is the sensational rather than the valuable which attracts most attention.[95]

'Bringing beauty home to the people'[96]

The Kyrle Society's aims of providing fresh air, art and music for the moral improvement of the poor were always contentious and even the society's

---

[92] NYPL, KSAR (1891), p. 11; NYPL, KSAR (1891), p. 12.
[93] Hill, *LFW*, 1879, p. 117.
[94] According to the notice of her death in NYPL, KSAR (1912), p. 8, 'No one had a greater dislike, a greater contempt of self-advertisement than she had; no one looked less to self and more to the object in view'.
[95] NYPL, KSAR (1901), p. 5; NYPL, KSAR (1910), p. 13. NYPL, KSAR (1905), p. 5, refers to the 'unpretentious and quiet manner which is habitual to the Society'.
[96] 'Taking as its aim "to bring beauty home to the people", [the Kyrle Society] has ever interpreted that aim in the widest and most catholic sense; and it may be said that all that tends to brighten, better, and beautify the lives of the poorer members of the community, has the full sympathy of the Society' (NYPL, KSAR (1879), p. 5).

'Nobler imaginings and mightier struggles'

own members expressed reservations about the compatibility of the society's artistic and didactic aims. Lord Leighton warned, at its first public meeting in 1881, that 'the Society must be careful not to flood them [the poor] with rubbish'.[97] In a letter written in 1887, he asked members of the society to consider 'how far the idea of purely and directly didactic painting ... is compatible with the *adornment* of the spaces, with a view to training the eye of the people to a sense of *Beauty*'.[98] Leighton's concern was that 'the inculcation of moral and religious truths must be admitted not to be the object of Art, as such, nor moral edification its appointed task'.[99] Partly because of the inherent tension between the society's artistic and didactic aims, and partly because of more practical constraints, the quality of the Kyrle's artistic endeavours was probably uneven – and the members who performed *Messiah* in Leytonstone Baptist Chapel,[100] painted copies of Walter Crane's illustrations of *Aesop's Fables* for the workhouse in Poland Street,[101] and sent books and illustrated magazines to the coastguards in the Beachman's Shed at Palling in Norfolk,[102] were probably under no illusions about that. The Kyrle Society's work and that of similar initiatives was always open to opposition (particularly, for example, from Sabbatarians) and ridicule: Henrietta Barnett recalled the comment of one visitor who witnessed her interpreting the message of a canvas to its working-class audience that 'It was worth a journey to East London, for the joke of hearing Mrs. Barnett point out the motherhood in a cow's eye to a crowd of Whitechapel roughs'.[103] Yet, taken on its own terms, and considering the small scale of its operation, its permanent shortage of funds, and the unprofessional nature of it all, the Kyrle Society's achievement was astonishing. The 1911 report – the last produced during Hill's lifetime – contains a 'Summary of work accomplished': 87,847 books and 152,667 magazines distributed to 1,431 institutions by the Literature Distribution Branch; 423 concerts, 148 oratorios and 493 entertainments given by the Musical Branch; 415 institutions adorned by the Decorative Branch; and so many open spaces preserved by the Open Spaces Branch, in collaboration

[97] E. I. (Mrs. Russell) Barrington, *Leighton and John Kyrle ('The Man of Ross')* (Edinburgh, 1903), p. 18, copy in Leighton House Museum, London.
[98] Barrington, *Leighton and Kyrle*, p. 20.
[99] Barrington, *Leighton and Kyrle*, p. 44. From Leighton's second address to the Royal Academy students in 1881.
[100] NYPL, KSAR (1892), p. 19.
[101] NYPL, KSAR (1891), p. 9.
[102] NYPL, KSAR (1890), p. 29.
[103] H. Barnett, *Canon Barnett: his Life, Works and Friends* (2 vols., 1918), ii. 160, quoted in Borzello, p. 71. See Maltz, *British Aestheticism,* for a summary of the most frequently voiced criticisms.

with 'the Commons Preservation Society, the National Trust for Places of Historic Interest and Natural Beauty, and other Associations', that they are not numbered.[104] The scale of the Kyrle's activity forms a remarkable tribute to a brave and challenging venture that began with Miranda Hill's talk to a small group of girls in Marylebone in 1875.

[104] NYPL, KSAR (1911), p. 24.

6. Octavia Hill: the reluctant sitter

Elizabeth Heath

As Octavia Hill's reputation and the appreciation for her work grew, she remained persistently averse to commemoration of any kind. She even declined to allow blocks of buildings to bear her name as a reflection of her successful housing schemes. In comparison with public figures in differing arenas of late nineteenth-century society, few known portraits of Hill exist. This is peculiar in light of the widespread demand for portraiture during the period, and consequently the professional portraitist's highly valued status. Margaret Stetz observes that portrait painters were sought out not merely by fellow visual or literary artists – sitters who rapidly grasped the potential for representation and display of their images to increase their own personal recognition as geniuses – but by large numbers of those able to afford their services.[1] Indeed, the genre's appeal extended throughout the social sphere.

Christopher Newall maintains that there was a continuous queue of people, 'from the Queen and court through to hundreds and thousands of self-made men, who wished themselves or their families to be commemorated in paint'.[2] The Royal Academy endorsed portraiture and promoted it as one of the central achievements of British art. Its summer exhibitions showed portraits in large numbers and served as an important forum for generating further commissions from individuals with a desire to be preserved for posterity. The burgeoning of the periodical press ensured the dissemination of likeness by way of engravings after paintings and other means of illustration, not least photography which developed rapidly as an art form from the 1850s. Portrait photographs in the format of *cartes de visite* and cabinet cards were extensively circulated and collected by members of the public, becoming an important tool in advancing celebrity, as was the publication of this imagery in contemporary newspapers and magazines. By analysing the variety of these reproduced likenesses, their proliferation and the frequency with which they were published, it is now possible to trace

---

[1] M. D. Stetz, *Facing the Later Victorians: Portraits of Writers and Artists from the Mark Samuels Lazner Collection* (Newark, Del., 2007), p. 9.

[2] C. Newall, 'The Victorians: 1830–1880', in *The British Portrait: 1660–1960*, ed. R. C. Strong and B. Allen (1991), p. 324.

the trajectory of an individual's public reputation.³ To do this with Hill, however, is problematic as her iconography is unusually short, restricted to one extant oil painting and a handful of drawings and photographs not known to have been reproduced during her lifetime.

In this chapter I will examine a selection of the few Hill portraits that do or did exist, considering how much her response to them illustrates her lack of interest in celebrity for its own sake. I will also investigate how her attitude drove a group of friends and supporters to memorialize her in portrait form against her wishes, and especially why they felt it was so important to do so. Furthermore, I will outline the circumstances under which particular images were produced and propose that such instances are revealing with regards to her character and outlook. The very brevity of her collected portraits is indicative of Hill's rejection of such personal celebration, and leads me to consider her thoughts in relation to the real purpose of art.

As a good example of Hill's reluctance, I begin with the (now untraced) portrait that, unusually, she allowed amateur artist Emilie Barrington to paint in 1889. It is not known how Mrs. Barrington persuaded Hill to sit for the lifesize picture, but Emilie's sister Eliza Wilson recorded seeing it in a brief diary entry: 'March 28 1889 ... Lady Grant Duff ... lunched here and there were 26 visitors [in the] afternoon. All went to Emilie's studio to see her portrait of Octavia Hill'.⁴ The author of Barrington's obituary in *The Times* is confident that sittings did occur, asserting that 'It was while Miss Hill was sitting to Mrs Barrington for her portrait that she explained the scheme for creating the National Trust'.⁵ Barrington became closely involved with Hill's work in 1888 when she helped with the latter's housing project in Southwark: the development of the Red Cross Hall and cottages. As a founder member of the Kyrle Society, which endeavoured to bring beauty to the homes and lives of the poor, Barrington exercised her considerable connections within the London art world, enlisting artist and designer Walter Crane to create a series of murals for the hall's interior.

The idea for a decorative programme commemorating heroic deeds by ordinary men, women and children was first devised by the artist George Frederic Watts, Barrington's close friend and neighbour in Holland Park.

---

³ See, e.g., the list of 'All known portraits' for Sir Henry Morton Stanley in the National Portrait Gallery's (NPG) Later Victorian Portraits Catalogue <http://www.npg.org.uk/collections/search/personextended.php?linkid=mp04254&tab=iconography> [accessed 11 June 2014].

⁴ As quoted in M. Westwater, *The Wilson Sisters: a Biographical Study of Upper Middle-class Victorian Life* (Athens, Ohio, 1984), p. 134.

⁵ 'Mrs. Russell Barrington', *The Times*, 11 March 1933, p. 12.

Watts lent his support to the Red Cross project while his own scheme for a memorial in Postman's Park in the City of London, to be decorated with ceramic tiles designed by William De Morgan, was not unveiled until 1900.[6] Barrington began working up Crane's preliminary cartoons for Red Cross Hall herself, and intended her portrait of Hill to be displayed alongside the murals. This appears to have been widely reported; in September 1890 a writer for the *North-Eastern Daily Gazette* understood that 'A portrait of Miss Octavia Hill is about to be presented to Red Cross Street Coffee Hall in South London, with which that indefatigable worker's name is so much associated. The painter is Mrs. Russell Barrington'.[7] Hill's feelings towards the picture itself are not known. However her strident opposition to the artist's intentions has been documented. It was an idea that she simply would not entertain. In a letter to Sydney Cockerell, she makes her position clear: 'I see from the papers that Mrs. Barrington proposes giving my portrait to Red Cross Hall. Now I can't have this done, and I write to ask you, as a friend, to help, so that the Committee should respect my wish about it and back me up in saying that this cannot be'.[8] The portrait's fate remains unknown, but although Barrington was a strong and determined character, Hill's words are likely to have put an end to this particular ambition. This is the clearest indication we have of her aversion to memorialization of this type. It is with this in mind that we can begin to interpret her elder sister Miranda's insistence that she was not a 'public woman' but instead was 'always dwelling on the importance of quiet individual effort'.[9] Although willing to write for the press and speak to the public to promote her cause, she had little interest in personal recognition as an end in itself, desiring simply to carry on with her work with steady determination and without fuss.

In 1887 Hill was offered a seat in Westminster Abbey for Queen Victoria's Golden Jubilee. Although impressed by the invitation, she wrote to her mother describing her bewilderment: 'I cannot think why I, who have done so simply, and at no great cost, just what lay before me, should be singled out in this kind of way. I always feel as if I ought to do, or be, something more, in order to deserve it'.[10] Even at this advanced stage of her life she was

---

[6] Hill, *LFW*, 1900, pp. 456–7.

[7] *North-Eastern Daily Gazette*, 2 Sept. 1890, with thanks to Dr. John Price for providing this reference, Oct. 2012 (who also notes that the Crane murals were not executed *in situ*, but on portable supports which were later affixed to the hall's walls). See also 'Another "People's Picture Gallery"', *Pall Mall Gazette*, 8 Oct. 1890, no. 7973.

[8] O. Hill to S. Cockerell, quoted in E. M. Bell, *Octavia Hill* (1942), p. 241.

[9] NPG Archive, RP1746, transcript, M. Hill, 'Account of the presentation of Sargent's portrait', *c*.1898.

[10] 2 July [?] 1887, reproduced in *Life of Octavia Hill as Told in Her Letters*, ed. C. E. Maurice (1913), p. 474.

Figure 6.1. Octavia Hill, by John Singer Sargent, oil on canvas, 1898.

uncomfortable with her celebrated status; a deep-seated modesty in relation to her career prevented her from allowing that she was in any way more extraordinary than the next person. E. Moberly Bell points out that this was not affectation, but an established attitude of mind. In her 1942 biography she writes, 'The art of publicity had not in those days the vogue it has since acquired. Octavia knew nothing of it, and with what to modern minds must appear a strange perversity, took as much trouble to avoid being in the public eye as many take to-day to be in it'.[11]

Perhaps because of Hill's experience with the Barrington painting, no subsequent formal portraits are known to have been executed until 1898,

[11] Bell, *Octavia Hill*, p. 240.

when a group of her supporters commissioned society portraitist John Singer Sargent to produce an oil to mark the occasion of her sixtieth birthday (Figure 6.1). The subscribers were led by Mary Booth, Charles Stewart Loch and Lady Frederick Pollock. A list of almost 200 names was gathered, including many from the USA and colleagues from all branches of her activities.[12] The presentation portrait was a common form of commission throughout the nineteenth and early twentieth centuries. These were variously produced for country houses as a gift from loyal tenants or clansmen, 'to embellish clubs and government offices, paid for by subscription of the members or by the Exchequer, or as a token of appreciation for a particular individual by a group of friends'.[13] Predictably, Hill was reluctant to agree to the scheme, insisting that funds could be better spent elsewhere. Writing anxiously to Loch in 1898, she argued that it was 'almost impossible ... to prevent memorials, presentations and testimonials ... from becoming a real oppression and pain to the contributors'.[14] However, as Bell records, 'Octavia ... could not always have her own way. There comes a point when to refuse to friends the opportunity of expressing their affection and appreciation in the way they desire, becomes ungracious and ungenerous. Octavia could never be either'.[15] Hill's supporters persisted with this endeavour, despite her protestations, because they felt compelled to celebrate her substantial achievements. Furthermore, they recognized the importance of leaving a tangible reminder of her presence for posterity. Miranda Hill's lengthy account of the Grosvenor House presentation ceremony on 1 December 1898 is particularly interesting in the fact that it outlines the friends' grateful attitude in relation to the portrait commission. Loch, among others, was called to speak on behalf of the group:

> He said what very great pleasure they all had in giving the picture as a mark of their respect and affection, and thanked Octavia for having leant her face to the artist; for he was sure she had felt some reluctance in so doing, and they felt that she was giving them a present rather than giving it to her. Her face was engraven on their minds and her character on their hearts; but they were anxious that those that would come after, and who had never had the privilege

---

[12] G. Darley, *Octavia Hill* (1990), p. 268. See also the handbook accompanying the presentation ceremony, copy in the Octavia Hill Birthplace Museum, Wisbech, Cambridgeshire.

[13] Newall, 'The Victorians', p. 316. Commissions of this sort are represented elsewhere in the NPG's collection (see, e.g., 'Sir George Scharf' by Walter William Ouless [NPG 895] and 'Sir (William Mathew) Flinders Petrie' by Philip Alexius de Laszlo [NPG 4007]).

[14] O. Hill, as quoted in Darley, *Octavia Hill*, p. 267.

[15] Bell, *Octavia Hill*, p. 241.

of knowing her should be able to realise something of what she had been and how she had looked.[16]

It is for this reason that, in addition, Hill's supporters pressed for the portrait to reside ultimately in a museum or gallery. The Revd. B. Alford voiced this hope during the ceremony: 'he looked forward to the picture one day becoming national property, and liked to think that it might hang in the same gallery with the great men (including F. D. Maurice and John Ruskin), who had so much influence on her character'.[17] This was indeed to be the case. Hill bequeathed it to the National Portrait Gallery (NPG) and it was accepted by the trustees in February 1915. Given her opposition to memorialization, as outlined above, the donation probably resulted from Hill's feeling of obligation to her friends and respect for their clear wishes with regard to the portrait. She expressed deep gratitude for its intended presentation, extending her thanks to those who were not at the ceremony: 'Let them be sure that this proof of their remembering kindness must ever be deeply valued by me; that it will speak to me of them; that it will be a proof of their sympathy in all that I have tried through life to do'.[18] Hill's decision to bequeath the portrait to the NPG may also suggest that, by the end of her life, she had changed her opinion about her deserved place in the national collection. Before her death the picture had apparently hung for many years behind her desk at 190 Marylebone Road – an indication that she was not displeased with the likeness.[19] Hill certainly recognized its importance as a portrait by Sargent; during her lifetime she controlled its reproduction tightly, as evidenced in a letter to Sydney Cockerell in 1899:

> I feel strongly that I should like myself to retain the control of the decision. I have therefore arranged with Mr Hollyer that after July 1901 the entire and exclusive copyright is in my hands. He also assures me that he certainly would not allow reproduction of it without my written authority.[20]

In any case Hill would have been aware that the gallery's trustees were to decide her fate. Although by the beginning of the 1900s the collection's increasingly comprehensive nature allowed more consideration of artistic merit, inclusion based on the sitter's significance and his or her contribution

---

[16] M. Hill (transcript, RP1746, NPG Archive).
[17] M. Hill (transcript, RP1746, NPG Archive).
[18] As quoted in Hill, *LFW*, 1898, p. 421.
[19] Information provided by Peter Clayton, Octavia Hill Birthplace Museum, Wisbech, Cambridgeshire, 2012.
[20] Westminster Archives Centre, D. Misc. 84/2, volume of letters compiled by Cockerell, O. Hill to S. C. Cockerell, 11 Nov. 1899.

to British history remained central to the acquisition process.[21] It is therefore testament to Hill's already-established reputation that Cockerell, acting on behalf of Hill's younger sister Emily (Emily S. Maurice), successfully petitioned the trustees to waive their usual practice at that time of leaving a ten-year interval before accepting a portrait.[22] In a letter to Cockerell, Emily explained:

> I suppose you know that my sister Octavia left her portrait by Sargent to the National Portrait Gallery. They have postponed any answer as to their acceptance of it, on the grounds that 10 years must elapse before a decision be given. We know, however, that this rule is not always kept and that thro' private influence portraits are admitted sooner ... Personally I do not admire the portrait, so I am not so very anxious that it should be accepted; but so many people wishing it to be in the gallery, and Octavia having left it for that purpose one wishes to carry out the plan.[23]

Arguably Sargent had been a strange choice for the commission; the glamour and lustre imparted by his brush not quite according with his sitter's lack of pretention. Merlin Waterson concedes that 'her plain brown dresses offered little scope for Sargent's slick technique'.[24] It is interesting to note that George Frederic Watts, in many ways a more appropriate artist, was not considered for the portrait. Hill thought highly of his work. In 1880 she wrote to Samuel and Henrietta Barnett, who were considering artists for the decoration of St. Jude's Church in Whitechapel:

> Watts might be the best man to go to. He cares for idealization, personification, Time, Death, struggle between Death and Love, mistake of a woman's life & all sorts of modern abstract and really noble ideas, cares for them earnestly ... Of course it is a great deal to ask, but he cares more than almost any man I know for art to be used to teach great lessons.[25]

Portraiture was the other mainstay of Watts's career and he approached it with the same intensity he directed towards his allegorical paintings.

---

[21] This was fundamental to the rules governing acquisition, clearly stated in the trustees' first and subsequent annual reports (see *NPG Report of the Trustees 1858* (NPG Library)).

[22] A period deemed appropriate for the rational assessment of an individual's contribution to the nation (see NPG Archive, RP1746, S. C. Cockerell to C. J. Holmes, 24 Nov. 1914: 'I imagine the portrait is one that the Trustees are pretty certain to wish to have, both on account of the sitter and of the painter. If this is so, is there any way of shortening the interval?').

[23] NPG Archive, RP1746, E. S. Maurice to S. Cockerell, 23 Nov. 1914.

[24] M. Waterson, *The National Trust: the First Hundred Years* (1994).

[25] LSE, COLL.MISC.512, O. Hill to H. Barnett, 19 Sept. 1880, quoted in V. F. Gould, *G. F. Watts: the Last Great Victorian* (2004), pp. 151–2.

'Nobler imaginings and mightier struggles'

The result was a series of highly wrought yet compositionally simplistic portraits, through which the artist sought to express the heroic virtues of his sitters 'not by accentuating or emphasizing, but rather keeping in mind those lines which are noblest'.[26] Watts selected a number of social reformers and philanthropists (including Josephine Butler and John Passmore Edwards) for inclusion in the hall of fame, his collected portraits of eminent Victorians ultimately presented to the NPG, but Hill was not among them.[27] His project to record the likenesses of prominent figures of the age was conceived as early as 1850, and Watts continued to add to his collection throughout his lifetime in an attempt to create a national pantheon of famous contemporaries. Usually these pictures originated from private portrait commissions; it became his practice to complete two versions, one of which he kept. Richard and Leonée Ormond observe that 'Watts's circle of great men was quite circumscribed, and often prompted by personal friendship'.[28] Obvious omissions include John Ruskin, with whom his relationship had cooled, and Charles Dickens. Although Watts was not anti-feminist, the only woman included in the series is Butler, whom he invited to sit in 1894. The selection of Sargent for Hill's portrait might well have been influenced by the personal preference of the commissioners, namely Pollock and Loch, whom he portrayed in 1900.[29] Sargent's reputation as the painter of an international elite grew throughout the 1890s and the demand was such that, by the middle years of the decade, he was painting up to three sitters a day.[30] Loch maintained that Hill's friends 'hoped that as the picture was the work of a great artist it might speak to the hearts of those who should look upon it, and that it should bring them something of the strength which she had brought to her friends'.[31] Perhaps also, the friends had in mind the portrait's future public display within a national institution and reasoned that a portrait by Sargent, at this time at the height of his powers as a society portraitist, would be an enticing prospect. Certainly the artist held the potential to convey the nature of Hill's character through his vigorous painterly style. On its exhibition at the Royal Academy in 1899, criticism of the portrait focused upon the efficiency of his technique. A reviewer for *The Spectator*

---

[26] G. F. Watts, quoted in Newall, 'The Victorians', p. 344.
[27] NPG, London (see NPG 2194 and NPG 3958).
[28] L. and R. Ormond, *G. F. Watts: the Hall of Fame: Portraits of his Famous Contemporaries* (2012), pp. 12–13.
[29] See R. Osmond and E. Kilmurray, *John Singer Sargent: Portraits of the 1890s* (New Haven, Conn. and London, 2002), nos 387 and 388.
[30] E. Kilmurray and R. Ormond, 'Sargent, John Singer (1856–1925)', *ODNB*.
[31] M. Hill (transcript, RP1746, NPG Archive).

praised the success of Sargent's bold handling with regard to the sense of immediacy and vivacity he imparted, remarking:

> the painter's magic reveals a face illuminated by an expression of graciousness which only the painter's art can arrest and fix. One cannot but pity the numbers of people who in their search for what they call 'honest work' will overlook the picture to fix on some tiresome accumulation of petty details miscalled 'finish'.[32]

Inevitably, sittings for the portrait began uneasily. They occurred during August and September 1898, presumably in Sargent's studio at 33 Tite Street, Chelsea; the Italian seventeenth-century-style chair in which Hill sits is likely to have been one of the artist's studio accessories.[33] Mary Booth recalled that Hill was reserved with strangers, 'putting down a veil, as it were, between her own personality and theirs and hardly allowing a glimpse of herself to show through'. However, Sargent employed his considerable experience to break through these defences. Booth noted: 'He engaged her in conversation, and had the happy instinct to differ with her categorically on a point where she felt strongly ... her face lit with all her characteristic force and fire'.[34] A contemporary critic argued that the picture was to be admired on stylistic grounds and also for its subject, 'which must have been a delight to a portrait painter tired of the characterless expressions of commonplace sitters'.[35] Hill's biographer and kinsman William Thomson Hill provides a useful evaluation of the painting:

> Beneath the wide brow, silvered with parted hair, the eyes glow with a fire that has nothing of old age in it. They express ardour and something more. These are very sane eyes, shrewd, serene and kindly, but eyes which you feel nothing could escape. The large mouth and chin are those of a very determined person – but for the suggestion of a humorous twist at the corners.[36]

However, praise for the portrait was not universal. While Booth enthused that 'Our modern Velazquez seized his chance and he succeeded in transferring to his canvas ... something of the inward spirit which we have reverenced', Harriot Yorke claimed compositional inaccuracy, maintaining that 'Octavia never looked sideways'. Gillian Darley observed that almost

---

[32] *The Spectator*, 6 May 1899, p. 641.

[33] It appears in a number of the artist's portraits during that period; see Kilmurray and Ormond, 'Sargent', p. xxii, no. 9.

[34] University of London, MS.797/II/67/1, M. Booth, draft of foreword for proposed publication by Charity Organization Society in Hill's memory (as quoted in Darley, *Octavia Hill*, p. 267).

[35] *The Athenæum*, 3 June 1899, p. 693.

[36] W. T. Hill, *Octavia Hill, Pioneer of the National Trust and Housing Reformer* (1956), p. 21.

all accounts referred to her large dark eyes and the effect of her direct gaze.[37] W.T. Hill qualified his admiration by conceding that despite the vivacity of the artist's representation, Sargent failed to capture and express the essence of her personality: 'Those who remember her feel this to be an authentic likeness – but not the whole Octavia ... we miss something of the sympathy that lives within those eyes; the enthusiasm which could kindle others'.[38] It is not known whether Sargent provided some of the garments that Hill wore for the sittings. There are photographs of Hill in her later years wearing lace collars and cuffs, but they are not so prominent as in Sargent's work, nor do they have the same effect.[39] In her reminiscence of Hill, Henrietta Barnett confirmed that 'she did not dress, she only wore clothes, which were often unnecessarily unbecoming'.[40] Hill's belief in want as a stiffener of character was outwardly reflected in the frugality of her dress. According to Darley, Hill was wilfully dowdy in her later years, determined to play on the image of herself that others presented to her.[41] Mary Stocks, who as a young woman visited Hill, believed that the artist was especially flattering in this respect: 'She was somewhat shapeless and wore strange Victorian clothes with very wide sleeves. But she was certainly impressive'.[42]

Sargent was interested in the framing of his paintings and during the 1890s in London showed a taste for seeking out antique frames to complement his commissions.[43] For Hill's portrait he chose one carved with leaves and fruit, probably seventeenth-century Italian, a style widely fashionable at the time. Darley noted that the frame for the painting was Sargent's gift, 'his own contribution to the celebration of a life of such extraordinary achievement'.[44] The artist himself articulated his approval of the portrait's eventual transfer to the NPG, writing dryly to the director Charles Holmes in 1915, 'I'm glad to hear that Miss Octavia Hill is received into Valhalla'.[45]

---

[37] M. Booth and H. Yorke (letter 21 Feb. 1989, University of London), as cited in Darley, *Octavia Hill*, p. 267.

[38] Hill, *Octavia Hill*, p. 21.

[39] A full list of Octavia Hill portraits has been compiled for the NPG's Later Victorian Portraits Catalogue (see <http://www.npg.org.uk/collections/search/personextended.php?linkid=mp02186&tab=iconography> [accessed 11 June 2013]).

[40] H. Barnett, *Canon Barnett: his Life, Work and Friends* (2 vols., 1918), i. 31.

[41] Darley, *Octavia Hill*, p. 266.

[42] M. Stocks, *My Commonplace Book* (1970), p. 56.

[43] J. Simon, 'John Singer Sargent and picture framing' (<http://www.npg.org.uk/research/programmes/the-art-of-the-picture-frame/john-singer-sargent-and-picture-framing.php> [accessed 11 June 2014]). See also J. Simon, *The Art of the Picture Frame: Artists, Patrons and the Framing of Portraits in Britain* (exhibition catalogue, 1996), p. 182, no. 107.

[44] Darley, *Octavia Hill*, p. 268.

[45] NPG Archive, RP 1746, J. S. Sargent to C. J. Holmes, 23 Feb. 1915.

Further known portraits of Hill are less formal in character, being either intended as private images, or executed as drawings and other works on paper. Some were produced by individuals within her immediate circle who were to prove pivotal to the direction of her life. An early example is the portrait by the Scottish artist Margaret Gillies (1803–87) painted in the early 1840s. Unfortunately the original is untraced, although it is reproduced in C. E. Maurice's *Life of Octavia Hill* (1913).[46] She is shown here as a young girl, her large upward-looking eyes hinting already at the focus and resolve which became a distinguishing feature of her adult character. Gillies was a pupil of miniature painter Frederick Cruikshank and moved in a social circle of nonconformists and academics, including William and Mary Howitt and Richard Henry Horne (all of whom she painted). She developed a close friendship with Hill's grandfather, physician and sanitary reformer Thomas Southwood Smith. From 1846 they set up an unconventional household together with her sister Mary at Hillside in Hampstead. This became a welcoming second home to the Hill family and it is likely that the portrait was executed during one of their visits. The composition's relaxed nature – the up-close pose and the open expression of the sitter – attests to the intimacy shared with family members. Gillies probably encouraged Hill to develop her own artistic talents: when the question of Hill's employment arose, the artist offered to teach her to draw in her London studio.[47] Almost certainly this exposure to the art world paved the way to the development of Hill's early career as a copyist of old master pictures. This she embarked on from 1855, under the guidance of John Ruskin, who had a lasting influence upon her life. Ruskin believed the dedicated studying of art works was an important first step towards her becoming an artist herself. Hill's dedication to the task is evident in her version of the National Gallery's *Doge Leonardo Loredan* by Bellini, copied in 1859 (now in the Collection of the Guild of St. George, Museums Sheffield).[48] Her work as a copyist also proved a vital source of income right up until 1864. In a letter to a friend written in December that year Hill explained the delay in purchasing her first property:

> since I saw Ruskin, I could not attend to the matter at all: for every moment of light time has been occupied by a drawing for the Society of Antiquaries; and the dark has been little enough for teaching, accounts, and all my various extra work. This drawing I should like you to see; it is a copy of the earliest dated portrait of an Englishman, – 1446.[49]

---

[46] Maurice, *Life of Octavia Hill*, between pp. 13–14.

[47] Maurice, *Life of Octavia Hill*, p. 13.

[48] CGSG00778 (<http://collections.museums-sheffield.org.uk/view/objects/asitem/search@/0/title-asc?t:state:flow=6d450dbf-4ee6-4848-97d1-211581efebc9> [accessed 11 June 2014]).

[49] O. Hill to 'Miss Baumgartner', 11 Dec. 1964, as quoted in Maurice, *Life of Octavia Hill*, pp. 215–16.

'Nobler imaginings and mightier struggles'

The quality of her work had been noticed by the National Gallery keeper who referred her to George Scharf, first secretary (and later director) of the NPG and active fellow of the Society of Antiquaries. The watercolour copy of Edward Grimston's portrait was to be reproduced as a chromo-lithograph in the society's journal *Archaeologia* and then kept at the society after the original was returned to the owner. Hill's estimate for the replica was ten guineas.[50] However, it is clear that this was more than simply paid work; in the process of copying the picture, her response to the original was profound:

> It is of an ancestor of Lord Verulam; one of the Grinstones [*sic*]; such a quiet, steadfast face, looking out from under a perfectly black hat, with quiet thoughtful eyes, like a person who went slowly and steadily on his way, without either hurry or doubt. I should never have done, were I to tell you of all the importance attached to his shield and chain and necklace, and all the accessories of the picture; how the antiquaries glory in each detail and understand from them each, who and what he was. To me his quiet face comments in its silence on our hurry and uncertainty; and, as I sit drawing him, I hope to gather reproach enough from his still eyes to teach me to live quietly.[51]

In this volume, William Whyte posits that it is exactly such sympathy with the work of art that Ruskin wished to engender in his students, so that they might then be encouraged to communicate this truth. It goes some way to justify the unconventional training to which he subjected them. In carefully copying great pictures, Hill was in fact learning a visual language to equip her with the skills to 'speak to – to teach – the heart'.[52] Although ostensibly her vocation lay elsewhere, Hill never lost her appreciation for art. She continued to find time to visit art exhibitions, being very impressed, for example, by the painter Edward Burne-Jones's *The Wheel of Fortune* and *Love among the Ruins* when she saw them on show at London's Guildhall in 1892.[53] Whyte convincingly argues that, far from representing a change of direction, Hill's earlier artistic training continued to inform her approach

---

[50] The illustration appeared in *Archaeologia*, xl (1866), 451. Hill's fee is recorded in the society's council minutes, 31 March 1868 (probably incorrectly transcribed for 1864; Society of Antiquaries, London). Octavia Hill's copy is still in the collection (Prints and Drawings Collections, Society of Antiquaries of London). The original portrait is now in the National Gallery, on loan from the earl of Verulam (L3). Hill is known to have executed a further copy for the society of a portrait of the Empress Leonora, then in the 5th Earl Stanhope's collection. When published as a chromolithograph, it illustrated George Scharf's article on the picture for the journal (see *Archaeologia*, xliii (1870), 1, 10).

[51] As quoted in Maurice, *Life of Octavia Hill*, pp. 215–16.

[52] See William Whyte's chapter in this volume.

[53] Maurice, *Life of Octavia Hill*, p. 522.

to social work. Yet beyond her commonly held ideal of promoting beauty among the poor for its own sake, her real interest lay in art's potential spiritually and emotionally to enrich her tenants' lives. For Hill, art remained a potent tool for instruction. Indeed, the sustained importance she placed on the symbolic power of art is clear from her opinions regarding Watts's painting, as quoted above. Likewise, she would have valued Crane's murals in Red Cross Hall for their ability to 'teach great lessons'. Considered in this light, her refusal to allow Barrington's portrait to hang alongside these works makes perfect sense. Personal commemoration played no part in her understanding of the function of art. Arguably, her formative artistic training under Ruskin contributed to her future reluctance to sit for portraits intended for this personal commemoration.

Frederick Denison Maurice was another significant figure in Hill's early life. She first met Maurice in 1852 through his involvement with the newly founded Ladies Guild, a craft workshop for unskilled women and girls in Holborn, to which she had just been appointed as manager of the toymakers. In 1856 she accepted a further post as secretary to the women's classes at the nearby Working Men's College, another of his educational ventures. Maurice's teaching and religious values made a lasting impression on Hill, who frequently attended his London sermons. Having been brought up a Unitarian, she was baptized and confirmed into the Church of England in 1857. Despite this, she remained pointedly undogmatic; her religious beliefs were private, although increasingly important to her. In a letter to her friend Mary Harris, a Society of Friends member, she indicated her developing awareness of the value of liturgy during this period:

> Do you remember that dear church at West Ham? The church service, which gains for me a new meaning, a fresh glory, as I hear it under fresh circumstances ... has become infinitely more precious to me since that day ... I should very much like to know what you think about fixed services, forms of prayer, &c.; but I feel, Mary, you will prize them when I tell you how much I have learnt from them how much joy and comfort they have given me.[54]

Maurice is likely to be the link between Hill and the artist of a second portrait in the NPG's collection, a pencil drawing attributed to a 'member of the Barton family' (Figure 6.2).[55] In 1951 the vendor, J. H. Money, wrote to the NPG about this work:

---

[54] O. Hill to M. Harris, Nov. 1856, as quoted in *Octavia Hill: Early Ideals, from Letters*, ed. E. S. Maurice (1928), p. 26.

[55] With thanks to Peter Clayton, Octavia Hill Birthplace Museum, Wisbech, Cambridgeshire, for assistance with this connection, March 2012.

Figure 6.2. Octavia Hill, possibly by a Barton family member, pencil, *c*.1864.

In a collection of mid-Victorian drawings, which I acquired the other day, I discovered a sketch of Octavia Hill, dated 1864 and to judge from the collection as a whole, by a contemporary member of the Barton family (of 'The Waterford [*sic*], Letter, Co. Fermanagh'). I am wondering if the National Portrait Gallery would be interested to acquire it – and, if so, could call in at some convenient time.[56]

Maurice's first wife Anna Barton (1810–45) came from an army family and had six siblings. Both her parents hailed from County Fermanagh, now Northern Ireland. In 1799 her father, Lieutenant-General Charles Barton, married Susanna Johnston, whose place of birth is listed as 'The Waterfoot'.

---

[56] NPG Archive, RP3804, J. H. Money to NPG, 21 June 1951. The method of acquiring this collection is not known. In another letter to Money, dated 25 June 1951, Adams writes: 'I shall be very interested to see the sketch of Octavia Hill which you have inherited'. However there is no documentary evidence to confirm this was the case.

Maurice and his friend John Sterling went to Cambridge with the third Barton son, Charles Barton (1805–56); Maurice's biographer Florence Higham describes his first tentative visits to the Barton family's London home:

> [Sterling] took him round sometimes to see the Bartons ... whose chief attraction was the possession of two pretty daughters. Susannah, languishing and elegant, had a vast admiration for John Sterling [whom she later married]; with her Maurice was tongue-tied, but forgot to be shy and forgot too his metaphysical problems when the schoolgirl sister Annie, with her gay beauty and teasing ways, appeared on the scene and smiled at him.[57]

Although Anna Barton died of tuberculosis as early as 1845, it is possible that Barton family members continued to visit Maurice in London into the 1860s. Hill's relationship with Maurice – and potentially with the Barton family – continued well beyond the early 1850s; in 1872 her younger sister Emily married his second son Charles Edmund. Another close contemporary of Maurice was Lieutenant-Colonel Hugh William Barton (1800–70), the eldest Barton son. In 1862 his occupation was recorded as 'Magistrate' and his address as 'The Waterfoot, County Fermanagh'.[58] This makes him, as well as Charles Barton, a candidate for authorship of the portrait; it is possible that the collection of drawings from which the sketch comes was stored in some sort of album, inscribed on the cover with the artist's address, which was mistranscribed by Money in his 1951 letter to the NPG. Also close in age to Maurice was the second son Colonel Nathaniel Dunbar Barton (c.1803–85). He is recorded in the 1861 census as living with his family in Paddington, London (before moving to Torquay and then Brighton). Potentially he too visited his late sister's husband, although it seems less likely that a collection of drawings by Nathaniel would be held at the family home in Ireland (which does not appear to have been his residence). Unfortunately, there is no evidence through which this early profile sketch can be attributed to a particular Barton sibling. Neither is there a record of Hill's providing sittings for the portrait. However, the careful representation of the face suggests that it was taken from life. Delicate cross-hatching across the forehead and around the eyes and nose indicates close observation on the artist's part. Although the rendering of the features is somewhat naive, a concerted effort has been made to communicate the salient points; for example, the strong contour of the upper lip and wide curve of the left nostril. If the attributed date is correct, the portrait shows Hill in her mid twenties. She turned twenty-six in 1864, which was a pivotal

---

[57] F. Higham, *Frederick Denison Maurice* (1947), p. 25.
[58] Barton database (see <http://www.bartondatabase.com/getperson.php?personID=I25120&tree=gbtree> [accessed 11 June 2014]).

'Nobler imaginings and mightier struggles'

year for her schemes for housing management. The date cannot be firmly established, however. After the NPG acquired the portrait, the director Charles Kingsley Adams wrote a letter to Money enquiring about the work, to which no response has been documented:

> This is about the drawing of Octavia Hill … I see that in the letter in which you first brought it to our attention you said that it was dated 1864, and probably by a contemporary member of the Barton family. I would be most grateful if you put down for our records anything you may know of its past history. I am also baffled by the date, of which there is no trace on the drawing.[59]

In 1914 Hill's sister Emily offered the gallery another profile portrait which was executed in 1877 and shows the sitter, aged thirty-nine (Figure 6.3). It was provisionally offered in place of the Sargent portrait, in the event that the latter proved too large, although, given Hill's dislike of the painting, she might have preferred the 1877 portrait to be the representative likeness. It was previously in the possession of Miranda Hill, who possibly shared this opinion, desiring that it too be presented to a public gallery after Hill's death.[60] Edward Clifford's pencil drawing (now with Sheffield Galleries & Museums Trust) has since been widely reproduced and is generally regarded as a successful portrait, capturing the long nose and distinctive arched brows evident in contemporary photographs. Clifford was a portraitist and illustrator, but he also acted as honorary secretary of the Church Army, an evangelical organization within the Church of England. In this latter role he became closely involved with attempts to control leprosy, travelling to India and Kashmir to this end. In 1868 he visited the leper colony in Kalaupapa, Hawaii, where he met Father Damien whose name became synonymous with the fight against the disease. The artist's original pencil profile of the Catholic priest, aged twenty-eight, is now in the Honolulu Museum of Art. It appears to have formed the basis of a more finished drawing, reproduced as an engraving for the frontispiece to an account of his journey, published in 1889.[61] Comparison between Hill's likeness and Clifford's portrait of Father Damien confirms that confident handling and economy of line characterized his style; he employed both to express his two sitters' ardency in their unwavering devotion to their respective causes. Further examples of his work in the NPG's collection confirm that he favoured a simple head-and-shoulders profile as a portrait format, with attention focused on the

---

[59] NPG Archive, RP 3804, C. K. Adams to J. H. Money, 17 June 1952.
[60] See NPG Archive, P1746, letters from E. S. Maurice to C. J. Holmes, 7 Dec. 1914, 8, 13 Feb. and 2 March 1915.
[61] E. Clifford, *Father Damien: a Journey from Cashmere to his Home in Hawaii* (1889).

Octavia Hill: the reluctant sitter

Figure 6.3. Octavia Hill, by Edward Clifford, pencil, 1877.

delineation of facial features.[62] The precise motivation for his portrait of Hill is not known, although Clifford seems to have been on friendly terms with her and Miranda. At the start of 1878 he wrote to Hill, on a European sojourn for the sake of her health, as 'one of the many friends who are thinking pretty often of you, and longing for the time when you can come back, revived, to all the folks who need you here'.[63] As late as 1880, writing to Miranda from Rome, Hill expressed interest in her sister's account of Clifford's 'discussions', presumably a talk he gave in the cause of the Church Army.[64] In the published portrait of Father Damien, the artist's signature is also visible bottom right and he inscribed the sitter's name and date of the work at top left, styled in a similar manner to Hill's name as included

[62] E.g. see NPG 1479 and NPG D37628.
[63] As quoted in Maurice, *Life of Octavia Hill*, p. 357.
[64] See Maurice, *Life of Octavia Hill*, pp. 397–8.

above her likeness. This indicates that the drawing was likewise intended for reproduction in an – as yet – unidentified publication.

In contrast to this tightly-worked, elegant portrait, the Barton sketch was perhaps conceived as a private record of the younger Hill who appears still girlish in appearance, her face fuller and her features not yet defined by maturity. It is particularly interesting, being one of only two identified images of Hill from this early stage in her life. The other is a group photograph taken in 1864, which shows her seated with her four sisters.[65] Comparison between the photographic image and the Barton drawing reveals the youthful pencil likeness to be accurate. Hill's preference for the modest nature of these more personal images became apparent as the idea for the Sargent oil began to take shape; she maintained that if the friends were firm in their intention, a simple well-executed chalk drawing would suffice.[66] Yet conceivably we can read in this instruction a concern beyond her desire to side-step the project, or keep costs to a minimum. Christopher Newall has examined a shift in Victorian portraiture in the middle of the century away from the dominant apparatus of the Grand Manner, designed to command the spectator's respect, towards an 'alternative tradition, which dealt in terms of directness and intimacy'. By stripping back the conventions of large-scale portraiture, the artist was able to 'draw closer to the sitter and to reveal as much as possible both physically and psychologically'.[67] He uses as examples two unassuming chalk portraits by the artist George Richmond of John Ruskin and Charlotte Bronte, both in the NPG collection.[68] Newall credits the success of these images, over Richmond's attempts at more formal portraiture, specifically to their power to provide insight into his sitters' inner lives. Arguably, it is the simplicity of this pictorial language which appealed most to Hill; the capacity in its straightforwardness to communicate an essential truth. With this in mind we can return to her profound response to the process of copying the Edward Grimston portrait at the Society of Antiquaries in 1864. In a letter to a friend she set herself apart from the antiquaries who possessed the skills to read the historical signs (i.e., the portrait's apparatus) and establish 'who and what he was'. Significance lay for her in the careful rendering of the sitter's face, and the potential of his reproachful 'still eyes' to teach her 'to live quietly'. This was perhaps for Hill, the real value of portraiture.

---

[65] Large format photogravure (Octavia Hill Birthplace Museum, Wisbech, Cambs., reproduced in Darley, *Octavia Hill*, between pp. 128–9).
[66] As cited in Darley, *Octavia Hill*, p. 267.
[67] Newall, 'The Victorians', p. 327.
[68] NPG 1058 (*c*.1857) and NPG 1452 (1850).

Octavia Hill: the reluctant sitter

In an age fascinated with the painted face and its role as a tangible marker for posterity – and throughout which the commercial demand for likenesses grew exponentially – Hill's view might be considered unusual. The NPG itself was established in 1856 to celebrate through portraiture individual lives and achievements, which collectively constituted the nation's history. Yet, as Newall identifies, for the later Victorians the portrait's attractiveness went beyond its function as an instrument of personal propaganda.[69] A good portraitist held the ability to elucidate character through the outward depiction of facial features, to make the invisible visible, or at least readable.

In this chapter I have focused on some key portraits of Octavia Hill and have considered what these tell us about her personality, but also how the circumstances surrounding their production reveal something of her attitude towards public life, and her thoughts about the purpose of art. This much is clear, but less easy to grasp is exactly why she adopted such an approach. A comparison with the iconographies of contemporaries in the field of social reform is arguably useful in this regard. Ready examples are those of Samuel and Henrietta Barnett, her close friends and long-term associates, who moved in many of the same social and professional networks. Despite their substantial achievements, including founding Toynbee Hall in Whitechapel (1884) and the planned community of Hampstead Garden Suburb (1903), just two known formal portraits of each exist. Watts painted Samuel for his Hall of Fame series (NPG 2893) and Henrietta is the subject of a late oil, now at the Henrietta Barnett School, although the primary image is a joint portrait by Hubert von Herkomer painted in 1908. Like Sargent's picture of Hill, the commission resulted from efforts made by a group of the Barnetts' friends and admirers, who presented the painting to the pair in the same year. The work was intended for display at Toynbee Hall, with which they were 'so long and intimately associated', and where the painting still hangs today.[70] Prime Minister Herbert Asquith unveiled it at an official ceremony at the hall on 20 November 1908. Overall, both their iconographies resemble Hill's in the scarcity of likenesses, the few other known portraits comprising more modest drawings, etchings and photographs. In light of this, I propose that an unflinching dedication to their work set in place a common pattern of behaviour among these three like-minded individuals which, at its core, excluded self-promotion. Certainly Hill was single-minded in her sense of purpose, and from an early age set a hazardous working pattern to the point of exhaustion and collapse.

---

[69] Newall, 'The Victorians', p. 351.
[70] 'The prime minister at Toynbee Hall', *The Times*, 21 Nov. 1908, p. 13; see BBC Your Paintings <http://www.bbc.co.uk/arts/yourpaintings/paintings/samuel-and-henrietta-barnet-135229> [accessed 11 June 2014].

Henrietta Barnett confirmed that Hill's life's work was all-encompassing, her vision unfaltering: 'She was strong-willed – some thought self-willed – but the strong will was never used for self. She was impatient in little things. Persistent with long-suffering in big ones'.[71] In accepting the Sargent portrait in 1898, Hill encouraged her audience not merely to hallow her personal achievements but to look ahead and see how her work might be successfully continued. She simply wished to inspire action in others: 'When I am gone, I hope my friends will not try to carry out any special system, or to follow blindly in the track which I have trodden. New circumstances require various efforts, and it is the spirit, not the dead form that should be perpetuated'.[72]

---

[71] Barnett, *Canon Barnett*, i. 30.
[72] As quoted in Bell, *Octavia Hill*, p. 242.

ns of nature
III. 'The value of abundant good air': Octavia Hill and the meanings of nature

7. Octavia Hill, nature and open space: crowning success or campaigning 'utterly without result'

Elizabeth Baigent

Octavia Hill is rightly remembered as one of the great British open space and nature campaigners of the nineteenth century.[1] Trained as a visual artist, she was alive to the beauty of nature and, influenced by Ruskinian and Arnoldian views of culture, she was persuaded of the moral work such beauty could accomplish.[2]

Awakening others to a love of nature was part of Hill's practical social work from an early age. As a young teenager she organized outings into green spaces for the toymakers in her charge.[3] When she was eighteen she marvelled at how an outing to Epping Forest affected some tailors and their families.[4] As a young adult she incorporated exercise and fresh air in Regent's Park into the curriculum of her Nottingham Place school[5] and, when she was successfully managing many houses, 'one of the pleasantest customs of all was common throughout the properties, that of meeting for a long half day together in the fields in summer'.[6] She combined such practical work with campaigning on the platform, in the press and in correspondence to preserve natural open spaces and secure poor people's access to them.[7] Her views on natural open spaces sprang from her own

---

[1] The literature on open space reform is voluminous. For London, see citations to the secondary literature throughout this chapter; and for contemporary views, see, e.g., Mrs. Basil Holmes [Isabelle Gladstone], *The London Burial Grounds* (1896); R. Hunter, *Gardens in Towns* (1915); *A Brief Statement of the Objects of the Metropolitan Public Garden, Boulevard, and Playground Association* (1883); J. F. B. Firth, *Municipal London; Or, London Government as it is, and London under a Municipal Council* (1876), pp. 243–7.

[2] D. Maltz, *British Aestheticism and the Urban Working Classes, 1870–1900: Beauty for the People* (Basingstoke, 2006).

[3] E. M. Bell, *Octavia Hill: a Biography* (1942), p. 28.

[4] Hill to Mary Harris, 3 Aug. 1856, in *Octavia Hill: Early Ideals, from Letters*, ed. E. S. Maurice (1928), pp. 26–7.

[5] Bell, *Hill*, p. 64.

[6] E. Chase, *Tenant Friends in Old Deptford* (1929), p. 14.

[7] *LFW* gives a taste of her more public correspondence. Various articles cited below give a sense of her broader publications. For women's public roles in social action and the open space movement, see H. Meller, 'Women and citizenship: gender and the built environment in British cities 1870–1939', in *Cities of Ideas: Civil Society and Urban Governance in Britain*

feelings, gained strength as she saw that poor city dwellers enjoyed nature, and finally became part of a coherent moral schema. The schema examined in this chapter threatened to lead her to conclusions more radical than she could ultimately contemplate or at least voice, but it tempers views of her as moralistic, reactionary and obsessed with an individualistic view of society – views which Garnett and Readman in this volume also suggest are superficial or partial. It also explains why, despite her hard-won authority on the subject of nature, her persuasive speaking voice and writing style, and the fact that her contemporaries largely agreed with her that time spent in nature was beneficial, she thought her open space work in some respects a failure: 'I think I never spent so much heart, time and thought on anything so utterly without apparent result', she declared to her fellow workers in 1876 after a series of open space failures which led her to feel she struggled against apathy as well as opposition. Her failure to persuade rich Londoners to open their private squares to their poor neighbours when they were out of town, or for an annual flower show, was a continuing source of frustration; and she was baffled by rich people's failure to give land for the benefit of all.[8] Elsewhere, of course, she rejoiced in her own and others' open space successes, but this chapter examines why she also spoke of failure – not simply because she sometimes failed to secure individual sites, but because her open space work was bound up in a scheme for the moral transformation of society.

Nature in England's nineteenth-century cities

The prevailing narrative of the open space movement tells how poor city dwellers were at first deprived of nature and open space but got some access to both as a result of it.[9] We can see this too in public monuments.

1800–2000. Essays in Honour of David Reeder, ed. D. A. Reeder, R. Rodger and R. Colls (Aldershot, 2004), pp. 208–31; H. Meller, *Leisure and the Changing City, 1870–1914* (1976); J. Lewis, *Women and Social Action in Victorian and Edwardian England* (Aldershot, 1991).

[8] First quotation and more comment about failure, in Hill, *LFW*, 1876, p.75; in Bell, *Hill*, pp. 147–8, Bell noted Hill's general frustration at her limited success and added her own that London squares still remained closed in 1940; second quotation from Octavia Hill, 'Space for the people', in Hill, *Homes of the London Poor* (1875), pp. 209–10, esp. pp. 196–212. She makes the same point about London squares at length in 'Open spaces', in O. Hill, *Our Common Land* (1977), pp. 105–51, at pp. 137–40.

[9] E.g., S. Sörlin and P. Warde, 'The problem of the problem of environmental history: a re-reading of the field', *Environmental History*, xii (2007), 107–30. Contemporary accounts include G. J. Shaw Lefevre, *English Commons and Forests: the Story of the Battle for Public Rights* (2nd edn., 1894); Baron Eversley, *Commons, Forests, and Footpaths* (1910); R. Hunter, *The Epping Forest Act 1878, with an Introduction, Notes, and Index by R. Hunter* (1878), as well as Hill's writings cited in this chapter. More recent accounts which stress the agency of

The Octavia Hill stained glass memorial window in Holy Trinity church, Crockham Hill, for example (see Figure 1.5), depicts on the right the densely packed, grey, grimy city, empty of plants and animals, on the left the verdant countryside. Given the lack of nature in the city, so the argument goes, city dwellers had to visit the adjoining fields or urban parks, preserved by Hill and her peers, for their contact with it.

In contrast to the sterile city in the window, however, nineteenth-century London, like contemporary towns the world over, was full of nature.[10] It was full of people and other animals, and poor people in particular came into close contact with those animals in their daily life and work. Poor people drove, fed, watered, groomed and cleaned up after the horses and donkeys on which passenger and goods transport depended; they kept rabbits, chickens, goats, pigs and cows for food, since freshness often depended on proximity;[11] and they sold or worked with animal products including meat, fish, shellfish, fur and feathers.[12] Though poor people's main exposure to animal nature was via work, leisure also brought contact. Children played with animal

---

poor people in the open space movement include B. Cowell, 'The Commons Preservation Society and the campaign for Berkhamsted common, 1866–70', *Rural History*, xiii (2002), 145–61; N. MacMaster, 'The battle for Mousehold Heath, 1857–1884: "popular politics" and the Victorian public park', *Past & Present*, cxxvii (1990), 117–54; P. Readman, 'Preserving the English landscape, c.1870–1914', *Cultural and Social History*, v (2008), 197–218; P. Readman, 'Landscape preservation, "advertising disfigurement" and English national identity, c.1890–1914', *Rural History*, xii (2001), 61–83; H. L. Malchow, 'Public gardens and social action in late Victorian London, *Victorian Studies*, xxix (1985), 97–124; H. L. Malchow, 'Free water: the public drinking fountain movement and Victorian London', *London Journal*, iv (1978), 181–203; A. Taylor, '"Commons-stealers", "land-grabbers" and "jerry-builders": space, popular radicalism, and the politics of public access in London, 1848–1880', *International Review of Social History*, xl (1995), 383–408. Some recent scholarship on the subject focuses again on the importance of the actions of the movement's middle-class leaders, e.g. M. J. D. Roberts, 'Gladstonian liberalism and environment protection, 1865–76', *English Historical Review*, cxxviii (2013), 292–322; and E. Baigent, 'A "splendid pleasure ground [for] the elevation and refinement of the people of London": geographical aspects of the history of Epping Forest 1860–1895', in *English Geographies: Historical Essays on English Customs, Cultures, and Communities in Honour of Jack Langton*, ed. E. Baigent and R. J. Mayhew (Oxford, 2009), pp. 104–26.

[10] P. Atkins, *Animal Cities: Beastly Urban Histories* (Farnham, 2012); J. H. Winter, *Secure from Rash Assault: Sustaining the Victorian Environment* (Berkeley, Calif., 1999), esp. ch. 10; H. Ritvo, *The Animal Estate: the English and other Creatures in the Victorian Age* (Cambridge, Mass., 1987).

[11] P. Atkins, *Liquid Materialities: a History of Milk, Science and the Law* (Farnham, 2010); S. Friedberg, *Fresh: a Perishable History* (Cambridge, Mass., 2009); A. Harding, *East End Underworld: Chapters in the Life of Arthur Harding*, ed. R. Samuel (1981), e.g. pp. 26 and 129 for cows, goats, pigs, horses, rabbits and chickens in the Nichol.

[12] Chase notes 'men hawking ... rabbits dangling from the end of a stick ... Italian women with cages of fortune-telling canaries' (*Deptford*, p. 23).

products, such as oyster shells,[13] while adults kept animals for a mix of profit and sentiment. Profit came from prize money for which pigeons were raced,[14] dogs were raced, fought and used for ratting,[15] and birds were entered in singing competitions, for example;[16] while sentiment governed the keeping of pets, including some such as the Deptford oystercatcher which later sensibilities deem unsuitable.[17] There were chance glimpses of exotic animals, such as circus animals, dancing bears, or beached whales, and all too many contacts with animals classed as vermin.[18] Contact with animal nature varied very considerably across London. Hill's tenants in central Marylebone, for example, lived in a press of people but had less contact with other animals, while those in Deptford, on London's edge, found the press of people less intense but had more contact with non-human animals.[19]

Poor Londoners' contact with vegetable nature was similarly extensive and varied. The extent to which they grew their own vegetables on allotments, in gardens or on scraps of waste land awaits full investigation, but research from other cities suggests that potato growing in particular may have been substantial.[20] Certainly vegetables were widely eaten by poor people in mid Victorian cities, though this perhaps decreased by the late Victorian period.[21] Many poor street vendors sold products such as watercress, oranges, cut flowers or roots;[22] decamped to the surrounding countryside to harvest hops

---

[13] Chase, *Deptford*, p. 36.

[14] M. Johnes, 'Pigeon racing and working-class culture in Britain, *c.*1870–1950', *Cultural and Social History*, iv (2007), 361–83. For horse and dog racing, see, e.g., Harding, *East End Underworld*, ch. 14.

[15] Harding, *East End Underworld*, pp. 14–16.

[16] E.g., Harding, *East End Underworld*, p. 6.

[17] Chase, *Deptford*, p. 29.

[18] Chase, *Deptford*, pp. 39, 58.

[19] Chase, *Deptford*; O. Hill, 'Four years' management of a London court', *Macmillan's Magazine*, Oct. 1871, reprinted in O. Hill, *Homes of the London Poor* (1875), pp. 33–66.

[20] J. Matheson, 'Common ground: horticulture and the cultivation of open space in the East End of London, 1840–1900' (unpublished Open University PhD thesis, 2010); M. Willes, *The Gardens of the British Working Class* (New Haven, Conn., 2014), though the 19th-century sections of this book are largely based on Matheson; H. Mayhew, *London Labour and the London Poor* (4 vols., 1864), ii. 336, on allotments <http://books.google.co.uk/books?id=iBIIAAAAQAAJ&> [accessed 30 Aug. 2013]; D. Crouch and C. Ward, *The Allotment* (1988). See bibliography in A. Björklund, *Historical Urban Agriculture: Food Production and Access to Land in Swedish Towns before 1900* (Stockholm, 2010).

[21] P. Clayton and J. Rowbotham, 'An unsuitable and degraded diet?', *Journal of the Royal Society of Medicine*, ci (2008), 282–9, 350–7, 454–62; P. Clayton and J. Rowbotham, 'How the mid-Victorians worked, ate and died', *International Journal of Environmental Research into Public Health*, vi (2009), 1235–53.

[22] P. Sanders, *The Simple Annals: the History of an Essex and East End Family* (Gloucester, 1989), pp. 133–4.

and fruit;[23] or worked with fodder crops to sustain the transport system. As with animals, contact with vegetable nature came mainly through work, but leisure activities included growing flowers and other plants for ornament and sometimes for prize money at competitive shows.[24]

For all Victorian Londoners, but particularly poorer ones, the weather and the seasons were close neighbours. Poor people's houses and clothes let in wind, rain, and cold in winter, and were stuffy and hot in summer. Poor Londoners often worked outdoors, as hawkers, crossing sweepers or prostitutes for example, and faced unremitting exposure to the weather. Work was often seasonal: poor people picked fruit or fished in season, and sold seasonal flowers or fruits. Poor Londoners, then, far from being cut off from nature were in repeated, daily close contact with it. The same was often true of open space. As noted above, many poor people worked in open spaces and, living in houses which were hot, small and airless, they often took their leisure outside: in an urban park or neighbouring rural open space, or, more likely, in building sites, yards, fountains, canals and particularly the street, 'the great recreation room' of the slums which was 'spacious, lively and exhilarating'.[25]

The kind of nature and open space described here is obvious in memoirs and novels by working-class people,[26] but also in accounts by Octavia Hill and her fellow workers, notably Ellen Chase who managed the houses in Green Street, Deptford, which had been in Hill's charge since 1884.[27] Marylebone was inhabited by 'mainly costermongers and small hawkers'

[23] Sanders, *Simple Annals*, p. 115; J. London, *The People of the Abyss* (1903; this edn. 1963), pp. 73–5.
[24] For ornamental plants, see, e.g., Harding, *East End Underworld*, pp. 22–4; Matheson, 'Common ground'; J. Matheson, 'Floricultural societies and their shows in the east end of London 1860–1875', *London Gardener*, viii (2002–3), 26–33; J. Matheson, '"A new gleam of social sunshine": window garden flower shows for the working classes, 1860–75', *London Gardener*, ix (2003–4), 60–70; S. M. Gaskell, 'Gardens for the working class: Victorian practical pleasure', *Victorian Studies*, xxiii (1980), 479–501.
[25] R. Roberts, *The Classic Slum: Salford Life in the First Quarter of the Century* (Harmondsworth, 1973), p. 124; C. Chinn, *Poverty Amidst Prosperity: the Urban Poor in England 1834–1914* (Lancaster, 2006); Harding, *East End Underworld*, pp. 32–8.
[26] E.g., and with particular respect to nature and open space, Harding, *East End Underworld*; Sanders, *Simple Annals*; A. Morrison, *A Child of the Jago* (1896); S. Newens, *Arthur Morrison: the Novelist of Realism in East London and Essex* (Loughton, 2008), p. 10; [A Journeyman Engineer] T. Wright, *Bill Banks' Day Out* (1868). Interpreting such texts is, of course, problematic, but nature is so clearly present in all that they may be relied on in this matter. Later memoirs describe a working-class experience of nature that much more closely resembled the middle-class one (e.g., rambling in Roberts, *Classic Slum*, p. 235; F. Bell, *At the Works: a Study of a Manufacturing Town (Middlesbrough)* (1907)).
[27] Bell, *Hill*, p. 181.

selling foodstuffs or flowers.[28] At Deptford the 'main industry' was cattle,[29] while hawkers sold primrose roots, groundsel roots or oranges.[30] As Chase described it:

> All that side of London [round Deptford] is bordered by market gardens, and not a few Green-Streeters look forward regularly to a week's 'fruiting' as a season of pleasure, while a still larger number go 'hopping' … every September our people flocked off in shoals, taking midnight excursion trains down toward Maidstone, where they led a merry, gipsy life in the field for a week or two.[31]

As Chase and her helpers made up the accounts, they heard 'a pair of cocks fighting on the window-ledge at our back, or a nanny-goat bleating in the yard below'.[32]

This kind of nature, however, although ubiquitous, did not disrupt the narrative that poor people lacked nature. The meaning of 'nature', as of all words, depends on its historical context and 'the idea of nature contains … an extraordinary amount of human history'.[33] 'There is no ahistorical ecological consciousness that transcends human constructions of nature.' Instead people 'envision nature … through competing … ideological lenses'.[34] Nature is simultaneously Other (wild, remote and distinctly apart from humanity) and Not Other (moulded by people and in relationship with them).[35] On the whole, the less people encounter non-human nature and open space in their daily working lives, the more those things become Other and have transcendent qualities ascribed to them.[36] Thus, while poor nineteenth-century Londoners generally encountered and formed their views of nature and open space via the daily close contact provided by work, middle-class reformers, including Hill, encountered and formed their views through

---

[28] O. Hill, 'Landlords and tenants in London', originally in *Macmillan's Magazine*, Oct. 1871, reprinted in O. Hill, *The Homes of the London Poor*, pp. 67–107, quotation at p. 71.

[29] Chase, *Deptford*, p. 33.

[30] Chase, *Deptford*, pp. 23, 117, 183.

[31] Chase, *Deptford*, p. 102.

[32] Chase, *Deptford*, p. 30.

[33] R. Williams, 'Ideas of nature', in *Problems in Materialism and Culture* (1980), quotation at p. 67; R. Williams, *Keywords: a Vocabulary in Culture and Society* (1976).

[34] T. Lekan, *Imagining the Nation in Nature: Landscape Preservation and German Identity, 1885–1945* (Cambridge, Mass., 2004), p. 263.

[35] D. E. Cooper, 'The idea of environment', in *The Environment in Question: Ethics and Global Issues*, ed. D. E. Cooper and J. A. Palmer (1992), pp. 165–80; B. McKibben, *The End of Nature* (1990).

[36] See, e.g., A. Offer, *Property and Politics, 1870–1914: Landownership, Law, Ideology, and Urban Development in England* (Cambridge, 1981). Baigent, 'Splendid pleasure ground', describes how one of Victorian England's most famous natural open spaces was remade to align with an urban and middle-class view of nature.

leisure informed by literature, the visual arts, history, theology, science or social science, which together created Nature and Open Space as aesthetic, ideological and moral goods. While poor Londoners had plenty of nature and some open space in their daily working lives, they had very little Nature or Open Space. In the second half of the nineteenth century middle-class reformers made concerted efforts to replace or control nature in poor people's working lives (for example, via sanitary reforms to regulate livestock in cities);[37] to provide Nature for poor people's leisure time (for example, by creating parks); and to discipline their behaviour in Nature (for example, by installing parkkeepers). The substitution of Nature for nature could be strikingly direct. For example, when Epping Forest in Essex was preserved for open air recreation, poor people lost their profitable rights to lop its trees for firewood – it made them look Unnatural – and people's recreation was regulated to make it appropriate for Nature's backdrop.[38]

The substitution of Nature for nature, and Open Space for open space was limited by technology, middle-class self-interest and, in some cases, working-class opposition. Draft animals and dairy cows (and their fodder and droppings) remained part of city life until innovations in transport and refrigeration made them obsolete; middle-class people were, with some notable exceptions, slow to establish parks when the same land might be built on for profit; and working people continued to take their leisure in open spaces which were not designated for that purpose.[39] The trend towards making nature and open space into Nature and Open Space was, however, clear.

Octavia Hill, nature and Nature: from cowsheds to cowslips?

Hill was a vocal and busy campaigner in the remaking of nature and open space. She joined the Ladies' Sanitary Association and the Sanitary Laws Enforcement Society, and lectured to the National Health Society.[40] She promoted housing sanitation, fitness and health, for example in her cadet

---

[37] Atkins, *Animal Cities*; *Sanitary Reform in Victorian Britain*, pt. i, ed. T. Y. Choi (2012), pt. ii, ed. C. S. Hamlin (2013).

[38] Baigent, 'Splendid pleasure ground'; and for similar examples, see MacMaster, 'Mousehold Heath'; G. Tyack, *Sir James Pennethorne and the Making of Victorian London* (Cambridge, 1992), pp. 90, 93; Malchow, 'Free water'; D. Reeder, 'The social construction of green space in London prior to the second world war', in *The European City and Green Space: London Stockholm, Helsinki, and St. Petersburg 1850–2000*, ed. P. Clark (Aldershot, 2006), pp. 41–67; N. Dreher, 'The virtuous and the verminous: turn-of-the-century moral panics in London's public parks', *Albion*, xxix (1997), 246–67, 251.

[39] Harding, *East End Underworld*, pp. 37–8; Malchow, 'Free water', p. 200.

[40] Atkins, *Animal Cities*; E. Hart, 'The National Health Society of London', *Public Health*, xix (1893), 71–3.

force, established in 1889,[41] and particularly the reworking of natural open spaces as leisure sites for poor people. At Freshwater Place, for example, she wanted to make a playground for her tenants' children from a 'bit of desolate ground, occupied with wretched dilapidated cowsheds, [and] manure heaps',[42] despite the 'neighbours who resented the clearing up of a waste space, which they had been accustomed to use as a place for fighting or loafing or throwing out their rubbish'.[43] Her playground project thus took a site of work (cow keeping and waste disposal) and unrespectable leisure (fighting and loafing by adults who should have been working), and turned it into one for respectable leisure enjoyed by more suitable people (children for whom play was legitimate).[44] Cowsheds were replaced by cowslips for Hill's May Day celebrations, in a classic example of profitable work's being replaced by folkloric rituals evacuated of material significance.[45] A maypole was erected and the usually rather down-to-earth Ellen Chase became whimsical in describing the scene. The balcony was

> threaded with boughs of blooming gorse and laburnum, topped with bunches of bluebells and red may, from out of which the women lean forward to look down upon the slim pole, with masses of wild hyacinths at its base, and cowslips, beech boughs, lilacs, meadow-sweet, and buttercups twining all the way up to where the whole is capped by a flower crown. Generally the children of the property sing a carol at the outset, the girls wearing fresh frocks with cowslip wreaths for the occasion, and the boys Sherwood green blouses with quivers at the shoulder to look like Robin Hood's band. Then, the music striking up, several rings are formed, the pole standing straight and beautiful in the middle, catching the light and making the whole air sweet, as tenants and helpers turn and double before it.[46]

Hill's biographer, Enid Moberley Bell, was so taken by the celebrations that she wrote in a triumph of wishful thinking over observation that, 'except for one or two boys, the flowers interested [the children] more than the cakes'.[47]

Hill's tenants were systematically moved away from self-provisioning towards flower growing (ironically thus impairing their nourishment and the economic 'self-sufficiency which was a necessary condition of

---

[41] Bell, *Hill*, pp. 195–9.

[42] Bell, *Hill*, p. 77. This phrase was the one used in the *Times* obituary, 'Death of Miss Octavia Hill', *The Times*, 15 Aug. 1912, p. 7.

[43] Bell, *Hill*, p. 92.

[44] See Malchow, 'Public gardens', p. 120, for 'loafing' and the unpopularity of clearing work sites for gardens.

[45] E. P. Thompson, *Customs in Common* (1993), pp. 3, 182.

[46] Chase, *Deptford*, pp. 101–2.

[47] Bell, *Hill*, p. 96.

respectability' and the independence preached by the Charity Organization Society).⁴⁸ There was an annual flower – not vegetable – show at Red Cross cottages.⁴⁹ Ellen Chase urged

> the laying out of gardens … A competition among the yards for the best show of flowers is worth trying for, and is far better for all than that rabbits or pigeons should be kept. Pigeons are wholly undesirable, as the men bet on their flight, and the birds, if at liberty, peck and destroy mortar. Fowls, too, are always getting loose, and their pens crowd the already straightened [*sic*] space: successive rows of sunflowers, irises, and scarlet beans running over the fences have a directly contrary effect, making the yards seem larger.⁵⁰

The only edible plants Chase approves – runner beans and herbs – were valued for their flowers, not their nutritional impact. Flower growing was heavily moralized: 'the places began to look homelike'; gardens 'became more and more our pride, as the people shifted less frequently'. Flower gardens were emblem and consequence of ordered lives, as tenants turned their backs on 'dreary wastes'.⁵¹

Hill thus unquestionably did remake nature into Nature, and open space into Open Space, and did 'impose her own uncontested aesthetic subjectivity in the design of outdoor sites, and … dictate recreations such as gardening and ordered children's games';⁵² but this was not the end of the story. First, we should not assume that her views were at odds with those of her tenants. Though some local people pulled down the walls of her playgrounds and stole the bricks, others – or perhaps the same people – enjoyed the flower shows.⁵³ Second, as a working woman from a family of working women, Hill always considered work when planning Open Space.⁵⁴ Her Marylebone Road playground was used as a drying ground for laundry during the school day.⁵⁵ Other Open Spaces were 'summer nurseries' where women looked after small children while mending and

---

⁴⁸ P. Bailey, '"Will the real Bill Banks please stand up?" Towards a role analysis of mid-Victorian working-class respectability', *Journal of Social History*, xii (1979), 336–53, at 338; G. Best, *Mid-Victorian Britain, 1851–1875* (1971), pp. 256–63.

⁴⁹ Bell, *Hill*, p. 193; and see Matheson, 'Floricultural societies'.

⁵⁰ Chase, *Deptford*, p. 207.

⁵¹ Chase, *Deptford*, pp. 11, 28–9; Gaskell, 'Gardens for the working class'.

⁵² Maltz, *British Aestheticism*, pp. 42–3.

⁵³ Two of Hill's undated letters to Mary Harris, cited in Maurice, *Hill*, p. 197; Matheson, 'Common ground'; Bailey, '"Will the real Bill Banks please stand up?"'.

⁵⁴ G. Darley, *Octavia Hill* (1990); Bell, *At the Works*, pp. 131, 166.

⁵⁵ Maurice, *Hill*, p. 188; by contrast in St. James Churchyard, Bermondsey, airing clothes was banned after the MPGA laid it out as a garden (Holmes, *London Burial Grounds*, p. 240, cited in Malchow, 'Public gardens', p. 120).

sewing.[56] She preferred cottages to flats not just for their rustic resonances, but because they facilitated work ('space in courtyards for drying clothes, standing a barrow').[57] Third, her involvement with the everyday lives of her tenants made her attitudes to Open Space practical and gave value to the space cottages afforded for 'the separate yard for chair for invalid, swing for child, place for creepers and bulbs, space for man to make a little workshop, the separation from other families'.[58]

The fourth reason that Hill's Open Space work defies caricature is that she paid more than lip service to the fundamental parity of poor and rich people – 'the human heart, which is the same everywhere' – which her theology preached.[59] She avoided structural analyses which treated poor people as a mass; sensationalist descriptions which treated them as spectacle; and naturalistic accounts of them as swarming, breeding or degenerate.[60] While Ruskin appeared to reserve 'delight' in 'natural scenery' to 'men of true feeling', Hill thought that everyone could share it;[61] and perhaps that those to whom Nature was unfamiliar might appreciate it more. Ada Vachell, who worked with disabled poor people in Bristol, suggested that 'we should ourselves have to live in ... a workhouse to fully realise what ... a country holiday must mean', and Hill suggested something of the same when, having conceded that 'To us [middle-class people] the [bank holiday] Common or forest looks indeed crowded with people', her conclusion was that, 'to them [working-class people who live in cramped, greenless places] the feeling is one of sufficient space, free air,

---

[56] O. Hill, *Colour, Space, and Music for the People* (1884), originally published in *Nineteenth Century*, xv (1884), 7.

[57] O. Hill, 'Space for the people', originally published in *Macmillan's Magazine*, Aug. 1875, reprinted in Hill, *Homes of the London Poor* (1875), pp. 196–212, at p. 196. Harding, in *East End Underworld*, p. 4, writes of the many sheds in courts for costermongers' donkeys; for lack of space for barrows in model flats, see G. Stedman Jones, *Outcast London: a Study in the Relationship between Classes in Victorian Society* (Harmondsworth, 1976), p. 204.

[58] Bell, *Hill*, p. 188.

[59] Hill, *Colour, Space, and Music*, p. 3.

[60] Cf. Sir Reginald Rowe, 'Foreword', pp. ix–xiii to Bell, *Hill*, who describes Hill's tenants as 'pig-like' at p. x. Hill does rely on 'types' and in 'Landlords and tenants in London', pp. 71–2, gives a scalar account of poor people. S. Koven, *Slumming: Sexual and Social Politics in Victorian London* (Princeton, N.J., 2004); R. Livesey, 'Reading for character: women social reformers and narratives of the urban poor in late Victorian and Edwardian London', *Journal of Victorian Culture*, ix (2004), 43–68; J. Lewis, 'Social facts, social theory and social change: the ideas of Booth in relation to those of Beatrice Webb, Octavia Hill, and Helen Bosanquet', in *Retrieved Riches: Social Investigation in Britain, 1840–1914*, ed. D. Englander and R. O'Day (Aldershot, 1995), pp. 49–67. Swenson in this volume cites some less attractive comments about restricting access to nature to those who deserved it.

[61] J. Ruskin, *The Stones of Venice* (3 vols., 1851–3), ii. ch. 6, para. 30.

green grass, and colour'.[62] Her writings show a constant tussle between her aesthetic and moral recoil from poor people's bad behaviour in Nature and Open Space, and her belief in people's fundamental parity. Criticism of appearance is immediately followed by a reproof to herself (and her middle-class audience) for missing the essence.[63] Thus she condemned the row made by 'eleven vans of schoolchildren going into the country shouting with wild glee … but then again I knew they fulfilled God's will in their joy'.[64] She recoiled from the children in her playground, exclaiming, 'No one can imagine … the[ir] disgustingness … Yet, when I see their joy and reflect from what they are being kept, it seems to me a thing for which I shall rejoice all my life'.[65] Bank holiday throngs were 'undisciplined but heartily happy'.[66] Crowds carried 'London noise and vulgarity into woods and fields', but observers should 'Look at the happy family groups … watch the joy of eager children … notice the affectionate father bringing out the pot of ale to the wife'.[67] On bank holidays poor people presented 'really bad sights … at every public-house on the road, [with] wild songs and boisterous behaviour, and reckless driving at night', but then again 'how much intense enjoyment the day gives!'[68] Certainly Hill regretted poor people's loudness and drunkenness, but her reproof was reserved for herself and her middle-class audience for missing the children's joy, the father's affection and the families' happiness. Brace argues that, 'With the power of articulation resting firmly with [middle-class observers], the diabolical behaviour of day-trippers [in Nature] becomes a source of profound disquiet articulated through the language of class'.[69] For Hill, however, poor people in Nature were the literal opposite of diabolical, for they fulfilled God's will.[70]

---

[62] F. M. Unwin, *Ada Vachell of Bristol* (Bristol, 1928), p. 110; Hill, 'Our common land', p. 4, in O. Hill, *Our Common Land and other Short Essays* (1877), pp. 1–17.

[63] For other middle-class observers who were not censorious of poor people's behaviour in nature, see Baigent, 'Splendid pleasure ground'; E. Baigent, '"God's earth will be sacred": religion, theology, and the open space movement in Victorian England', *Rural History*, xxii (2011), 31–58.

[64] Hill to Mary Harris, 25 June 1865, in Maurice, *Hill*, p. 86.

[65] Undated letter, Hill to Mary Harris, in Maurice, *Hill*, p. 199.

[66] Hill, 'Our common land', p. 3.

[67] Hill, 'Our common land', p. 3.

[68] Hill, 'Our common land', p. 2.

[69] C. Brace, 'A pleasure ground for the noisy herds? Incompatible encounters with the Cotswolds and England, 1900–1950', *Rural History*, xi (2000), 75–94, quotation at p. 81.

[70] It seems likely that the sympathy which Hill shows here was more common than is generally thought. The cliché has Hill evicting tenants for non-payment of rent, but Chase, with Hill's approval, was flexible and sympathetic when there was good cause for lateness, e.g. when a tenant had just had a baby or was ill (Chase, *Deptford*, pp. 152, 175).

Hill's general philosophy

The fifth reason that Hill resists caricature in her open space campaigns is that her theology made her avoid the middle-class tendency to elevate Nature and Open Space to transcendental goods.[71] This can be seen in a rare attempt she made to explain her general philosophy. Hill considered there to be 'two primary blessings, the power of entering into divine and human love' and then 'secondary gifts – music, colour, art, nature, space, quiet'.[72] Unremarkably for her time she gave priority to religious matters but, under F. D. Maurice's influence, she emphasized divine love (rather than, for example, divine judgement) and considered divine and human love to be common possessions: 'we all possess [the primary blessings] – high and low, rich and poor'.[73] Contemporary middle-class readers would have recognized that she was citing Psalm 49, the whole of which makes unsettling reading for rich people. In the context of this psalm, her exclamation, 'how unequally these [secondary gifts] are divided', is less a disinterested observation than one of her many rebukes to rich people.[74] The judgement that Hill had an 'unshakeable belief in the moral superiority of the middle and upper classes' entirely misjudges those whom she here criticized.[75]

Nature and space, separately identified, were just two of Hill's secondary gifts. Though she valued nature for its types ('The bramble is to me so full of signs, as well as beauties'),[76] her sacramental view of the world extended far beyond it: 'outward objects and events are *all* connected with inward life …. illustrations, and even interpreters of it'.[77] She used catechism language to describe earthly life (a sacrament being there defined as the outward sign of inward grace). She reiterated, having been inspired by one of Maurice's sermons on the real presence (of Christ in the host at communion), that she understood Christ to be really present 'here and everywhere', so that the whole human world was thus sanctified.[78] Nature and open space were

---

[71] Offer, *Property and Politics*.

[72] Hill, *Colour, Space, and Music*, p. 1.

[73] Hill, *Colour, Space, and Music*, p. 1.

[74] Hill, *Colour, Space, and Music*, p. 1. She was instinctively suspicious of some rich people: 'As I am thrown among "*ladies*" I hope I may discover some good in them', she wrote of voluntary workers at Maurice's Working Men's College (Bell, *Hill*, p. 41). She was particularly wary of 'slumming' ('the want felt by those who have little of this world's goods is too solemn to disclose to those who haven't imagination enough to feel it other than as an exciting show' (*Colour, Space, and Music*, p. 6)).

[75] P. Malpass, 'Octavia Hill', in *Founders of the Welfare State*, ed. P. Barker (1984), pp. 31–6, esp. 32.

[76] Letter, Hill, 31 July 1858, cited in Maurice, *Hill*, p. 54.

[77] Maurice, *Hill*, p. 216 (my italics).

[78] Hill to Mary Harris, 2 May 1869, cited in Maurice, *Hill*, pp. 101–2.

thus parts, but not unique ones, of Hill's sacramental understanding of the world. This, and the fact that she understood God to be immanent in nature, not nature to be transcendent, prevented her from joining some other open space campaigners in expecting exposure to Nature to transform society.[79]

Hill is widely castigated for her view that unsystematic charity corrupted, though it is rarely noted that she thought it perverted donors as much as recipients.[80] However, she thought that secondary gifts, being initially free from God, could be presented again without corrupting donor or recipient, and should be so given: 'it is ... a giving back to men that which God gives most freely and generally to all his children – blue sky, pure earth, bright water, green grass'.[81] Thus independently and through the Kyrle Society, Hill organized her better-off friends to provide poor Londoners with works of music and visual art (as Robert Whelan and John Price describe in this volume), and with nature, space and, to a certain extent, quiet as they opened their gardens to parties of her tenants, or sent them flowers from their gardens or greenhouses. 'All must know how much pleasure it gives', she wrote concerning the gifts of flowers, and obviously considered this pleasure free from corruption.[82]

The re-giving of secondary gifts was rarely free of instrumentalism; Hill like many other reformers unquestionably hoped that providing nature, space, music, art and the like would turn poor people away from drink and towards God, and improve their physiques and morals.[83] Hill thus noted that giving flowers enabled reformers to go 'into the homes of those

[79] Baigent, 'God's earth will be sacred'.

[80] O. Hill, 'The work of volunteers in the organisation of charity', originally published in *Macmillan's Magazine*, Oct. 1872, reprinted in Hill, *Homes of the London Poor*, pp. 108–42; Malpass, 'Octavia Hill', p. 34; Jones, *Outcast London*; R. Humphreys, *Poor Relief and Charity 1869–1945: the London Charity Organization Society* (Basingstoke, 2001); R. Livesey, 'Reading for character: women social reformers and narratives of the urban poor in late Victorian and Edwardian London', *Journal of Victorian Culture*, ix (2004), 43–68; Bell, *Hill*, pp. 279–80; *Supplement to the Report of an Attempt to raise a Few of the London Poor without Gifts, being a Letter from John Ruskin MA* (1870), with a rejoinder by Octavia Hill.

[81] O. Hill, 'More air for London', *Nineteenth Century*, xxiii (1888), 181–8, quotation at p. 187.

[82] Hill, *Colour, Space, and Music*, p. 6.

[83] E.g., B. Harrison, *Drink and the Victorians* (1971), pp. 320–,3 for drink, and Tyack, *Pennethorne*, p. 88, for other 'low and debasing pleasures'; D. A. Reid, 'Playing and praying', in *The Cambridge Urban History of Britain*, iii, ed. M. Daunton (Cambridge, 2000), pp. 745–807; and P. Bailey, *Leisure and Class in Victorian England: Rational Recreation and the Contest for Control 1830–1885* (1978), for the relationship between recreation and religion; Meller, *Leisure and the Changing City*.

who for various reasons are not going to any school, chapel, or mission room'.[84] Providing poor people with open space gave them 'that sense of quiet in which whispers of better things come to us gently'.[85] Natural open spaces kept poor people out of the pub ('I have seen dozens of men take their dinners into these gardens in hot weather instead of going to the public house'),[86] though sometimes it was a close run thing ('I took the B Court people to Woodford ... We feared, all day, they would wander off to the public-house').[87] Her playground at Freshwater Place allowed Hill to discipline the children's play.[88] She even advocated natural open spaces as the opium of the people: by ensuring that 'our small open places look well cared for', middle-class people could replace working people's 'passionate longing for more' with the reigning of 'a great [and very convenient] peace'.[89]

However, for Hill the significance of secondary gifts went far beyond the instrumental, and it was in considering nature and space that she developed the free gift idea most explicitly. She wrote of natural, accessible, open space that,

> To most men it is an inheritance to which they are born, and which they accept straight from God as they do the earth they tread on, and light and air its companion gifts ... This space – where it is not easily inherited it seems to me that it may be given by the city, the state, the millionaire, without danger of destroying the individual's power and habit of energetic self help.[90]

Hill, notorious for her resistance to state provision and many aspects of charity, thus urged municipal and national authorities and millionaires to give natural open space for poor people to use, and declared it an integral part of such uncorrupting gifts, not an unfortunate side effect of them, that poor people would not be grateful, but accept them as of right. Nor is this quotation an isolated instance. Elsewhere she stated, 'The space, the quiet, the sight of grass and trees and sky, which are a common inheritance of men ... are accepted as so natural, are enjoyed so wholly in common, that, however largely they were given, they could be only helpful

---

[84] Hill, *Colour, Space, and Music*, p. 7; M. Smith, 'The mountain and the flower: the power and potential of nature in the world of Victorian evangelicalism', in *God's Bounty? The Churches and the Natural World*, ed. P. Clarke and T. Claydon (Woodbridge, 2010), pp. 307–18.
[85] Hill, 'Space for the people', pp. 211–12.
[86] Hill, *Colour, Space, and Music*, p. 9.
[87] Hill to Mary Harris, undated, in Maurice, *Hill*, p. 204; Chase, *Deptford*, p. 120, for the same problem.
[88] Bell, *Hill*, p. 93.
[89] Hill, 'Space for the people', p. 201.
[90] Hill, 'Space for the people', pp. 199–200.

[unlike demoralizing charity]'.[91] And in yet another essay she wrote of the importance of common land which gave 'our people the sense that they have [a] share in the soil of their native England'.[92]

It is impressive that Hill attempted a structural and general analysis of the ills of society and their remedies – unlike many other women reformers, and despite her reputation as 'one of the least theoretical of Victorian reformers'.[93] But her analysis is problematic. First, she did not press it home. She rejoiced that poor people considered open land to be theirs by right, given by God, but she did not quite say that the land was 'the people's' by God-given right. Commenting on the unequal distribution of land she quoted Psalm 49 to warn of God's judgement on those who store up earthly riches, but she did not press home her own judgement. In a practical sense, this is hardly surprising: she wanted not to alienate those with earthly riches, but to persuade them to give her some of them. Moreover her early life led her to shy away from philosophically coherent but impracticable schemes, as Gillian Darley shows in this volume. However, the argument's intellectual force was weakened as she shied away from its conclusions.

Second, although Hill regretted the present unsatisfactory distribution of secondary gifts such as nature and space, she did not specify what a better distribution would look like. Although she considered commons 'the only portion of the land of England which remains in a living sense of the birthright of the people of England',[94] she had no vision of an ideal past before the land was wrested from 'the people' (unlike, for example, George Shaw Lefevre's and Robert Hunter's idealization of England's pre-Norman past).[95] And, although she thought that 'the special feature' of the garden created from the St. George's in the East churchyard was 'the evident sense of its being common property', she did not argue from this for an ideal future, where land, flowers and the like were indeed common property.[96] Lacking a general vision of a better distribution, and largely isolated from contemporary debates about, for example, land taxation,[97] Hill could not

---

[91] Hill, *Colour, Space, and Music*, p. 11.

[92] Hill, 'Our common land', p. 15.

[93] R. McKibbin, *The Ideologies of Class* (Oxford, 1991), cited in J. Welshman, *Underclass: a History of the Excluded, 1880–2000* (2006); Maltz, *British Aestheticism*, p. 63; Symonds, *Far Above Rubies*, p. 37.

[94] O. Hill, 'Open spaces', pp. 105–51, in O. Hill, *Our Common Land and other Short Essays* (1877), quotation at p. 148.

[95] Offer, *Property and Politics*, p. 339, for the 'original sin' of conquest; Cowell, 'The Commons Protection Society', p. 157.

[96] Hill, 'Open spaces', pp. 116–17.

[97] Unlike, e.g., Stuart Headlam, the Christian Socialist supporter of Henry George's single land tax.

'Nobler imaginings and mightier struggles'

tell how or even if her open space campaigns advanced that improved distribution. Just as in her housing work she never effectively answered Ruskin when he asked, 'My Question, a very vital one, is, whether it really never enters your mind at all that all the measures of amelioration in great cities ... may in reality be only encouragements to the great Evil Doers in their daily accumulating Sin?',[98] so, in the land question, she did not ask whether making some land accessible to poor people effectively licensed the better-off comfortably to hold tight to the rest of it. Indeed, as we have seen, on at least one occasion she seemed to advocate exactly such an outcome. Hill's failure to press her argument home or specify what a general solution would look like weakened its force, and if she held back from doing so to avoid offending potential donors of land, by her own admission she had limited success.

Inasmuch as Hill had a solution to the general problems of society, including the unequal distribution of secondary gifts such as nature and open space, she looked not to time (past or to come), but to place: her 'ideal was ... the close relations between the landlords and tenants ... in the quiet of an English countryside'.[99] Many Victorian reformers shared this country parish ideal, which David Mole argues was a vision of order, not of contact with nature, since its key elements were that rich and poor people knew each other, and the former regulated the latter.[100] Although there is much truth in Mole's argument, the vision was, however, just that – an image rather than an analysis, and thus needed Nature as backdrop. Maltz criticizes the 'narrow village aesthetic' on which Hill's conceptualization rested;[101] but Hill's vision did admit that poor as well as middle-class people could experience pleasure in nature. When she rejoiced that 'the tiny children tumble on the soft grass' and poor children enjoy collecting 'feathers, sticks, leaves, clover, etc.', she celebrated *their* sensory pleasures, not her own – after all, we have seen that she found many of the children aesthetically disgusting.[102]

However, if Nature was necessary to the country parish ideal, nature could play havoc with it, as Hill found in Deptford. 'Deptford was

[98] John Ruskin to Hill, 8 June 1876, cited in Maurice, *Life of Octavia Hill*, p. 341, and in Malchow, 'Public gardens', p. 120.
[99] Chase, *Deptford*, p. 10; Hill, 'Landlords and tenants in London', originally published in *Macmillan's Magazine*, Oct. 1871, reprinted in Hill, *Homes of the London Poor*, pp. 67–107, at p. 68.
[100] D. E. H. Mole, 'The Victorian town parish: rural vision and urban mission', in *The Church in Town and Countryside*, ed. D. Baker (Oxford, 1979), pp. 361–71.
[101] Maltz, *British Aestheticism*, p. 42.
[102] Hill, *Colour, Space, and Music*, p. 11; 'Space for the people', p. 206; Maurice, *Hill*, p. 193. See Maltz, *British Aestheticism*, for the connections between aestheticism and social reform, including a very critical analysis of Hill.

uncommonly like a small country community in some ways, not a few of our people even spoke familiarly of "Squire" Evelyn, and went to his country seat regularly for the hop-picking'.[103] While Hill had had to invent May Day celebrations in Marylebone, Deptford tenants, many with rural occupations, spontaneously formed Christmas waits, wassailed and beat the bounds of the parish.[104] If nature were the solution to the 'problem' of poor people, Hill should have had crowning success with her Deptford tenants, but in fact she found them singularly problematic, in part because of their contact with nature.[105] With more opportunities for self-provisioning, the Deptford tenants were more independent than their inner city peers, and when closest to nature they were least disciplined. Fruit and hop picking times were a heady mix of work, drink and unregulated life in the fields. One Deptford tenant, Mrs Blagdon, epitomized the problematic nature of nature. She hawked goods all over the country, including to sites such as the Lake District and Cornwall which middle-class Nature-lovers idealized. Observant and discriminating enough to distinguish and rank her preferences for these natural sites, she drank 'more and more' in order to feel able to do the work that got her to them in the first place – curiously something that Hill's friend Chase described as 'natural'.[106]

If Hill thought Nature incapable of redeeming society, neither did she think it able to redeem individuals: 'I don't think that ... even among the hills, people, who thought to escape evil, found rest; for surely ... evil must be fought with and conquered'.[107] However, Nature could, along with the other secondary gifts, mitigate society's ills since it provided a means of expressing and experiencing untainted human love (by giving flowers or land or as a site for innocent family pleasures); to experience divine love because of its sacramental quality; and to feel innocent sensory pleasure.

In some ways Hill's schema was resolutely hierarchical – a feature common to many open space reformers, for all their invocation of community ideals.[108] The relationship between God the giver and people the recipients was inescapably asymmetrical and hierarchical, but Hill is also often remembered as having reinforced asymmetrical and hierarchical relationships between people. Thus, her murals at Red Cross Hall, though

---

[103] Chase, *Deptford*, p. 31.
[104] Chase, *Deptford*, p. 36.
[105] Bell, *Hill*, pp. 182–4.
[106] Chase, *Deptford*, pp. 115–18; Sorlin and Warde, 'The problem of the problem of environmental history'.
[107] Hill to Ruskin, Apr. 1857, cited in Maurice, *Hill*, p. 124.
[108] Malchow, 'Public gardens', p. 118.

'Nobler imaginings and mightier struggles'

they depicted working-class heroes, are remembered as having been painted by rich and famous people for poor and obscure ones. Hill is known for having persuaded visual artists to exhibit their works to uplift the onlooking poor, and musicians to perform edifying works such as the *Messiah* for them ('beautiful music given by friends').[109] She is also remembered for having secured open spaces 'by the great kindness of donors';[110] and for having policed the art, music and nature produce by her tenants: no pigeons or cows however natural, and no children's traditional singing games ('questionable sentences') but rather competitive, disciplined ball games.[111]

All these things are true and indeed, some of the secondary gifts she presided over seem wilfully to have emphasized the gulf between donor and recipient. What must the Southwark residents have made of *Popping the Question*, performed for them by the young gents of Dulwich College, or *The Girton Girls and the Milkmaid*, staged by those of King's College, Cambridge?[112] But they are not the whole story. Hill's scheme contained radical elements, although they are less well remarked and certainly less well remembered. Rich and poor people, she wrote, were equally capable of enjoying the primary blessings of divine and human love and, with equal encouragement and training, the secondary gifts of nature and the like, while the rich should share secondary gifts with the poor or face God's judgement. Moreover, she thought poor people, if taught, could independently produce art, music and particularly nature. Thus at the Red Cross Hall annual exhibition poor women showed embroideries and men the products from their carvings. The hall, with its Walter Crane murals, was 'still further enriched' by the men's carved clock case;[113] Boys from Red Cross Cottages helped execute a panel designed by Crane.[114] Children from Marylebone acted in plays from an early date and the Red Cross children eventually followed suit.[115] The Red Cross cadet corps had a band.[116] Other

---

[109] Hill, *LFW*, 1891, p. 303; *LFW*, 1908, p. 595; *LFW*, 1909, p. 621.

[110] Hill, *LFW*, 1910, p. 639.

[111] O. Hill, 'Four years' management of a London court', originally published in *Macmillan's Magazine*, July 1869, reprinted in Hill, *Our Common Land*, pp. 33–66, at p. 43; K. J. Brehony, 'A socially civilising influence? Play and the urban "degenerate"', *Paedagogica Historica*, xxxix (2003), 87–106; K. Cranwell, 'Street play and organized space for children and young people in London 1860–1920', in *Essays in the History of Community and Youth Work*, ed. R. Gilchrist, T. Jeffs and J. Spence (Leicester, 2001).

[112] Hill, *LFW*, 1906, p. 562 n 14.

[113] Hill, *LFW*, plate 11 opposite p. 161; *LFW*, 1891, p. 303.

[114] Chase, *Deptford*, p. 213.

[115] Hill, *LFW*, 1889, p. 265, *LFW*, 1909, p. 621.

[116] Hill, *Letters*, p. 263; pupils from the Normal school at Dulwich came to sing to the tenants. Chase, *Deptford*, p. 213; 'Death of Miss Octavia Hill', *The Times*, 15 Aug. 1912, p. 7.

children learnt the violin in fulfilment of Hill's 'long cherished hope of training the working people to join in the performances as well as listen to them', and they later formed an orchestra.[117] The Red Cross Thursday entertainments increasingly relied on local clubs rather than imported performers.[118]

Hill's desire that poor people should independently produce and enjoy natural beauty was longstanding and strong, and she devised practical ways to accomplish her goals. She taught poor people how to grow their own flowers and provided a flower show to encourage them.[119] She helped them to get into nature within their budget: her middle-class helpers mapped Kent and Surrey so that the poor could find (free) green routes along which to walk to open spaces;[120] and considered that 'One of the best things the institute [for women and older girls in one of her courts] has done has been to arrange expeditions every Saturday during the summer to park, or field, or common ... to places they can reach by walking, or for a very cheap fare'.[121] Hill also gave them the confidence to get into nature: 'They must be invited to come out in little companies for a walk, taken out again, and again, and again during the summer'.[122]

Although these initiatives undoubtedly disciplined poor people's leisure time, the aim was to enable them to enjoy nature independently of capitalist entrepreneurs ('Your excursion trains and vans only carry noise into the country: let the people stroll from their own homes up the hilly fields, and you may be sure it will do them good')[123] and, ultimately, middle-class supervisors ('I have a strong belief that ... we have made great mistakes from believing that we have to manage and direct the poor ... we have mainly to take care to remove all obstacles to their living nobly').[124] Moreover, she saw poor people as campaigners for, not just enjoyers of, open spaces. Her Kent and Surrey committee of the Commons Preservation Society was, unlike some other conservation societies, socially inclusive.[125] With a membership fee of only 1s, 'the agricultural labourers have found us out.

Further information on her work with the cadets is in a letter from Major L. W. Bennett to *The Times* at 'Deaths', *The Times*, 20 Aug. 1912, p. 7.

[117] Hill, *LFW*, 1897, p. 402, *LFW*, 1898, p. 417; *LFW*, 1910, p. 638.
[118] Hill, *LFW*, 1910, p. 638.
[119] Chase, *Deptford*, p. 213.
[120] Bell, *Hill*, pp. 223, 230.
[121] Hill, 'Space for the people', p. 200.
[122] Hill to Mary Harris, undated, cited in Maurice, *Hill*, p. 196.
[123] Hill, *Colour, Space, and Music*, p. 11.
[124] Hill to Mary Harris, undated, cited in Maurice, *Hill*, p. 196.
[125] P. Mandler, 'Against "Englishness": English culture and the limits to rural nostalgia, 1850–1940', *Transactions of the Royal Historical Society*, 6th ser., vii (1997), 155–75.

Many a hard-earned shilling reaches us in postal orders from a village, many an illiterate but burning letter'.[126] The permanent reminders of Hill's work – the panels designed by influential artists or the churchyards opened by the established church – preferentially record the contributions of the well-known, influential and powerful, while the tenants' transitory flowers and performances on the violin have been forgotten, and Hill's insistence on poor people as producers of secondary gifts is overlooked.

While all secondary gifts could, in Hill's view, be produced as well as enjoyed by poor people, nature and open space were in her view unique in that she eventually advocated action by public institutions to secure them. In 'Why the Artisans' Dwellings Bill was wanted' she admitted that 'individual interest and effort' alone could not make poor people's housing acceptable, and that changes to the law were needed to curtail landlords' and entrepreneurs' rights over their land and freedom to build as they chose by regulating access to space, with its concomitant light and fresh air, among other things.[127] Elsewhere she argued in favour of the Disused Burial Grounds Bill and by-laws to regulate the amount of space to be left behind all new dwelling houses.[128] She praised the value of the judiciary and legislature in promoting commons preservation, and rejoiced that Larksfield, her retirement home, gave her common rights allowing her to use the law to frustrate potential enclosure schemes.[129] After the failure of Evelyn's efforts to give land in Deptford for the public, described by Cowell in this volume, she was fully persuaded of the need for parliamentary and legislative action to enable future gifts to be held for the public benefit. Robert Hunter revealed that, towards the end of her life, she thought that 'in towns the local authority should be left to supply appropriate open spaces', while private efforts should concentrate on wilder areas.[130] These small steps do not show Hill to have abandoned her commitment to individual rather than state or municipal action, any more than her comments about land's being a common possession show her to be a land nationalizer: but they suggest that she regarded nature and space as in some ways remarkable, and that her attitude to both was complex.

---

[126] Bell, *Hill*, pp. 228–9.

[127] O. Hill, 'Why the Artisans' Dwellings Bill was wanted', originally published in *Macmillan's Magazine*, June 1874, reprinted as pp. 162–95 in Hill, *Homes of the London Poor*. One of her main objections to municipal, subsidized, housing was that it enabled employers to pay inadequate wages (Bell, *Hill*, p. 257).

[128] Hill, *Colour, Space, and Music*, p. 9.

[129] Bell, *Hill*, pp. 143, 180–1, for Larksfield; Hill, 'Our common land'.

[130] R. Hunter, 'Miss Octavia Hill and open spaces', *The Times*, 17 Aug. 1912, p. 8.

Hill the radical failure?

Hill's theological view of nature helps to explain why she thought her open space work in some respects a failure. Rich people and institutions proved much readier to give her houses to manage than land for open space – unsurprisingly since the former was designed to bring a financial return, and the latter not even gratitude.[131] But a more fundamental philosophical reason was that her open space work had a much higher criterion for success since it was so radical. Because she aimed to lead in housing by example, the scale of her endeavours was in some senses irrelevant: a successful model could be small scale, even unique. Moreover, she warned housing reformers: 'Do not aim too high. Be thankful to make any reasonable progress'.[132] Housing success was thus relatively easy since any improvement counted.[133] When it came to nature and open space, however, Hill advocated not caution, but radical societal change. If given practical expression, her open space philosophy would have seen at least open land held in some unspecified way in common, having been willingly transferred to common ownership by its erstwhile owners – private individuals, municipalities and the central state – with everyone having equal rights over it, and all behaving as though this were the morally right state of affairs. These startlingly radical aims make it hard to write Hill off as a reactionary, and easy to see why, for all the recent celebrations of her open space work, Hill was less sure of her success. In concrete terms she, and others, of course achieved much after she made her comment in 1876: though she never managed to get rich Londoners to open their squares to their poorer neighbours and saw open fields round London built over, she was part of movements which saw significant tracts of land in town and countryside preserved for ever and opened to all. However, the more profound changes she advocated in individuals and society as a whole as part of her open space philosophy seem as distant now as they were then.

---

[131] E. L. Birch and D. S. Gardener, 'The seven-percent solution: a review of philanthropic housing, 1870–1910', *Journal of Urban History*, vii (1981), 403–36.

[132] Hill, 'Artisans Dwellings Bill', p. 193.

[133] Although, as Garnett illustrates in this volume, Hill was always concerned with changes to individual and societal morality which were to accompany housing reform.

8. Octavia Hill and the English landscape

Paul Readman

Octavia Hill's interest in open spaces was central to her ideals and activities, intersecting with her housing work as well as being reflected in her involvement with the National Trust. This preoccupation was evident from an early stage. To her long-standing enjoyment of nature, she added in adulthood a strong conviction as to the moral benefit of contact with the verdant outdoors. This belief was galvanized into energetic activism by her ultimately unsuccessful efforts to save Swiss Cottage Fields in north London, in 1875, also the year in which she became a member of the Commons Preservation Society (CPS).[1]

Over the years that followed, she developed the open spaces work of her sister Miranda's Kyrle Society.[2] Indeed, such was her success in directing the Kyrle's attention towards open spaces that in the mid 1880s some members complained to Robert Hunter, then the society chairman: '[s]he does distinctly care for Open Spaces more than for the other parts of the work ... by being always ready to appeal for funds for open spaces – but not for General Purposes'.[3] Hearing of these complaints, Hill contemplated resignation.[4] In the 1890s and 1900s she was similarly insistent on the value of the National Trust's open spaces work, being relatively unenthusiastic about the preservation of buildings. She originally suggested 'The Commons and

---

[1] W. T. Hill, *Octavia Hill: Pioneer of the National Trust and Housing Reformer* (1956), pp. 102–3. This chapter is based on the paper I gave in Sept. 2012 to the conference, '"Nobler imaginings and mightier struggles": Octavia Hill and the remaking of British society'; it has been much improved by helpful comments from my fellow delegates, particularly those offered by Elizabeth Baigent on an earlier draft. I also thank Ben Cowell and Daz Beatson for their assistance in searching for material in the National Trust Archives. Some of the research on which the chapter is based was presented in papers delivered at the Institute of Historical Research (Oct. 2012) and the University of East Anglia (Nov. 2012); I am most grateful for the input of my audiences on these occasions. I must also thank King's College London for granting me study leave to research and write this chapter. Finally, I wish to thank Martha Vandrei for her enthusiastic participation in Octavia Hill-themed walks in London and south-east England.

[2] O. Hill, 'Colour, space, and music for the people', *Nineteenth Century*, xv (1884), 747.

[3] Surrey History Centre, Robert Hunter papers 1621/7/1, M. Pickton to R. Hunter, 10 Dec. 1884.

[4] Surrey History Centre, Hunter papers 1621/7/1, O. Hill to R. Hunter, 28 Nov. 1885.

Gardens Trust' as a name for the body that became the National Trust, and in 1898 threatened to resign if its work 'was to include more house property'.[5] As in the case of the Kyrle Society, however, resignation proved unnecessary. Approximately two-thirds of the National Trust's acquisitions before 1914 were open spaces, with about one-fifth being buildings and the rest monuments.[6]

This chapter explores why Hill attached such importance to open space, with particular reference to the types of natural landscape she most valued. It argues that Hill's preferences reflected a patriotic agenda common to the early landscape preservationist movement, and in her case closely associated with a Christian Socialist emphasis on cross-class 'fellowship' in communion with the natural world. Although these preferences were based on an understanding of access to 'wild' nature, and particularly commons, as the historic 'inheritances' of all English men and women, it is suggested here that they did not express a retrogressive ruralism, but rather a forward-looking ethos directed, as with Hill's Christian Socialism generally, towards the benefit of ordinary people in the urban-industrial present.

Octavia Hill and open spaces

Hill's concern for open spaces sprang from a belief in their value to all classes of the community, especially the poor. In 1886 she suggested to her long-standing colleague Robert Hunter that the Society for Improving the Condition of the Labouring Classes might 'devote its income to Open Spaces'. Although it came to nothing, this was a revealing suggestion. Hill evidently saw open spaces as sufficiently important for their provision to be the whole purpose of a society dedicated to the general benefit of the poor; she thought the 'improvement of the condition of the labouring classes' could be advanced in no better way.[7] Such a position explains why Hill so strongly emphasized the importance of open spaces appeals in the Letters to fellow-workers she sent to her supporters each year, and why she participated so energetically in these appeals herself – the National Trust's campaigns for land at Ullswater and Gowbarrow in the English Lake District being two notable cases in point.[8] In her personal correspondence

---

[5] G. Darley, *Octavia Hill* (1990), pp. 298, 302, 309; see also J. Gaze, *Figures in a Landscape: a History of the National Trust* (1988), p. 87. As Gaze points out, it is significant that the Society for the Preservation of Ancient Buildings was absent from the initial list of bodies nominating members to the trust's council.

[6] This estimate is derived from the acquisitions list given in National Trust *Annual Reports* (Swindon, National Trust Archives).

[7] Surrey History Centre, Hunter papers 1621/1/5, O. Hill to R. Hunter, 21 Dec. 1886.

[8] E.g. see Hill, *LFW*, 1904, pp. 525–7 [Ullswater]; *Manchester Guardian*, 24 June 1905, p. 6 [Gowbarrow].

with donors she was not above slyly guiding their generosity toward open spaces. Writing to one benefactor in December 1906, for example, Hill coupled an acknowledgement that 'I gather that you are not, this time, thinking of open space,' with the caveat that 'in case I am mistaken I send you the paper about Purley Beeches', a tactic that resulted in a donation for the latter object.[9] In this light, it is perhaps not surprising that, when it came to raising funds to restore the National Trust's first building, Alfriston clergy house in Sussex, Hill reported, 'All my friends seem keener about beautiful open space'.[10]

In the 1870s and 1880s Hill was primarily concerned with open spaces in urban areas, particularly London, regarding their provision as inextricably linked to her housing work. The establishment of what Hill termed 'open air sitting-rooms' would, she felt, not only bring nature and beauty to poor Londoners, but install them as fixtures in their everyday lives. Small areas of open space in close proximity to the dwellings of the poor, and thus affording daily access – such as disused graveyards – would in her mind function as communal recreational areas for people who had no private gardens of their own.[11] Believing that '[t]he natural complement of the house is the garden', Hill felt that establishing communal gardens fostered a more complete and wholesome domesticity.[12] Over time, however, she became more concerned with what she called 'unappropriated space' outside the inner London area.[13] Having long appreciated the recreational value of common land,[14] she saw its preservation as especially important. But as is evident from her Letters to fellow-workers,[15] she also became increasingly involved in the preservation of footpaths – not least when she established the Kent and Surrey committee of the CPS in 1891, which took upon itself the task of drawing up a map showing all rights of way in the two counties.[16]

---

[9] Westminster City Archives, DMisc 84/1/9-10, O. Hill to Miss Schuster, 12 and 14 Dec. 1906. Purley Beeches, a small area of mature beech woodland in Croydon, was preserved as an open public space in 1907.

[10] Swindon, National Trust Archives, Ref. 6074103, Hill to H. D. Rawnsley, 22 March 1897. Raising funds for Alfriston, Hill found, was 'a much more difficult problem' (Westminster City Archives, DMisc 84/2/208, letter to S. Cockerell, 26 Oct. 1896).

[11] O. Hill, 'Space for the people', *Macmillan's Magazine*, xxxii (1875), 328–32; O. Hill, 'Open spaces', in Hill, *Our Common Land* (1877), esp. pp. 106–8, 111–12; O. Hill, 'More air for London', *Nineteenth Century*, xxiii (1888), 181.

[12] O. Hill, 'Natural beauty as a national asset', *Nineteenth Century and After*, lviii (1905), 937; O. Hill, 'The open spaces of the future', *Nineteenth Century*, xlvi (1899), 27.

[13] Hill, 'Open spaces of the future', p. 32.

[14] O. Hill, 'The future of our commons', in Hill, *Our Common Land*, pp. 175–206.

[15] E.g., Hill, *LFW*, 1897, p. 405.

[16] E. M. Bell, *Octavia Hill: a Biography* (1942), pp. 228–31.

'Nobler imaginings and mightier struggles'

Throughout her career Hill was concerned with providing access to the beauties of nature. In her early years as a reformer, she paid some attention to the physical health benefits of parks, playgrounds and commons, but this faded into the background as time passed. In this respect, Hill's perspective on the benefits of open space contrasts with that of the Metropolitan Public Gardens Association (MPGA), with which her work is often associated. Founded in 1880 by Reginald, Lord Brabazon, later twelfth earl of Meath, the MPGA encouraged organized physical exercise, and provided parks and children's playgrounds for Londoners. Animated by strong patriotic feeling, the MPGA was principally concerned with the physical condition of the common people, the steady deterioration of which was, as Brabazon put it, 'an evil which would ultimately lead to a degeneration of the race and to national effacement'.[17] Hill took a different line. Indeed, despite Brabazon's involvement in the Kyrle Society, by the mid 1880s Hill's differences with the MPGA were such that she told Hunter she 'could not work with Lord B's association', as she 'neither like[d] their spirit or way, & whenever any of us approach them I think we all feel this, to such a degree that we feel fellow-work impossible'.[18] Hill, Hunter and their friends did not agree that a few tracts of greensward on which slum dwellers could exercise their enfeebled bodies would be all that was needed. What they thought important in urban areas was not open space *qua* open space, but rather the preservation of distinctively English landscape – or at least something of its quality – in the heart of towns and cities, as well as on the fringes of urban areas and in the countryside. To Hill's mind, it was about 'bring[ing] the sense of country nearer to the town',[19] at the same time as preserving distinctive natural scenery and features of England. As she put it in 1897:

> Give the city dwellers ... for exercise, by all means the flat cricket-field, the place for football and skipping rope, and the asphalt playground with swings. Provide the formal garden and park. But keep as well English commons and moors and footpaths, and purchase here and there sites of natural beauty, whether seashore or cliff, limestone valley, reach of meadow by river or stream, or slope to mountain summit.[20]

---

[17] Lord Brabazon, 'Decay of bodily strength in towns', *Nineteenth Century*, xxi (1887), 674; also Brabazon, *Social Arrows* (1886) and 'Open spaces and physical education', *National Review*, viii (1886), 483–90.

[18] Surrey History Centre, Hunter papers 1621/7/1, O. Hill to R. Hunter, 30 Jan. 1885.

[19] Hill, 'More air', p. 185.

[20] *Manchester Guardian*, 8 May 1897, p. 6; also Hill, 'Natural beauty as a national asset', p. 938.

Future founder of the Empire Day movement,[21] Brabazon was something of a super-patriot; the MPGA reflected this patriotism, with its assumption that British national greatness was a function of physical – and by extension racial – strength. Hill's patriotism was of a different order, being more focused on the needs and people of England than those of Britain, let alone the British empire. In this respect it correlated with the patriotic spirit animating much early preservationist and open spaces activism, which, excepting James Bryce's access to mountains campaign, was largely concerned with English landscapes.[22] (While the National Trust's first acquisition was in Wales, it garnered no more than four more properties in the principality before 1914, none at all in Scotland, but at least fifty-seven in England.)[23] Hill's England-centred sense of patriotism was founded on a conviction that, as she put it in 1905, 'love of and intercourse with wild nature' is 'the spirit which keeps a nation free and vigorous', and, this being the case, it was a spirit to be nurtured in the breasts of rich and poor alike.[24] The wildness of the nature so engaged with was particularly important for Hill. Although formal parks and playgrounds, such as those championed by the MPGA, conferred some benefits they were insufficient on their own, as they did not grant access to what she called the 'wild beauty' of nature, such as that which she enjoyed in the meadowland near her country home at Crockham Hill, in Kent.[25] Religion played a part here, as Elizabeth Baigent has shown.[26] For the Christian Socialist Hill, only through contact with an at least relatively untamed version of the natural world could men and women learn to know the varied wonders of divine creation, which – as in the case of Ullswater, for example – offered a means by which one might 'commune' with God.[27] In this way Hill felt – here influenced by F. D. Maurice – that the poor and the rich might combine in fellow appreciation of the

---

[21] See J. English, 'Empire Day in Britain, 1904–1958', *Historical Journal*, xlix (2006), 247–76, esp. pp. 248–9.

[22] For this patriotism, see P. Readman, 'Preserving the English landscape, c.1870–1914', *Cultural and Social History*, v (2008), 197–218 and Readman, 'Landscape preservation, "advertising disfigurement", and English national identity, c.1890–1914', *Rural History*, xii (2001), 61–83.

[23] Calculations based on listings in National Trust *Annual Reports* (Swindon, National Trust Archives).

[24] Hill, 'Natural beauty as a national asset', p. 938.

[25] O. Hill to C. S. Hill, 23 June 1889, in *Life of Octavia Hill as Told in her Letters*, ed. C. E. Maurice (1913), p. 495.

[26] E. Baigent, '"God's earth will be sacred": religion, theology, and the open space movement in Victorian England', *Rural History*, xxii (2011), 31–58.

[27] Hill, *LFW*, 1904, p. 527.

Figure 8.1. Churchyard Bottom Wood (later Queen's Wood), Highgate.

natural world and hence gain access to the kingdom of Christ now, in the temporal realm, rather than having to wait until the hereafter.[28]

Hill's Christian Socialist stress on 'fellowship' was inextricably connected to her sense of patriotism. For her, that rich and poor should unite in veneration of divinely created nature demonstrated national solidarity and common moral purpose. In this respect, her patriotic agenda was in line with that dominant in contemporaneous political culture which – largely because of the impress of mid Victorian Liberalism – placed heavy emphasis on class harmony and reconciliation, and continued to do so into the twentieth century.[29] Yet Hill's valorization of (relatively) wild nature

---

[28] H. Jones, '"Recognising fellow-creatures": F. D. Maurice, Octavia Hill, Josephine Butler', in *Shaping Belief: Culture, Politics and Religion in Nineteenth-Century Writing*, ed. V. Morgan and C. Williams (Liverpool, 2008), pp. 21–38; also Baigent, '"God's earth will be sacred"'.

[29] See J. Parry, *The Rise and Fall of Liberal Government in Victorian Britain* (1993); J. Parry, *The Politics of Patriotism: English Liberalism, National Identity and Europe, 1830–1886* (Cambridge, 2006); P. Readman, 'The Liberal party and patriotism in early twentieth century Britain', *Twentieth Century British History*, xii (2001), 269–302. For the persisting importance of liberalism generally in understandings of Englishness, see R. Colls, 'Englishness and the political culture', in *Englishness: Politics and Culture 1880-1920*, ed. R. Colls and P. Dodd

was also connected to mainstream patriotic discourse in that she prized individual freedom and liberty, widely understood by Victorians to be key characteristics of English national identity.[30] These characteristics, she felt, were embodied and promoted by unenclosed landscapes. It was for this reason that, in 1897, when Churchyard Bottom Wood (later Queen's Wood) in Highgate was saved, Hill expressed the hope that the local authorities 'will … be sensible enough to leave it unspoiled in its natural beauty, instead of turning it into a conventional park', and urged that it remain unfenced by railings and was easy to access at any point along its perimeter.[31] Another key asset of Churchyard Bottom Wood was the view it afforded. In describing the place in her Letter of that year, she declared: 'A view is a great refreshment to those of us who live habitually enclosed by near and high walls'.[32] She understood publicly accessible land with expansive views to be unenclosed in a double sense. It was open to the feet of all and gave visual access to a surrounding landscape which was otherwise largely inaccessible, being fenced off as private property. This, she felt, gave hilly land a 'special value': it offered a sense of personal liberation and breezy freedom while connecting its visitors with the landscape beyond, the natural beauty of which was part of their patrimony as English men and women.[33] Appealing for funds to help the National Trust buy more open space on Mariners Hill in Kent in 1907, Hill noted that:

> Such vantage points of view all along the chain of hills in Kent and Surrey are being sought, occupied, and enclosed by the richer purchaser, and many a happy home is growing up on them. But it would seem well that some portion of them should be kept for the enjoyment, refreshment, and rest of those who have no country house, but who need, from time to time, this outlook over the fair land which is their inheritance as Englishmen, whose view is too often bounded by houses the other side of the street, and from whom more and more, woods, fields and hills are closed, as residences spring up in the country.[34]

Being the quintessential unenclosed landscape, and often offering undulating terrain, commons were especially important here. As Hill wrote in 1899, 'a great part of [the] charm' of metropolitan commons such as those at Blackheath, Wimbledon and Hampstead was 'the freedom

---

(Beckenham, 1986), pp. 29–61.
[30] P. Mandler, *English National Character: the History of an Idea from Edmund Burke to Tony Blair* (2006), ch. 3.
[31] Hill, *LFW*, 1897, p. 404.
[32] Hill, *LFW*, 1897, p. 404.
[33] Hill, 'More air', p. 185; Hill, *LFW*, 1907, p. 579.
[34] Hill, *LFW*, 1907, p. 579; see also Maurice, pp. 567, 573–4.

'Nobler imaginings and mightier struggles'

which being unenclosed gives: they look unfettered, you can gain access to them or leave them when you like'.[35] This conferred a personal sense of freedom, of being able to wander where one pleased and do largely what one wished. These were benefits which undoubtedly helped to explain the popularity of places such as Hampstead Heath for Bank Holiday excursions (incidentally, Hill was by no means especially censorious of the disorder and 'vulgarity' which usually attended such holidays) and, as she told Sydney Cockerell in 1875, she had 'seen the poor there from all the poor places around for years with [her] own eyes'.[36] But more than this, and as was widely appreciated at the time, commons also evoked the deep-rooted idea that ordinary English people had a substantial inherited stake in the soil of their native country.[37] Hill appreciated this keenly; as early as 1877 she described common land as 'the only portion of the land of England which remains in a living sense of the birthright of the people of England'.[38] In thinking this, she did not really have in mind the old agricultural economy of common land, with its smallholding cottagers and user rights. Although she supported the CPS's pragmatic defence of these rights as a means of preserving commons from enclosure by landlords, and thus as open spaces, she worried, characteristically, that such rights might somehow be bartered for 'doles' or other material inducements (as they had in fact been under the provisions of past enclosure schemes).[39] In any case, Hill thought it far better for commons to be seen as part of the heritage of all English men and women, whether rights-holders or not (after all, formal rights of common were not enjoyed by all, and in many cases were restricted to rather few individuals).[40] As she told one correspondent in April 1881, commons were

---

[35] Hill, 'Open spaces of the future', p. 30.

[36] Westminster City Archives, DMisc 84/3/19, letter to S. Cockerell, 18 July 1875: 'To a Cockney "'Ampstead 'Eath" is *par excellence* the place to spend a happy day. He ... finds here more liberty than in the trim elegance of the parks. It is irksome for him to be ordered to keep off the grass, or to be told that his dog must be tied with a string or some other suitable fastening; and so Bank Holiday sees even this huge recreation-ground of the northern heights uncomfortably crowded ... As many as 100,000 have been known to come to the heath on a Bank Holiday' (J. J. Sexby, *The Municipal Parks, Gardens, and Open Spaces of London* (1898), p. 375). See also H. Conway, *People's Parks: the Design and Development of Victorian Parks in Britain* (Cambridge, 1991), pp. 183–5. For Hill's relaxed attitude to 'undisciplined but heartily happy' Bank Holiday trippers, see Baigent, '"God's earth will be sacred"', p. 43.

[37] For comments on this, see P. Readman, *Land and Nation in England: Patriotism, National Identity, and the Politics of Land, 1880–1914* (Woodbridge, 2008), pp. 113–16.

[38] Hill, 'Open spaces', pp. 148–50.

[39] O. Hill, 'Our common land', *Macmillan's Magazine*, xxxiii (1876), 536–9.

[40] Of the commons around Coventry, near where he grew up in the early 19th century, the ribbon weaver Joseph Gutteridge recalled that although the original intention of the

Octavia Hill and the English landscape

Figure 8.2. West Wickham Common, Kent.

'national treasures', of concern not only – indeed 'less and less' – to 'the towns or villages nearest to which they happen to be', but to England as a whole.[41] Free access to commons and to the God-given beauties of nature generally was thus for Hill a means of uniting the national community in a cross-class patriotic fellowship – a fellowship, moreover, that reached back into the past to connect present English men and women with their predecessors, and by extension the nation. Speaking at a meeting in 1892 to support the preservation of West Wickham Common, in Kent, Hill made this clear, presenting commons and footpaths as embodiments of national unity and popular continuities:

> As our great men, as our ancient buildings, as our national institutions, as our Royal family, as our British flag, being possessions of all, unite us, so do our forests, our commons and our foot-paths; and far may the day be when

---

land donors had doubtless been 'to benefit the community … the common rights over these lands, owing to the conditions attaching to the freedom of the city, ultimately became restricted to comparatively very few people, who regarded their privileges with a very jealous eye' (J. Gutteridge, *Lights and Shadows in the Life of an Artisan* (Coventry, 1893 [1891]), p. 5).

[41] Maurice, *Life of Octavia Hill*, p. 442.

Figure 8.3. A footpath through bluebells in April at Mariners Hill, near Crockham Hill, Kent.

these open spaces and little threads of path wandering by brook and through meadow shall cease to be the inherited possession of the Englishman, which he receives with memories definite, or subtly felt, of those who in ages past have wandered by the same footpaths, or trod the same heathery slope, or rested in the same forest glen. Let us preserve them as the common inheritance of Englishmen and women and children.[42]

Preservationism and the people

As well as being consistent with Christian Socialist ideas of reciprocal bonds of unity and fellowship between people of all classes, Hill's perspective also

[42] Kent and Surrey Committee of the Commons Preservation Society, *Preservation of Commons: Speech of Miss Octavia Hill at a Meeting for Securing West Wickham Common* ([1892]), [p. 1].

reflected the patriotic agenda that she shared with other preservationists and campaigners for open spaces. It was predicated on the belief, as she put it in 1876, that 'the right to roam over the land' was closely 'connected with the love of it, and hence with patriotism'.[43] For Hill and her associates, the preservation of public open spaces and footpaths offered a means of maintaining a popular stake in the land of the country – the country generally envisaged here as England rather than Britain, for all that emblems of British identity were also invoked (as in her West Wickham speech). Maintaining this sense of common interest in the national territory, Hill felt, was especially important at a time when land ownership was being concentrated in progressively fewer hands. Lord Derby's 1876 *Return of the Owners of Land* revealed to her that 'one quarter of the land in England [was] owned by only 710 persons', a statistic she regarded with some alarm.[44]

This patriotic desire to reconnect a progressively landless people to the national domain can be seen as an attempt at social control by upper-middle- and middle-class reformers who felt threatened by the increasing pace of democratization, the growth of organized labour and socialism, and other unwelcome developments associated with urban-industrial modernity. Indeed, some scholars have taken this view. For John Walton, to give one example, the preservationism of Hill, H. D. Rawnsley, Hunter and the like was animated by what he terms the 'noblesse oblige' and 'authoritarian paternalism' of 'high tory Ruskinianism', the National Trust to which it led celebrating and sustaining the 'preserved enclaves' of 'a deeply conservative vision of England'.[45]

Anxieties about social trends were not absent from the open space movement, it is true. The artist George Frederic Watts welcomed the establishment of the National Trust as an acknowledgement that 'the wisest laws and the firmest enforcement of them will be powerless to remove discontent', and that 'trades unions must be supplemented – for they cannot be put down – by unions among the thoughtful, to promote

---

[43] Hill, 'Our common land', p. 539.

[44] Hill, 'Our common land', p. 539; *Return of the Owners of Land 1873 (England and Wales)* (Parl. Papers 1874 [C. 1097], lxxii). The *Return* was actually published in 1876.

[45] J. K. Walton, 'The National Trust centenary: official and unofficial histories', *The Local Historian*, xxvi (1996), 86; J. K. Walton, *The National Trust Guide to Late Georgian and Victorian Britain: from the Industrial Revolution to World War I* (1989), p. 255; Walton, 'The National Trust: preservation or provision?', in *Ruskin and the Environment: the Storm-cloud of the Nineteenth Century*, ed. M. Wheeler (Manchester, 1995), pp. 158–62. For similar perspectives, see P. C. Gould, *Early Green Politics: Back to Nature, Back to the Land, and Socialism in Britain 1880–1914* (Brighton, 1988), pp. 88ff.; N. P. Thornton, 'The taming of London's commons' (unpublished University of Adelaide PhD thesis, 1988).

'Nobler imaginings and mightier struggles'

pleasure and contentment'.[46] But any application of a 'social control' paradigm to the movement as a whole is problematic. Indeed, as F. M. L. Thompson showed over thirty years ago, such an interpretative framework is of dubious utility for middle-class-led reform movements generally, since their aims often correlated with the independently formed aspirations of poor people. Many working-class men and women valued 'respectability', and preferred 'rational recreation' to rumbustious fairs and carnivals, and so on.[47] *Mutatis mutandis*, the campaign to preserve public access to footpaths and open spaces was less marginal to the mainstream of either high or low British culture than some scholars have suggested.[48] True, it drew a good deal of middle-class support, not least from those such as Hill who saw it as a means simultaneously of improving the lot of the lower orders and of mobilizing a sense of status-transcending fellowship. But at the same time the campaign was also in line with the autonomous preferences of working-class people, many of whom were active participants in protests over commons and rights-of-way.[49]

Like Rawnsley and many others associated with the preservationist movement, including politicians such as Bryce and C. P. Trevelyan, access to mountains champions, Hill had no doubt that even the very poor could appreciate nature.[50] They were not misguided in this. Gardening was popular among the poor, with many contemporaries noting a love of cultivating flowers, even in slum areas, from the 1850s on.[51] Nature study was an established feature of working-class culture from mid century, particularly in and around large urban and industrial centres.[52] Elizabeth Gaskell's

[46] Swindon, National Trust Archives, Acc. 42/7.
[47] F. M. L. Thompson, 'Social control in Victorian Britain', *Economic History Review*, 2nd ser., xxxiv (1981), 189–208.
[48] E.g., by Peter Mandler (see his '"Against Englishness": English culture and the limits to rural nostalgia', *Transactions of the Royal Historical Society*, 6th ser., vii (1997), 155–75).
[49] See below.
[50] See, e.g., Hill, 'Natural beauty as a national asset', pp. 935–41; H. D. Rawnsley, 'Footpath preservation: a national need', *Contemporary Review*, i (1886), 373; Hill, 'Colour, space and music', p. 743; R. Evans, 'Landscape and legislation', *Cornhill Magazine*, new ser., xxiii (1907), 816–18; speech of C. P. Trevelyan on the second reading of the Access of Mountains Bill, *Hansard*, 4th ser., clxxxviii (15 May 1908), 1440–3. James Bryce had told the Commons in an earlier Access to Mountains debate that educational advances had inculcated in ordinary people a 'taste for poetry and beauty' (cited in J. Winter, *Secure from Rash Assault: Sustaining the Victorian Environment* (Berkeley, Calif., 1999), p. 78). On Bryce's access to mountains campaigning, see H. Taylor, *A Claim on the Countryside: a History of the British Outdoor Movement* (Edinburgh, 1997), pp. 143–4, 146–8.
[51] See Winter, *Secure from Rash Assault*, pp. 200–3.
[52] A. Secord, 'Science in the pub: artisan botanists in nineteenth-century Lancashire', *History of Science*, xxxii (1994), 269–315; Taylor, *A Claim on the Countryside*, pp. 93–6;

hugely successful novel *Mary Barton* (1848) featured an autodidact artisan botanist, Job Legh, and opened with a description of factory workers out for a ramble in the countryside near Manchester one 'early May evening'.[53] Gaskell had observed such scenes in and around Manchester, as had Hill in and around London. A 'love of rural rambles' is clear from the testimonies of working people themselves.[54] With the coming of bank holidays and improved and cheaper transport facilities (not least the bicycle, widely affordable by the 1890s),[55] this love became still more general. Far from being predominantly the concern of middle-class intellectuals, as some accounts have suggested,[56] the late nineteenth- and early twentieth-century 'outdoor movement' involved men and women of all social backgrounds: Leslie Stephen's highbrow walking group the 'Sunday Tramps', though well known because its writerly members recorded its doings in detail, was not representative of the phenomenon generally.[57] Many working men and women spent their days off walking in the countryside.[58] Others joined organizations such as the Clarion Cycling Clubs or the staunchly proletarian

---

Winter, *Secure from Rash Assault*, p. 97. By 1871 there were eight working-class societies dedicated to the study of butterflies in Epping Forest alone; by 1883 the radical MP J. Thorold Rogers reckoned there were 10,000 working-class botanists in London (B. A. K. McGaffey, 'Three founders of the British conservation movement, 1865–1895: Sir Robert Hunter, Octavia Hill, and Hardwicke Drummond Rawnsley' (unpublished Texas Christian University PhD thesis, 1978), p. 7; T. Stephenson, 'Footpath stoppers and early ramblers', *Rucksack*, ix (1977), 8; *Hansard*, 3rd ser., cclxxvii (12 March 1883), 166–8).

[53] E. Gaskell, *Mary Barton: a Tale of Manchester Life* (Harmondsworth, 1970 [1848]); ramblers at pp. 39ff; A. Secord, 'Elizabeth Gaskell and the artisan naturalists of Manchester', *Gaskell Society Journal*, xix (2005), 34–51.

[54] As Thomas Oliver (b. 1830) recalled at the end of a long life, 'Often when taking my walks abroad with no other company than my little dog, I have been so much delighted with the beauties around me, had it not been that I should be afraid to be heard, I should jump aloud for joy' (T. Oliver, *Autobiography of a Cornish Miner* (Camborne, 1914)). For other accounts of mid 19th-century artisans enjoying walking in nature, see, e.g., N. Cooke [*b*. 1831], *Wild Warblings* (Kidderminster, 1876), pp. 4–5, at p. 4; K. Wilson, *My Days are Swifter than a Weaver's Shuttle: Richard Ryley's* [*b*. 1821] *Diary, 1862* (Barnoldswick, 1980), pp. 77, 87; Gutteridge [*b*. 1816], *Lights and Shadows*, pp. 6, 8–9, 18–21, 54–6.

[55] D. Rubinstein, 'Cycling in the 1890s', *Victorian Studies*, xxi (1977), 47–71.

[56] Compare H. Walker, 'The popularisation of the outdoor movement, 1900–1940', *British Journal of Sports History*, ii (1985), 141–3 with A. Offer, *Property and Politics, 1870–1914: Landownership, Law, Ideology and Urban Development in England* (Cambridge, 1981), pp. 333–8.

[57] For the Sunday Tramps, see W. Whyte, 'Sunday Tramps (*act.* 1879–1895)', *ODNB*. For a balanced account of the development of recreational walking in the later 19th century as an organized activity involving all social classes, see Taylor, *A Claim on the Countryside*, pp. 54–90. Taylor's book is valuable for its overall – and compelling – argument as to the socially varied character of the British 'outdoor movement'.

[58] For one example, see J. Lawson, *A Man's Life* (1944), pp. 77–80.

Sheffield Clarion Ramblers, which by 1914 was probably the largest walking club in England.[59] Still others took advantage of bodies which provided cheap rural holidays and excursions, destinations such as the Lake District and Isle of Man having proved popular with working people from the mid Victorian period.[60] These included Church of England Missions, which put on trips to Epping Forest and elsewhere, as well as organizations such as T. Arthur Leonard's Countrywide Holiday Association, which had 14,000 members by 1911, and Hill's own Charity Organization Society, which provided holidays for around 20,000 boys and girls each year by 1889.[61]

Since engagement with the countryside and the natural world was so popular, it is not surprising that preservationism attracted significant popular support, even if this was necessarily limited in scale given the movement's still-emergent status before 1914. The campaign to save Epping Forest, described in the second edition of *Murray's Handbook* as 'a very favourite resort in summer time of people from the East End of London', provides a case in point.[62] Members of Parliament for working-class London seats lined up to affirm the affection their constituents felt for the forest

---

[59] Inspired by *The Clarion*, Robert Blatchford's eponymous newspaper, its Scouts combined political propaganda dissemination with enjoyment of the English countryside, into which they took regular trips (see Taylor, *A Claim on the Countryside*, pp. 157–74, and D. Pye, *Fellowship is Life: the National Clarion Cycling Club 1895–1995* (Bolton, 1995), esp. pp. 50–1). One working-class Bolton woman remembered joining the *Clarion* cyclists in the 1900s so she could enjoy 'the beauty and excitement of a countryside as yet unspoiled by the advent of motor transport' (A. Foley, *A Bolton Childhood* (Manchester, 1973), p. 72). For the Sheffield Clarion Ramblers, see D. Prynn, 'The Clarion Clubs, rambling, and the Holiday Associations in Britain since the 1890s', *Journal of Contemporary History*, xi (1976), 65–77; H. Hill, *Freedom to Roam: the Struggle for Access to Britain's Moors and Mountains* (Ashbourne, 1980), esp. p. 32; M. Tebbutt, 'Rambling and manly identity in Derbyshire's Dark Peak, 1880s–1920s', *Historical Journal*, xlix (2006), 1123–53.

[60] Winter, *Secure from Rash Assault*, pp. 211–12.

[61] *A List of the Historical Records of the Countrywide Holiday Association*, comp. P. Bassett (Birmingham and Reading, 1980), p. i. See also T. A. Leonard, *Adventures in Holiday Making: Being the Story of the Rise and Development of a People's Holiday Movement* ([1934]); P. Horn, *Pleasures and Pastimes in Victorian Britain* (Stroud, 1999), p. 142. The Charity Organization Society is often portrayed as prescriptive and moralistic, but its Holiday Fund was certainly popular with many of those it benefited. Walter Southgate remembers enjoying a two-week stay in Essex through the fund (W. Southgate, *That's the Way it Was: a Working Class Autobiography 1890–1950*, ed. T. Philpot (Oxted, 1982), pp. 69–70, and see also pp. 19, 26, 92, 130).

[62] *Murray's Handbook for England and Wales* (2nd edn., 1890), p. 154. For Epping Forest, see E. Baigent, 'A "splendid pleasure ground [for] the elevation and refinement of the people of London": geographical aspects of the history of Epping Forest 1860–95', in *English Geographies 1600–1950: Historical Essays on English Customs, Cultures, and Communities in Honour of Jack Langton*, ed. E. Baigent and R. J. Mayhew (Oxford, 2009), pp. 104–26.

when it was threatened by a railway bill in 1883, and the proposal was in the end soundly defeated in the House of Commons by 230 votes to eighty-two.[63] Similar proposals for railway construction in the Lake District were also abandoned due to strong popular opposition, much of it mobilized by the Lake District Defence Society (LDDS), a body founded in 1883 by Rawnsley and others, and with whose activities Hill was closely associated.[64] In addition, the closure (and threatened closure) of footpaths aroused strong popular protest. Grassroots local organizations mushroomed in defence of rights of way,[65] and the obstruction of paths was often met by stormy public demonstrations involving hundreds and sometimes thousands of people, as at Knole Park in Kent (1883–5), Latrigg, near Keswick in the Lake District (1887), Swaffham in Norfolk (1890), and Winter Hill, near Bolton (1896).[66]

Indeed, the issue of footpaths provides an especially good illustration of the extent to which the preservationist movement, middle-class-led though it may have been, accorded with popular sensibilities. Although John Walton has suggested that 'some campaigners ... were less forward than they might have been in footpath preservation because they feared that hordes of trippers might destroy the beauty and atmosphere of the high fells without deriving benefits themselves', there seems to be little evidence of this, and so far as Hill is concerned the charge seems peculiarly misplaced.[67] From an early age, Hill had great affection for footpaths, and if anything this affection deepened over the course of her life. By 1890 she was

---

[63] *Hansard*, 3rd ser., cclxxvii (12 March 1883), 160–1ff. Writing to his daughter Jenny, William Morris remarked that, 'I suspect by [James] Bryce moving the amendment, & Richie [*sic*: C. T. Ritchie] voting for it there is not much doubt about the opinion of the East End poor people on the subject; as they are the two members for the Tower Hamlets' (W. Morris to J. Morris, 14 March 1883, in *Collected Letters of William Morris*, ed. N. Kelvin (4 vols., 1984–96), ii. 175).

[64] Readman, 'Preserving the English landscape', pp. 203–4. Hill seems to have been an LDDS member from the outset, and by 1887 – if not before – she was on the General Committee of the Society (Carlisle Record Office, DSO/24/15/1, 'The Lake District Defence Society [1884]'; Carlisle Record Office, DSO/24/15/3, 'Lake District Defence Society: opposition to the proposed Windermere and Ambleside Railway [1887]').

[65] E.g., the Kendal and District Footpath Association, concerning which some documentation is preserved in Kendal, Cumbria Archive Centre, K.R.O., WDso 1/1/1–62.

[66] For Knole Park, see D. Killingray, 'Rights, "riot" and ritual: the Knole Park access dispute, Sevenoaks, Kent, 1883–5', *Rural History*, v (1994), 63–79. For Latrigg, see *English Lakes Visitor and Keswick Gazette*, 8 Oct. 1887. For Swaffham, see *Lynn News and County Press*, 24 May 1890, p. 5; 7 June 1890, p. 8; 21 June 1890, p. 5. As that newspaper reported at the outset of the controversy, 'the matter has been taken up by a large number of the working classes' (24 May 1890, p. 5). For Winter Hill, where demonstrators may have totalled 12,000, see P. Salveson, *Will Yo' Come O' Sunday Mornin': the 1896 Battle for Winter Hill* (Bolton, 1996), esp. pp. 13–14, 21, 26.

[67] Walton, *National Trust Guide*, p. 254.

supplying the naturalist magazine *Nature Notes* with extracts from William Howitt's *Book of the Seasons* (1830) which attested to his love of 'our real old English footpaths' and his indignation at their arbitrary closure by wealthy men.[68] It was a perspective with which Hill evidently sympathized, and one that bore a direct relationship to her campaigning activities – in particular her role in persuading the CPS to extend its involvement with the cause of footpath preservation. In an impassioned speech at a CPS meeting in June 1888 urging support of the defendants in the Latrigg footpath case, Hill told her audience that it was 'incumbent on us all … to preserve for our countrymen … the great common inheritances to which, as English citizens they are born, the footpaths of their native country'. These, she warned, were 'vanishing … closed by Quarter Sessions, the poor witnesses hardly daring to speak, the richer dividing the spoil; the public from a larger area hardly knowing of the decision which has for ever closed to them some lovely walk'.[69]

Hill's spirited defence of popular rights over the land can hardly be described as conservative. Rather, it accorded with the perspective of many radical liberal and socialist campaigners, including campaigners for land nationalization, many of whom supported the CPS and, later on, the National Trust.[70] Hill, of course, was no land nationalizer, and my intention here is not to recast her as some sort of quasi-socialist. But scholars have overlooked the radical trajectory – or at least the possible implications – of her preservationist ideals and activities, mesmerized perhaps by what they see as her laissez-faire and moralistic approach to housing reform.[71] This suggests an inconsistency in Hill's ideology. In later life, as she became ever more hostile to state intervention in housing, her views on land use became more radical. At any rate, in the sphere of landscape preservation, hers was an approach which recognized the existence of a popular stake in the land of England.

This was a perspective predicated on an inclusive understanding of nationhood. Hill was no advanced democrat (she opposed women's suffrage in parliamentary elections), but she did have a capacious understanding of

---

[68] 'Field paths', *Nature Notes: the Selborne Society's Magazine*, i (15 Sept. 1890), 138–9.

[69] Cumbria Archive Centre, K.R.O., WDX/422/2/4, 'Miss Octavia Hill on the duty of supporting footpath preservation societies [1888]'; R. Legg, *National Trust Centenary* (Wincanton, 1994), p. 15. See also Hill, 'Open spaces of the future', p. 32.

[70] See, e.g., *Land and Labour* (Sept. 1901), p. 108 [Derwentwater]; *Land and Labour* (Dec. 1893), 8. Parliamentary supporters of the CPS were almost entirely Liberal, and many of them were distinctly radical or 'advanced' (see M. J. D. Roberts, 'Gladstonian Liberalism and environment protection, 1865–76', *English Historical Review*, cxxviii (2013), 305–8).

[71] See, e.g., A. S. Wohl, 'Octavia Hill and the homes of the London poor', *Journal of British Studies*, x (1971), 105–31.

citizenship (a word of which she was fond),[72] and one that accorded with the democratizing trends of the time. She was appalled by the case of a rich landlord who, wanting to close footpaths on his land, demanded that local ratepayers vote to determine public opinion on the issue. In the poll the richer ratepayers had up to six votes each, so that, although the proposal's supporters were outnumbered nearly two to one, the landlord won the day. Hill wrote angrily to *The Times* and *The Standard*. 'These field paths', she declared, 'are ... the inheritance of the landless people, and it would seem an anomaly to give to the larger owners a preponderance of weight in deciding about these thin lines of path, which afford pleasant ways, and open a sight of wood, and field, and stream – highways of the Queen, and, therefore, of the least of her subjects – growing every year of greater value to them, yet the number of which is yearly being diminished'.[73]

Closure of footpaths and commons might have been understandable – if not acceptable – when the aristocratic landed interest predominated in Parliament, but times had changed. Late Victorian Britain was widely (if erroneously) understood to be a democratically governed nation: as the Liberal MP W.E. Forster told the Commons during the debate on the 1884 Representation of the People Bill, 'the doctrine of numbers pervades and must pervade the representative system ... On the passing of this measure, not property, not interests, but numbers – human beings – will be acknowledged even more clearly than by the Act of 1867 to be the basis of popular power.'[74] The preservationism of Hill and her associates was predicated on this 'doctrine of numbers' that the second and third Reform Acts had installed as orthodoxy. It rejected old claims that private property rights were always inviolate; the nation as a whole had a stake in the national domain, and Parliament – now representative of the whole people – had a duty to protect that stake. In a sense this was not a new argument: private property in land had for centuries been subject to considerations of national interest, exclusive or near-exclusive use rights being seen as likely to maximize output. What was new, however, was the assumption that the national interest in the land included consideration of what later generations would term amenity and heritage. Whereas earlier the patriot had been the man – as Jonathan Swift had put it – who 'could make two Ears of Corn, or two Blades of Grass to grow upon a Spot of Ground where only one grew before',[75] the mid Victorian patriot, in a country committed

---

[72] See, e.g., O. Hill, 'A word on good citizenship', *Fortnightly Review*, xx (1876), 321–5.
[73] *The Times*, 14 Sept. 1892, p. 6; *The Standard*, 16 Sept. 1892, p. 3.
[74] *Hansard*, 3rd ser., cclxxxvi (31 March 1884), 1196.
[75] J. Swift, *Travels into Several Remote Nations of the World. In four parts. By Lemuel Gulliver, First a Surgeon, and then a Captain of several ships* [*Gulliver's Travels*] (Dublin, 1726), p. 116.

'Nobler imaginings and mightier struggles'

to free trade in food as in other commodities, had a duty to consider factors other than food production on rural land. And in the city the preservation of at least some open land as public green space was increasingly seen – by Liberals especially – as essential for the well-being of a nation of town dwellers, on utilitarian, spiritual, aesthetic and patriotic grounds.[76]

Hill was in the forefront of this shift in sensibilities, giving voice to it as early as 1877 in *Our Common Land*.[77] She remained faithful to this idea, the National Trust being in some ways its logical culmination. Indeed, Hill saw the trust as a means of preserving common land in a new form, fit for modern-day needs. The first open space the National Trust acquired in England was Barras Head, a stretch of Cornish coastline that Hill described in her 1896 Letter as 'not quite the first, nor will it, I hope, be the last, of such places which shall thus become in a new and very real sense the common land of England'.[78] Whereas common land had previously been associated with peasant agriculture and cottagers' and smallholders' rights, it was now linked to the wider claims of the nation over what Hill termed 'the common playground'.[79]

Hill's determination to defend the nation's stake in common land, and in open spaces generally, did not reflect an emotional aversion to the modern world. Despite the assertions of some writers, the culturally reactionary rural-nostalgic mindset, famously identified by Martin Wiener, should not be seen as that which dominated the early preservationist movement generally, or Hill's approach in particular.[80] Hill combined practicality with sentiment. She acknowledged the realities of modern life, seeking to work within the parameters they imposed. She did not seek to turn back the clock, and was impatient with those whom she suspected of being so disposed. (Her opinion of a pamphlet by William Morris, sent to her by Sydney

---

[76] Readman, 'Preserving the English landscape'; Roberts, 'Gladstonian Liberalism and environment protection', pp. 292–322.

[77] See esp. Hill, 'Future of our commons', pp. 180–2.

[78] Hill, *LFW*, 1896, p. 393.

[79] Hill, *LFW*, 1896, p. 393.

[80] For P. D. Lowe, 'Common to all the preservation groups of the period was a moral and aesthetic revulsion to the contemporary industrial city'; for Paula Weideger, 'As the century ended, the idealistic new National Trust was created to protect countryside and historically important buildings and preserve them for ever – as they then were. However radical they were … conservation makes people conservative. And from its beginnings the National Trust seems to have been involved in stopping the clock' (see P. D. Lowe, 'Values and institutions in the history of British nature conservation', in *Conservation in Perspective*, ed. A. Warren and F. B. Goldsmith (Chichester, 1983), p. 339; P. Weideger, *Gilding the Acorn: Behind the Façade of the National Trust* (1994), p. 36). Cf. M. J. Wiener, *English Culture and the Decline of the Industrial Spirit, 1850–1914* (Cambridge, 1981); Mandler, '"Against Englishness"'; Readman, 'Landscape preservation'.

Cockerell, was that 'the miseries of the middle ages' were 'slurred over in a marvellous manner'.)[81] Unlike some other preservationists, Hill knew that urban-industrial modernity could not be undone, that, for example, as she put it in 1899, 'the garden attached to every house has, in London, become a thing of the past'.[82] But her response to this state of affairs was neither despair nor nostalgia, but recognition that there was a need to mitigate the negative aspects of contemporary life to benefit present and future generations. Saving publicly accessible open spaces and footpaths was a key means through which this might be effected. Not only did these amenities confer health benefits by providing 'lungs' for cities and opportunities for physical exercise, recreation and days out in the 'country', they also offered the spiritual refreshment that only contact with nature could give – and such contact, Hill felt, would do much to help ordinary English men and women face the day-to-day challenges of modernity. Such a perspective was of a piece with her Christian Socialist belief that the communion with God, and access to his kingdom, was accessible in the here-and-now for everyone, rich and poor alike. As she wrote in 1877, 'the words God speaks to us on the moorlands proceed, indeed, from His mouth with audible power, and memories of them haunt us with ennobling and consoling thought in the bustle, the struggle, and the pain to which we must return'.[83]

As shown in her preservationist activities, Hill's Christian Socialism was suffused with patriotic purpose. These activities were designed to maintain, in modified form, the popular stake in the national domain for which commons and footpaths stood as synecdoches. As with her ideas about fellowship, Hill wanted to promote a sense of common belonging to a larger national community, through access to the shared heritage of that community and also, crucially, through combined action to preserve this heritage for the benefit of future generations (hence the significance she attached to donations from across the social spectrum).[84] She felt this goal to be particularly important in the context of late Victorian England, a place increasingly democratic in spirit, yet simultaneously one where, as Lord Derby's *Return* showed, fewer and fewer people had personal proprietorial interests in the soil; in London, only about 3 per cent of households owned any land.[85] For Hill, the circumstances of British modernity demanded recognition of what she termed

---

[81] O. Hill to S. Cockerell, 21 Aug. 1891, in Maurice, *Life of Octavia Hill*, p. 517.
[82] Hill, 'Open spaces of the future', p. 28.
[83] Hill, 'Future of our commons', pp. 179–80.
[84] See, e.g., Hill, *LFW*, 1878, p. 104; 1901, pp. 473–5; 1902, p. 489; Bell, pp. 225–6, 228–9.
[85] P. H. Lindert, 'Who owned Victorian England? The debate over landed wealth and inequality', *Agricultural History*, lxi (1987), 35. Outside London the figure was under 13% (p. 33).

the value of those possessions in which each of a large community has a distinct share, yet which each enjoys only by virtue of the share the many have in it; in which separate right is subordinated to the good of all; each tiny bit of which would have no value if the surface were divided amongst the hundreds that use it, yet which when owned together and stretching away into the loveliest space of heather or forest becomes the common possession of the neighbourhood, or even of the County or Nation.

The preservation of such possessions

> will give a share in his country to be inherited by the poorest citizen. It will be a link between the many and through the ages, binding with holy happy recollections those who together have entered into the joys its beauty gives—men and women of different natures, different histories, and different anticipations—into one solemn joyful fellowship, which neither time nor outward change can destroy—as people are bound together by any common memory, or common cause, or common hope.[86]

Conclusion: Hill, landscape and national heritage

In 1985 David Cannadine suggested that 'The very idea of a "national" heritage, which is somehow "threatened", and which must be "saved", is often little more than a means of preserving the artefacts of an essentially élite culture, by claiming – in most cases quite implausibly – that it is really everybody's'.[87] Cannadine was writing about the late twentieth-century idea of heritage, and although a case exists for seeing some aspects of the modern-day 'heritage industry' as predicated on a socially conservative and partial conceptualization of the national past – being overly concerned with country houses, castles and the like – the merit of this view is debatable, at least as far as the National Trust is concerned. Indeed, the trust's most successful fundraising initiative has been its Neptune Coastline Campaign, which has raised £65 million over the fifty years to 2015 for the purchase of 545 miles of coastal landscape.[88] (It is also worth pointing to the trust's deepening commitment to the non-aristocratic built environment, as evidenced by its

---

[86] Hill, 'Future of our commons', pp. 204–6.
[87] D. Cannadine, 'Nostalgia' [1985], in *The Pleasures of the Past* (1989), p. 259.
[88] 'Neptune in pictures: highlights from 50 years spent looking after Britain's coastline', *National Trust Magazine*, cxxxvi (2015), 30. One notable recent success achieved by the campaign was the 2012 'White Cliffs of Dover Appeal', which – in the teeth of a global recession – raised £1.2 million from over 16,000 people in just 133 days, the money going towards the purchase of 0.8 miles of coastline (see 'Neptune in pictures' and <http://www.nationaltrust.org.uk/get-involved/donate/how-youve-helped/white-cliffs-of-dover-appeal/> [accessed 29 Sept. 2015]); also P. Readman, '"The cliffs are not cliffs": the cliffs of Dover and national identities in Britain, c.1750–c.1950', *History*, xcix (2014), 265, 266–7.

recent stewardship of such properties as Mr. Straw's house in Worksop, semi-detached home to a family of mid twentieth-century grocers; Rainham Hall in Havering, the residence of an eighteenth-century merchant and master mariner; and the once-neglected Sutton House in the heart of East London, where the artwork of the squatters who lived there in the 1980s is preserved alongside Tudor fixtures and fittings.)[89] But irrespective of the contemporary merit or demerit of any reading of the trust's work as socially conservative, such an assessment cannot be made of Hill's work in this area. When it came to preserving what she called the 'common inheritances' of Englishmen and women, she was less interested in the built environment – and not at all interested in stately homes – than she was in open spaces, commons and footpaths. Hers was a popular – even democratic – understanding of national heritage, and one which regarded the natural world to be as much a part of this heritage (or inheritance) as any fine house or castle. Her priorities were not those of some later preservationists who understood heritage as primarily concerned with buildings.[90]

Hill's views also contrast with the more recent idea of heritage as being predicated on a declinist view of history – the glorious past, commodified as heritage, juxtaposed with a dolorous present and future. There might be some truth to this for the later twentieth century onwards, in the context of the eclipse of British world power and perceptions of social and economic decline.[91] But Hill and her associates did not see heritage (or its contemporaneous equivalent) as offering a means of imaginative retreat to a necessarily better past; conditions of life in the present were not seen as normatively inferior in all aspects, for all that they might be improved in some. Rather, they understood inheritances such as common land and footpaths as amenities that offered real benefits in the here and now, not least by acting as reminders of the long continuities of popular access rights to the land. For all that such a perspective may have lost prominence in later years (though it is undoubtedly still present), it yielded real results at the time, and these successes call into question some scholars' claims that late Victorian and Edwardian preservationism was culturally marginal.[92]

---

[89] <http://www.nationaltrust.org.uk/mr-straws-house/>; <http://www.nationaltrust.org.uk/sutton-house/history/> [both accessed 29 Sept. 2015]; J. Collett, 'Who's living at Rainham Hall?', *National Trust Magazine*, cxxxvi (2015), 41–4.

[90] E.g. *Preserving the Past: the Rise of Heritage in Modern Britain*, ed. M. Hunter (Stroud, 1996). This almost completely ignores the natural landscape, heritage being associated with the built environment.

[91] R. Hewison, *The Heritage Industry: Britain in a Climate of Decline* (1987); P. Wright, *On Living in an Old Country* (1985).

[92] Cf. Mandler, '"Against Englishness"'; D. Cannadine, *Making History, Now and Then: Discoveries, Controversies and Explorations* (Basingstoke, 2008), pp. 118–19.

Organizations such as the CPS or the Kyrle Society may have had small memberships, but their activism helped to save large quantities of open space, directly by spearheading appeals, and indirectly through their effect on public opinion. Between 1865 and 1897 8,579 acres of open space were preserved – more than thirteen square miles – in the Greater London area, 5,531 acres in Epping Forest, and at least 15,000 acres in provincial towns and cities.[93] Hill was, of course, just one individual prominent in effecting these successes, with Robert Hunter a perhaps overlooked other, but hers was a very significant contribution. Quite apart from her fundraising activities, she gave vital publicity to the cause and its guiding ideals. For all that she is remembered as a housing reformer, her contribution to landscape preservation was as least as important.

---

[93] Sir R. Hunter, 'The movements for the inclosure and preservation of open lands', *Journal of the Royal Statistical Society*, lx (1897), 400–2.

IV. 'A common inheritance from generation to generation': Octavia Hill and preservation

9. 'To every landless man, woman and child in England': Octavia Hill and the preservation movement[1]

Astrid Swenson

Introduction: the construction of a national treasure

Octavia Hill is increasingly commemorated as a key figure of Britain's heritage movement. Indeed, she is virtually the only nineteenth-century woman to be thus celebrated. Her enduring place in the collective consciousness owes much to the energetic efforts of friends and family to keep her memory alive after her death by publishing her letters and several biographies.[2] They also put her centre stage in textual and visual accounts of the National Trust's early years. A 1924 watercolour depicting the trust's executive committee meeting, held on 15 April 1912, the year Hill died, is symptomatic of the creation of a founding narrative (see Figures 9.1 and 9.2). Beneath a portrait of George Shaw-Lefevre, initiator of the Commons Preservation Society (CPS) – an important headspring for the National Trust – the committee sits around a table listening to a paper read by the botanist Francis Oliver. Hill was too ill to attend the meeting, but the painter shows her in her usual chair in a prominent position to the right of the other two founders, Canon Hardwicke Rawnsley and Sir Robert Hunter.[3]

Octavia Hill's memory was also preserved more publicly through the acquisition of land. Hydon Heath in Surrey was bought for the National

---

[1] I would like to thank the participants of the Sutton House Conference for the inspiring discussion, and Elizabeth Baigent, Ben Cowell, Inge Dornan, and Monica Fernandes for their comments on the chapter.

[2] See esp. *Life of Octavia Hill*, ed. C. E. Maurice (1914); *Octavia Hill: Early Ideals, from Letters*, ed. E. S. Maurice (1928); E. M. Bell, *Octavia Hill* (1942); and with increasing emphasis on her preservation work, W. T. Hill, *Octavia Hill: Pioneer of the National Trust and Housing Reform* (1956). For a broader discussion of the early works, see E. Baigent, chapter 1 in this volume.

[3] For further discussion see M. Waterson, *The National Trust: the First Hundred Years* (rev. edn., 1997), pp. 54–5; G. Murphy, *Founders of the National Trust* (2002), illustration 10 between pp. 64 and 65; A. Swenson, *The Rise of Heritage: Preserving the Past in France, Germany, and England, 1789–1914* (Cambridge, 2013), p. 94. On Hill's reluctance to be transformed into a national treasure during her lifetime, see Heath, chapter 6 in this volume.

'Nobler imaginings and mightier struggles'

Figure 9.1. National Trust Executive Committee Meeting on 15 April 1912. Watercolour by Thomas Matthews Rooke (1924).

Octavia Hill and the preservation movement

Figure 9.2. Reverse of watercolour of National Trust Executive Committee Meeting on 15 April 1912.

Trust as a memorial to her, and 300 acres were added to Crockham Hill 'to preserve the view so dear to Octavia Hill'.[4] As the trust's membership and influence grew between the world wars, Hill maintained her place as a venerated founder. The trust's golden jubilee book, edited by James Lees-Milne, was dedicated to the memory of 'Miss Octavia Hill, Canon Rawnsley and Sir Robert Hunter. Founders of the National Trust'. Her ideas, however, became progressively less important as guiding principles for the trust. The book noted that her 'housing work had led her to a vivid appreciation of such places as Parliament Hill Fields to the urban working classes', but said nothing else about her motivation.[5]

After its founders had died the trust's preoccupations shifted from improving the lives of the urban poor to preserving England's great mansions. For the country house scheme, which developed during the interwar years and took off fully after the second world war, Hill's ideas offered little guidance. By 1994, when the trust's centenary engendered the next round of official histories, Hill's 'moral tone' with its biblical metaphors could even 'seem unsympathetic'.[6] Although later generations of scholars and practitioners never criticized her preservationist activities as they did her housing work, her language was perceived as 'certainly unfashionable'.[7]

Yet, the National Trust's centenary also provided an opportunity 'for its past and future role to be assessed, for its achievements and ideals to be scrutinised'.[8] The 1980s 'heritage debate' had led to widespread criticism of the 'heritage industry's' commodification of the national past, and some even mocked the trust as the 'Society for the Preservation of the Aristocracy'.[9] In light of this critique the trust's 'earlier values' were perhaps

---

[4] H. Batsford, 'Country and coast', in *The National Trust: a Record of Fifty Years' Achievement,* ed. J. Lees-Milne (3rd edn., 1948), pp. 9–28, at 25; see also G. Darley, *Octavia Hill: Social Reformer and Founder of the National Trust* (2010), p. 316.

[5] See D. M. Matheson, 'The work of the National Trust', in Lees-Milne, *The National Trust,* pp. 122–5, at 122.

[6] J. Jenkins and P. James, *From Acorn to Oak Tree: the Growth of the National Trust, 1895–1994* (1994); Waterson, *The National Trust; The National Trust: the Next Hundred Years,* ed. H. Newby (1995). For slightly earlier appraisals, see R. Fedden, *The Continuing Purpose* (1967); R. Fedden, *The National Trust: Past and Present* (1968; rev. edn., 1974) and G. Murphy, *Founders of the National Trust* (1987; new edn., 2002). Quotation from Waterson, *The National Trust,* p. 268.

[7] See, for instance, Gareth Stedman Jones's criticism in *Outcast London* (1971) and *Languages of Class* (1983), discussed above by Baigent, chapter 1 in this volume. Quotation from Waterson, *The National Trust,* p. 268.

[8] Waterson, *The National Trust,* p. 269.

[9] R. Hewison, *The Heritage Industry: Britain in a Climate of Decline* (1987); P. Wright, *On Living in an Old Country: the National Past in Contemporary Britain* (1985; rev. edn., Oxford, 2009); for the trust as the 'Society for the Protection of the Aristocracy', see P. Weideger, *Gilding the Acorn: Behind the Façade of the National Trust* (1994).

'not to be despised'.[10] Of all the Victorian founders, Octavia Hill, whose idealism and practicality had by then been reappraised in scholarly works such as Gillian Darley's biography and Robert Whelan's editions of essays and letters, offered the best vision on how to make the trust a more diverse and participatory organization.[11] 'I have felt the spirit of Octavia Hill sitting on my shoulder', reflected Dame Fiona Reynolds about her time as the National Trust's director-general:

> When I joined the National Trust as Director-General, I concluded that while being proud of our many achievements, Octavia Hill might have questioned whether we had sufficient focus on 'benefit for the nation'. We are world-class conservationists – and must always remain so. But we had drifted a little away from the 'everlasting delight of the people' that had been Octavia's watchword. I felt we needed to become more 'arms open' if we were to meet her vision.[12]

Hill was seen no longer as an interfering and dour if well-meaning Victorian spinster, but as a 'focused, determined and passionate woman'. Talk of her old fashioned language gave way to praise for her extraordinary foresight. Fiona Reynolds again:

> She was a visionary, ahead of her time in the links she made between access to fresh air and physical and spiritual wellbeing. This is a philosophy with which we are only now getting to grips. One hundred years after her death we are only beginning to develop ways of measuring national happiness as well as gross domestic product. In the age of capitalism's birth, her views were truly revolutionary.[13]

The commemorative events and media coverage of 2012 further popularized Hill's contribution, but her rise to iconic status has led to her appearing as a lone visionary.[14] She now outshines not only the two men commonly named

---

[10] Waterson, *The National Trust*, p. 269; D. Cannadine, 'The first hundred years', in Newby, *The National Trust*. Attention is also drawn to the founders' Christian Socialist and liberal ideas at pp. 11–31.

[11] G. Darley, *Octavia Hill: a Life* (1990), rev. as *Octavia Hill: Social Reformer and Founder of the National Trust* (2010); G. Darley; 'Hill, Octavia (1838–1912)', *ODNB*; *Octavia Hill and the Social Housing Debate: Essays and Letters by Octavia Hill*, ed. R. Whelan (1998); Hill, *LFW*, ed. R. Whelan (2005).

[12] Dame Fiona Reynolds, 'Octavia Hill and the National Trust', in *"To the utmost of her power...": the Enduring Relevance of Octavia Hill*, ed. S. Jones (2012), pp. 169–75, quotations at pp. 171, 174.

[13] Reynolds, 'Octavia Hill and the National Trust', p. 169.

[14] See *inter alia* Jones; J. Rossiter, *Nobler and Better Things: Octavia Hill's Life and Work* (2012); T. Hunt, 'Octavia Hill revisited', *The Guardian*, 6 May 2008 <http://www.theguardian.com/commentisfree/2008/may/06/past.housing>; T. Hunt, 'Octavia Hill,

with her as the 'three founders' of the National Trust, but arguably also most other Victorian preservationists.[15] Yet she did not act or develop her ideas about preservation in isolation. In her chapter in this book Melanie Hall shows the need to examine Hill's role in the trust more carefully by paying closer attention to the trust's wider epistemic community.[16] My contribution complements hers by looking beyond the National Trust's institutional history to situate Hill within the broader national and international preservation movement.

Despite growing scholarly work on Hill and her prominence in institutional histories, she features little in the wider historiography on heritage published in the last three decades. While Raphael Samuel drew attention to the relation between her social work and her preservation, later histories of Britain's heritage movement usually mention Hill only in passing as 'founder of the National Trust', and discuss neither her ideas nor her other contributions to the preservation movement.[17] For reasons that will become apparent below, many internationally focused histories of heritage preservation, especially those in languages other than English, ignore Hill

---

her life and legacy' <http://www.nationaltrust.org.uk/article-1356393664070/>; M. Bragg, 'Octavia Hill', BBC Radio 4 'In Our Time', 7 Apr. 2011 <http://www.bbc.co.uk/programmes/b0100jpz>; T. Hunt and S. Marling (prod.), 'Octavia', BBC Radio 4, 13 Aug. 2012, <http://www.bbc.co.uk/programmes/b01lswvg>; 'Heritage! The battle for Britain's past', BBC Four, ep. 1, 10 Oct. 2013 <http://www.bbc.co.uk/programmes/p014fxzv> [all accessed 25 Feb. 2015].

[15] It was Sir Robert Hunter's misfortune, in particular, that the centenary of his death occurred only a year after the festivities for Hill. Although he was finally memorialized in B. Cowell, *Sir Robert Hunter: Cofounder and 'Inventor' of the National Trust* (2013), he was further eclipsed in 2013 by the heritage community's focus on celebrating the 1913 Ancient Monuments Act for which he had laboured tirelessly. Gerald Baldwin Brown is similarly overlooked (see M. Cooper, 'Gerald Baldwin Brown, Edinburgh, and the care of ancient monuments', *The Historic Environment*, iv (2013), 156–77).

[16] See also M. Hall, 'The politics of collecting: the early aspirations of the National Trust', *Transactions of the Royal Historical Society*, xiii (2003), 345–57; and A. Swenson, 'Founders of the National Trust (*act.* 1894–1895)', *ODNB*.

[17] R. Samuel, *Theatres of Memory*, i: *Past and Present in Contemporary Culture* (1994), pp. 225, 295–6 and ii: *Island Stories* (1998), pp. 143, 303. For mentions of Hill as the National Trust's founder, see *Preserving the Past: the Rise of Heritage in Modern Britain*, ed. M. Hunter (Stroud, 1996), p.182; P. Mandler, *The Fall and Rise of the Stately Home* (1997), p. 171; D. Evans, *A History of Nature Conservation in Britain* (1997; rev. edn. 2002), pp. 38, 42; *Representing the Nation: a Reader. Histories, Heritage, and Museums*, ed. D. Boswell and Jessica Evans (1999), p. 124; *The Heritage Reader*, ed. G. Fairclough, R. Harrison, J. H. Jameson Jnr. and J. Schofield (2008), p. 279 (a reprint of Samuel's work from *Theatres of Memory*). Hill is not mentioned at all in S. Thurley, *Men from the Ministry: how Britain Saved its Heritage* (New Haven, Conn., 2013). A notable exception to this trend is B. Cowell, *The Heritage Obsession: the Battle for England's Past* (Stroud, 2008), pp. 93–7.

entirely and present John Ruskin's and William Morris's condemnation of restoration and their development of conservationist principles as the sole British contributions to nineteenth-century international preservationist thought.[18] It is time to re-inscribe Hill in these histories, for only then can we appreciate what was unique about her contribution. Examining her place in the national and international preservation movement can help to explain the contradictions often observed in Hill's work and personality, and draw attention to how she shaped and benefited from differences between British and continental European preservation movements. Focusing on Hill's role as a 'hub' in the British movement, the first part of this chapter compares her ideas with those of other preservationists. Tracing her national and international connections through personal networks and the reception of her publications in the second part, however, reveals commonalities and differences between the British preservation movement and its European counterparts – differences that provided the structural framework for Hill's contribution.[19]

Octavia Hill's place in the British preservation movement

Octavia Hill's route to preservation is well known, but it is useful to recall the main steps to frame the assessment of her place in national and international movements.[20] It started with her housing work and her transforming cemeteries into gardens and playgrounds for the urban poor. In 1875 she consulted Robert Hunter at the CPS on how to save the Swiss Cottage Fields in relation to one of her projects. Thereafter she joined the CPS and, with Hunter, helped to broaden its mission from the preservation of commons to protecting the countryside more generally. In parallel she became involved in locally focused preservation societies, including her sister Miranda's Kyrle Society for the diffusion of beauty (discussed by Robert Whelan in this volume) and the Hampstead Heath Extension Committee, headed by the duke of Westminster, who was later the National Trust's

---

[18] See for instance D. Lowenthal, *The Past is a Foreign Country* (Cambridge, 1985); D. Gillman, *The Idea of Cultural Heritage* (2006); or D. Poulot, *Une histoire du patrimoine en occident, XVIIIe–XXIe siècle: du monument aux valeurs* (Paris, 2006). Hill is also absent from key 'critical heritage studies' textbooks, e.g. L. Smith, *Uses of Heritage* (2006); and *Understanding the Politics of Heritage*, ed. R. Harrison (Manchester, 2010). A brief mention is made in R. Harrison, *Heritage: Critical Approaches* (2012), pp. 22, 46.

[19] Since Melanie Hall's chapter examines the trans-Atlantic links, my focus here is mainly on Europe, with particular emphasis on France and Germany, and allusions to Italy, Spain, the Netherlands, Russia and the USA to provide a broader comparative framework.

[20] See above nn. 3 and 4. For further discussion of Hill's view on heritage and her contributions to the preservation movement, see the chapters by Baigent, Hall, Readman, Whelan and Whyte in this volume.

first president, and she raised money by private subscription to safeguard numerous other locations. It was the failure of several such campaigns – one she and Hunter ascribed to the absence of a body that could acquire and care for land – that led to the National Trust being founded, with its mission to hold property 'for ever, for everyone'. Although the land she saved and the institutions she created are arguably her biggest legacy, she also left a rich body of writings on preservation, spread across essays such as *Our Common Land*, her Letters to fellow-workers and a plethora of articles in the national press.

Hill's biographers have highlighted how her love for the open countryside was rooted in childhood experiences. She took refuge in nature after her father's bankruptcy. As a child what she wanted most was not a dolls' house but a field 'so large that I could run in it for ever'.[21] Some of the first places she fought to preserve were those she had roamed as a girl – the Hill sisters spent so much of their childhood outdoors they became known locally as 'the young ladies who are always up in the hedges'.[22] The loss of the countryside plunged the fourteen-year-old Octavia into melancholy, but also fostered a determination to retain open spaces not only for herself but also for every man, woman and child in England.

Hill's housing work in places bereft of the country air, space and greenery she valued explains her emphasis on the preservation of nature. Compared with the leaders of Victorian preservation bodies, such as the Society of Antiquaries of London (SAL) and the Society for the Protection of Ancient Buildings (SPAB), Hill's focus was on the preservation of nature rather than culture, activism rather than antiquarianism and, arguably, public access rather than the aesthetics of (anti-)restoration championed by William Morris.[23]

This does not mean, however, as is often argued, that historic, aesthetic and artistic values meant less to her – not least because she, like Morris and most other preservationists, took such inspiration from Ruskin. The latter's influence on her has long been highlighted, but his prediction that she would one day stop copying the great masters, which she had taken up under his supervision, with the words 'Hang drawing!! I must

---

[21] Murphy, p. 50.

[22] Quotation in *Life of Octavia Hill*, p. 4; see also Murphy, p. 50.

[23] On Morris and the history of the SPAB, see C. Miele, '"A small knot of cultivated people": William Morris and the ideologies of protection', *Art Journal*, liv (1995), 73–9; C. Miele, 'The first conservation militant: William Morris and the Society for the Protection of Ancient Buildings', in *Preserving the Past: the Rise of Heritage in Modern Britain*, ed. M. Hunter (Stroud, 1996), pp. 17–37; *From William Morris: Building Conservation and the Arts and Crafts Cult of Authenticity, 1877–1939*, ed. C. Miele (2005).

go to help people', has often been interpreted too literally.[24] As William Whyte discusses in this book, Hill thought that the act of copying and the attention to artistic detail that it brought were crucial to her housing work.[25] Other contributors to this book also demonstrate the strong links between artistic creation and Hill's social work. Elizabeth Baigent, for example, highlights how the secondary gifts of 'music, colour, art, nature, space and quiet' were linked to the primary blessings of entering 'into divine and human love'.[26]

Thus, although Hill's preservationist activities focused on open spaces, they were part of a broader fight to preserve and create beauty in all its forms. The integrative approach is reflected in the National Trust's early acquisitions, which included many buildings alongside open space, and also in Hill's role in creating links among organizations with different concerns.[27] Unlike in some continental European countries, where umbrella organizations tried to co-ordinate preservationist efforts, Britain's national preservation societies had specific aims, with the CPS responsible for legal questions, the SPAB for restoration, and the National Trust for landscapes and acquisitions, while local societies championed research and particular sites.[28] Yet the frequent collaborations among societies created an increasingly organized movement. In particular, lacking the money or power to hold buildings, the SPAB saw in the National Trust a source of help and often suggested buildings for acquisition. In turn, the trust often sought conservation advice from the SPAB.[29] Collaborations were facilitated by shared principles and overlapping membership, with a few individuals – notably Hill – acting as special connectors. She joined many local groups, as well as the three core national preservation societies. She was a CPS member for two decades before the trust's inception, and was made honorary member of the SPAB in 1897 following a long collaboration with Morris in the Kyrle Society. Over several decades she brought societies together for numerous campaigns, formalized support by linking bodies through advisory functions, and enlisted contacts from her charitable work for preservationist efforts.[30]

---

[24] Quoted in Maurice, *Octavia Hill*, pp. 129–31. On the reception, see Murphy, pp. 52–3.
[25] Whyte, chapter 3 in this volume.
[26] Baigent, chapter 7 in this volume.
[27] Hall, 'The politics of collecting'; Hall, chapter 10 in this volume.
[28] Swenson, *Rise of Heritage*, pp. 93–4.
[29] Weideger, *Gilding the Acorn*, pp. 38–9; J. Gaze, *Figures in a Landscape: a History of the National Trust* (1988), pp. 31, 36, 87; Jenkins and James, *From Acorn to Oak Tree*, pp. 18–19, 29.
[30] Jenkins and James, *From Acorn to Oak Tree*, p. 21. On the personal and affiliate ties that connected the preservation movement, see Swenson, 'Founders'; Swenson, *Rise of Heritage*, ch. 2.

Like many other leading preservationists, Hill championed preservation not as an end in itself but as a means to mitigate inequality. Although she did not theorize her ideas in the same way as Ruskin or Morris did, and never produced a manifesto, her views expressed in *Our Common Land* were strongly critical of established privileges. She fervently defended 'our common birthright to the soil' against the 'seven hundred and ten persons' who owned a quarter of the English land.[31] Her critique was in many ways no less radical than Morris's, but was expressed in more acceptable language: following Hugh Miller she pointed out 'how intimately the right to roam over the land is connected with the love of it, and hence with patriotism'.[32] While Morris alienated many of the SPAB's supporters by contending that preservation should pave the road to socialism, Hill steered clear of linking politics and preservation.[33] Instead she successfully used the connections established through her charitable work to get backing for preservationist ventures from the most respectable and influential circles.

Yet, despite her ability to harness support, Hill was criticized for how she put her preservation principles into practice, such that she can now appear rigid and even reactionary. However, she was very much a child of her time. How best to use sites that had lost their original purpose and who should have custodianship were new and contentious questions for the preservation movement, and have remained so ever since. Hill's responses were sometimes contradictory, but so were those of the wider British (and continental) movement. A disagreement over the use of the Court House in Long Crendon between Hill and the Arts and Crafts designer Charles R. Ashbee, who was active in the SPAB and the National Trust, epitomizes difficulties about the museification of the past. The Court House was among the vernacular buildings that Hill treasured for the 'quaint picturesque out-of-the-world' feelings they inspired, evoking 'memories of England as our ancestors knew it'. Although 'nothing very striking', these buildings greeted 'the eye with a sense of repose'.[34] She also believed that such buildings should be used and so was initially keen for Ashbee to move in with his wife and make the house a holiday home for London boys connected with Ashbee's art classes. Yet the boys' boisterousness and Ashbee's transformation of the house into a showcase for his Guild of Handicraft furniture was not quite what she had in mind. She was not amused when Ashbee inscribed the

---

[31] O. Hill, *Our Common Land* (1877), p. 14.

[32] Hill, *Our Common Land*, p. 16. On patriotism and preservation more broadly, see P. Readman, *Land and Nation in England: Patriotism, National Identity, and the Politics of Land, 1880–1914* (Woodbridge, 2008).

[33] Miele, 'A small knot', pp. 73–9.

[34] Darley, *Octavia Hill: Social Reformer*, p. 285.

guild's emblem over a historic fireplace and, fearing that the occupants would damage the delicate old house, she did not renew Ashbee's tenancy. He bitterly noted that the boys 'would have given it such a soul as no dead museum in the Trust's charge can … possibly have'.[35] As Darley comments, 'It was an early instance of a familiar criticism'.[36]

In natural spaces too Octavia Hill struggled to reconcile increasing access with preventing destruction by growing visitor numbers. Publicly she expressed the belief that the trust's properties belonged 'to every landless man, woman and child in England',[37] but privately she said that the trust 'by no means plans to give access to the tramp, the London rough, the noisy beanfeaster'. Instead, the objective was to 'preserve land in its natural beauty for the artist, the professional man, and such of the public as appreciate and respect natural beauty'.[38] While she regularly organized excursions for London's East End tenants, she was wary that 'picnic parties carry London noise and vulgarity out into woods and fields, giving no sense of hush or rest'.[39] The distinctions she drew between deserving and undeserving poor in her housing work also applied to her preservationism, and echo widely expressed anxieties about the 'cocknification' of travel, deplored for instance by Henry James.[40] Many conservative preservationists used similar language to justify keeping cultural and natural heritage the preserve of the elite. Yet to ascribe fears about the potentially destructive impact of increasing visitor numbers solely to class snobbery is too easy. Such fears were also connected with a profound change in attitude towards 'authenticity', which sacralized the creations of the past and demanded that they be passed unaltered to future generations. Ruskin's dictum that '[w]e have no right whatever to touch [old buildings]. They are not ours. They belong partly to those who built them, and partly to all the generations of mankind who are to follow us', influenced conservationists of buildings and nature alike.[41] Like most other reform-minded preservationists of her generation, Hill did not really resolve the tensions between preservation and transformation through use and as a result appeared at times radical and at others reactionary.[42]

---

[35] Darley, *Octavia Hill: Social Reformer*, p. 287.
[36] Darley, *Octavia Hill: Social Reformer*, p. 287
[37] Weideger, *Gilding the Acorn*, p. 385.
[38] Darley, *Octavia Hill: Social Reforme*r, p. 292
[39] Waterson, *National Trust*, p. 58.
[40] H. James, 'In Warwickshire', *The Galaxy* (1877), p. 671; see P. Mandler '"The wand of fancy": the historical imagination of the Victorian tourist', in *Material Memories*, ed. M. Kwint, C. Breward and J. Aynsley (Oxford and New York, 1999), pp. 125–41, at p. 127.
[41] J. Ruskin, *The Seven Lamps of Architecture* (repr. New York, 1989), p. 197.
[42] See A. Swenson, 'Popular heritage and commodification debates in nineteenth- and early twentieth-century Britain, France, and Germany', in *Popularizing National Pasts, 1800*

Similar contradictions run through Hill's responses to decision-making in preservation, and the role of the aristocracy and the state in particular. Despite writing about the common ownership of land by the people, she enlisted the mightiest aristocrats for the trust's cause. Despite being known for her small-scale, individualistic, communitarian method and her rejection of statist approaches in her housing work, she was not against a legislative framework when it came to preservation. Though she valued the leadership provided by individuals of integrity, believing that the National Trust's leadership should 'consist of men and women who should be free from the tendency to sacrifice such treasures to mercenary considerations, or to vulgarizing them in accordance with popular cries', she embraced the need for legislation to prevent the enclosure of commons and to safeguard the land the trust had acquired.[43] As such, she was again in tune with prevailing sentiment in Britain and Europe as a whole.

Octavia Hill's international networks and her reception abroad

While Octavia Hill was creating new societies in Britain, a plethora of voluntary associations was being formed across the Channel and the Atlantic, working in tandem with state administrations. Some of these bodies, like the National Trust, still shape preservation today, while others, like the Kyrle Society, were more ephemeral. In some places, like Britain and the USA, the idea of a landholding trust gained lasting ground, while in others it did not. In Germany, for example, the Association for Protected Nature Parks purchased some land, but, because of different property-owning regimes and greater state involvement, there was less need for a private landholding body, and the National Trust model was imitated only in the late twentieth century when more value was put on private involvement in preservation.[44] Despite differences in organization, the purpose of preservation was widely agreed. Activists everywhere saw the preservation of nature and culture as intertwined, and as part of a broader drive to reform art, land and life in the face of a common challenge from modernization. They also shared ideas and methods through correspondence, publications, international exhibitions, congresses and personal meetings.[45]

---

to the Present, ed. S. Berger, C. Lorenz and B. Melman (New York and Abingdon, 2011), pp. 102–24; Swenson, *Rise of Heritage*, pp. 134–43.

[43] Quoted in Darley, *Octavia Hill*, p. 297.

[44] Founded in 1909, the *Verein Naturschutzpark* purchased 4,000 hectares of land on the Lüneburg Heath between 1910 and 1920 (see M. Jefferies, 'Heimatschutz: environmental activism in Wilhelmine Germany', in *Green Thought in German Culture: Historical and Contemporary Perspectives*, ed. C. Riordan (Cardiff, 1997), pp. 42–54, at p. 42).

[45] Swenson, *Rise of Heritage*, passim.

Although Octavia Hill was connected to most preservation ventures in Britain, she remained on the edge of developments in continental Europe. Unlike some of her male preservationist colleagues, such as Canon Rawnsley, Charles R. Ashbee or William Morris, Hill used her travels abroad to recover from exhaustion and not for promotional tours. She did, however, take inspiration from developments she saw on her travels. From Nuremberg, for instance, she wrote:

> The town looks very comfortable and flourishing, as if the old things had been taken into use and would stay; – not like Italy or Constantinople as if every breath of purer or more living thought would sweep away some of the beauty, and substitute hideous Paris or London models. Trees grow among the houses; and children play round them, and clean industrious women knit at their doors; and comfortable little shops are opened in them; and you see 'Bürger Schule' put up over their doors; and yet they aren't all torn down and replaced with rows of houses, like Camden Town, and shops like Oxford Street; and still these gardens for the people everywhere look reproach on me, when I think of England, and every tree and creeper and space of green grass in the town reminds me of our unconsumed smoke, and how it poisons our plants, and dims the colour of all things for us. … We hope to make a few useful outlines here for windows &c. in possible future houses in London.[46]

Despite her interest in foreign practices, Hill's main centre of operation always remained London, but by the mid 1880s visitors from across the world came to the city to see her methods and be trained by her.[47] The awe she inspired was such that some of her admirers feared, 'if ever, I have the pleasure of standing before you, all my courage will evaporate, and I will be utterly unable to express the feelings with which I look up to you, much as a raw recruit on the general who has led victory in many a good fight'.[48] She took training seriously and in turn demanded serious commitment. When German visitors wished to study her schemes in order to implement them in Munich, she wrote 'I would gladly show and tell them all I could', but 'I am afraid that I should have to ask that whoever came should devote a minimum of three months to steady work. *Nothing* could be learnt under that time, and it is a great upsetting of work to arrange it for less'.[49]

Hill's reputation abroad – across Europe, the USA and the British empire – was facilitated by personal contacts, her writings, and by those

---

[46] Octavia Hill to her mother, Nuremberg, 24 May 1880, in *Life of Octavia Hill*, p. 437.
[47] The following draws on *Life of Octavia Hill*, pp. 440–1, 449–50, and Darley, *Octavia Hill*, pp. 152–62, 209–10, 240.
[48] 'A Russian lady' to Octavia Hill, 23 Apr. 1884, in Maurice, *Life of Octavia Hill*, p. 449.
[49] Octavia Hill to Miss Howitt, 10 June 1896, in Maurice, *Life of Octavia Hill*, pp. 537–38 (original emphasis).

'Nobler imaginings and mightier struggles'

who discussed her work. Some of the earliest and most sustained interest came from the USA. From the 1870s her housing work was emulated in Boston by Henry Bowditch, Massachusetts Board of Health chairman, and by Ellen Collins and Alice Lincoln in New York and Boston. As the decade progressed, Hill's ideas on charity, as well as on housing, became more widely known in the USA, thanks to Louisa Lee Schuyler, founder of the State Charities Aid Association of New York. Schuyler published five of Hill's articles as *The Homes of the London Poor* in 1875, before the book was republished in England.[50] *Our Common Land* was republished in 1880 for the Associated Charities of Boston. Interest in Hill was also increased by the reports of Bostonian Ellen Chase, after she had returned to Massachusetts, having worked for Hill in Deptford. In 1896 the Octavia Hill Association of Philadelphia was set up by two other Americans who had worked for Hill in the 1880s.[51]

While the common language facilitated exchanges with the USA and the British empire – resulting, for instance, in some of Hill's ideas being implemented in South Africa – correspondence also arrived from Europe, including Scandinavia and Russia.[52] The Netherlands and Germany were perhaps 'the most fertile ground for her ideas', but they were also well received in Catholic France, Italy and Spain.[53] As in the USA, in Europe personal visits and friendships made Hill's ideas known. A 'charming young lady, Mis Ter Meulen from Amsterdam', whom Octavia Hill described to Ellen Chase as 'full of power, brightness and sweet human sympathy', spent a few months with Hill in England 'to prepare for taking up houses in her own country'.[54] In Germany Hill's ideas were particularly influential due to her friendship with Princess Alice of Hesse-Darmstadt, Queen Victoria's third child and a social reformer and organizer of the 'Parliament of women', which furthered topics of interest to women, including educating and employing the poor.[55] Hill's sister Florence went to Darmstadt in the 1860s to help the princess's housing work.[56] Princess Alice had *The Homes of*

---

[50] Maurice, *Life of Octavia Hill*, pp. 264–5.

[51] Darley, *Octavia Hill*, p. 209; on Hill's relationship with Chase, see also Hill, *LFW*, 1893, p. 339.

[52] Hill, *Octavia Hill*, pp. 13–14; C. Morrell, 'Housing and the women's movement, 1860–1914' (unpublished Oxford Brookes University PhD thesis, 1999), pp. 129–30, Oxford Brookes University Research Archive and Digital Asset Repository <https://radar.brookes.ac.uk/radar/file/0405ebda-1b5b-ef73-2ec5-7c17e773d075/1/morrell1999housing.pdf> deposited 23 Nov. 2012 [accessed 20 May 2014].

[53] Darley, *Octavia Hill*, p. 209.

[54] Octavia Hill to Ellen Chase, 22 Nov. 1893, in Maurice, *Life of Octavia Hill*, p. 527.

[55] Darley, *Octavia Hill*, pp. 152–3.

[56] Hill, *Octavia Hill*, p. 185.

the London Poor translated and, at Octavia's request, wrote the introduction to the German edition.[57] The translation was widely reviewed in the press, and subsequent works on housing reform provided regular updates on developments in London.[58]

Despite language differences, the broader reception of Octavia Hill's work in Germany took off almost as early as in the USA, peaking in the 1880s and 1890s.[59] Hill was described enthusiastically as an 'unusually gifted and hardworking lady', and as 'one of the noblest philanthropists in England', a turn of phrase that sounded particularly affectionate when 'philanthropist' was Germanized and feminized as 'Menschenfreundin'.[60] As in the USA, her ideas were emulated in Germany, particularly by a society in Berlin, the *Frauenverein* Octavia Hill, and also in Aachen and Dresden.[61] Her thoughts about housing reform were widely discussed in German publications on social reform, and in specialized economic, administrative and theological publications, and reached the general reader via noted political periodicals such as the *Preußische Jahrbücher* and through Germany's first successful mass-circulation newspaper *Die Gartenlaube*, which aimed to address all members of the middle-class family.[62]

The French periodical press published translations of some of her works in the 1880s and 1890s, and the articles were also full of praise for this 'young girl who appears frail, pale, and weak', but who is 'great hearted'.[63] The Académie Française's director called her the 'personification of thoughtful charity'; and a historian of charity even claimed that 'all the governments of the world, with all their means of action, with all their enormous resources, have not accomplished what this woman has done alone, because her heart,

---

[57] Darley, *Octavia Hill*, p. 159; O. Hill, *Aus der Londoner Armenpflege* (Wiesbaden, 1878).

[58] For instance *Deutsche Rundschau*, xxviii (1881), 212; W. Ruprecht, *Die Wohnungen der arbeitenden Klassen in London* (1884), p. 109.

[59] The analyses of peaks in German, French, Spanish and Italian publications are indicative rather than absolute. They are based on statistics compiled using the Google Ngram <https://books.google.com/ngrams> [accessed 1 March 2014] and the French digitization project Gallica.

[60] 'selten begabte und arbeitstüchtige Dame', *Schriften des Vereins für Socialpolitik*, xxviii–xxx (1884), 139; 'eine der edelsten Menschenfreundinnen in England', *Der Arbeiterfreund: Zeitschrift des Centralvereins in Preußen für das Wohl der arbeitenden Klassen*, xxii (1884), 134.

[61] W. Vietor, *Die neueren Sprachen* (Diesterweg, 1915), p. 101; N. Bullock, *The Movement for Housing Reform in Germany and France 1840–1914* (1985; rev. edn., Cambridge 2011), p. 233.

[62] *Johaniter Ordensblatt: Amtliche Monatsschrift der Balley Brandenburg*, xix–xx (1878); *Preußische Jahrbücher*, xlv–xlvi (1880), 371; *Die Gartenlaube*, xxvii (1889), 648.

[63] 'Jeune fille frêle, pâle et faible d'apparence' (*Revue britannique, ou Choix d'articles traduits des meilleurs écrits périodiques de la Grande-Bretagne* (1885), p. 280); 'grande par le coeur' (*Bulletin des séances de l'Académie de Nîmes* (1886), p. 153).

her sympathy, her whole soul are in her work'.[64] Hill's housing work was initially discussed in books and journals on economics and sanitary reform, was then reviewed in works concerned with social reform, including Catholic and socialist periodicals, and finally won wide praise in the main bourgeois newspapers, from *Le Figaro* to the *Petit Parisien,* and the most prestigious intellectual magazines, such as the *Revue des Deux Mondes*.[65] Following discussion by the Académie des Sciences Morales et Politiques, her work even featured in the Académie Française's annual public lecture, diffused nationally in the Republic's organ, the *Journal Officiel*.[66]

Similarly enthusiastic responses to Hill can be traced in other European countries, including Italy (where citations peaked in the 1890s and 1900s, mainly in economic and social reform publications) and Spain (where reception was strongest in municipal centres preoccupied with urban reform, such as Barcelona, and where feminists were particularly interested in Hill). From the late 1880s onwards international congresses for hygiene, housing reform and female philanthropy took increasing notice. At the 1889 Paris Universal Exhibition, at least three international congresses discussed her work and helped to spread her ideas across the globe.[67] Her international reputation was such that when she died, 'although no formal invitation to the funeral had been sent, friends … gathered from far and near', including 'one of her Dutch friends coming from Amsterdam'. Tributes were paid to her in newspapers 'both English and foreign'[68] and her work was discussed in specialized and general publications in foreign countries during the twentieth century.

Throughout and beyond her lifetime, Hill's work excited extraordinary interest among people as diverse as economists, doctors, lawyers, politicians, sanitation boards, Jesuits and feminists, and in fields including housing,

---

[64] 'Personnification de la charité réfléchie', in L. Say, 'Rapport sur les prix de vertu, lu dans la séance publique annuelle de l'Académie française', *Journal Officiel*, 22 Nov. 1890, 5659; 'Tous les gouvernements du monde, avec tous leurs moyens d'action, avec leurs dépenses énormes, n'ont pas fait ce que cette femme seule a accompli, parce que son cœur, sa sympathie, son âme entière, étaient dans son œuvre', in L. Lefébure, *La Charité privée en France* (Paris, 1900), p. 165.

[65] *Le Figaro. Supplément littéraire du dimanche* (1884); P. Leroy-Beaulieu, 'Etudes sociales – Le luxe: la fonction de la richesse', *Revue des Deux Mondes*, cxxvi (1894), 570; R. de La Sizeranne, 'La religion de la beauté: étude sur John Ruskin', *Revue des Deux Mondes*, cxxxii (1885), 585.

[66] *Séances et travaux de l'Académie des sciences morales et politiques: compte-rendu* (Paris, 1889); Say, 'Rapport', p. 5659.

[67] *Congrès international des habitations à bon marché* (Paris, 1889); *Congrès international d'assistance tenu du 28 juillet au 4 août 1889* (Paris, 1889); *Actes du Congrès international des œuvres et institutions féminines* (Paris, 1890).

[68] Maurice, *Life of Octavia Hill*, p. 582.

sanitation, charity, child protection and women's work. This reception across European countries complicates the question of whether Hill was reactionary or radical. Contemporaries certainly mobilized her for diverse political and social positions. German, French, Italian and Spanish publications reveal that she inspired religious groups (Protestant and Catholic), socialists and feminists alike. In France, for example, in the highly divided political climate between the Dreyfus affair and the separation of church and state, Hill inspired Catholics and anti-clericals, conservatives and socialists.[69] Her work was used equally to promote private charity and to prepare legislative drafts for state regulation.[70]

Yet what is striking about the reception of Hill's work is that, in the European countries examined here, interest focused almost entirely on her housing projects, and references to Hill's publications were largely limited to *Homes of the London Poor*. The only German citations of her preservationist writings I could find were the listing of her essay on 'Colour, space and music for the people' in the German Yearbook for National Economy and Statistics' list of noteworthy foreign publications, and a brief commendation of her emphasis on fresh air and gardens by a natural history society in the north German town of Emden.[71] There was no mention of her work in preservationist periodicals such as *Heimatschutz*, the organ of the National League for the Protection of the Homeland, Germany's largest preservationist organization, which, like Hill, championed the protection of nature and culture.

In countries where Hill's preservationist work was discovered largely after the National Trust was founded her ideas on preservation were still little cited. In France, for instance, the discussion of her work in the *Revue des*

---

[69] For Catholic reception see wide reporting in *La Croix* and 'Bulletin des questions sociales', *Etudes religieuses, historiques et littéraires par les Pères de la Compagnie de Jésus* (1891), p. 524; G. Wampach, 'La maison de l'ouvrier', *Revue des sciences ecclésiastiques* (1896), p. 817. For socialist reception, see especially publications by the independent socialist Benoît Mahon, for instance 'Les habitations ouvrières en Allemagne', *La Revue Socialiste* (1890), p. 294; B. Mahon, *Le socialisme intégral. Deuxième partie: des reformes possibles et des moyens pratiques* (Paris, 1891), p. 389.

[70] The leading periodical for international legal development, the *Bulletin de la Société de législation comparée*, wrote about her as early as 1883. Legislative drafts referring to her work came from across the political spectrum: e.g., M. R. Bompard, 'Rapport présenté au nom de la 5e Sous-Commission du Comité du budget et du contrôle, sur les dépenses du service des secours à domicile', *Conseil Municipal de Paris, Rapports et Documents* (1891), p. 12; *Journal Officiel*, 25 July 1896, p. 4262; G. Wampach, *Un projet de loi sur les maisons à bon marché: extrait de la science catholique* (Paris, 1899). On her uses for private charitable work, see for instance Lefébure, *La Charité privée*.

[71] *Jahrbücher für Nationalökonomie und Statistik*, xlii (1884), 27; *Jahresbericht der Naturforschenden Gesellschaft in Emden*, lxviii–lxxvi (1884), 23.

deux mondes coincided with the French discovery of Ruskin and the *Revue* picked up on their connection – but it was Ruskin's help with her housing work rather than her own ideas about preservation that were reported in the late 1890s and early 1900s.[72] As in Germany, French bibliographic works listed some of her preservationist essays, including 'Space for the people' and *Our Common Land*,[73] but there was little discussion of them; and when the National Trust was examined it was Rawnsley's name that was mentioned, not hers.[74]

How can this lack of notice be explained? Not by any anti-British sentiment. The German preservation movement's leaders were generally highly anglophile and well acquainted with British developments. The architect Herman Muthesius, an attaché to the German embassy in London, and collaborator with the SPAB, had done much to acquaint German audiences with English ideas about preservation, and especially Ruskin's and Morris's views on restoration.[75] The conservator of the Prussian province of the Rhineland, and arguably the most influential man in monument preservation, Professor Paul Clemen, published the first monograph on Ruskin and corresponded with Gerald Baldwin Brown, professor at Edinburgh and National Trust council member – each man wanting to make foreign preservationist practices known in his own community through publications and congress speeches.[76] Interest in British developments was also strong among proponents of garden cities. From the 1880s Ernst Rudorff and Paul Schulze Naumburg, who founded the nationwide *Heimatschutz* association in 1904, promoted England's 'feeling for the charm of the landscape' as an example which Germany should emulate.[77] French preservationist periodicals and congresses were as cosmopolitan and anglophile as their German counterparts.

Hill's refusal to allow her *Letters to fellow-workers*, in which she outlined many of her preservationist practices, to be translated might have limited

---

[72] de la Sizeranne, 'La religion de la beauté'; R. de la Sizeranne, *Ruskin et la religion de la beauté* (Paris, 1898), p. 65.

[73] For instance, *Polybiblion: revue bibliographique* (1875) mentions 'Space for the people' and *Our Common Land* (1876).

[74] For instance, in *Congrès international pour la protection des paysages* (Paris, 1909).

[75] P. Alter, 'Hermann Muthesius: Die englischen Jahre', in *Rivalität und Partnerschaft: Studien zu den deutsch–britischen Beziehungen im 19. und 20. Jahrhundert*, ed. G. Ritter and P. Wende (Paderborn, 1999), pp. 53–68.

[76] P. Clemen, *John Ruskin* (Leipzig, 1900).

[77] E. Rudorff, 'Das Verhältnis des modernen Lebens zur Nature', *Preußische Jahrbücher*, xlv (1880), 261–76; A. Knaut, 'Ernst Rudorff und die Anfänge der deutschen Heimatbewegung', in *Antimodernismus und Reform: Zur Geschichte der deutschen Heimatbewegung*, ed. E. Klueting (Darmstadt, 1991), pp. 20–49.

knowledge of her ideas on nature. Over many years she sent the letters to foreign 'fellow-workers' including Princess Alice, but she would not allow the princess to translate them into German:

> I fear I feel just a little differently about my letters to my fellow-workers, and that slight difference of feeling makes all the difference in action. Though they are printed, and pretty widely circulated among certain circles of people, they have never been published. I have refused more than once to let them be published either in America or here. For this reason. They are meant for, and written to my fellow-workers and though they contain passages which are entirely public, there are other parts I could not write exactly as they stand if I felt I were writing to the world in general.[78]

As a result, many of her thoughts on preservation remained confined 'to my own friends'. But the fact that her letters were not translated does not adequately explain why her ideas did not spread more widely, since the preservationists who shaped national and international movements were usually multilingual and highly mobile. They exchanged ideas through correspondence and personal encounters and read foreign language texts, as is evident in their knowledge of English preservationism, and especially Ruskin and Morris.

It might have mattered that, unlike the British preservation movement's leading figures, such as the National Trust's Robert Hunter, Hardwicke Rawnsley, Charles R. Ashbee or Gerald Baldwin Brown, and leaders of the SAL and the SPAB, Hill did not go on promotional tours abroad or attend foreign congresses.[79] Her travels abroad certainly also provided inspiration, as shown in her comments above on Nuremberg and her letters from France, Italy and Greece with their thoughts on developments in politics and art. She occasionally met well-placed people overseas, for example the German head of excavations Herr Kurzius, at Olympia, but she did not systematically use her travels to connect with foreign campaigners or spread news about her work.[80] Yet such reticence did not prevent her housing work from becoming internationally known, and she was not the only preservationist who interacted with the outside world mainly through correspondence and publications.

Another possible reason for Hill's strikingly poor links to continental preservationist circles was that legislation and restoration, which dominated the correspondences of her fellow trust leaders, were not at the

---

[78] Quoted in Darley, *Octavia Hill*, p. 159.
[79] On their travels and promotional tours, see Swenson, *Rise of Heritage*, chs. 2, 4.
[80] See Hill's letters while travelling, in Maurice, *Life of Octavia Hill*, pp. 134–43, 234–42, 354–86, 398–437.

forefront of her fight.[81] Although she did not correspond with continental preservationists interested in landscape preservation or land reform, she did discuss preservationist matters with American correspondents and used, for instance, her contact with Ellen Chase to find out whether the Trustees of Reservations, established in Boston in the early 1890s, could serve as a model for the National Trust.[82]

A likely explanation for Hill's lack of exchange on preservation with continental Europe is the dearth of female representation among preservationist movement leaders in France and Germany, compared to the Anglo-Saxon countries. Hill's foreign correspondents were mainly women, who, like the Russian correspondent who wrote on 'The homes of the London poor' in the *Journal of St. Petersburg*, took 'pleasure and pride' in the fact that achievements in housing reform were women's.[83] While women were prominent in housing reform across Britain, Europe and America, only in Britain and the USA were they prominent in preservation. There were some in German and French associations at the end of the nineteenth century, and some connections existed between the garden city movement and the women's movement in Germany,[84] but the founders and members of executive committees or councils of the large national preservation societies were exclusively male. Due to the earlier professionalization of preservation in France and Germany, civil servants, conservators and architects dominated state institutions and private movements alike. By the time preservation movements in Britain (and the USA) were institutionalized and professionalized, they included women who were already active in the feminized voluntary and religious spheres.[85] The lesser female presence in

---

[81] On these networks, see Swenson, *Rise of Heritage*, passim.

[82] Octavia Hill to Ellen Chase, 22 Nov. 1893, in Maurice, *Life of Octavia Hill*, pp. 527–8, and Darley, *Octavia Hill: Social Reformer*, p. 279. On the links between the trust movements on both sides of the Atlantic, see M. Hall, 'Niagara Falls: preservation and the spectacle of Anglo-American accord', in *Towards World Heritage: International Origins of the Preservation Movement*, ed. M. Hall (Aldershot, 2011), pp. 23–43; M. Hall, 'Plunder or preservation? Negotiating an Anglo-American heritage in the later nineteenth century in the Old World and the New: Shakespeare's birthplace, Niagara Falls, and Carlyle's house', in *From Plunder to Preservation: Britain and the Heritage of Empire, 1800–1950*, ed. A. Swenson and P. Mandler (Oxford, 2013), pp. 241–65.

[83] 'A Russian lady' to Octavia Hill, 22 Apr. 1884, in Maurice, *Life of Octavia Hill*, pp. 449–50; Darley, *Octavia Hill: Social Reformer*, p. 209.

[84] T. Harris, 'The garden city movement: architecture, politics, and urban transformation, 1902–1931' (unpublished Columbia University PhD thesis, 2012), Columbia University Academic Commons <http://hdl.handle.net/10022/AC:P:12406> [accessed 20 May 2014].

[85] For figures and a brief discussion of the literature, see Swenson, *Rise of Heritage*, pp. 131–3; M. Holleran, 'America's early history preservation movement (1850–1930) in a transatlantic context', in Hall, *Towards World Heritage*, p. 194.

continental Europe meant that Hill's ideas did not reach the preservation movement via her female correspondents, who were neither as active nor as well placed as Hill across the two types of movements. Unlike housing reform, which was largely seen as a domestic, 'women's affair', continental European preservation was a professionalized, male world, and male preservationist leaders, who customarily picked up on interesting foreign developments, might have simply not considered it worthwhile to report Hill's work in areas they considered masculine.[86]

Conclusion

Situating Octavia Hill in the national and international heritage movement highlights that she was part of a broader current and yet exceptional. Her work appertained to a wider drive to preserve the heritage of the past and create a better, more equal future. She was one of many preservationists who never managed to reconcile access with protection, or belief in small-scale private endeavours with the realization that a long-lasting framework for protection could be provided only by legislation. The same concerns animated debates within movements in all countries. Though favoured solutions might be unique, as with the National Trust's position as property holding trust, say, ideas about preservation were largely held in common.

A comparison of Octavia Hill's international networks and those of other preservationists highlights her unique place in Britain and internationally. Hill, more than anyone else, married housing reform with preservation, practically and ideologically: but while she was connected to virtually every important preservationist venture in Britain, and often acted as a nodal point, she was marginal to the international movement. Her network of (mostly female) correspondents extended from Boston to St. Petersburg, but scarcely overlapped with those of international preservationists. While other leading National Trust figures, such as Hunter and Rawnsley, were in constant contact with preservationists from Europe, Hill was not. Although her housing work was internationally discussed and emulated, her preservationist work was not. A lack of promotional activity on her part might have been a contributing factor, but the different gendering of housing reform and preservation seems at least as important.

I have argued elsewhere that, at the turn of the century, similarities outweighed differences in the aims, structures and numbers of British, French and German preservation movements; but a close look at Octavia Hill and her international reception reveals some noteworthy distinctions.

---

[86] Morrell, 'Housing and the women's movement'; U. Terlinden and S. von Oerzen, *Die Wohnungsfrage ist Frauensache! Frauenbewebung und Wohnreform 1870 bis 1933* (Berlin, 2006).

A properly gendered history of the European, including the British, preservation movement is 'yet to be written'.[87] Octavia Hill's biography certainly points to substantial differences in the public role of women. Whereas the earlier professionalization of the heritage sector in continental Europe seems to have excluded women from leadership, in British preservationism, with its slightly later drive towards institutionalization, women known for their contribution to the arts, religion and philanthropy were more prominent. The comparison of Octavia Hill's networks with those of some leading male preservationists in Britain also suggests that, due to the reduced female presence, preservation and social housing reform were less close in continental Europe than in Britain, lacking a figure like Octavia Hill to connect the two areas – although more sustained research on this topic would be desirable. In all the countries discussed, ties existed among reform movements that focused on housing standards, sanitation, open spaces, national monuments and even naturism and vegetarianism.[88] The substantial literature on these 'life reform' movements has long acknowledged how interconnected ideas and people were, but it seems worth exploring why ties between areas were closer in some countries than in others and how these thicker connections could be created.

Yet, while structural reasons help to explain why a woman could gain such influence and importance in the British preservation movement, it took the extraordinary woman that Octavia Hill was to establish a lasting link between the need for decent housing and for air, beauty, nature and history. Although she is not the only woman whose contribution to the preservation movement should be celebrated, Hill made a unique contribution. Her prominence as a housing reformer, her talent as a campaigner, her ability to find the right words (proposing for instance to call the National Trust a 'trust' rather than a 'company'), and her connection in the highest circles enlisted support for radical ideas about natural and architectural property as common goods, even from conservative landowners who otherwise objected to seeing such properties as anything other than family heritage. Her emphasis on the right of access to beauty, nature and history as an essential element towards fulfilment and well-being for 'every man, woman and child' was indeed revolutionary and remains worth fighting for to 'the utmost of our power'.

---

[87] Holleran, 'America's early history preservation movement', p. 194.

[88] For a discussion of links between the garden city movement and housing reform, and between garden city and *Heimatschutz* movements, see Bullock, *Housing Reform in Germany and France* and Harris, 'The garden city movement'.

10. Octavia Hill and the National Trust*

Melanie Hall

'Seldom in the world's history has one woman, quietly and unobtrusively, effected so much to make her fellow-beings happier, and left behind so permanent an impress of her own personality.'[1]

Mary Lumsden

Octavia Hill was an inspiring woman with a loyal following whose contribution to society was often made beyond the public gaze, as 'fellow-worker' Mary Lumsden's tribute attests. In a period when few women gained prominence for their work, her name is known from her accomplishments in housing and campaigns to preserve open space. She is also recognized as one of the founders of the National Trust for Places of Historic Interest and Natural Beauty, as the institution was known at its inception in 1894. Now known simply as the National Trust, it has become the most successful preservation organization anywhere, with a membership exceeding four million.[2] As more information comes to light about the trust's early years, we can begin to tease out her part in shaping the organization.

The founders of the National Trust

Recent accounts of the trust's origins focus on three founders: Octavia Hill, Sir Robert Hunter (1844–1913) and Canon Hardwicke Drummond

---

* This chapter is part of my current study of the National Trust's origins. It is, inevitably, a partial view of a complex topic. I am grateful to Peter Clayton, director, Octavia Hill Birthplace Museum Trust and Patricia McGuire, archivist, King's College, Cambridge, for access to and assistance with archives in their care, as well as to many individuals at the National Trust who have shared their expertise. Thanks are due to Elizabeth Baigent and Ben Cowell for organizing the conference from which this publication originated; to Polly Atkin and Jeff Cowton for references to James Russell Lowell and the Lake District; and to David Antiss and Commons Licence for permission to reproduce his photograph of the Caroline Southwood Hill memorial seat.

[1] 'A fellow-worker' [Mary Lumsden], obituary of O. Hill, *Edinburgh Review*, Apr. 1913.

[2] NT Annual Report (2011–12) <http://www.nationaltrust.org.uk/about-us/annual-reports/> [accessed 28 July 2013].

Rawnsley (1851–1920).³ These three, described as a 'trinity' and (oddly, given the importance of Hill's gender as is discussed below) a 'triumvirate', are remembered as high-minded philanthropists who promoted open space as a means of societal regeneration in a period of change.⁴ Members of the trust itself, together with Hill's family and friends, helped to shape this perception, as Astrid Swenson points out in this volume.⁵ As Robin Fedden explained, 'Members of the Trust have been taught to revere the trinity which brought it into being: properly so, for they were remarkable'.⁶ However, accounts by National Trust supporters and family members have often been designed to enhance its later mission rather than to explain its early years.

While biographical accounts of the three founders and their interests provide a useful framework for considering the National Trust's origins, they do not adequately explain how it came into being. To understand more

---

³ H. D. Rawnsley, *A Nation's Heritage* (1920); R. Fedden, *The Continuing Purpose: a History of the National Trust, its Aims and Work* (1968); J. Gaze, *Figures in a Landscape* (1988); M. Waterson, *The National Trust: the First Hundred Years* (1994); J. Jenkins and P. James, *From Acorn to Oak Tree: the Growth of the National Trust 1895–1994* (1994); G. Murphy, *Founders of the National Trust* (1987; new edn., 2002); A. Swenson, 'Founders of the National Trust (*act.* 1894–1895)', *ODNB*. See also G. Darley, *Octavia Hill: a Life* (1990), pp. 297–332; (rev. edn., 2010), pp. 277–94; L. W. Chubb and G. Murphy, 'Hunter, Sir Robert (1844–1913)', *ODNB*; B. Cowell, *Sir Robert Hunter: Co-Founder and 'Inventor' of the National Trust* (Stroud, 2013); E. F. Rawnsley, *Canon Rawnsley: an Account of his Life* (Glasgow, 1923). Studies of the National Trust's early years that place its origins in broader socio-political contexts include D. Cannadine, 'The first hundred years', in *The National Trust: the Next Hundred Years*, ed. H. Newby (1995), pp. 11–31; J. K. Walton, 'The National Trust: preservation or provision?', in *Ruskin and the Environment: the Storm Cloud of the Nineteenth Century*, ed. M. Wheeler (Manchester, 1995), pp. 144–64; M. Hall, 'Affirming community life: preservation, national identity and the state, 1900', in *From William Morris: Building Conservation and the Arts and Crafts Cult of Authenticity 1877–1939*, ed. C. Miele (New Haven, Conn., 2005), pp. 129–57; S. Gill, *Wordsworth and the Victorians* (Oxford, 1998), pp. 235–59; M. Hall, 'The politics of collecting: the early aspirations of the National Trust, 1883–1913', *Transactions of the Royal Historical Society*, vi (2003), 345–57; C. Judy, '"Unbroken towards the sea", the National Trust and the rise of coastal preservation in late nineteenth and twentieth century Britain', *Voices Novae, Chapman University Historical Review*, ii (2011), <http://journals.chapman.edu/ojs/index.php/VocesNovae/article/view/204/503> [accessed 1 Apr. 2012].

⁴ Fedden, *Continuing Purpose*, p. 6, described a founding 'trinity'; Cannadine, 'The first hundred years', p. 15, referred to a 'triumvirate'. The useful construct has been repeated in Gaze, *Figures in a Landscape*, p. 12; Waterson, *National Trust*, p. 14; Jenkins and James, *From Acorn to Oak Tree*, p. 1; Murphy, *Founders* (1987; new edn., 2002).

⁵ See esp. *Life of Octavia Hill as Told in Her Letters*, ed. C. E. Maurice (1913); *Octavia Hill: Early Ideals, from Letters*, ed. E. S. Maurice (1928); E. M. Bell, *Octavia Hill* (1942); and W. T. Hill, *Octavia Hill. Pioneer of the National Trust and Housing Reform* (1956). For a broader discussion of the early works see E. Baigent, chapter 1 in this volume.

⁶ Fedden, *Continuing Purpose*, p. 6.

fully Hill's contribution to the trust, this chapter first considers the broader context of the organization's origins and then discusses Hill's involvement with specific properties, particularly Alfriston Clergy House, Long Crendon Court House, Brandelhow Park and Mariners Hill.

The emergence of the National Trust

The National Trust was among numerous small pressure and interest groups and voluntarist societies that emerged during the nineteenth century's later decades in response to extraordinary changes in social conditions and the historical environment brought about by industrial capitalism, urbanization and political modernization.[7] As Peter Stansky has observed, activists who joined groups were not only concerned with change, they wanted to do something about it.[8] Hill, who participated in several societies, was among them.

During the 1880s and 1890s the administration of British town and county government and social welfare underwent its most sweeping transformation since Tudor times.[9] The reforms had consequential effects on the landscape, compounding the radical change brought about by railway construction. New legislation made redundant the institutions and societies (and their ancient buildings) associated with earlier forms of welfare administration, while the London and county council reform acts facilitated changes to cross-county administration and hence road and reservoir construction. Simultaneously, the UK's domestic and international relationships were changing, notably in response to an increasingly powerful USA. In the face of so much transformation, the National Trust was among several new bodies and initiatives that helped to suggest new identities through commemoration, legislation, conservation and education. It sought to ameliorate change to the environment and encourage stability through preservation.[10]

The National Trust did not emerge in a vacuum. In 1910 George Shaw Lefevre (later Baron Eversley, Gladstonian Liberal MP, long-serving first

---

[7] G. Wootton, *Pressure Groups in Britain, 1720–1970* (Hamden, Conn., 1975), pp. 1–12, 75–91, 100–11; P. Stansky, *William Morris, C. R. Ashbee, and the Arts and Crafts* (1984), p. 1; H. Malchow, *Agitators and Promoters in the Age of Gladstone and Disraeli: a Biographical Dictionary of the Leaders of British Pressure Groups Founded Between 1865 and 1888* (New York and London, 1983); P. Levine, *The Amateur and the Professional: Antiquarians, Historians, and Archaeology in Victorian England, 1835–1886* (Cambridge, 1986).

[8] Stansky, *William Morris*, p. 1.

[9] Hall, 'Affirming community life', pp. 129–58.

[10] Cannadine, 'First hundred years', pp. 11–31; Hall, 'Politics of collecting', pp. 345–57; Hall, 'Affirming community life'.

commissioner of the Board of Works and a barrister) emphasized its emergence from the Liberal-leaning Commons Preservation Society (CPS), which he had helped to found in 1865.[11] He explained that several leading CPS members were important to the trust's foundation. They included Shaw Lefevre himself and James (later Viscount) Bryce, Gladstonian Liberal MP, regius professor of civil law at the University of Oxford, and ambassador to the USA (1907–13); both were presidents of the CPS.[12] The duke of Westminster, the National Trust's first president, was a member of the CPS's general committee, as was Octavia Hill.[13] (Sir) Robert Hunter was particularly closely involved with that society. An expert on law relating to common land, he served as its honorary solicitor and vice-president.[14] In 1884 Hunter first proposed a land-holding company that became the precursor of the trust and, with assistance from Bryce and Shaw Lefevre, circulated the idea to CPS members for comment.[15] In response Hill suggested calling this new venture the 'Commons and Gardens Trust', stressing the idea of a 'Trust' rather than 'Company' to bring forward its 'benevolent [rather] than its commercial character'.[16] From this suggestion, Hunter began to consider a 'National Trust', although it took another ten years for the idea to come to fruition.[17]

Between 1884 and the launch of the trust a decade later, Hill continued her engagement with the CPS, which also expanded its interest to the Lake District.[18] Canon Rawnsley, a Lake District vicar who was active in those campaigns, first announced a 'National Trust for places of historic interest and natural beauty' on 16 November 1893 at a meeting held in the CPS offices.[19] For several weeks, in a well-organized drive, publicized largely through the Liberal-leaning *Daily News*, Rawnsley and others had enlisted

---

[11] Lord Eversley, G. Shaw Lefevre, *Commons, Forests and Footpaths: the Story of the Battle During the Last Forty-Five Years for Public Rights over the Commons, Forests, and Footpaths of England and Wales* (rev. edn., 1910), pp. vi–vii. Eversley refers to the importance of the CPS's James (later Viscount) Bryce, C. Edmund Maurice (Hill's brother-in-law and the son of F. D. Maurice), and himself. Gaze, *Figures in a Landscape*, p. 12, notes the importance to the early National Trust of Hugh Lupus Grosvenor, first duke of Westminster.

[12] Hall, 'Politics of collecting'.

[13] CPS, Report of Proceedings, 1876–80 (1880), Loeb Design Centre, Harvard University, Cambridge, Mass.

[14] Cowell, *Sir Robert Hunter*, pp. 11–14; Bishopsgate Institute, London, Howell Collection Reports, 2.8, Commons and Footpaths Preservation Society, annual report (1908). The first page indicates that Hunter was a vice-president of the CPS by at least 1908.

[15] Murphy, *Founders*, pp. 101–2; Hall, 'Politics of collecting', p. 351.

[16] Hill, *Octavia Hill*, pp. 144–5; Murphy, *Founders*, p. 102.

[17] Murphy, *Founders*, p. 102.

[18] Murphy, *Founders*, pp. 73–98.

[19] 'A National Trust for Places of Beauty and Interest', *Daily News*, 17 Nov. 1893, p. 5.

support for a new body able to hold property as a 'National Trust' to be incorporated under the Joint Stock Companies Act.[20] An influential list of supporters including 'the Duke of Westminster, Lord Dufferin, Lord Rosebery [the prime minister], Sir Frederick Leighton, Professor Huxley, the Master of Trinity, Cambridge [Henry Montagu Butler], [and] Mr. Shaw Lefevre' was amassed and publicized.[21] James Hornby, provost of Eton College, Walter Besant 'and a number of others distinguished in art, letters or practical affairs' were included.[22] The prevalence of prominent Liberal names suggests political influence behind the scenes. Among this roster of men, 'Miss Octavia Hill' stood out for her gender.[23]

Press reports of the proceedings noted several properties recently for sale, indicating the types of property the National Trust might collect and their associations with poetry and painting. These included the Lake District estate containing the Falls of Lodore, painted by J. M.W. Turner, poeticized by Robert Southey, and described by Samuel Taylor Coleridge; and Grasmere, as well as areas near Snowdon's summit. Acknowledging that 'Local authorities can hardly be expected to help the public to preserve the beauty of its great pleasure grounds', the trust aimed 'to promote the preservation of places that are of value to the nation, on account of their natural beauty, their historic associations, or any other desirable quality'.[24] *The Times* urged the National Trust to educate 'the sight-seeing public' in the genteel art and practice of viewing.[25] Such accounts were regularly supplemented by letters from Hill, Rawnsley, Bryce and the duke of Westminster. From the outset the organization aspired to hold many properties, and it was a female philanthropist, Mrs. Fanny Talbot, a friend of Ruskin, Rawnsley and Hill, who provided the first. Her promised gift of Dinas Oleu, in Barmouth, a Welsh headland, was announced at the November meeting.[26]

Between November 1893 and July 1894, when the trust was officially inaugurated, much work was done behind the scenes: a provisional council was formed and public support engaged.[27] Preliminary publicity shows that Hill had already become the National Trust's public face: her name

---

[20] *Daily News*, 17 Nov. 1893, p. 5; 'The National Trust for Places of Historic Interest', *The Times*, 17 Nov. 1893, p. 9; 'Places of beauty and interest', *Huddersfield Daily Chronicle*, 22 Nov. 1893, p. 4.
[21] *Daily News*, 17 Nov. 1893, p. 5.
[22] 'The National Trust for Places of Historic Interest', *The Times*, 17 Nov. 1893, p. 9.
[23] *Daily News*, 17 Nov. 1893, p. 5.
[24] 'Places of beauty and interest', *Huddersfield Daily Chronicle*, 22 Nov. 1893, p. 4; 'The National Trust for Places of Historic Interest', *The Times*, 17 Nov. 1893, p. 9.
[25] 'The National Trust for Places of Historic Interest', *The Times*, 17 Nov. 1893, p. 9.
[26] Murphy, *Founders*, p. 107.
[27] 'The preservation of objects of natural beauty', *Daily News*, 17 July 1894, p. 3.

was constantly mentioned beside those of well-known politicians, cultural luminaries, and institutions and societies that had pledged support.[28] At the inaugural meeting, presided over by the duke of Westminster at his London residence, Grosvenor House, the initial resolution was proposed in two stages by Hill and Hunter supported by others.[29] Hill proposed the motion that the organization be able to accept gifts; Hunter proposed the next legal step.[30] Each founder played a role, undoubtedly co-ordinated to encourage confidence in the new organization's procedural methods. Hill represented the philanthropic principle, a broad outreach and public trust; Hunter represented legal acumen and reliability; while Rawnsley, the publicity man, gave a progress report of the National Trust's work to date. Marking transatlantic interest, he noted the successful New England precedent, the Trustees of [Public] Reservations (TPR), a landscape preservation society founded in Boston in 1890.[31] The fact that Hill presented one motion helped to distance the organization from the Liberal party; however, she was not necessarily privy to the backroom manoeuvrings that raised such high-level political support. When, at the meeting's close, the duke of Westminster declared 'Mark my words ... this is going to be a very big thing', he understood the political backing the initiative had received.[32] Hill's gender and, perhaps, her avoidance of high politics allowed her to say without the charge of sentimentalism that might have been levelled against men that, 'the inauguration of the ... Trust ... was due to the belief ... that man ... was enobled [sic] by beauty around him ... recalling a great past'.[33]

Hill and the National Trust's transatlantic links

Rawnsley's mention of a New England preservation society, the TPR, at the National Trust's inaugural meeting merits further explanation since Octavia Hill provides a link to it. Hill had an American following. Her correspondence confirms the trust's early co-operation with American social reformers and preservationists, while affirming her own involvement with it from its planning stages.[34] A November 1893 letter from Hill to Ellen Chase (one of her fellow workers in Deptford who had returned to her

---

[28] E.g., 'In trust for the people', *The Leeds Mercury*, 7 Apr. 1894, p. 4.
[29] Waterson, *National Trust*, p. 37; Darley, *Octavia Hill*, p. 280; Murphy, *Founders*, p. 103.
[30] It would be empowered to produce by-laws, 'The National Trust for Places of Historic Interest', *The Times*, 17 Nov. 1893, p. 9.
[31] *Daily News*, 17 July 1894, p. 3.
[32] Quoted in Waterson, *National Trust*, p. 37.
[33] O. Hill, 'Natural beauty as a national asset', *Nineteenth Century*, lviii (1905), 935.
[34] D. T. Rodgers, *Atlantic Crossing: Social Politics in a Progressive Age* (Cambridge, Mass., 1998), pp. 33–75.

home in Brookline, on the outskirts of Boston, Massachusetts) illustrates the complex and interwoven associations between the National Trust founders and the Boston area.[35] In the letter Hill related the 'unveiling of [James Russell] Lowell's Memorial at [Westminster] Abbey', to which she had been invited.[36] Lowell, the noted poet, Harvard professor and, from 1880 to 1885, America's popular minister (ambassador) to the court of St. James's, was an erstwhile Episcopalian and self-confessed Wordsworthian, who had dubbed the Lake District 'Wordsworthshire' for its associations with the poet.[37] Hill's letter describing the occasion exemplifies her and the National Trust's association with Anglicanism alongside topical interests in protecting the Lake District's literary landscapes, and Harvard University's cultural milieu. Hill met Lowell several times through Julia, countess of Ducie.[38] Lowell's Westminster Abbey memorial was one of several Anglo-American friendship-building initiatives taking place on the fringes of diplomacy during the 'great rapprochement' between the two countries in which literature and the Anglican church played important roles.[39] Comprising two windows, one of which illustrated his famous poem 'Vision of Sir Launfal' – a line from which was later inscribed on a seat commemorating Hill's mother – the Lowell memorial represented an extraordinary expression of friendship.[40] Hill much admired Lowell's 'greater poetry' and reinforced these connections with the National Trust.[41]

In her letter Hill also thanked Chase 'for [the most useful] report of Public Reservation [*sic*] of which Chase was a founder-member.'[42] Hill continued,

---

[35] E. Chase, *Tenant Friends in Old Deptford with a Preface by Octavia Hill* (1929). Long Hill, Beverley, Massachusetts, TRA Archive, 'Report of the Standing Committee to the Trustees of Public Reservations and their Associates', p. 12, lists Chase as founder member.

[36] Hill to Chase, 22 Nov. 1893, quoted in Maurice, *Life of Octavia Hill*, pp. 527–8.

[37] For Lowell's designation of 'Wordsworthshire', see W. Wordsworth, *The Poetical Works of William Wordsworth* (7 vols., Boston, 1854), unsigned 'Sketch of Wordsworth's life' (by Lowell), i p. xxxviii. For his associations with Episcopalianism, see Lowell to Charles Eliot Norton, 21 Sept. 1875, in *Letters of James Russell Lowell*, ed. C. E. Norton (2 vols., New York, 1894), ii. 148.

[38] Darley, *Octavia Hill*, p. 239.

[39] Arthur Penrhyn Stanley was prominent among those who organized such commemorations (see B. Perkins, *The Great Rapprochement: England and the United States, 1895–1914* (1969), pp. 130–7; Hall and Goldstein, 'Writers, the clergy, and the "diplomatization" of culture', in *On the Fringes of Diplomacy: Influences on British Foreign Policy, 1800–1945*, ed. J. Fisher and A. Best (Aldershot, 2010), pp. 127–54).

[40] *Boston Daily Globe*, 29 Nov. 1893, p. 10.

[41] Loch, 'In memoriam', pp. 220–1. Hill quoted 'Sir Launfal' in 'Natural beauty', p. 939.

[42] Hill to Chase, 22 Nov. 1893, quoted in Maurice, *Life of Octavia Hill*, pp. 527–8. For the TPR, see C. W. Eliot, *Charles Eliot, Landscape Architect* (Amherst, Mass., 1999), pp. 331–5, 753.

'Mr Rawnsley has taken up the idea of a similar trust; we are getting it up, and had a first meeting this month'.[43] There was already an association between the TPR's founders and those involved with the National Trust. The TPR founder was Charles Eliot, a young landscape architect and preservationist who was the son of James Bryce's friend, Charles W. Eliot, president of Harvard University. Charles Eliot was influenced by Bryce and informed by Hunter's 1884 proposal for a landholding society.[44] At Bryce's suggestion, Eliot had visited Rawnsley in the Lake District in August 1886, where they had discussed landscape preservation and national parks.[45] Rawnsley was already known to Chase's wider circle, including Charles Eliot Norton, Harvard University's professor of art history, a friend of Lowell and Ruskin, and Eliot's cousin. This group already supported each other's campaigns.[46]

Although Hill never visited the USA, her reputation and support base for voluntary philanthropic work inspired confidence that spread to Europe (as Astrid Swenson discusses in this volume) and to the USA. Preservation's transatlantic community was closely knit. In the USA, as in Britain, various interests intersected with preservation. These included settlement housing, women's education, often with an arts and crafts bias, and nascent planning initiatives. While some developed these interests as distinct professions, the approach of others has been likened to a 'civil religion' in which women played an active role.[47] Hill was among their role models. By 1894 Ellen Collins had founded a New York housing association on Hill's London model; the artist Mrs. Alice N. Lincoln established another in Boston following earlier, unsuccessful attempts to institute Hill's methods in the city.[48] An Octavia Hill Association in Philadelphia (founded in 1896) emerged from earlier housing initiatives organized by the wealthy philanthropists Hannah Fox and Helen Parrish.[49] They, like Ellen Chase,

---

[43] History of Hilly Fields, Lewisham <http://www.lewisham.gov.uk/inmyarea/openspaces/parks/Pages/hilly-fields.aspx> [accessed 25 July 2013]. The purchase was completed in 1896.

[44] Murphy, *Founders*, p. 101.

[45] Hall, 'American tourists', pp. 103–6.

[46] Carlisle, Cumbria Record Office (CRO), papers of the Lake District Defence Society, WDX/422/2/3, 'Proposal for a Permanent Lake District Defence Society', 1883, notes that Norton was a member; Murphy, *Founders*, pp. 82–7, 96, 121; Hall, 'American tourists', p. 107; H. Ritvo, *The Dawn of Green: Manchester, Thirlmere, and Modern Environmentalism* (Chicago, Ill., 2009).

[47] J. Lindgren, *Preserving Historic New England: Preservation, Progressivism, and the Remaking of Memory* (New York, 1995), esp. pp. 35–42; West, *Domesticating History*, esp. pp. 5–37.

[48] Darley, *Octavia Hill*, pp. 209–10, 222; S. Driscoll, 'Practical preservation in Philadelphia: the Octavia Hill Association 1896–1912' (unpublished University of Pennsylvania MA dissertation, 2011), pp. 1–2.

[49] Driscoll, 'Practical preservation', pp. 7, 27–9.

were among Hill's American fellow workers in London.[50] The Philadelphia Association remained in contact with Hill until her death, and presumably others did too; it seems likely that these groups regularly exchanged reports about their civic activities.[51]

Hill's leadership qualities and transatlantic status were acknowledged at Chicago's 1893 World's Fair, held the year before the National Trust's launch. Emily Janes, honorary organizing secretary of the National Union of Women Workers, in considering 'the associated work of women in religion and philanthropy', noted that:

> Women have followed the lead of Miss Octavia Hill as rent-collectors; they join local committees of the Charity Organization Society, they look after boarded-out children, they start girls' clubs, they become Poor-law guardians. Hardly a girl leaves some of our women's colleges – e.g. Cheltenham and Westfield – without interesting herself in some aspect of philanthropy. There are settlements of women-students under able guidance in Southwark, at Mayfield House, Bethnal Green, and at Victoria Park.[52]

They also engaged in preservation. The Women's Building in Chicago housed an exhibition on city planning; the Metropolitan Public Gardens Association (MPGA) award for open space work affirmed Hill's interest in preserving urban gardens.[53] An account in the popular American magazine *Harper's Bazaar*, written by women associated with the fair, linked Hill to Lady Dufferin and Princess Louise, both wives of governors General of Canada.[54] Such associations encompassed several intersecting interests. The women's husbands were well known for promoting national parks at Niagara Falls, and in the Rocky Mountains (created 1885); and Lake Louise, situated between Banff and Windermere, in Alberta, Canada, was named in 1881 to memorialize the princess.[55] Both Lord Dufferin and Princess Louise were National Trust presidents.

Sometimes associations between American and British preservationists came through family connections. The American society painter John Singer

---

[50] Driscoll, 'Practical preservation', p. 24.

[51] Driscoll, 'Practical preservation', p. 29.

[52] E. Janes, 'On the associated work of women in religion and philanthropy', in *Woman's Mission: a Series of Congress Papers on the Philanthropic Work of Women, by Eminent Writers. Royal British Commission, Chicago Exhibition, 1893*, ed. A. Burdett-Coutts (1893), p. 146.

[53] *Eleventh Annual Report of the Metropolitan Public Gardens Association* (1893), pp. 15–16.

[54] L. Whiting, 'A group of interesting foreign women', *Harper's Bazaar*, xxvii (1894), 34.

[55] M. Hall, 'Niagara Falls: preservation and the spectacle of AngloAmerican accord', in *Towards World Heritage: International Origins of the Preservation Movement 1870–1930*, ed. M. Hall (Farnham, 2011), pp. 34–6.

Sargent (then living in Chelsea), who was chosen to paint Hill's portrait (1898), as Elizabeth Heath describes in this volume, was a cousin of Charles Sargent, the TPR's representative to the National Trust. Hill's American supporters, mostly from Boston and Philadelphia, gave generously to the commission, which now hangs in the National Portrait Gallery, London.[56] An early aim of the trust was to form links with several North American city beautification societies and, it would seem, to establish 'national parks' of some description in the UK.[57] Between 1899 and 1901 Rawnsley and Ashbee both made fact-finding, fundraising and promotional tours to North America on the National Trust's behalf.[58]

The National Trust hoped its properties would prove attractive not only to Britons at home but also to those 'sons who, far away, are colonising the waste places of the Earth', and to Americans abroad.[59] American tourists and tour groups, often keen to see progressive social initiatives while visiting the land of their ancestors, were regular visitors to Britain. The trust's executive committee (of which Hill was a member) hosted a group of 'descendants of the Pilgrim Fathers' visiting 'their old homes' in 1896, and noted that 'in America, there is a strong and growing feeling for the preservation of those features of this country which, whether from association or from inherent beauty, go to make it interesting and inspiring'.[60] Americans had given so generously to the campaign to preserve Thomas Carlyle's Chelsea home as a museum in 1894 that the American ambassador was invited to chair its board.[61] The National Trust had raised funds for the house, C.R. Ashbee helped to restore it, and it came to the trust in 1938.

---

[56] Hall, 'Politics of collecting'; OHBMT Archive, WISOH, 2005.60, *Presentation of Miss Octavia Hill's Portrait, Grosvenor House, December 1 1898*, pp. 16–17. Subscribers included Mrs. C. R. Lowell and Misses S. and H., and Mr. R. T. Paine, from Boston.

[57] C. R. Ashbee, *American Sheaves and English Seed Corn* (1901), appendix for a list of affiliated American societies; M. Hall, 'American tourists in Wordsworthshire: from "national property" to "national park"', in *The Making of a Cultural Landscape: the English Lake District as Tourist Destination, 1750–2010*, ed. J. K. Walton and J. Wood (Aldershot, 2013), pp. 105–6.

[58] Hall, 'Politics of collecting'; R. W. Winter, 'American sheaves from "C.R.A." and Janet Ashbee', *Journal of the Society of Architectural Historians*, xxx (1971), 317–22.

[59] NTA, Interim Report of the Executive Committee (1896), pp. 12–13.

[60] NTA, Interim Report of the Executive Committee (1896), pp. 12–13.

[61] M. Hall, 'Plunder or preservation? Negotiating an Anglo-American heritage in the later nineteenth century in the Old World and the New: Shakespeare's birthplace, Niagara Falls, and Carlyle's house', in *From Plunder to Preservation: Britain and the Heritage of Empire, 1800–1950*, ed. A. Swenson and P. Mandler (Oxford, 2013), pp. 262–5.

The National Trust and political neutrality?

Nigel Bond, long-serving secretary to the trust, explained of its founders: 'it was their object ... to give confidence to *the nation* that the National Trust was going to do something nobody else was doing or was then capable of doing'.[62] The object he described demanded that the trust be seen as an unusual organization associated with three volunteers and as above party politics, yet in practice its ties to other establishment organizations and to the Liberal party were close. While it has become extraordinarily successful, the National Trust, with an initial membership of around 250, began as a small organization that required support from other more established groups and institutions, including one in the USA, as has been shown.[63]

The National Trust's initial strength lay in its council, which was responsible for its policies.[64] This body of forty-nine members demonstrated political and establishment influence and an interconnected network of influence. It included representatives of national institutions and established amenities societies, including the Royal Academy, the British Museum, the Society of Antiquaries and, of course, the CPS.[65] While the universities of England, Scotland and Ireland, and public schools were represented by their leaders, other National Trust council members had attended those institutions and sometimes continued to be professionally affiliated to them. Learned societies were well represented, and trust council members often belonged to several groups. The National Trust sought affiliations with a variety of other voluntary societies, as well as national institutions. Hill was active in several civic improvement societies that are often regarded as influential precursors to the trust. These include the CPS; the Conservative-led MPGA; and the Kyrle Society, formed by Octavia Hill's sister Miranda and examined by Robert Whelan in this volume.[66] All were represented on the National Trust's council, as was the Society for the Protection of Ancient Buildings (SPAB), founded in 1877 by William Morris, which made Hill an honorary member in 1897.[67] The TPR was represented by Charles Sprague

---

[62] OHBMT Archive, Ouvry papers (OU) 22 pt. 1 of 2, 1996.7.29 (8), 'Octavia Hill and open spaces, by Sir Lawrence Chubb, Mr Nigel Bond, and Mr Lionel Curtis', published by the Association of Women House Property Managers, London, speeches delivered by the association in the hall of the Royal Society of Arts, 13 June 1930, pp. 6–7 (my italics).

[63] Hall, 'Affirming community life', p. 138.

[64] Waterson, *National Trust*, p. 53.

[65] NTA, Acc 42/12, 'National Trust for Places of Historic Interest or Natural Beauty, Council (Provisional)' printed leaflet; National Trust, Interim Report of the Executive Committee (1896), p. 4; P. Venning, 'The first hundred years. National Trust and SPAB', *SPAB News*, xv (1995), 13.

[66] Malchow, *Agitators and Promoters*.

[67] Whelan, *Octavia Hill's Letters*, p. 393.

Sargent, director of Harvard University's Arnold Arboretum and professor of arboriculture.[68]

Hill's lack of political affiliation was important to her influential position. The council displayed a distinct Liberal presence. Some fifteen of its members were either Liberal MPs or Liberal members of the House of Lords; they included Bryce and Shaw Lefevre, as well as the leader of the new County Councils Association, Sir John Hibbert.[69] The duke of Westminster sat as a Liberal in the House of Lords. Several were also imperial federationists or members of Anglo-American societies, which enhanced the National Trust's American interests.[70] Hunter, 'a sturdy Liberal', was closely connected to Liberal party politics, helping to draft preservation legislation and being appointed solicitor to the Post Office under a Liberal government.[71] Rawnsley had Liberal leanings, and joined Cumberland County Council as an Independent Liberal in 1888–9.[72] The high-level influence wielded by the CPS members Shaw Lefevre mentioned helps to explain how so many powerful institutions came to be affiliated to a new society, as well as the National Trust's association with the Liberal party; in turn, the high level of influence represented on its council also helps to explain the trust's distinction from many other pressure groups.

In contrast to the many National Trust men with their clear and strong Liberal party links, Hill was politically unattached, as she carefully avoided partisan allegiance. Her presence thus suggested that the trust's national role was similar to that of the church or the monarchy: above the political fray. When the Society for Promoting Women as County Councillors (SPWCC) had sought to field candidates in the London County Council election (1888), Hill was among those pressed to stand, but she refused.[73]

[68] See H. D. Rawnsley, 'The National Trust', *Cornhill Magazine* (Feb. 1897), p. 245. For a list of council members, see National Trust, Report of the Provisional Council (1895), i; National Trust, Report of the Council (1896), p. i. M. Hall, 'Affirming community life', pp. 142–3. For Sprague Sargent's involvement, see Rawnsley, 'The National Trust' (1897), p. 246; *Proceedings of the Linnaean Society*, i (1926–7), 96–8 (obituary).

[69] Hall, 'Politics of collecting', pp. 350–1.

[70] J. Mackenzie, *Propaganda and Empire: the Manipulation of British Public Opinion, 1880–1960* (Manchester, 1984). It is noted on pp. 151–2 that important members of the Imperial Federation League (1884–93) included Lubbock and the dukes of Westminster and Argyll.

[71] Canon Rawnsley, 'A national benefactor – Sir Robert Hunter', *Cornhill Magazine*, new ser., xxxvi (1914), 239. Further information on Hunter's political views from Dorothy Hunter, quoted in Gaze, *Figures in a Landscape*, p. 20; also see, NTA, Acc 14, D. Hunter, 'Sir Robert Hunter, draft biography by Dorothy Hunter', pp. 47–73.

[72] G. Murphy, 'Rawnsley, Hardwicke Drummond (1851–1920)', *ODNB*.

[73] P. Hollis, *Ladies Elect* (Oxford, 1987), pp. 72–3, 303–17, 491; W. Stokes, 'Missing from the picture: women's initiatives in English local government', in *Women and Representation in Local Government: International Case Studies*, ed. B. Pini and P. McDonald (Abingdon and New York, 2011), pp. 95–8.

Hill, affiliated to both the Liberal-leaning CPS and the Conservative-inclined MPGA, helped to suggest that preservation was above party political interest or, at least, bi-partisan. During 1884 Hill sat on the Royal Commission on Housing at the request of Conservative prime minister Lord Salisbury, who knew her housing work and her opposition to state and municipal housing provision.[74] Salisbury's interest in Hill came, perhaps, partly from a sense of party obligation: her grandfather, Dr. Southwood Smith, had been supported by Conservative MP Anthony Ashley Cooper (later earl of Shaftesbury) when he was appointed commissioner on the first Board of Health.[75] Salisbury's personal endorsement of Hill undoubtedly helped to make the National Trust attractive to Conservatives who might otherwise have been wary of it, given its many more obvious connections to Liberalism. The relationship between party politics and preservation was mitigated and, perhaps, disguised by Hill, unenfranchised yet an active participant in public life through societies, as well as through her relationship with the ecclesiastical commissioners, for whom she had ably managed 133 houses in Deptford since 1884.[76]

The National Trust, Hill and the female public sphere

While women's presence in American preservation initiatives has been acknowledged, less attention has been devoted to their role in British preservation.[77] Their presence in the early National Trust was important, if sometimes shadowy. Hill in some ways epitomized women's role in the voluntary sphere, but in other ways was exceptional. Many of her female contemporaries who had time, skills and disposable income were active in voluntary work in organizations that focused on welfare, and which provided spaces where women could gain influence.[78] Hill was an

---

[74] J. A. Yelling, *Slums and Slum Clearance in Victorian London* (1986), pp. 13, 23, 31–5, 141.
[75] *Octavia Hill and the Social Housing Debate: Essays and Letters by Octavia Hill*, ed. R. Whelan (Bury St. Edmunds, 1998), p. 1.
[76] 'Ecclesiastical and Church Estates Commissioners for England', *Encyclopaedia Britannica*, 11th edn. (1910); C. E. Crowther, *Religious Trusts: their Development, Scope, and Meaning* (Oxford, 1954); K. Gleadle, *Borderline Citizens: Women, Gender, and Political Culture in Britain 1815–1867* (Oxford, 2009); S. Richardson, *The Political Worlds of Women: Gender and Politics in the Nineteenth Century* (New York, 2013), pp. 15–18, 155–6, 257–67; Darley, *Octavia Hill*, pp. 233, 240, 271, 305.
[77] P. West, *Domesticating History: the Political Origins of America's House Museums* (Washington, DC, 1999); M. Holleran, 'America's early historic preservation movement (1850–1930)', in Hall, *Towards World Heritage*, pp. 193–4.
[78] Richardson, *Political Worlds of Women*; S. Morgan, '"A sort of land debatable": female influence, civic virtue, and middle-class identity, *c*.1830–1860', *Women's History Review*, xiii (2004), 183–209; also Gleadle, *Borderline Citizens*, pp. 77–82.

exemplary figurehead, in part because she enjoyed a more secure position than did most contemporary female voluntary workers, who often 'enjoyed but borderline political status as their position could never be assured'.[79] Hill's position was buttressed by the national and international reputation she had achieved by the late nineteenth century.[80] Her presence as a role model encouraged the participation and financial contributions of many other women to the National Trust.

Hill's politically neutral presence and unusual social status received Queen Victoria's endorsement. The monarch invited her to the 1887 Jubilee celebrations in Westminster Abbey; in turn, the endorsement facilitated the participation in the National Trust of another 'exceptional' woman, HRH Princess Louise. As vice-president 1898–1902 and president from 1902, the princess buttressed the impression that the trust was above party politics.[81] Trust secretary Nigel Bond explained that 'from its earliest days, the Princess took a sympathetic and encouraging interest in the aims of the Trust. I believe [this] interest … was first aroused by her admiration of the work of Octavia Hill', particularly in the Kyrle Society, of which the princess was president, and housing.[82] When the question of the National Trust's presidency arose Princess Louise took the initiative, but it was Hill whom she approached. Hill recounted to her sister and mother 'The Princess was most kind, and really deeply interested in the National Trust work'.[83] 'She asked me whom we were going to make President and added, "I hoped you should ask me, I should really like to do more for the work, and I should like Lord Carlisle as Vice President"'.[84]

Fledgling volunteer organizations need volunteers. Hill engaged the support of her mother and sisters. She also mobilized her extensive network of women, named and unnamed, those 'devoted and steady fellow-workers'.[85] They included the self-effacing Harriot Yorke, Hill's loyal companion who served as trust treasurer from 1895–1924, and Paula Schuster, Hill's fellow

---

[79] Gleadle, *Borderline Citizens*, p. 59.

[80] For Hill's reputation, see Maurice, *Life of Octavia Hill*, p. 525; Swenson, chapter 9, this volume, and Baigent, chapter 1, this volume.

[81] N. Boyd, *Josephine Butler, Octavia Hill, Florence Nightingale: Three Victorian Women Who Changed Their World* (1982), pp. 118–19; NTA, Report of the Council, 1897–98 and 1902–3. The princess was marchioness of Lorne when she became vice-president, and duchess of Argyll when president. For Princess Louise and the Kyrle Society, see Maurice, *Life of Octavia Hill*, p. 317.

[82] Bond, quoted in Darley, *Octavia Hill*, p. 282.

[83] Hill to E. Maurice, in Maurice, *Life of Octavia Hill*, p. 553.

[84] Hill to Caroline S. Hill, quoted in Darley, *Octavia Hill*, p. 283.

[85] OHBMT Archive (OU), 22 pt. 1 of 2, 1996.7.29 (21), Hill, *LFW*, 1872, p. 11; also see Hill, *LFW*, 1894, pp. 361–2.

worker, who became a contributing member.[86] Hill maintained her network through her annual Letters to fellow-workers.[87] She also put her notable skills as a letter-writer to the service of the National Trust's preservation campaigns through the pages of the press, acting invariably as a voice for charitable, religious, voluntaristic community life, while Hunter and others expressed the legal and political aspects of the trust's work.[88]

Through her Letters, Hill led her fellow workers to the National Trust's campaigns:

> I am, naturally, deeply interested in the foundation of the National Trust for the Preservation of Places of Historic Interest and Natural Beauty. It gives for the first time a body able to hold such places for the nation, and, I hope, likely to treat them with taste and thought. It is delightful to think that one beautiful sea-cliff has already been given to them – a bit of British coast held in trust for the nation. Will there be more such gifts to record this time next year? Let us hope so; and let us resolve that we for our own part will not be wanting. It may not be given to us to make our offering by contributing to the purchase of land or building, but in some form, tangible or invisible, let us resolve that some sacrifice shall be made, some lasting gift devoted, by us, for our own dear England.[89]

As her mother Caroline Southwood Hill explained to American philanthropist and social reformer Georgina Schuyler, 'Her heart is chiefly interested just now in saving beautiful spots in England, securing them in their beauty for future generations'.[90]

Hill often took the lead in raising funds for properties and, as Sir Robert Hunter attested, her 'remarkable power of raising money was an invaluable means of supplying the means of action'.[91] Women provided the driving force in donating and fundraising for several properties. Following Fanny

---

[86] For Paula Schuster and Harriot (sometimes Harriet) Yorke, see Darley, *Octavia Hill*, pp. 200–2, 212, 242, 263–4, 266–7, 277, 279, 311, 332.

[87] For Hill's active correspondence, see *LFW*; Maurice, *Life of Octavia Hill*; Swenson, chapter 9 in this volume.

[88] Hill, 'Natural beauty', pp. 935–41; Hunter, 'Places and things of interest and beauty', *Nineteenth Century*, xliii (1898), 570–89.

[89] Hill, *LFW*, 1894, pp. 361–2.

[90] C. Hill to Schuyler, 28 July 1897, quoted in Maurice, *Life of Octavia Hill*, p. 539. Georgina Schuyler was the sister of Louisa Lee Schuyler, who had arranged publication of Hill's *Homes of the London Poor* in the USA in 1875, ahead of the London edition the same year, and an American edition of *Our Common Land* for the Associated Charities of Boston (1880). The sisters had connections to preservationists associated with the Trustees of [Public] Reservations.

[91] OHBMT Archive (OU) 22 pt. 1 of 2, 1996.7.29 (6), Commons and Footpaths Preservation Society, Proceedings of General Meeting, 7 May 1913, p. 10.

'Nobler imaginings and mightier struggles'

Talbot's example, Catherine Johns of Boscastle bought the Old Post Office, a Tintagel manor house, in 1896, and maintained it through sales of local artists' paintings before vesting it in the National Trust in 1903.[92] Hill described it as 'a picturesque fourteenth-century cottage' during one of her fundraising lectures.[93] In 1906, after a seven-year negotiation by 'enthusiastic guardian' of the village Mrs. Childers Thompson, the trust acquired Winster Market House, a testament to commercial and mercantile activities before the industrial revolution.[94] The dowager countess of Egmont donated Kanturk Castle, in County Cork, Ireland (1899–1900).[95] Beatrix (Potter) Heelis continued this trend, donating Lake District farms to the National Trust, notably the Monk Coniston estate (1930–1 and 1944).[96] Preservation empowered women in the public sphere, continuing a long-standing pattern of females becoming patrons of churches, schools, almshouses and the like.

The National Trust, Hill and the Church of England

Hill, Hunter and Rawnsley were all closely connected to the Church of England: at the time of the National Trust's launch, Rawnsley had just been installed as a canon of Carlisle cathedral; Hunter was a practising Anglican; and Hill, under the influence of Christian Socialist clergyman and theologian F. D. Maurice, had moved from her family's Unitarian background to the Church of England.[97] The three founders' denominational affiliation, tinged with natural theology, moral philosophy and an appreciation of Romantic poetry, informed their work and helped to influence the early trust collection. Hill's religious faith permeated her work for the National Trust. To her, it was founded on a 'creed' of 'securing ... the blessings of beauty'. Invoking the poet John Keats and her God, 'Our Father', she described their aim to 'preserve a thing of beauty to be a joy forever' as

---

[92] NTA, Minutes of the Executive Committee, March 1899, 29 Sept. 1899, Apr. 1900, May 1900, 9 Feb. 1903; SPAB, Twentieth Annual Report (1897), p. 63; NTA, Annual Report (1899), pp. 9–10, (1900), pp. 8–9; Hall, 'Affirming community life', p. 142.

[93] OHBMT, WISOH, 2005.48, 'Miss O. Hill's address on National Trust'.

[94] NTA, Annual Report (1906), p. 7.

[95] NTA, Annual Report (1900), p. 7. This property was transferred to An Taisce in July 2000 <http://www.antaisce.org/properties/kanturk-castle> [accessed 12 Apr. 2015].

[96] Waterson, *National Trust*, pp. 93–7; National Trust, *Properties of the National Trust* (1992), pp. 60–1. Heelis had helped the trust to acquire half of the estate in 1930–1; she bequeathed the rest on her death.

[97] When the National Trust was formed Rawnsley was vicar of Crosthwaite; he was installed as a canon of Carlisle cathedral in November 1893 (Murphy, *Founders*, pp. 88, 98). For Hunter's religious practice see NTA, Acc 14, D. Hunter, 'Sir Robert Hunter, draft biography by Dorothy Hunter', pp. 41–6, typed MSS. B. M. G. Reardon, 'Maurice, (John) Frederick Denison (1805–1872)', *ODNB*.

a freewill offering by those who are conscious of great blessings in their own lives, and of the manifold goodness of Him Who has created this wonderful world and has made England rich in historic memories which are recalled by the interesting buildings that have come down to us.[98]

Religion was an important and overlooked factor in the open spaces movement, as Elizabeth Baigent has argued elsewhere, and among the National Trust's early holdings are several buildings and monuments associated with Christianity's role in local and vernacular English life.[99] These include Alfriston Clergy House and Muchelney Priest's House (two village clergy houses); Sharrow Cross (a wayside preaching cross), Ripon; and Westbury College Gatehouse, Bristol, noted for its association with John Wyclif, who translated the bible into the vernacular language.[100] All of these buildings had become redundant to the Church of England but for Hill conjured imagined 'memories of a simple life long ago'.[101] For her, the communal act of volunteers uniting in preserving such locations as 'thankofferings' was as important to the nation's social welfare as was the recreational use of open space to health.[102]

Hill's relationships and personal endorsement by significant contemporaries within a 'small knot of cultivated people' (as William Morris defined preservationists) added to her credibility and almost iconic parochial persona.[103] Many of those with whom she associated were Christian (not all were Anglicans), and a religious culture permeated their thinking. She had acquired a quasi-religious status as a female in a predominantly male sphere (Ruskin called her 'the finest lady abbess you can have for London work')[104] and she brought that religious sense to the National Trust.[105] Her religious conviction was noted by her fellow worker Mary Lumsden, for many years a trust executive committee member, who witnessed that, 'Her religion, like her sympathy, ran deep'.[106] Thomas Carlyle, the 'sage of Chelsea', also praised her.[107] Hill's 'intense love of Nature' was partly

---

[98] Hill, 'Natural beauty', pp. 936, 939.
[99] E. Baigent, '"God's earth will be sacred": religion, theology and the open space movement in Victorian England', *Rural History*, xxii (2011), 31–58.
[100] Hall, 'Affirming community life', pp. 142–4.
[101] Hill, 'Natural beauty', p. 939.
[102] Hill, 'Natural beauty', p. 939.
[103] J.-M. Schramm, *Testimony and Advocacy in Victorian Law* (Cambridge, 2000), pp. 24–32; C. Miele, '"A small knot of cultivated people": William Morris and the ideologies of protection', *Art Journal*, liv (1995), 73–9.
[104] Quoted in Rawnsley, *Canon Rawnsley*, p. 29.
[105] Gleadle, *Borderline Citizens*, pp. 192–3, 216–24.
[106] 'A fellow-worker' [Mary Lumsden], *Edinburgh Review*, Apr. 1913.
[107] Darley, *Octavia Hill*, p. 139.

attributed to 'Ruskin's writings [in his] … quieter mood of reverence' and served further to associate her with the ideal of a 'natural citizen' in the mould of Wordsworth or Rousseau.[108] While for some 'nature' provided an alternative to religion, others still considered nature to be a manifestation of God's presence in the world and its proper management to the social good to be an indication of divine will.[109]

In a period when the relationship between 'identity, trust, and faith' was a topical indicator, Hill made her career in the charitable sector and was a recipient of philanthropy herself.[110] To acquire property the National Trust relied on donations. Hill brought a reputation for sound financial management and trustworthiness. She was careful never to appear to be extravagant, and her celebrity included a 'commitment to the virtues of frugality and economy'.[111] In addition to funding her housing work, her wealthy supporters established a trust for her personal provision in 1874, and this probably strengthened her sense of obligation to benefactors.[112] She was further supported by Harriot Yorke, whose lifestyle was similarly modest.[113] Hill's dependence on others and lack of personal extravagance brought an unusual degree of authenticity to her fundraising, enhancing her trustworthiness and sense of vocation. Her links to personal charity and religion enabled donations to the National Trust to be re-embedded in a context of existing charitable, philanthropic relationships. Lionel Curtis, a public servant associated with the Liberal party and Poor Law reform and an early trust supporter (he described himself as an honorary secretary), later articulated a general perception among her supporters of Hill's personal integrity: 'No one ever suggested or thought for one moment that Miss Hill in any of her projects had any personal or ulterior motive. Her aim was to better the conditions of the working classes, to which end she put the whole strength of her personality, clear sightedness, singleness of purpose, unbounded enthusiasm, and above all her great attention to detail'.[114] The combination of skills, modesty, faith and public reputation helped to inspire trust which, in turn, helped her to further those causes with which she was associated.

---

[108] Loch, 'In memoriam', ii. 219.
[109] Baigent, '"God's earth will be sacred"'.
[110] B. Maurer, 'The anthropology of money', *Annual Review of Anthropology*, xxxv (2006), 15–36, at p. 28.
[111] Murphy, *Founders*, p. 50.
[112] Darley, *Octavia Hill*, p. 147.
[113] Darley, *Octavia Hill*, pp. 200–2.
[114] Chubb, Bond and Curtis, 'Octavia Hill and open spaces', pp. 8–11; A. May, 'Curtis, Lionel George (1872–1955)', *ODNB*.

Alfriston Clergy House

Of some thirty sites which Jan Marsh identifies as being under investigation by the National Trust from 1895 to 1899, at least six were associated with the church.[115] The trust did not aspire to purchase them all but supported their preservation and conservation by various means, often in conjunction with the SPAB.[116] The first building it acquired was a thirteenth-century Clergy House in Alfriston, which the local vicar, the Revd F. W. Benyon, had drawn to the SPAB's attention in 1891.[117] In 1885, as the ecclesiastical commissioners modernized their holdings of medieval properties, the church authorities sought permission to demolish it.[118] The Clergy House is one of several buildings in the trust's initial portfolio that reflect its interest in rural parish life. To buy the property the National Trust needed approval from the lord chancellor (as patron of the living), the bishop of Chichester and the ecclesiastical commissioners.[119] That Hill already managed properties for the ecclesiastical commissioners doubtless helped its case.[120] As the commissioners 'knew of no means by which the Building could be transferred to the Trust other than by Purchase', active executive committee members (Hill, Hunter, Yorke, Hill's brother-in-law, C. Edmund Maurice, and John St. Loe Strachey) offered 'a nominal sum ... viz £10 or £20'.[121] Although the commissioners accepted £10, repairs to the dilapidated building amounted to £700.[122] The committee resolved 'That restoration means such work as may be necessary to the Preservation of the building with as little new work as possible'.[123] This approach helped to engender a sensibility of continuity which contrasted with more modern restoration principles.

Hill set to work raising funds and public awareness by undertaking lecture tours and writing to her friends and the press for support.[124] The

---

[115] J. Marsh, *Back to the Land: the Pastoral Impulse in England from 1880 to 1914* (1982), p. 57.

[116] Venning, 'The first hundred years', pp. 11–14.

[117] NTA, Report of the Provisional Council (1895), p. 5.

[118] <http://www.nationaltrust.org.uk/alfriston-clergy-house/history/> [accessed 9 Apr. 2015].

[119] NTA, Report of the Provisional Council (1895), p. 56; NTA, Minutes of the Executive Committee, 19 Feb. 1895, p. 250.

[120] Darley, *Octavia Hill*, pp. 233, 240, 271, 305.

[121] NTA, Minutes of the Executive Committee, 23 Apr. 1895. Strachey was editor of *The Spectator*.

[122] TNA, LCO 2/166, H. D. Rawnsley on behalf of the National Trust to the lord high chancellor, 20 March 1895.

[123] NTA, Minutes of the Executive Committee, 25 March 1895, p. 255, 9 Jun. 1896, p. 298.

[124] E.g., see Hill to Sydney Cockerell, 26 Oct. 1896, in Maurice, *Life of Octavia Hill*, p. 538.

Clergy House exemplified an antiquarian and a 'domesticated' approach to the past, then popular in Europe and the USA, in which houses were romantically regarded as witnesses to a nation's history and community by a process of association with and transference from their occupants' lives, enhanced by visual appeal.[125] At Alfriston the focus was not on a famous individual, but on generations of unknown clergymen around whom parish life had revolved. At an Oxford fundraising lecture Hill invoked a nostalgic vision, describing it as one of their 'small houses, steep in roof and gable, mellowed with the colour of ages, picturesque in outline, rich in memories of England as our ancestors knew it ... [a] prereformation clergy house nestled below the downs of Sussex'.[126] In more business-like fashion the National Trust's annual report explained that it was among the 'only old timber vicarages of the kind in England, if not the only one in the southern counties'.[127] Hill's desire for open spaces near to her housing settlements is well known. The Clergy House, close to the parish church and an ancient oak, fronted the village green. It represented rural, domesticated Anglicanism and an ideal of community life in which the vicarage, rather than a secular building, was the village's focal point. However, it proved easier to raise money for landscapes, as Hill explained to Rawnsley:

> Nothing comes in for it [Alfriston Clergy House], I wonder how it will be possible to start [work on] it again. We *can* hold our hand now, but it seems a pity. All my friends seem keener about beautiful open space, and of course Churchyard Bottom Wood is more urgent. – We don't seem to reach the antiquarians and artists. However it is a great point that walls and roof will stand weather.[128]

Questions of new functions for trust buildings arose at Alfriston Clergy House. The vicar's request to use it for 'parochial purposes' brought Rawnsley's response that, 'while they would possibly be willing under proper safeguards to favourably entertain any proposals ... for suitable use', they could not 'place the Trust under any legal obligation with reference to the future use

---

[125] S. Bann, *The Clothing of Clio: a Study of the Representation of History in Nineteenth-Century Britain and France* (Cambridge, 1984); H. Hendrix, *Writers' Houses and the Making of Memory* (New York and Abingdon, 2007); B. Anderson, *Imagined Communities: Reflections on the Spread and Origin of Nationalism* (2006). While attention has been paid to literary associations, the impact of houses with religious associations is less well considered.

[126] OHBMT, WISOH, 2005.48, 'Miss O. Hill's address on National Trust and preservation of Gowbarrow at Oxford', MSS. n.d. (*c*.1904); NTA, Report of the Provisional Council (1895), p. 5. For nostalgia and heritage see D. Lowenthal, *The Past is a Foreign Country* (Cambridge, 1985).

[127] OHBMT, WISOH, 2005.48, 'Miss O. Hill's address on National Trust and preservation of Gowbarrow at Oxford', MSS. n.d. (*c*.1904); NTA, Report of the Provisional Council (1895), p. 5.

[128] NTA, Acc 6/13 (copy), Hill to Rawnsley, 22 March 1897.

for the same'.[129] Hill sought a solution, proposing parish use under 'proper supervision' by trust members and thought a suitable activity in the Clergy House would be taking tea.[130] She had earlier managed Ruskin's experiment in bringing reasonably-priced tea to Marylebone's poor at 'Mr. Ruskin's Tea Shop'.[131] Tea-drinking, an unassailable symbol of British domestic life, featured in Hill's Southwark housing. At Red Cross Hall, Ellen Chase recorded, 'tea, coffee, warm drinks, cakes and oranges are sold and the hall becomes a bright drawing room for the neighbourhood and pleasant groups congregate at various tables and look at illustrated papers and books'.[132] Doubtless the National Trust's famous tea shops would have delighted her.

As the Clergy House was located 'about eight miles from Eastbourne', the National Trust suggested to its members that 'a visit to it forms a pleasant excursion for visitors to that town'.[133] The trust's sites were intended to attract individual tourists and organized groups including those from churches and Sunday schools, Christian associations such as the Young Men's Christian Association, mechanics' institutes and the professions.[134] At a time when religious and literary tourism were growing pastimes, Hill hoped their properties would attract the 'artist, naturalist, hard-worked ... smoke-grimed city dweller, workman and child'; the 'manual workers, the large multitudes of professional men, of shop-keepers, and of other dwellers in towns'.[135] As she explained, National Trust properties provided locations for a 'Saturday afternoon' or even a 'yearly holiday'.[136] Hill's tradition of arranging outings for her pupils and tenants offered a model for how prospective citizens could engage with national landscapes.[137]

---

[129] NTA, Minutes of the Executive Committee, 18 Feb. 1896, p. 283.

[130] SPAB, *Alfriston Clergy House*, Hill to Thackeray Turner, 2 March 1896.

[131] J. S. Dearden, *John Ruskin: an Illustrated Life 1819–1900* (Princes Risborough, 2004), p. 43; Darley, *Octavia Hill*, p. 180.

[132] R. Ray, *Under the Banyan Tree: Relocating the Picturesque in British India* (New Haven, Conn., 2013), pp. 53–96. Hill quoted in P. Clayton, *Octavia Hill, Social Reformer and Co-Founder of the National Trust* (Stroud, 2012), p. 19.

[133] NTA, Seventh Annual Report (1901–2), appendix A, p. 12.

[134] K. Hanley and J. K. Walton, *Constructing Cultural Tourism: John Ruskin and the Tourist Gaze* (Bristol, 2010), esp. pp. 167–70; Snape, 'The Co-operative Holidays Association'; M. Hall and E. Goldstein, 'Writers, the clergy, and the "diplomatization" of culture: sub-structures of Anglo-American diplomacy, 1820–1914', in Fisher and Best, *On the Fringes of Diplomacy*, pp. 127–54.

[135] OHBMT Archive (OU), 22 pt. 1 of 2, 1996.7.29 (21), Hill, *LFW*, 1904, p. 11; see also 'Trust for Historic and Beautiful Places', *Morning Post*, 17 July 1894, p. 2.

[136] OHBMT Archive, Ouvry Papers (OU), 2005 Box 2, WISOH, 2005.48. 'Miss O. Hill's address on National Trust and preservation of Gowbarrow at Oxford', MSS. n.d., p. 8; Hill, 'Natural beauty', p. 941.

[137] Chase, *Tenant Friends*, p. 14.

'Nobler imaginings and mightier struggles'

Figure 10.1. Alfriston Clergy House after restoration, photograph by C. R. Ashbee, c.1898.

For the Clergy House the National Trust sought suitable tenants to defray costs and oversee repairs (see Figure 10.1).[138] Its first tenant was SPAB member and art historian Sir Robert Witt.[139] The founders hoped the buildings would provide artistic inspiration as an extension of the Arts and Crafts education practised at Toynbee Hall.[140] Other tenants included Lionel Curtis, who recorded that he and 'The artist Max Balfour ... rented ... the Clergy House at Alfriston, where we often spent our weekends'.[141] C. R. Ashbee and his wife Janet honeymooned there in 1898.[142] Ashbee, a follower of Morris and Ruskin and a member of the trust's executive committee since 1896, had founded a Guild of Handicraft (1888) to which he apprenticed settlement 'boys' as he called them.[143] The couple stayed

---

[138] NTA, Report of the Council (1897–8), p. 5.

[139] Waterson, *National Trust*, p. 42.

[140] S. Meacham, *Toynbee Hall and Social Reform, 1880–1914* (New Haven, Conn., 1987).

[141] W. T. Hill, *Octavia Hill: Pioneer of the National Trust and Housing Reformer* (1956), foreword by L. Curtis, p. 14. In 1902 Balfour designed a window for St. Christopher's Church, Alfriston.

[142] F. Ashbee, *Janet Ashbee, Love, Marriage, and the Arts and Crafts Movement* (New York, 2002), p. 34.

[143] NTA, Executive Committee Minutes, 28 Apr. 1896. For Ashbee and Morris, see F. MacCarthy, *William Morris: a Life for Our Time* (1994), pp. 27–8, 195–6, 430, 454, 523,

there again at Easter, 1900, with several of the Guild, 'a fine roaring party ... eleven of us, and all in a holiday humour', as Janet Ashbee recorded.[144]

Hill, Ashbee and Long Crendon Court House

On his return from the USA in 1901, where he had been touring on behalf of the National Trust, C.R. Ashbee rented another of its buildings – Long Crendon Court House – for his Guild of Handicraft. The episode led to conflict with Hill, but helps to reveal the trust's and her own approach to their properties.

The National Trust acquired its second building, Long Crendon Court House, dating from about 1500, in 1899–1900 from another female benefactor, Lady Kinloss, together with All Souls College, Oxford, and the ecclesiastical commissioners.[145] Hill sought donations, describing it to Paula Schuster in a letter that highlights her personal engagement with sponsors:

> a beautiful place, which ... may inspire your sympathy ... a lovely old manor house, on a common, near Thame ... used for hundreds of years for the Manor Courts. It would have been pulled down but for the action of the National Trust which is purchasing the quaint old place. But to prevent its falling to ruin, and to render it usable, about £300 is needed ... at once, or rain and wind and decay will impair it.[146]

This time, parish use was assured:

> The top room, a large one, will be used as a Sunday School [as] there is no parish room in the village. The Rector, and member of Commee of course pay rent, but the initial cost must be met by donations, and few care to help about these lovely old places so I am anxious.[147]

A different model of use had been negotiated and the building was also to 'be always available for holding the Manorial Courts'.[148] As Hill explained to Miss Schuster, in addition:

593–6, 621; A. Crawford, *C. R. Ashbee: Architect, Designer, and Romantic Socialist* (New Haven, Conn., 2005), esp. pp. 19–20, 24–31, *et passim*; A. Briggs and A. Macartney, *Toynbee Hall, the First Hundred Years* (1984), pp. 34–5; Meacham, *Toynbee Hall*, pp. 45, 46, 82.

[144] KCC, Ashbee papers, CRA/1/6. Janet Ashbee in C. R. Ashbee, *Journal*, 'Easter at Alfriston 1900'.

[145] NTA, Minutes of the Executive Committee, 12 March 1900, 14 May 1900, 29 July 1899. All Souls and Lady Kinloss each asked for a nominal £5.

[146] CWAC, Octavia Hill papers, D Misc. 84/1/1, Hill to Schuster, 7 Apr. 1900 (Hill's abbreviations).

[147] CWAC, Octavia Hill papers, D Misc. 84/1/1, Hill to Schuster, 7 Apr. 1900 (Hill's abbreviations).

[148] NTA, Minutes of the Executive Committee, 12 March 1900.

'Nobler imaginings and mightier struggles'

Figure 10.2. Long Crendon Courthouse, Buckinghamshire.

> A member of our [General Purposes] Committee [Ashbee] will rent the rest of the house partly for his wife and himself to go down to, partly to use as a holiday home for London boys connected with his Art Classes. They will go in groups through the summer, fortnight by fortnight. – It is a <u>great</u> blessing to get these lovely old buildings into the hands of the Nat. Trust.[149]

Although Ashbee's perception of an 'Arts and Crafts' holiday came into conflict with Hill's model of recreation, as Astrid Swenson describes in this volume, her influence in establishing patterns of use prevailed.

During Whitsuntide 1901 Janet Ashbee recorded her enjoyment of the building: 'How cosy the low length of its roof makes one feel, with the great gothic chimney rising at the end – the chimney up which so many witches have flown. & plenty room for them you would say through that stupendous flue from the ingle nook!'[150]

---

[149] CWAC, Octavia Hill papers, D Misc 84/1/1, Hill to Schuster, 7 Apr. 1900 (Hill's abbreviations).

[150] KCC, Ashbee papers, CRA/1, Ashbee, *Journals*, viii (Jan.–July 1901), 79–81, Whitsuntide, Long Crendon Court House.

For Ashbee historic houses in rural settings provided an ideal location for a kind of communal life, which he saw as essential to co-operative relationships between craftsmen and trainees, that he sought for his Guild of Handicraft.[151] During their recent tour of the USA on the National Trust's behalf, Janet had explained their vision of establishing such a lifestyle in the country to a sceptical Henry Whitney in Boston.[152] The Ashbees and their visitors and artisan apprentices rode around the village on haycarts, shirtless and singing. They relished the idea that their Bohemian appearance and activities made locals think them 'queer folk in barefeet and sandals … faith healers and fortune tellers'.[153] One visitor, Beatrice Creighton, the bishop of London's daughter, found these antics unusual, telling Janet, 'I never did anything quite so mad as this before'; she wondered 'what my maiden aunts would say if I told them that we brushed our teeth out of the windows and that the front door opened into our bathroom!'[154] To Hill, herself a maiden aunt, the Court House was associated with law, order and 'Queen Katherine, wife of Henry the Fifth'.[155] Hill had developed clear policies about tenant behaviour in the houses under her management; tenants were to be respectful and law abiding or, if troublesome to the community, to be removed.[156]

A representational tussle ensued at Long Crendon for the use of the National Trust's buildings as either artistic or antiquarian resources, as well as over appropriate tenant use.[157] Ashbee, who saw the Court House as an inspirational workshop and exhibition space for the Guild of Handicraft, hoped that the American architect Frank Lloyd Wright would join them in the 'romantic little place'.[158] According to his wife, Ashbee planned to place six coats of arms above the chimney beam; four associated with the building's previous owners; 'a blank shield for the National Trust whose spurs are not yet won'; and another for his own Guild of Handicraft, 'whose reign began there today'.[159] Whether these were fittings rather than fixtures or were simply never made is not known as there is no evidence of them

---

[151] Crawford, *Ashbee*, pp. 99–105, 149.
[152] KCC, Ashbee papers, CRA/1/, Ashbee, *Journals*, viii, 16 Jan. 1901. See also Hall, 'Politics of collecting', pp. 345, 352–6; Winter, 'American sheaves', pp. 317–22.
[153] KCC, Ashbee papers, CRA/1, Ashbee, *Journals*, viii, 81.
[154] KCC, Ashbee papers, CRA/1, Ashbee, *Journals*, viii, 80.
[155] Hill, 'Natural beauty', p. 940.
[156] Chase, *Tenant Friends*, p. 9.
[157] O. Wetterberg, 'Conservation and the professions: the Swedish context 1880–1920', in Hall, *Towards World Heritage*, pp. 201–20.
[158] Quoted in Crawford, *Ashbee*, p. 102.
[159] KCC, Ashbee papers, CRA/1, Ashbee, *Journals*, viii (Jan.–July 1901), 79–81, Whitsuntide, Long Crendon Court House.

'Nobler imaginings and mightier struggles'

today.¹⁶⁰ Simultaneously Patrick Geddes (also on the trust council) was developing the aesthetic principle that local character was best conserved 'in active sympathy with the essential and characteristic life of the place concerned'.¹⁶¹ However, the building belonged to the National Trust, not the guild. For Hill, the Court House, 'used since the time of Henry V', was a historical record and its value was to carry 'the mind back to the days of our Fathers, and to that [past] out of which England has grown'; its ability to do so lay in its 'uninjured' state.¹⁶²

While Ashbee recorded his frustration with 'the obstinacy of a certain little old woman' who curtailed his activities, Hill, referring to Ashbee's general attitude, wrote to Hunter that 'I fear it has not been helpful either in America or here'.¹⁶³ Simultaneously, Ashbee left Long Crendon and resigned from the National Trust's Council over the 'quarrel', which he saw as entirely with Hill.¹⁶⁴ He was replaced as tenant by Sir Laurence Gomme, FSA, London County Council's chief administrative officer, with local family connections and a trust supporter whom Hunter described as 'an antiquary of high repute'.¹⁶⁵ Gomme's son Austin, who worked in Ashbee's architectural office, continued the restoration work.¹⁶⁶ Ashbee found Hill 'imperious', recording that when some of 'the boys' visited 'the new tenants of the ... little lady in the mushroom hat', they found 'that the dear old National Trust was still sticking in the mud'.¹⁶⁷ Perhaps Ashbee thought that some of his boys, especially the 'mad hatter', would seem undesirable tenants to Hill.¹⁶⁸ He later recalled how:

> the dear old Lady's way of ordering things grew to be intolerable – something akin to an English Govt. Department and a seaside lodging house land lady – and as one must leave a woman in command of the fixed and so certain

---

¹⁶⁰ I am grateful to local historian Eric Sewell for this information.
¹⁶¹ P. Geddes, *Cities in Evolution* (1915), p. 397. For Geddes and the National Trust, see Hall, 'Affirming community life', pp. 145–52.
¹⁶² OHBMT, WISOH, 2005.48, 'Miss O. Hill's address on National Trust'; Hill, 'Natural beauty', p. 939. Hill was speaking about National Trust buildings in general, not just Long Crendon Court House.
¹⁶³ KCC, Ashbee papers, CRA/1, Ashbee, *Journals*, ix (2 Aug. 1901).
¹⁶⁴ KCC, Ashbee papers, CRA/1, Ashbee, *Journals*, viii (Jan.–July 1901), 7 June 1901.
¹⁶⁵ NTA, Council minutes, 14 Oct. 1901. R. Hunter, *The Preservation of Places of Interest or Beauty* (Manchester, 1907), p. 15. Gomme founded the Folk-Lore Society, and was one of the originators of the Victoria County History of England (R. Gomme, 'Gomme, Sir (George) Laurence (1853–1916)', *ODNB*).
¹⁶⁶ Crawford, *Ashbee*, p. 217; N. Pevsner and E. Williamson, *The Buildings of England, Buckinghamshire* (1994), p. 446.
¹⁶⁷ KCC, Ashbee papers, CRA/1, Ashbee, *Journals*, ix (2 Aug. 1901), x (14 Nov. 1901).
¹⁶⁸ KCC, Ashbee papers, CRA/1, Ashbee, *Journals*, x, (Nov. 1901).

conditions, there was no other way out. The fact is she is getting too old, and she doesn't sympathise with or see what the younger ones are driving at.[169]

Lawrence Goldman in this volume describes how Hill failed to see what the younger ones were driving at in welfare reform: but whereas in welfare Hill was left looking 'too old', as Ashbee described it, in conservation matters hers reflected the 'authentic' approach favoured by the SPAB. At all events, at Long Crendon Hill's housing managerial style and an antiquarian ethos prevailed. Perhaps she pragmatically appreciated that fledgling organizations needed philanthropic and local goodwill. Her professional reputation for consistency and perseverance, and her concern with appropriate use of buildings and tenant behaviour was driven by her housing principles, by a more antiquarian sensibility, and by fundraising concerns. She explained her perspective to Paula Schuster 'One should follow the instincts of those who gave the money'.[170] Both Hill and Schuster had donated; Hill herself had been the largest single donor, having given twenty guineas.[171] She later mellowed, saying of the National Trust in 1911 'We are a body of many members … We have had no friction'.[172]

The Lake District: Brandelhow, Gowbarrow and Aira Force

The National Trust is known to many for its preservation (or conservation) of landscapes. Although preservation in the Lake District is particularly associated with Canon Rawnsley's efforts, Hill played an important role in promoting acquisitions there. Following Ruskin's death in 1900, the trust erected a 'simple stone … on Friar's Crag [at Derwentwater] where first he [Ruskin] learned the beauty of that nature he was to love as much and describe as eloquently', as Hill explained to an Oxford audience.[173] An appeal for the 100-acre Brandelhow estate overlooking Derwentwater raised sufficient funds for its purchase and Princess Louise (as the trust's vice-president) opened it as a park on 16 October 1902 during a rainstorm that blew away the marquee. As was customary, her husband, the duke of Argyll, spoke on her behalf. Describing the Lake District as England's 'national park', Argyll, an imperial federationist, associated the National Trust's work there with its work instituting national parks in Canada, saying it

---

[169] KCC, Ashbee papers, CRA/1, Ashbee, *Journals*, viii (Jan.–July, 1901), 117.
[170] CWAC, Octavia Hill papers, Hill to Schuster, 7 Apr. 1900.
[171] National Trust, *Sixth Annual Report* (1900–1).
[172] Hill quoted in Maurice, *Life of Octavia Hill*, p. 575.
[173] OHBMT, WISOH, 2005.48, 'Miss O. Hill's address on National Trust'. Hill's and Ruskin's well-known rift had been mended two years earlier.

should be preserved, not only for the people of this country, but for the inhabitants of the colonies, the great kindred nation on the other side of the Atlantic who in the future might resort here as the home of their leisure and as the place where they would enjoy what they had acquired by their labours.[174]

The princess's Canadian connections were useful to the trust's culturally federating mission.[175] Both Lord Dufferin and the duke of Argyll had helped to form national parks in Canada – Windermere, a new settlement in one of these, invoked associations with the Lake District where the trust aspired to promote a similar park.[176] Such an area would form, it was claimed, 'the finest national park in England'.[177]

The Lake District already attracted the Co-operative Holidays Association (CHA), founded in 1891–3 by Lancashire Congregationalist minister, the Revd. T. A. Leonard as an extension of the Home Reading Groups which had been based on Ruskinian principles.[178] Two years later Hill appealed for funds for the Gowbarrow Estate and Aira Force, also in the Lake District, once again invoking sentimental, artistic, literary and historical associations. As she explained in *The Spectator*, the estate 'commands views of lake, islands, and of the head of the lake which Turner has drawn for us … [where] Wordsworth wrote on this very land his poem on the daffodils'.[179] The appeal was successful and the National Trust acquired Gowbarrow as a park in 1906.

Hill's hills: the Kentish Weald

Hill was always 'on the lookout' for landscapes which might be preserved, as Ashbee noted in June 1900:

> I have been trying to get Octavia Hill to take up the Ruislip matter, and purchase the Kings' [*sic*, College, Cambridge] Forests to throw them into the Common. But the little old lady is either too busy, or hunting other game at present of a like nature. She said to me the other day, 'I am interested in this Ruislip idea of yours, because, curious as it may seem, I happen to be on the lookout for an open space to preserve.'[180]

---

[174] *The English Lakes Visitor and Keswick Guardian*, 18 Oct. 1902, p. 5.

[175] Cannadine, 'First hundred years', pp. 11–31; see also Hall, 'Politics of collecting', pp. 345–57.

[176] M. Hall, 'Niagara Falls: preservation and the spectacle of Anglo-American accord', in Hall, *Towards World Heritage*, pp. 57–90.

[177] Quoted in Rawnsley, *Canon Rawnsley*, p. 112.

[178] R. Snape, 'The Co-operative Holidays Association and the cultural formation of countryside leisure practice', *Leisure Studies*, xxiii (2004), 143–58.

[179] OHBMT, WISOH, 2005.59, 'Ullswater and the National Trust', *The Spectator*, n.d. press cutting.

[180] KCC, Ashbee papers, CRA/1, Ashbee, *Journals*, xiii (June 1900), 129–30.

Hill and her family ultimately acquired three hilltops for the National Trust on Kent's High Weald: Ide Hill, Toys Hill and Mariners Hill, where her generous, commemorative and poetical approach to preserved sites is best seen. They might be called 'Hill's hills'. She characteristically described each as forming

> a vantage ground for looking over what Rudyard Kipling calls the 'blue goodness of the Weald.' The blue of the Ashdown Forest range beyond the meadows and woods, seen across the near slopes of wild hyacinth, or meadow grass, the sight of sunset and moonrise, the free right to wander and to gather, spaces accessible to many a London worker on Saturday afternoon holiday is a possession anyone may be thankful to have helped to secure for now and the years to come.[181]

A stone seat on Mariners Hill dedicated in her mother's memory (see Figure 10.3) is inscribed with a line adapted from Lowell's 'Vision of Sir Launfal' – the poem illustrated in Lowell's Westminster Abbey memorial which had so impressed Hill at its unveiling; it reads, 'for never shall their aureoled presence lack'. The stanza, written to commemorate lives given in the service of the nation, reads:

> SALUTE the sacred dead,
> Who went and who return not. –Say not so! ...
> We rather seem the dead, that stayed behind.
> Blow, trumpets, all your aureoled presence lack ...
> They come transfigured back,
> Secure from change in their heigh-hearted ways,
> Beautiful evermore, and with the ray
> Of morn on their white shields of Expectation.[182]

Conclusion

Hill's position in the early National Trust reveals that she was in many ways an exceptional and unusual presence, recognized by her contemporaries in describing her as 'original'.[183] Her permanent contributions to the trust came through her fundraising abilities, her part in the choice of acquisitions, and her own gifts of landscapes. She was also a figurehead for a far larger female presence in preservation than is usually recognized, whose contributions this volume has helped to reveal. Her influence lent the trust a sense that theirs

---

[181] OHBMT, WISOH, 2005.48, 'Miss O. Hill's address on National Trust', pp. 8–9.

[182] James Russell Lowell, 'Ode recited at the Harvard commemoration, July 21, 1865', pp. 260–8.

[183] 'In memoriam: Miss Octavia Hill', pt. 2, *The Charity Organisation Review*, xxxii (1912), 122.

Figure 10.3. Stone bench to Caroline Southwood Hill, on Mariners Hill, Kent.

was a voluntary and communal mission of 'fellow-workers', rather than an enterprise; and her very presence helped to lift the organization above the party political fray. She remains a figurehead for many, continuing to exert an exemplary encouragement.

Hill's engagement with the National Trust was personal, familial and, to some extent, broadly inclusive. Her approach to preservation was influenced by her deep religious sensibility, tinged with a persistent natural theology and patriotism that saw selected historic buildings and landscapes as gifts from her God to be set aside for others and maintained as memorials. Appreciation of them would be guided by recollected poetry (she knew much by heart) and historical associations.[184] Hers was both an act of Christian faith and a deeply Romantic vision that incorporated a sense of the past into an understanding of the present and as a projection of hope for the future. For her, the trust's sites were locations, hallowed by memories of those she loved and others whose work she admired. Acquiring these locations for the trust was, for her, 'a great blessing'.[185]

---

[184] 'In memoriam: Miss Octavia Hill', pt. 2, *The Charity Organisation Review*, xxxii (1912), 120.

[185] CWAC, Octavia Hill papers, D Misc 84/1/1, Hill to Schuster, 7 Apr. 1900.

Octavia Hill and the National Trust

While Hill was not the only founder of the National Trust, nor was her understanding of the past's utility to the present unequivocally shared, she was an eloquent and persuasive spokeswoman for the organization. Explaining how the trust came into being, Hill evoked Ruskin's delight in 'the joy in beauty, in association [with] … the memories wh[ich] gather round things [and evoke] the thoughts of the past', continuing: 'The National Trust … has been formed for the definite purpose of preserving these sources of joy and inspiration'.[186] For her, its mission was to acquire locations where such memories were made and affirmed, personally and as a nation. Such a charge benefits from shared reference points, sensibilities and aspirations, which was not and is not always the case for preservationists. The trust has become a notable institution with a large and varied collection of buildings and landscapes. Its membership exceeds that of the nation's political parties; it is a very different organization to the one that Hill helped to found.[187] The early acquisitions that she helped preserve were invariably small-scale, rural and folkish. Memorials to her own sources of joy and inspiration, as well as to her desire to 'make her fellow-beings happier', they remain as an enduring impress of a remarkable personality.[188]

---

[186] OHBMT WISOH, 2005.48, 'Miss O. Hill's address on National Trust and preservation of Gowbarrow at Oxford', MSS. n.d., p. 1.
[187] Cannadine, 'First hundred years', p. 11.
[188] 'A fellow-worker' [Mary Lumsden], *Edinburgh Review* (Apr. 1913); Maurice, *Life of Octavia Hill*, p. 566.

V. 'The loving zeal of individuals which cannot be legislated for by Parliament': Octavia Hill's vision in historical context

11. At home in the metropolis: gender and ideals of social service

Jane Garnett

The closing image of John Ruskin's famous lecture, 'Of Queens' Gardens' is of Mary Magdalene coming upon Jesus in the garden, the closing words a plea for the exercise of queenliness:

> Oh – you queens – you queens! Among the hills and happy greenwood of this land of yours, shall the foxes have holes, and the birds of the air have nests; and in your cities, shall the stones cry out against you, that they are the only pillows where the Son of Man can lay His head?[1]

On 11 December 1864 Octavia Hill reported having had 'such a grand talk with [Ruskin], quietly, just before he went [to Manchester] to deliver the lecture'.[2] She was later to adopt his language in urging her fellow workers to 'take up the position of *queens*, as well as *friends*, each in her own domain'.[3] I want here to analyse in more detail than one usually sees the sort of influence exerted by Ruskin's ideas on Octavia Hill, relating it to that of her other acknowledged mentor, Frederick Denison Maurice. In doing so, I will suggest that the commonplace perception that she was, in a recent commentator's words, 'fiercely anti-theoretical'[4] needs some qualification, and that attention to the substance, not just the fact, of her theological seriousness opens up a more complex understanding of the gendered theory underpinning her ideals of social service. Octavia Hill's attention to the personal and the individual, and her mistrust of the state, which undermined her legacy in the welfarist heyday of the twentieth century, have made her more attractive to the politics of the recent past. But in both contexts more attention has been paid to her method and her organizational

---

[1] *The Library Edition of the Works of John Ruskin*, ed. E. T. Cook and A. D. O. Wedderburn (39 vols., 1902–13), xviii. 144.

[2] *Life of Octavia Hill as Told in her Letters*, ed. C. E. Maurice (1913), p. 217. Cf. her reported discussion about Greek myths with Ruskin in 1869 – especially 'the goddess of the air', the 'inspirer' – and his citation of what she described as 'curious parallel thoughts from the Bible' (Maurice, *Life of Octavia Hill*, p. 249).

[3] Hill, *LFW*, 1874, p. 38.

[4] K. Hughes, 'Octavia Hill and the values of the home', in *The Enduring Relevance of Octavia Hill*, ed. S. Jones (2012), pp. 117–23, at p. 117.

principles than to the depth of the convictions which drove her. Although a scholar in the 1980s could straightforwardly deplore her writing as 'dripping with Victorian piety',[5] contemporaries as well as early twenty-first-century post-secularists would take more seriously the religious framing of both her life and her theory of life. Furthermore, a related problem has been the tendency to take at face value nineteenth-century constructions of women as concerned with the concrete rather than the abstract,[6] and uncritically to accept binary gendered distinctions between the intellectual and the practical which were often framed for strategic rhetorical effect, and were rarely stable in the mid/late nineteenth century.[7] Albeit from a partial perspective, Octavia Hill's brother-in-law's preface to his 1913 edition of her life and letters already pointed to such a problem of stereotyping. Reflecting on recent controversy over Florence Nightingale, and the argument that too much sentimental talk about the 'lady of the lamp' had obscured recognition of her power of organization and practical reform, he observed: 'Perhaps twentieth-century hardness may be as blinding as nineteenth-century sentiment'. He feared that the risk in relation to Octavia Hill went in the opposite direction – that she might purely be remembered for her practical skills. Hence his desire to illustrate through publishing her letters Hill's quality of sympathy, and his citation of Samuel Barnett's comment that 'she brought the force of religion into the cause of wisdom and gave emotion to justice'.[8]

Although Octavia Hill's debt to Ruskin is well established, persistent and misleading reference is made to his *Sesame and Lilies* as a literal blueprint for confining women to a domestic sphere.[9] But as Ruskin

---

[5] P. Spicker, *Social Policy: Themes and Approaches* (1985), p. 39.

[6] E.g., see F. Prochaska, *Women and Philanthropy in Nineteenth-century England* (Oxford, 1980), pp. 133–4, 223; M. Brion, *Women in the Housing Service* (1995), p. 12; J. Lewis, *Women and Social Action in Victorian and Edwardian England* (Aldershot, 1991), pp. 24–82. An exception is E. Yeo, *The Contest for Social Science: Relations and Representations of Gender and Class* (1996). For different mid Victorian positions, see F. Power Cobbe, 'Female charity: lay and monastic' [reprinted from *Fraser's Magazine*, Dec. 1862], in *Essays on the Pursuits of Women* (1863), pp. 102–41, at pp. 107–8; and T. H. Buckle, 'The influence of women on the progress of knowledge', read to the Royal Institution, 14 March 1858, and published in *Fraser's Magazine* the following month.

[7] The contingency of such a distinction has been more broadly problematized and contextualized by historians and social scientists concerned with embodiment (see, e.g., C. Lawrence and S. Shapin, *Science Incarnate: Historical Embodiments of Natural Knowledge* (Chicago, Ill., 1998); and S. Mahmood, *Politics of Piety: the Islamic Revival and the Feminist Subject* (Princeton, N.J., 2005)).

[8] Maurice, *Life of Octavia Hill*, pp. vi–vii.

[9] Including by Hughes, 'Octavia Hill and the values of the home', p. 121. See, however, for different perspectives, *Ruskin and Gender*, ed. D. Birch and F. O'Gorman (Basingstoke

himself made clear in his 1882 preface to a re-edition of the essays, their message was to be understood by reading them alongside his radical critique of political economy, *Unto this Last*, as related demands for the profound transformation of the values of contemporary society.[10] The essays in *Sesame and Lilies* – 'Of kings' treasuries' and 'Of queens' gardens' – were equally concerned with the need to probe behind words' conventional meanings – those 'masked words droning and skulking about us in Europe just now',[11] masquerading as fact and misleading people into setting up false gods. Ruskin's critical weapon was to probe language, and to point to the ways in which apparently uncontentious and innocuous assumptions could be absorbed unthinkingly, and could then go unexamined, uncontested. From *The Political Economy of Art* in 1857 and *The Queen of the Air* in 1869 to his edition of Xenophon's *Book of the Household* in 1876, he constantly elaborated the metaphors of kingship and queenship, the household and the nation, in order to challenge these assumptions and to think holistically about economic, social and moral goods.[12] Ruskin's 'kings' treasuries' were to contain wisdom rather than gold, just as 'wealth' in *Unto this Last* was to signify life – not the headlong pursuit of money-making, into which was 'pour[ed] our whole masculine energy'. The original ending of 'Of kings' treasuries' prefigured that in 'Of queens' gardens': 'The treasuries of true kings are the streets of their cities'. The second essay builds rhetorically on the first – developing the metaphor of reading rightly to exploring *why* to read. The discussion is of the relationship between womanly and manly qualities, and of their true *correlation* rather than mere complementarity, in terms and language which were idiosyncratic rather than conventional. Ruskin's phrases – that woman's power 'is for rule, not for battle, – and her intellect … not for invention or creation, but for sweet ordering, arrangement, and decision' – are often cited reductively without what follows: that 'she sees the qualities of things, their claims, and their places', and that 'it would often be wiser in men to learn things in a womanly sort of way … and to seek for the discipline and training of their mental powers in such branches of study as will be afterwards fittest for social service'.

---

and New York, 2002), especially Dinah Birch's reprinted 1988 essay, 'Ruskin's "womanly mind"', pp. 107–20; *Sesame and Lilies*, ed. D. Epstein Nord (2002); and J. Garnett, 'Political and domestic economy in Victorian social thought: Ruskin and Xenophon', in *Economy, Polity and Society: British Intellectual History*, ed. S. Collini, R. Whatmore and B. Young (Cambridge, 2000), pp. 205–23, at p. 211.

[10] Cook and Wedderburn, *Works of John Ruskin*, xviii. 51–2.
[11] Cook and Wedderburn, *Works of John Ruskin*, xviii. 66.
[12] Garnett, 'Political and domestic economy', pp. 205–23.

'Nobler imaginings and mightier struggles'

Queenly power is power within the state 'to heal, to redeem, to guide, and to guard'. In a typically Ruskinian bit of etymology, the lecture moves to its culmination in defining 'lady' as 'loaf-giver', 'lord' as 'maintainer of laws', whereupon 'lady' is analogized with Christ in eucharistic imagery of the breaking of bread. The audience, provocatively gendered female in Ruskin's prose, is called upon to assume that Christ-like responsibility and agency, a point reinforced by the final focus on Mary Magdalene, the type of the repentant sinner and true believer, who goes to look for Christ and is the first to whom He reveals Himself after His death. Only by realizing such a role could a different spiritual and material reality be attained from the corrupted world in which foxes and birds find rest, but not the Son of Man – a condition transposed from St. Luke's Palestine to nineteenth-century London.[13]

Far from cosily conservative, this was richly allusive and intended to be radically challenging. It resonated with the theological emphases to which Octavia Hill was drawn in F. D. Maurice, especially his emphasis on divine order as constituted in the harmonious interdependence of the familial, the civil and the spiritual, and of Christianity as a reality which upholds one, rather than a set of dogmas which one holds. Maurice's lectures on *Social Morality*, given at Cambridge in 1868 and published in 1869, a sustained critique at one and the same time of atomistic individualism, Comtean positivism and Christian conventionality, drew attention to a faculty in the Greek 'intellect or imagination ... curiously combining the masculine and feminine qualities'.[14] His lectures counterposed this with medieval chivalric and Comtist worship of women which he saw as degrading the object of its idolatry. Characterizing domestic morality as not simply an integral part of social morality, but its starting point, he invoked the ideal of motherhood in distinguishing authority from dominion, and of fatherhood 'softened and deepened through notes of feminine devotion and self-sacrifice'.[15]

Maurice's penultimate lecture analysed the Sermon on the Mount, and addressed critics who considered it a counsel of perfection rather than a practical guide to ethics in that it encouraged indiscriminate almsgiving. Maurice's response was to affirm that it was the fundamental moral guide insofar as it encouraged people 'to acknowledge themselves to be like other men'.[16] The focus was thus more on the ethical understanding of the giver than on categorizing the receiver – in very similar terms to Octavia Hill's

---

[13] Cook and Wedderburn, *Works of John Ruskin*, xviii. 121–2, 128, 137, 138, 144.
[14] F. D. Maurice, *Social Morality: Twenty-one Lectures Delivered in the University of Cambridge* (1869; 1893), p. 48.
[15] Maurice, *Social Morality*, pp. 27, 41.
[16] Maurice, *Social Morality*, pp. 388–95, esp. 390.

distinction between 'people' and 'poor people'. She underlined the need to start with the desire of knowing the poor as people, without which it was impossible to help them appropriately, or to establish the right reciprocal interrelationship.[17] The issue here was not one of removing moral judgement, but of recognizing the risks of failing to train it on oneself. As Octavia wrote to her sister Gertrude in August 1858, discussing over-preoccupation with self, it was necessary 'to look at all, not as one standing aloof or above; but as fellow-worker, fellow-sufferer; to trace the same tendency to good and evil in oneself'.[18] The conclusion of Maurice's lecture referred to the 'passive or feminine character ... often ascribed to the Sermon on the Mount. It has been thought to discourage all the qualities which have been most conspicuous in heroes who have struggled for freedom; to commend the submission which is sought for by tyrants and paid by slaves'. He emphasized rather that it was expressly designed to create enduring courage, rather than the self-important, bragging spirit which passed for courage in the present. His rousing peroration asserted that

> The free and brave Spirit is the Spirit of charity and truth, the Spirit which fights in us with our selfishness; a Spirit which makes men feminine, if feminine means courteous, deferential, free from brutal and insolent pretensions; but which also gives women manliness, if manliness means the vigour to live for the cause of Humanity and die for it.[19]

This spirit was what underpinned Hill's calls for her visitors to give 'the greatest of all gifts you can make – that of yourselves, following in your great Master's steps, whose life is the foundation of all charity'.[20]

Although in practice most of her fellow workers were women, Hill called also for men to take on such responsibility, and in 1889, when addressing university extension students at Oxford, lamented the smaller number of male volunteers.[21] While she reckoned that women were particularly valuable as visitors, given their household training, and commended the combining of work within and outside the home, in fact much of what she said and published underscored *qualities* that contemporary social critics gendered female, especially using terminology given specific resonance by Ruskin – gentleness, courtesy, patience, hope, carefulness, accuracy – which could be applied to workers of either sex. The emphasis

---

[17] O. Hill, 'A few words to volunteer visitors among the poor', in O. Hill, *Our Common Land* (1877), p. 49.
[18] Maurice, *Life of Octavia Hill*, p. 112.
[19] Maurice, *Social Morality*, pp. 394–5.
[20] Hill, 'A few words to volunteer visitors among the poor', p. 61.
[21] O. Hill, 'A few words to fresh workers', *Nineteenth Century*, xxvi (1889), 459–60.

on building interrelationships between those living in different types of home was explicitly seen as a duty and a privilege for both sexes: 'men and women coming out from bright, good, simple homes, to see, teach and learn from the poor; returning to gather fresh strength from home warmth and love, and seeing in their own homes something of the spirit which should pervade all'.[22] In this respect, too, the model of Christ was fundamental. Thomas à Kempis's *Imitation of Christ* was an important point of devotional reference. In 1884 Hill wrote to her mother that she was poring over it (alongside the *Life of Frederick Denison Maurice*,[23] within which she noted a letter about his *Subscription no Bondage*, and Ruskin's 'Story of Ida'),[24] and never tired of it.[25] This text, multiple editions of which existed in the nineteenth century, was widely promoted as a model of spiritual discipline and sacrifice.[26] Matthew Arnold copied out the text 'Always place a definite purpose before you' in his notebooks each year for ten years;[27] the women's magazine *Mothers and Daughters* highlighted Thomas à Kempis's own qualities of endurance and patience.[28] Hill's regret, expressed in her 'Letter to fellow-workers' for 1874, that they had not taken 'as a rule, high enough ground to satisfy me' returned to the language of queenliness to embody this need for wider ambition – not aiming at perfection, but 'whether it can be well comprehended and

---

[22] O. Hill, 'The work of volunteers in the organisation of charity', *Macmillan's Magazine*, xxvi (1872), 441–9, at p. 449; cf. Hill, 'Amateur work', *Lend a Hand*, i (1886), 36.

[23] *Life of Frederick Denison Maurice, Chiefly Told in his own Letters*, ed. J. F. Maurice (2 vols., 1884).

[24] Maurice's pamphlet, published in 1835, was a contribution to the intense debate at that period on the status of subscription to the 39 Articles of the Anglican Church as a matriculation test at Oxford. Maurice's argument, consistent with his expansive and inclusive vision of Anglicanism, was that subscription should be seen as an educational device, not a test of faith. Such theological tests were modified in 1854 and abolished in 1871. Ruskin edited Francesca Alexander's *The Story of Ida: Epitaph of an Etrurian Tomb* (Orpington, 1883), a biographical memorial to a poor Florentine girl who died young. In his preface (pp. 4–5), Ruskin observed: 'The lives we need to have written for us are of the people whom the world has not thought of – far less heard of – who are yet doing the most of its work, and of whom we may learn how it can best be done'. Octavia Hill commented that, with its 'quiet undercurrent of unobtrusive feeling', it reminded her 'of the very early painters' work' (Maurice, *Life of Octavia Hill*, p. 451).

[25] Maurice, *Life of Octavia Hill*, p. 451.

[26] See W. van Reyk, 'Christian ideals of manliness in the eighteenth and early nineteenth centuries', *Historical Journal*, lii (2009), 1053–73, esp. pp. 1062–6 for discussion of gender in relation to the *Imitation of Christ* in a slightly earlier period.

[27] *The Note-Books of Matthew Arnold*, ed. H. F. Lowry, K. Young and W. H. Dunn (Oxford, 1952), for the years 1858–70; cf. M. Arnold, *Culture and Anarchy*, ed. J. Garnett (Oxford, 2006), editor's introduction, p. vii ff.

[28] C. Goslett, 'Papers for girls: Thomas à Kempis', *Mothers and Daughters*, ii (1893), 9–10.

persistently aimed at … all the kingdom is your own while you hold it, to make of it what good thing you can'.[29]

The relationship between the contemplative and the active, which *The Imitation of Christ* confronted, was one on which Octavia Hill constantly reflected, in ways which further complicate the assumption of her untheorized practicality. In February 1866 she wrote to her friend Mary Harris about the biblical models of Martha and Mary. Unsurprisingly, she observed that her pity and sympathy had always been with Martha, but she was very self-aware about both the difficulty of making time for quiet thought and the need to do so. She recognized that excessive preoccupation with detail could arise from pride – a 'lingering doubt whether God can really arrange the world without our help'.[30] This was a tension with which she wrestled, yet she did make time to look at pictures or draw plants, or to read and to discuss what she saw or read or sermons she had heard. Devotional attentiveness – a process of getting to the heart of things – had been cultivated by her work copying for Ruskin and imbibing his principle of learning to see rightly, both literally and metaphorically. Here Ruskin's example was both very practically active and contemplative. In 1880 she wrote to her sister about the work of Edward Clifford, an artist, author and Church Army evangelist, who travelled to India and Hawai'i to study and promote means of combating leprosy. She suggested that his discussions would be useful if they had the effect of showing 'people who are doing tangible good, or good less spiritual, that distinct teaching about God Himself [might] be needed', especially after a period of reaction against it – 'that I and many people need to be reminded of that deepest way of work', to cultivate it in themselves and look for it in others.[31]

Hill's scepticism about systems, especially those on a large scale, was not the product simply of a preference for personal and local relationships: it was rooted in the anti-systematic theology of Maurice, whose work was analogous to Ruskin's in its drive to expose the arrogance or unreflectiveness of parties or structures. As Maurice said:

> My business, because I am a theologian … is not to build, but to dig, to show that economics and politics must have a ground beneath themselves, and that society is to be regenerated by finding the law and ground of its order and harmony, the only secret of its existence, in God.[32]

---

[29] Hill, *LFW*, 1874, p. 38.
[30] *Octavia Hill: Early Ideals, from Letters*, ed. E. S. Maurice (1928), p. 92.
[31] Maurice, *Life of Octavia Hill*, pp. 397–8.
[32] *Life of Frederick Denison Maurice*, ed. J. F. Maurice (2 vols., 1884), ii. 137; cf. F. D. Maurice, *The Kingdom of Christ* (2 vols., 1853; repr. 1959), ii. 329.

'Nobler imaginings and mightier struggles'

Maurice's stress on the divine immanence underpinning social connection – on the finding of Christ on the streets of London – was inspiring to Octavia Hill. Just as Ruskin's radical focus on the meaning of words developed intellectual arguments against disembodied theoretical abstractions, so Maurice's theology appealed to the experienced reality of Christ's presence in terms which collapsed a trite distinction between theory and practice. When Hill observed that her principles of engagement with her poor tenants were not theoretical but worked out practically, she went on immediately to clarify the distinction she was making – that the principles were 'essentially living ... not mere dead rules'. What she was opposing was thus not the development of ideas (themselves rooted in moral and spiritual convictions), which should certainly frame activity, but theoretical nostrums elevated to (and frozen in) dogma, whether religious or secular.[33] As it did for Maurice, this principle underpinned both Hill's theology and her social ideals: the two were implicitly fused. At the end of an address on charity (delivered in the suburbs) arguing on the one hand for the sacrificial extension of the principle of Christian neighbourliness (the Sermon on the Mount's ethics) into London's East End, and on the other (contrary to some clerical practice) for the exemplification of Christian love as a blessing in itself, not as a bribe to get people into church, Hill cited a stanza from the prologue to Tennyson's *In Memoriam*. She put explicit stress on the last two lines to represent the culmination of the whole:

> Our special form of [God's truth], or application of it, may not commend itself to our neighbours. Do not let this disappoint us; let us with single-minded zeal try to get those neighbours to be and do what they see to be right, and then will be revealed to them gradually whatever form of truth they can comprehend and apply. They will help to form God's church, which is of many members: and if
> > 'Our little systems have their day,
> > They have their day and cease to be',
> we must remember that the words go on: -
> > 'They are but broken lights of Thee,
> > And Thou, O Lord, art more than they.'[34]

Hill's conception of friendship, which she juxtaposed with queenliness in her injunctions to fellow-workers, was mapped on to her understanding of her relationship with God. A long and very personal letter to Ruskin of November 1873, in response to his expressed reluctance to ask her for

---

[33] O. Hill, 'Blank Court; or, landlords and tenants', *Macmillan's Magazine*, xxiv (1871), 456–65, at pp. 458–9; cf. Hill, *LFW*, 1889, pp. 266–7.

[34] O. Hill, 'A more excellent way of charity', *Macmillan's Magazine*, xxxv (1876), 126–31, at p. 131. This address was reprinted in *Our Common Land*, pp. 63–87.

support, elaborated on the necessity for trust as a basis for the real sense of warmth and friendship which should in fact facilitate asking for help, as it would from God himself. She carried the analogy forward, embedding an ideal of human insight in the divine example in suggesting that Ruskin might have hesitated to ask her for help because 'The people who need to be asked are so dense and so useless, they can but clumsily follow one's expressed desire. How different are they who see all, know all, fulfil all with far, deep-piercing sight and swift action'.[35] Friendship was to be exercised among fellow-workers, as it should be between them and the poor whom they assisted. Here the concepts of wise rule and management interlocked with that of a reciprocal bond of fellowship, forged both in small acts of sympathy and courtesy, and in the realization that the gifts were not only given in one direction: in some cases, although support could be provided, 'in all-important things they do not need our teaching, while we may learn much from them'.[36] Hill echoed Ruskin in interrogating the terminology of 'landlady' and 'landlord', evoking rural estates where deferential rule embodied a two-way relationship of duty and trust between landlord and tenant. She characterized the joint principles of rule and friendship in her 'desolate little kingdom' in Marylebone in such terms – the duty owed by her tenants to her (above all in promptly paying rent) and the justice and patience owed by her to them, which alone could generate trust. As so often, she concluded her paper by underlining the divine model for 'cherishing human beings' and 'building up temples meet for Him to dwell in'.[37]

The anxiety about how best to maintain that connection, that spirit of fellow-workmanship, and to give it depth, was always present, and explains some of the twists of Hill's relationship with Ruskin. There were real tensions between the concepts of rule and of fellowship, especially between rich and poor, but even between friends of equal social standing. Both Hill and Ruskin were involved in the Charity Organization Society, and were aware of its dangers – the risks of mechanistic coldness and detachment – and the fact that injunctions against indiscriminate almsgiving could provide a cloak for selfishness and self-indulgence on the part of the givers. In response to Hill's 1869 address to the Social Science Association, Ruskin pushed for more consistency in setting out what he deemed to be principles they held in common – for her to be clearer and more combative about the fundamental Christian importance of charity in the broadest sense – as a spirit, an attitude of mind, which should issue in the gift not just of money

---

[35] Lancaster University, Ruskin Library Collection, L7, Octavia Hill to John Ruskin, 30 Nov. 1873.
[36] Hill, 'Blank Court', p. 461.
[37] Hill, 'Blank Court', pp. 458, 465.

but of time, care and sympathy.[38] The criticism of the wrong sort of giving should not inhibit more appropriate forms, or allow anyone the excuse not to give. As he suggested, she might have found herself expressing a more hard-line position for that particular Social Science Association audience, which would apply particular criteria of practicality.

In fact Hill's and Ruskin's preoccupations and concerns were very close at this point, each reflecting on ways of educating and refining their fellow-workers' consciences. When in 1877 Ruskin published correspondence with Hill, in *Fors Clavigera*, which exposed the fact she had advised a potential benefactor to decline donating to the Guild of St. George on the ground that Ruskin was hopelessly impractical, at stake were their respective reputations, influence and charismatic authority.[39] Both Ruskin and Hill believed in the power of example and personal connection, and a mutual fragility was present in their concern for that trust not to be broken, and for the underlying rationales of their projects not to be misunderstood. Nine years before, and clearly stung by the criticism, Hill had reported to Ruskin that Matthew Arnold had reproached her for having faith in machinery.[40] Her 'Letters to fellow-workers', although in a wholly different idiom, were in some respects designed to perform an equivalent function to Ruskin's serial production (1871–84) of *Fors Clavigera*, whose subtitle was *Letters to the Workmen and Labourers of Britain*. In terms both literary and personal, often highly metaphorical and allusive, Ruskin's work was designed to educate and to energize – to construct an ideal of fellow-workmanship.[41] Hill's letters were to pull together her diffused army of helpers, and to build a stronger support network through exemplifying progress and repeatedly exhorting appreciation of responsibility. For her, as for Ruskin, the letter form enacted a close and sometimes emotionally charged relationship. Ruskin reacted so sharply and so publicly in 1877 because Hill's criticism threatened to undermine the guild, support for which (mobilized through *Fors Clavigera*) had become emblematic of fellowship in Ruskin's inner community, itself a microcosm of wider social possibilities.

---

[38] Maurice, *Octavia Hill: Early Ideals*, pp. 179–81; Maurice, *Life of Octavia Hill*, p. 257; *Supplement to the Report of an Attempt to raise a Few of the London Poor without Gifts, being a Letter from John Ruskin M.A.* (1870). Hill's published essays and addresses of the 1870s certainly articulated this conception of charity.

[39] Cook and Wedderburn, *Works of John Ruskin*, xxix, letters 73–84.

[40] Maurice, *Octavia Hill: Early Ideals*, p. 177.

[41] *Fors Clavigera* was self-published and distributed through Ruskin's protégé George Allen, and its increasingly participative format was designed to reinforce subscribers' feeling that they were part of a common project.

For many mid Victorian male critics, challenges to the hegemony of values conventionally gendered male – competitiveness, military or commercial prowess, materialism, single-minded individualism – could give rise to the charge of futile effeminacy and sentimentality. Ruskin was both used to this and sensitive to it insofar as it implied that criticism was not an active and practical project. But he also played with gender categories to challenge and confront, sometimes deliberately casting his critical role in feminine terms in order directly to unsettle critical paradigms which accorded lower intellectual status to familial, domestic audiences.[42] For Matthew Arnold, too, the charge of developing an effete and over-refined concept of culture grew out of his critique of Hebraism's muscularity, and his privileging the 'feminine' qualities of the Indo-Germanic, Celtic and Catholic.[43] His essay on the function of criticism at the present time was designed to defend the critic as man of action, at the same time underlining the futility of action without thought.[44] Uncritical activity, restless busyness were all too characteristic of contemporary society, more particularly its Hebraic aspects. Octavia Hill defined the same 'curse of the time' as 'impatience';[45] she fought against it in her emphasis on training and the cultivation of understanding as a gradual and evolving process, which would in itself be socially and morally transformative. A frequent leitmotif was the significance of memory and association in consolidating fellowship. Her 'Letters to fellow-workers', acting also as the medium of memorialization, reinforced this point, positioning the everyday in an overarching sense of spiritual interconnectedness.[46] This, too, was grounded in her understanding of Maurice's theology, and his discussion of communion, which rejected what he saw as the limitations of Protestant notions of the eucharist as 'mere remembrance' in favour of a fuller conception of memory rooted in vital connection. He thus redefined and elaborated the Catholic concept of the *real presence* of Christ as a living sacrament linking the present and the past – those very near, who were at risk of being forgotten, as well as the far.[47]

---

[42] Cf. Birch, 'Ruskin's "womanly mind"'; and Garnett, 'Political and domestic economy', pp. 211–12, 218–19.

[43] M. Arnold, *Culture and Anarchy* (1869; Oxford, 2006 edn.), pp. 104–5, 155; *The Letters of Matthew Arnold*, ed. C. Y. Lang (6 vols., Charlottesville, Va. and London, 1996–2001), iv. 162–4, 199.

[44] M. Arnold, 'The function of criticism at the present time', [*National Review*, 1864], *Essays in Criticism, First Series* in *Complete Prose Works of Matthew Arnold*, ed. R. H. Super (11 vols., 1965), iii.

[45] O. Hill, 'Our poor', *Lend a Hand*, xii (1 Jan. 1894), 54–5, at p. 55.

[46] Hill, *LFW*, 1879, p. 115; 1888, pp. 247–8; 1890, pp. 291–2; 1903, p. 511; Maurice, *Life of Octavia Hill*, pp. 33, 535; Maurice, *Octavia Hill: Early Ideals*, pp. 31, 111.

[47] Maurice, *The Kingdom of Christ*, ii. 254–89; Maurice, *Octavia Hill: Early Ideals*, pp. 101–2. Cf. her reference to memories as Presences (thus capitalized) (Maurice, *Life of Octavia Hill*, p. 535).

The relationship between theory and practice, complicated by Hill's own controlling tendencies, was never straightforward. But it was important to her to reflect upon the inevitable but ultimately creative tensions, and to encourage others to do so. Here, as Ruskin suggested, lay the scope to move from the remedial to the radical cure of social evils – to assume queenly authority to 'feel the depths of pain and conceive the ways of its healing'.[48]

[48] Maurice, *Life of Octavia Hill*, pp. 348–9; Cook and Wedderburn, *Works of John Ruskin*, xviii. 115.

12. Octavia Hill, Beatrice Webb and the Royal Commission on the Poor Laws, 1905–9: a mid Victorian in an Edwardian world

Lawrence Goldman

Octavia Hill was a quintessential mid Victorian figure in her endeavours and social attitudes, whose continued involvement in the making of social policy into the early twentieth century demonstrates how far attitudes and outlooks changed in the seminal period from the 1880s up to the First World War. Her later career is studded with success and creativity; but in participating in the Royal Commission on the Poor Laws between 1905 and 1909, and in endorsing that famous investigation's Majority Report, she displayed an unchanging and, indeed, narrow-minded approach to problems of poverty and destitution.

Hill's opinions and approach form a fixed point that allows for an appreciation of the distinctiveness of social thought in the 1860s and 1870s and its supersession by new thinking in the Edwardian period. Explaining this intellectual development and Hill's relationship to it requires some discussion of changing conceptions of the state, and also of the role voluntary action played across the period. It will also entail examining the Royal Commission on the Poor Laws itself and a comparison between Octavia Hill and another commission member, Beatrice Webb. Most of this chapter, however, will focus on Octavia Hill's questions and comments. Drawn from the oral evidence taken by the commission, these present her in a less favourable light than recent discussions of her life and work have done, since they have largely ignored or glossed over many of her fundamental social attitudes.[1]

Historians have debated the extent of Victorian state interventions but have been hampered by non-agreement over the meaning of central concepts such as 'laissez-faire' and 'individualism'. The Victorians themselves were confused: according to John Stuart Mill in *On Liberty*, 'there is, in fact, no

---

[1] With the notable exception of the editor's own essay, e.g. see the laudatory contributions in *The Enduring Relevance of Octavia Hill*, ed. S. Jones (2012). For a more critical view of Hill, see R. Whelan, *Octavia Hill and the Social Housing Debate: Essays and Letters by Octavia Hill* (2000), p. 18.

recognized principle by which the propriety or impropriety of government interference is customarily tested. People decide according to their personal preference'.[2] It has been argued that the early interventions from the 1830s in public health, education and employment – factory regulation – undermine the idea that there ever was an 'age of laissez-faire'.[3] But those who have adopted a narrower definition of the term have argued for its continued relevance if it is accepted that there were some areas of national life, such as public health, which were never subject to its doctrines. Disease affected everyone, rich and poor, encouraging local authorities and then parliament to take measures from the early Victorian period onwards.[4] Other historians have noted a contradiction between the intention of some Victorian statutes that seemed consistent with active state regulation, and their implementation, which was sometimes irregular and unsystematic, giving the impression of an unregulated public sphere. In this view, 'laissez-faire' was the outcome but not the intention.

Chronological distinctions are also important. Most historians have accepted that state interventions were characteristic of the 1830s and 1840s, but have tended to take the view that laissez-faire was more evident at mid-century. Yet the most perceptive students of the mid Victorian decades have not concluded this was the age of the minimal state.[5] If laissez-faire was the 'default position' of central government, and the state would consider intervention only when local or voluntary action had failed, allowance was always made for exceptions. By the 1860s workplace regulation, so controversial in the age of the 'ten hours movement' in the 1830s and 1840s, was now widely accepted, even welcomed.[6] And the rhetoric of laissez-faire could not disguise a coercive state that did not hesitate to act against those who deviated from its norms, as is evident in the three Contagious Diseases Acts of the 1860s, which attempted to regulate prostitution and the treatment of venereal diseases in ports and towns with barracks, and which entailed negating the civil rights of any woman believed to be a prostitute.[7] The Habitual Criminals Act 1871 allowed known criminals to be apprehended on the slightest suspicion and demonstrated thereby how little

[2] J. S. Mill, *On Liberty* (1859; 1991 edn), p. 30.
[3] J. B. Brebner, 'Laissez-faire and state intervention in nineteenth-century Britain', *Journal of Economic History*, supplement viii (1948), 59–73.
[4] D. Read, *England 1868–1914* (1979), pp. 133–4.
[5] J. F. Harris, *Private Lives, Public Spirit: Britain 1870–1914* (1993; Harmondsworth, 1994 edn.), p. 196; W. L. Burn, *The Age of Equipoise: a Study of the Mid-Victorian Generation* (1964); O. MacDonagh, *A Pattern of Government Growth: the Passenger Acts and their Enforcement 1800–1860* (1961).
[6] B. L. Hutchins and A. Harrison, *A History of Factory Legislation* (1926), p. 167.
[7] P. McHugh, *Prostitution and Victorian Social Reform* (1980).

A mid Victorian in an Edwardian world

Figure 12.1. Beatrice Webb.

respect was accorded to libertarian arguments when defending property and moral good order.[8]

Mid Victorian Britain certainly reduced state interventions in matters economic and fiscal. A free economy was believed to be more productive and efficient than one which was subject to the protections and interventions

---

[8] M. J. Wiener, *Reconstructing the Criminal: Culture, Law, and Policy in England 1830–1914* (Cambridge, 1990), pp. 151–2; Harris, *Private Lives, Public Spirit*, p. 196.

of the state. All those who favoured free trade also argued that state intercession would assist one social group over another and so compromise the state's neutrality. And some of the governing elite's deeper-thinking members, whose confidence had been undermined by Chartism and the Anti-Corn Law campaign, recognized that to align the state with one or other economic interest ultimately risked the very stability of the state itself. But if this explains, to a large degree, why the Corn Laws were repealed in 1846, the age displayed no reluctance in appealing to the state as a regulator of the moral and social arenas.

Against this background, the mid Victorians turned reflexively to state action in three different contexts: to emancipate, to protect and, most significantly for Octavia Hill, to administer more efficiently. 'Emancipatory reforms', as they may be called, refer to those efforts by the state to equalize legal and political conditions as between classes, religious denominations and genders, and to create the conditions for unfettered economic competition. Examples include legal and political reforms to equalize the rights of Roman Catholics, non-conformists and Jews in the 1850s and 1860s, and also of women in the first Married Women's Property Act of 1870 which began equalizing property rights in marriage. By 'protective legislation' we should understand the Victorians' efforts to safeguard their material interests and enforce their moral code, often thereby stigmatizing, if not actually creating, social deviants who apparently threatened those interests. Penal reform in the 1850s and 1860s, for example, led to the widespread belief that a class of habitual criminals remained, beyond the reach of reformative penal discipline and prison regimes, who could be harried and cajoled without the time-honoured legal protections accorded to suspects.[9] But the most characteristic response was to improve the ways in which public administration was applied. The aim was to make public policy more efficient and expert, rather than extend the state's oversight into new areas or to tax more and spend the results on more extensive provision of social and educational support. There was no increase in the role the central state assumed, in other words, nor an increase in public expenditure, but the state was used to remodel institutions in accordance with new conditions, and this often entailed confrontation with traditional interests.[10] Boyd Hilton has summarized this high Victorian position:

> Legal improvements, constructive planning, permissive legislation and the efficient and systematic mobilization of private capital for philanthropic purposes,

[9] L. Goldman, *Science, Reform and Politics in Victorian Britain: the Social Science Association 1857–1886* (Cambridge, 2002), pp. 143–73.
[10] Goldman, *Science Reform and Politics*, pp. 266–7.

were expected to lead to improvements in society without any calls on tax and ratepayers' pockets or any un-British interference with individual freedom.[11]

In accordance with Peelite and Gladstonian orthodoxy, as it emerged in the 1840s and 1850s, reformers sought to construct an enabling framework of laws and institutions which would assist individuals to work out their own destinies.[12] This is where Octavia Hill fits in, of course, encouraging the use of private capital for small-scale, but exemplary, projects which might act as models for similar endeavours elsewhere – projects that expected a moral as well as a financial contribution from the tenants themselves, whose respectability was the condition for their residence and participation. Hill's approach was described thus by Henrietta Barnett in her biography of her husband, Samuel, who was one of Hill's closest collaborators and vicar of St. Jude's, Whitechapel and first warden of Toynbee Hall, the university settlement in the East End of London:

> Counting that the only method of improving social conditions was by raising individuals, she held that it was impertinent to the poor and injurious to their characters to offer them doles. They should be lifted out of pauperism by being expected to be self-dependent, and, in evidence of respect, be offered work instead of doles, even if work has to be created artificially.[13]

Hill's approach, and the mid Victorian consensus more widely, held until the 1880s when social problems were reconsidered in the context of a new view of the state and amid more challenging economic circumstances, a rise in class tensions, the rediscovery of poverty, and growing evidence that millions of Britons were simply unable to take advantage of the opportunities supposedly established by mid Victorian reforms. The research of Charles Booth in London, who was to be a colleague of Octavia Hill's on the Poor Law Commission, and of social investigators in other towns and cities, showed how many citizens lived in poverty through no moral fault of their own but as a consequence of low wages, poor health, sheer old age, or intermittent, casual labour. Moral regeneration, the goal of Hill's projects, simply was not relevant as a solution to poverty because immorality, back-sliding, bad habits and bad household management were not the causative problems. Moral and personal failings may have contributed but poverty was increasingly seen to have wider societal, structural and environmental causes.[14]

---

[11] B. Hilton, 'Whiggery, religion and social reform: the case of Lord Morpeth', *Historical Journal*, xxxvii (1994), 842.

[12] H. C. G. Matthew, *Gladstone 1809–1874* (Oxford, 1986), pp. 59–86, 103–48.

[13] H. Barnett, *Canon Barnett: his Life, Work, and Friends* (2 vols., 1919), i. 35.

[14] Goldman, *Science, Reform and Politics*, pp. 271–2.

'Nobler imaginings and mightier struggles'

A key battlefield where old and new conceptions of poverty clashed or, perhaps more accurately, moralistic and empirical approaches to deprivation did, was the famous Royal Commission on the Poor Laws and the Relief of Distress which sat between late 1905 and early 1909. Octavia Hill, in her old age, was a member.[15] She had previously given evidence to the Royal Commission on the Housing of the Working Classes in 1884, and the Royal Commission on the Aged Poor in 1893, as well as to a Select Committee of the House of Commons on Artisans' and Labourers' Dwellings Improvement in 1882.[16] She may be contrasted with the younger, radical Beatrice Webb, also a commission member, in order to appreciate how the understanding of poverty and its suggested remedies had changed.[17]

Of the commission's twenty members, six, including Octavia Hill, were Charity Organization Society (COS) members and their spokespersons were Helen Bosanquet, the society's leading theorist and publicist, and Charles S. Loch, its general secretary, although he was in ill-health by this time. Members also included leading civil servants, guardians of the poor and social investigators. The commission was exceptionally hard work for an elderly woman like Hill: in total, members visited some 200 Poor Law Unions and 400 Poor Law institutions, heard more than 400 witnesses and took in 900 statements of evidence. The resulting inquiry stretched to forty-seven volumes of Parliamentary Papers. In early 1909 Octavia Hill signed the Majority Report; Beatrice Webb (Figure 12.1), George Lansbury, later the Labour party leader in the 1930s, and two others signed a Minority Report.

Each of the two groups of commissioners in fact focused on a different subset of those who fell on the tender mercies of the Poor Law guardians: on the one hand, the able-bodied unemployed who could not find work, and on the other, the sick, the lame and the halt – the disabled, the chronically ill, the aged, young mothers, orphans and others unable to help themselves. Bosanquet and the majority focused on the able-bodied, the *un*deserving poor who should be made to work; the Webbs (for we must use the plural – Sidney Webb may not have been a commissioner but he co-authored the Minority Report with his wife) and their supporters focused on the many categories of the deserving and involuntary poor, arguing that, in considering the plight of these groups, it should be evident poverty was not a moral problem to be blamed on individual weakness, but a structural and environmental one with deep-rooted economic and social causes. As

---

[15] G. Darley, *Octavia Hill: Social Reformer and Founder of the National Trust* (1990; 2010 edn.), pp. 266–76.

[16] B. Webb, *My Apprenticeship* (1926), pp. 169, 224.

[17] J. Davis, 'Webb, (Martha) Beatrice (1858–1943)', *ODNB*.

Beatrice Webb put it, the research the commission undertook pointed 'away from bad administration as the cause of pauperism and towards bad conditions among large classes of the population as the overwhelmingly important fact'.[18]

The COS commissioners feared above all that indiscriminate public relief would create a permanent class of paupers and undermine the resolve of others to live honest lives of toil and self-support. Mrs. Bosanquet, who wrote much of the Majority Report herself, defended the role of organized private charity in public welfare, against the bureaucratic socialism of Beatrice Webb. The Minority, conversely, contending that a fifth of the London population died in workhouses and Poor Law hospitals simply because they had no other means of support or access to medical treatment, wanted to 'break up the Poor Law' once and for all, and address different problems by specific, targeted means. They called for a new public health authority to treat all sickness, including pauper sickness, outside the Poor Law, where the practice of good preventative medicine would prevail. They also advocated old age pensions and the humane treatment and education of pauper children under the existing Board of Education's auspices. As Beatrice Webb put it in 1907, playing on the image of old wine in a new bottle, 'Why not have the old thing standing and take the stuff out, drop by drop? – the sick first, and place them under the sanitary authority – then the children, placed under the education authority – then the aged – pensions – perhaps the unemployed and the vagrants'.[19] The Majority Report recommended thoroughly restructuring poor relief administration, but Beatrice Webb and the Minority Report signatories suspected that this would be only cosmetic change. In their view the Majority were suggesting ways of alleviating destitution but falling short of measures to abolish it altogether.[20]

The COS and its representatives on the Royal Commission exaggerated the problem of the unemployed; the Webbs, meanwhile, probably minimized their significance. But the Minority argued, presciently, for public investment and major capital projects to offset periods of cyclical unemployment and to mop up the able-bodied in productive labour – a novel and radical approach for the Edwardian period which became, after 1945, the social and economic orthodoxy that it remains to this day. The Minority were trying to think creatively about how to deal with the unemployed who fell on the parish, though in the absence of supporting economic

---

[18] Beatrice Webb's Diary (typescript version: <http://digital.library.lse.ac.uk/collections/webb> [accessed 15 Dec. 2015]) (hereafter BWD), 18 Jan. 1907, fo. 422.

[19] BWD, 10 Apr. 1907, fo. 436.

[20] M. E. Rose, *The Relief of Poverty 1834–1914* (1972), p. 45.

theory, for Keynesianism was more than a generation away. The Majority, on the other hand, were still essentially trying to deter them. They put their faith, as in the previous generation's administrative interventionism, in a new and better bureaucracy, so-called 'public assistance authorities'. They also 'envisaged the establishment in each area of voluntary aid committees composed of leading organizers of local charities. These, it was hoped, would work in close co-operation with the public assistance authority, and thus achieve the organized intermingling of public and private relief which the COS had been working for since the 1870s'.[21] The Majority favoured co-ordination of efforts, but were not prepared to support the interference in individuals' lives to the degree proposed by the Minority. It would be simplistic to characterize the Majority as backward-looking; but they were essentially still dedicated to making the Poor Law regime established under the 1834 New Poor Law work better in the context of primarily voluntary efforts to assist the poor. According to Beatrice Webb, on the contrary, the Minority had 'a philosophic basis in the whole theory of an enforced minimum of civilised life'.[22]

The Minority had expected a degree of public support and perhaps acclaim for their radicalism, but were disappointed when most of the attention and praise was reserved for the Majority. Beatrice and Sidney Webb and their supporters thus launched a famous two-year public campaign, from 1909 to 1911, under the auspices of the National Committee for the Promotion of the Break-Up of the Poor Law which they formed for the purpose.[23] The campaign ended in acknowledged failure, however, and the Poor Law remained intact for another generation.[24] In the event, the Liberal governments before the First World War chose to fight poverty caused by old age, low wages and unemployment by other means than the Poor Law and its reform – by introducing old age pensions, trade boards setting minimum rates of pay in sweated industries, and National Insurance from 1911. The problems in reforming the Poor Law administration were too great, and the workhouse stigma would have stuck to everything attempted in the name of the Poor Law, even a *reformed* Poor Law. Better to bypass it entirely by creating new welfare bureaucracies from scratch. In time the Poor Law *was* broken up, to be replaced ultimately by the strategy laid out in the 1942 Beveridge Report.

Beatrice Webb had been influenced by Octavia Hill in varied ways over three decades before the commission met. Indeed, Samuel Barnett once

---

[21] Rose, *The Relief of Poverty*, p. 45.
[22] B. Webb, *Our Partnership* (1948), p. 452; see also pp. 481–2.
[23] Webb, *Our Partnership*, pp. 422–91.
[24] Webb, *Our Partnership*, pp. 477–8.

told his wife that Miss Potter, Beatrice's maiden name, 'reminded him of Octavia Hill'.[25] In 1873 Beatrice's sister Kate had requested permission 'to take service under Miss Octavia Hill as rent-collector in East London', a request her parents acceded to two years later.[26] It was when staying with Kate in London that Beatrice Potter 'first became aware of the meaning of the poverty of the poor'.[27] Through Kate's employment, Hill herself was 'introduced into the [Potter] family circle'.[28] But Hill was a COS founder, which was part of a 'reactionary movement' as Webb later described it. To Webb the COS was 'my friend the enemy' – an interesting description – and 'one of the most typical of mid Victorian social offsprings'.[29] She granted that Hill and the society's other founders were distinguished by 'moral fervour and intellectual integrity'. However, she came to question the manner in which the society individualized poverty, placing responsibility for it on the shoulders of the poor, who were to be denied the financial support they needed more than anything else in favour of proverbial lectures on the efficacy of regular habits by one or other of the COS's agents.[30] Hill and her followers 'concentrated their activities on schooling the poor in industry, honesty, thrift and filial piety', and Beatrice Webb became contemptuous of 'the self-complacent harshness of doctrine of the COS'.[31] Working as a rent collector in the East End in the mid 1880s, she met Octavia Hill but once at the Barnetts' home and 'there was a slight clash between us' over the question of keeping careful tenant records. Webb thought this indispensable; Hill wanted action and less fastidiousness.[32] Beatrice criticized herself for her 'presumption' on the occasion, but two decades later she would be far less inhibited in dealing with doctrines she thought unsound, not to say immoral.

Historians have generally written their accounts of the Royal Commission from the progressive Minority's perspective, and have used Beatrice Webb's diaries for that task. Heavily excerpted in her second volume of autobiography, *Our Partnership*, the diaries provide a commentary on the commission's work and an insight into the arguments and divisions among the commissioners. Written in a forthright and also gossipy style, there is much ironic self-congratulation as she relates her petty triumphs over her

---

[25] Webb, *My Apprenticeship*, p. 183.
[26] Webb, *My Apprenticeship*, p. 63n.
[27] Webb, *My Apprenticeship*, p. 80.
[28] Webb, *My Apprenticeship*, p. 150.
[29] Webb, *My Apprenticeship*, p. 168.
[30] Webb, *My Apprenticeship*, p. 169.
[31] Webb, *My Apprenticeship*, pp. 177, 228–9.
[32] Webb, *My Apprenticeship*, p. 239.

benighted adversaries for whom she had little respect: as she confided at the very end of her account, 'If I ever sit again on a Royal Commission I hope my colleagues will be of a superior calibre – for really it is shockingly bad for one's character to be with such folk – it makes me feel intolerably superior'.[33] She was herself the cause of many a disagreement because she refused to be bound by committee work conventions and followed a highly independent line, both procedurally and intellectually. This included breaching the confidence of the commission by briefing friends and journalists. Arguably, this indiscreet and unscrupulous behaviour – both words that Beatrice used about herself – lost her several potential allies on the commission.[34] One of them told her that, because of her behaviour, her proposals were bound to fail.[35] Webb encouraged the commission's transformation 'away from being an enquiry into the disease of pauperism, into an investigation of the disease of destitution' – its widening, in other words, from the question of how to treat paupers to the problem of poverty itself.[36] On several occasions she explained that her real aim was not to contest points of detail over Poor Law administration workings, but to abolish the Poor Laws themselves, lock, stock and barrel. As she expressed it at the outset, 'my best work will be outside the Commission room … I will give my best thought, but scamp attendance'.[37]

Semi-detachment allowed her to consult far beyond the committee and to follow her own lines of enquiry, while also manipulating the commission over important points. She was, in her own account, aloof and indifferent, as well as 'comfortably and good-naturedly hostile'.[38] Having reached her own conclusions, she amused herself 'by promoting every dissension among [her] colleagues, backing up every proposal that separates one from the other'.[39] 'The game', she confided, 'is extraordinarily exciting'.[40] Octavia Hill is mentioned only rarely, although Webb sets her down as one of 'the COS party' and as a defender of the status quo.[41] Webb's real targets in debate were Bosanquet and Loch, the leaders of this faction, which confirms the impression to be gleaned from the many volumes of oral testimony taken by the commission: that Octavia Hill, at an advanced age, was not

---

[33] BWD, 15 Dec. 1908, fo. 528.
[34] BWD, 15 Sept. 1908, fo. 511–12.
[35] L. Radice, *Beatrice and Sidney Webb: Fabian Socialists* (New York, 1984), pp. 165, 169.
[36] Webb, *Our Partnership*, p. 369.
[37] BWD, 9 Jan. 1906, fo. 332; see also 17 July 1906, fo. 380.
[38] BWD, 10 Apr. 1907, fo. 438.
[39] BWD, 19 July 1907, fo. 454.
[40] BWD, 28 Sept. 1907, fo. 458.
[41] BWD, 8 Oct. 1907, fo. 460, 17 Feb. 1908, fo. 486.

a central figure in its deliberations, but was nevertheless a regular attender at its hearings (held in a Foreign Office room) who questioned witnesses relatively infrequently. When Beatrice Webb visited the commission's office in October 1908 and saw the Majority at work on their report, she described 'Miss Hill not intervening'.[42]

Questions and comments in a Royal Commission transcript have to be taken with care because the purpose of questioning is to unlock the views and experience of the witness for the commissioners' wider benefit, rather than to set out the questioner's opinions. Advocates must inevitably take positions in their questioning that they do not themselves hold but employ only instrumentally. That said, there is quite enough clear evidence of her views contained in Hill's questions and comments for us to form a firm impression of her undiluted attachment to the outlook she held half a century before, and of her unwillingness to open her mind to the evidence of new social research that the Royal Commission encountered.

We might start with her examination of Harry Quelch, who gave evidence in October 1906 on behalf of the Social Democratic Federation. The SDF was a *marxisant* grouping in London, formed in the 1880s, out of which many leaders of the organized labour movement were then emerging. Quelch was a village blacksmith's son and edited the federation's weekly paper, *Justice*, for two decades.[43] In these exchanges Hill made evident her strong attachment to the social policies and supposed achievements of the past. She vindicated the Poor Laws themselves by pointing to the diminished number over time of outdoor relief claimants per thousand of the population, the very aim of the 1834 system's architects: 'Surely as far as the objects of the Poor Law Commissioners of 1834 were concerned the very thing they wished, was it not, was to throw the people more on their own resources so that a large number should not have their wages supplemented by outdoor relief'. But this narrow view of the Poor Laws' efficacy – that they met their designers' financial and administrative aims – cut no ice with Quelch, who had quite other ways of assessing their 'success': 'That may have been their object', he replied, 'and as far as that was the object no doubt they have succeeded; but whether they have succeeded at the expense of the material well-being of those who were affected or not is, of course, another matter'.

Quelch made it clear that, in his view, 'the standard of housing general among working people in London now is lower than it was some years ago'. Her record and life's work called into question, Hill pointed to historic

---

[42] BWD, 16 Oct. 1908, fo. 518.
[43] J. Saville, 'Quelch, Henry [Harry] (1858–1913)', *ODNB*.

improvements in sanitation, which Quelch granted, and to the increase in living space now enjoyed by the working classes, which Quelch contested. Hill was not unnaturally convinced that 'the people are in better rooms and have more of them taking London as a whole, than they had certainly in my youth'. Quelch demurred: in his experience, 'the small houses in Bermondsey where [he] first lived when [he]came to London which would be fetching 9*s* or 10*s* a week then and which would be inhabited by two families now fetch 15*s* or 16*s* a week, and you will have three families living in the house'.[44]

In the knowledge that many paupers required medical, educational and social care, rather than the harsh regime of the workhouse, one group of witnesses before the commission advocated that public authorities assume genuine welfare functions. Faced with these arguments, Hill reiterated her lifelong attachment to the primacy of individual responsibility. Social order depended on personal endeavours and would be undermined by public welfare. Her most interesting opponent over these questions was one John Theodore Dodd, a barrister educated at Christ Church, Oxford, who for nearly ten years had been a Poor Law guardian in that city. Dodd was not opposed to the Poor Laws root and branch, but to their lamentable administration. He submitted a paper to the commission arguing for a better Poor Law medical service, removed from the hands of local boards of guardians, which in particular would reduce high infant mortality levels among the poor in general by providing medical relief including nutritional support for mothers and infants.[45] Hill understood the implication of Dodd's suggestions and rushed to defend a crude version of Victorian individualism:

> The whole assumption that lies at the root of your statement would be that you think these children would be better nourished and better attended to by a great State or parochial organisation coming in and feeding them and the mother, than they would be if you were merely to stimulate the energies and care of the parents? I suppose it is pretty clear that if that sort of thing were done, the parents would be relieved from a certain amount of responsibility?

Dodd agreed, leading Hill to carry on in the same vein:

> Surely one of the first things that the members of a family think about is the health of the mother and the children; if they have any good in them the first thing they care about is the food for them. But if they find a strong body

---

[44] Royal Commission on the Poor Laws and Relief of Distress (Parl. Papers 1909, xl), Appendix iii, minutes of evidence, 8 Oct. 1906 (hereafter RCPL), 25854–9.
[45] RCPL, 31–45.

coming in and supplying that food, surely you would withdraw one of the main stimulants to energy, and is that not a very serious consideration?

Dodd replied that 'you want to have your people well-fed to start with in order to make them energetic ... One of the reasons why you have so much pauperism now is that you have a large number of underfed people, and people who are not perfect and who are not physically healthy'. If the cause of poverty was ill-health, it was in the state's pecuniary, not to mention moral, interest to feed the young and the needy. But to Hill it was 'unnatural, inadvisable and undesirable ... that one of the very first duties of parents should be more or less taken off them by the State'. Reverting to her own experience, she claimed that 'the more charity, the more poor relief, the more State relief there is, the more money goes to the public house, and the idler the parents become'.[46]

Hill did not oppose charity in itself, of course, but only charity given to excess and in competition with thrift. In questioning Sir William Chance, she warmed to the idea of abolishing outdoor relief for paupers and replacing it with charity, believing that voluntary action could adequately replace public provision, that much less charity would be required than was commonly anticipated and hence, with less being expended, the number of recipients would fall, which was all to the good.[47] When she questioned the Revd. Bradley Hurt Alford, a long-term COS member who had extensive experience of ministering in poor London parishes, she focused – with approval – on the growing use that Poor Law authorities were making of local charities such as the Metropolitan Association for Befriending Young Servants and the Workhouse Girls' Aid Society. 'Our workhouses and schools ought to be more under the influence of volunteers', she opined, and the witness concurred.[48] But charity was inadvisable and could be positively destructive if it took away the need to be provident. In November 1906 Hill questioned two representatives from the London Hospital, the Hon. Sydney Holland and Mr. Ernest William Morris. Holland, afterwards second Viscount Knutsford, was the London Hospital committee chairman, an office he would fill for fully thirty-five years, making him one of the most notable hospital administrators and benefactors of that era. He had become a champion of progressive medicine when the 1889 dock strike took place, when, in defending the employers, he had first encountered ill-health in the East End.[49] Hill's questions focused on the contradiction between the

[46] RCPL, 25600–9.
[47] RCPL, 29380–5.
[48] RCPL, 31888–98.
[49] J. Gore, 'Holland, Sydney George, second Viscount Knutsford (1855–1931)', rev. P. Wallis, *ODNB*.

formation of a provident medical association, where people contributed to their healthcare by paying in regularly, and the parallel existence of free medical care provided by London hospitals, which she believed were undercutting the instinct to save and be thrifty. 'It is hardly possible, is it, for a provident system to attain any dimensions so long as there is an entirely free system going on: is that not so?', she asked.[50] Later, in questioning a Metropolitan Provident Medical Association representative, a Mr. C.H. Warren, she was exercised over competition from the Middlesex Hospital which had killed off a provident dispensary in nearby Marylebone.[51] She asked another witness if he saw 'any loophole of hope for the diminution of this vast number of free out-patients at hospitals?'[52]

It followed from this that, in the era of its creation, Hill was against the old age pension, at least in its non-contributory form. When she questioned Sir Edward Brabrook, the chief registrar of friendly societies between 1892 and 1904, she had a willing accomplice in making the case against state pensions, for they would undermine the role and the place of the friendly societies' movement in providing for old age through members' own contributions. Brabrook was the author of *Provident Societies and Industrial Welfare* (1898), 'the most comprehensive contemporary survey of working-class self-help institutions', and also of *Institutions for Thrift* (1905), 'a strong statement of his beliefs about the economic and moral advantages of self-help'. His opposition to non-contributory old age pensions was known and could be relied upon.[53] Brabrook and Hill thus agreed in favouring the 'thrift, energy and sobriety of the people ... themselves'. They also agreed that there was 'less tendency to look forward, except among the more self-controlled and energetic of the people'. They deprecated 'the general habit which is growing among the more careless of the working-people of rather hoping that something will turn up from the Government, or the municipality, or somebody else'.[54]

In a sensationalist style not unfamiliar to the tabloid journalism of today, Hill accused working-class Poor Law guardians of doling out relief to their friends and family. Referring to the abolition in 1894 of any qualifications for the office of guardian, she was concerned that 'guardians may now be drawn from a class which is really very closely connected with the pauper class', and hence that outdoor relief was being 'given in many cases to the

---

[50] RCPL, 32814–15.
[51] RCPL, 33728–30.
[52] RCPL, 35103 (the witness was Col. Emanuel Montefiore, medical committee secretary at the COS).
[53] P. Johnson, 'Brabrook, Sir Edward William (1839–1930)', *ODNB*.
[54] RCPL, 35308–12.

relations of guardians … that people are voting money to their own near relations'.[55] In a wholly conventional manner Hill was also concerned about drink, as her questions to a young Eleanor Rathbone showed. Rathbone was already at the centre of social work in Liverpool through her role in the Victoria Women's Settlement, and was the author of the 1904 *Report of an Inquiry into the Conditions of Dock Labour at the Liverpool Docks* that 'laid bare the inefficiencies as well as the hardships of the casual labour system'. In her questioning Hill was sure, and was evidently censorious, that Liverpool dockers consumed alcohol to help them work through physically demanding twenty-four-hour shifts.[56] In another hearing she blamed lunacy on drink, evidently unable to see that alcohol consumption might be a consequence as well as a cause of personal disability and mental handicap.[57]

When discussing the social stigma associated with the receipt of public relief, Hill displayed an almost wilful insensitivity to the attitude of men and women who, in Rathbone's words, 'will not apply for Poor Law relief, although their income is quite insufficient to bring up their families'.[58] The issue also came up in her exchanges with Percy Alden, the socialist-leaning, Liberal MP for Tottenham 1906–18. He had been warden at the Mansfield House settlement in Canning Town, West Ham for a decade after its foundation in 1891 and had published *The Unemployed. A National Question* in 1905.[59] Alden had submitted to the commission a paper critical of the Poor Law as 'not adapted to meet the needs of our present complex civilisation'.[60] Hill asked him if

> the thing which you call the stigma of poverty [is] the sense in people's minds that they have not, or their relations have not, made provision for themselves, and that therefore they are becoming a burden on their neighbours; or is it that they will not be sufficiently comfortably dealt with, and that they will lose their vote – because these are two very different things?

Alden replied that

> the real stigma is the feeling that they are being treated as persons who have disgraced themselves. That is where the real stigma comes in; they are regarded as people who are in disgrace, who have not deserved well of the community, and must be treated accordingly.

---

[55] RCPL, 29214–16 (evidence of Sir William Chance).
[56] RCPL, 83398–400, 11 Nov. 1907; S. Pedersen, 'Rathbone, Eleanor Florence (1872–1946)', *ODNB*.
[57] RCPL, 30113 (evidence of Mr. Thomas McKay).
[58] RCPL, 83417.
[59] M. C. Curthoys and T. Wales, 'Alden, Sir Percy (1865–1944)', *ODNB*.
[60] RCPL, 131.

When Hill asked subsequently whether the poor should be inculcated with the 'desire rather to be self-helpful and self-respecting men, supporting themselves and their families, than men having to come on other people for that support?', Alden replied in the affirmative, but with a significant addition: 'Yes, I think we wish to encourage that in everybody, rich as well as poor'.[61]

Hill thought it enough that British workmen's wages were 'fairly up to the wages in most countries'. The witness, in this case J. T. Dodd, applied another standard in reply: 'They are really in many cases not sufficient for the healthy life of the father, mother and children'.[62] The mounting evidence that poverty was caused by low wages in too many occupations had passed her by. The attempt by trade unions to raise wages, meanwhile, met with her veiled opposition. She dismissed the National Union of Dock Labourers, when examining James Sexton, its general secretary for nearly thirty years and later the Labour MP for St. Helens 1918–31, as 'simply an association for raising wages'.[63] Her questions, focusing on the benefits the union paid to its members in sickness and death, and for burial, suggest that she had more respect for the old craft unions and their provident functions, but little sympathy with the so-called 'new unions' of this period, organizing unskilled workers, with a more determined focus on wages.

One exchange in particular stands out as most revealing of Hill's approach to poverty in general and of her failure to understand, let alone assimilate, the implications of late Victorian and Edwardian research into its causes. It occurred during the questioning of a young R.H. Tawney, who had spent three years after Oxford at Toynbee Hall in Whitechapel, and who was then a temporary lecturer in economics at the University of Glasgow. While living in the city, Tawney carried on with social investigation, especially into the education of working-class children and the relationship of defective education to adolescent unemployment and casual labour.[64] He could see that the 'social problem' had to be solved when men were young or not at all. As he wrote to his close friend and later brother-in-law, William Beveridge, from Glasgow in April 1907, 'Personally when I survey the class of men who applies here [for relief] I am rather hopeless about doing anything with them now that they have grown up'.[65] From this early stage he advocated

---

[61] RCPL, 27892–97.
[62] RCPL, 25607–8.
[63] RCPL, 84382–5; G. A. Phillips, 'Sexton, Sir James (1856–1938)', *ODNB*.
[64] L. Goldman, *The Life of R. H. Tawney: Socialism and History* (2013), pp. 31–2.
[65] R. H. Tawney to William Beveridge, 13 Apr. 1907, quoted in J. R. Brooks, 'R. H. Tawney and the reform of English education' (unpublished University of Wales PhD thesis, 1974), p. 31.

raising the school-leaving age to at least fifteen and ensuring 'continuation education' for those leaving school at fourteen, none of whom should work more than thirty hours a week while they also learnt a skilled trade.[66] He presented a distillation of this research to the Poor Law Commission himself in 1907 in two papers, one on the problem of 'boy labour' in Glasgow and the other on the method of poor relief used in Strasbourg, which Tawney had investigated in person and found to be efficient and humane, without the stigma attaching to poor relief in Britain.[67]

Tawney's work in Glasgow centred on boys who left school at fourteen or younger, and were taken on in unskilled occupations as 'a messenger, a milk boy, or a van boy' throughout their adolescence, only to be sacked on reaching adulthood. Poorly educated and without skills, they were doomed to irregular, casual labour for the rest of their lives and were frequently pauperized. He was questioned intensively by Royal Commission members on both aspects of his research. The exchanges with Octavia Hill are almost more revealing about her attitudes than Tawney's.[68] She was incredulous that relief was offered in Strasbourg without reference to suitability and character. She also found it difficult to accept that boys were expendable in so many unskilled occupations: 'He leaves a place because he is tired of the job, or because he could not get on with the foreman, or because he wanted more money.' When Hill blamed casualization and unemployment on 'the want of discipline in the boy', Tawney countered that 'you cannot expect boys to rise above the average boy nature'. Hill praised the virtues of 'a loyal boy, a punctual boy, an obedient boy, a good-tempered boy and an industrious boy'. Tawney replied that 'the present conditions of workshop life tend to produce precisely the opposite type'. When she referred to unemployment as 'a personal thing', Tawney contradicted her: 'No, it is caused by the industrial system'. When she placed emphasis on 'the personal characteristics of the boy', Tawney blamed something much bigger: 'The general system degrades the whole class of boys, and puts an incentive in the way of all boys, good and bad, to make a mess of their lives'. Despite Tawney's arguments, she continued to believe 'that what these boys want is not so much industrial training as moral training'. These brief exchanges captured the essential difference between those wedded to the Victorian Poor Laws, who placed emphasis on individual responsibility, and those

---

[66] R. H. Tawney, 'The economics of boy labour', *The Economic Journal*, xix (1909), 517–37.

[67] R. H. Tawney, 'Unemployment and boy labour in Glasgow' and 'Labour exchanges and relief work in Strassburg', Royal Commission on the Poor Laws and Relief of Distress (Parl. Papers 1910 [Cd. ??] xlix), 329–46.

[68] Royal Commission on the Poor Laws and Relief of Distress (Parl. Papers 1910 [Cd. ??] xlix), 329–46, 96840–46.

who sought their reform, if not their total abolition, on the grounds that poverty was a social rather than an individual failing, the product of economic conditions and structures rather than personal weakness. Hill, however, was quite deaf to any but moralistic arguments.

It would be easy enough to ignore the doctrinaire and sometimes inhumane opinions that Octavia Hill expressed as a Royal Commission member in an assessment of her life. Her age, fatigue and perhaps also her unfitness for the intellectual task of reviewing and reforming a century of social legislation and administration might all, quite fairly, be used in her defence and the whole episode treated as a faintly embarrassing coda to an otherwise blameless life. But these exchanges are important to a full biographical appreciation of her, and also to the wider intellectual and social history of the half-century before the First World War, during which the attitudes (and also prejudices) Hill embodied were challenged and then surpassed by people of wider experience, deeper knowledge and more expert command of the economic and social facts of poverty, unemployment and ill-health.

We should note, in fact, that Hill was up against some notable and impressive opponents of the Poor Laws and of her whole political economy, whose answers often stretched her intellectually and demonstrated the limitations of her experience and outlook. Harry Quelch and James Sexton were famous autodidacts and seasoned leaders of the emerging labour movement. Eleanor Rathbone and R.H. Tawney would become two of the twentieth century's leading socialists, devoted, respectively, to the progress of public welfare and education. Percy Alden was at the centre of social work and social policy for half a century. There were many less well-remembered experts in public health, education, employment and Poor Law administration, such as J.T. Dodd, who gave back as good as they got from Hill. In comparing her to Beatrice Webb, meanwhile, we pitch a mid Victorian sensibility focused on limited government, philanthropy and exemplary, private initiatives against one of the leading late Victorian intellectuals, whose life was dedicated to revealing the inadequacies of such a world-view and such expedients. The division between Octavia Hill and Beatrice Webb over the reform of the Poor Law is instructive, therefore – if not as a turning point in itself, then as a signpost to modern welfare without moralism, its universality in contrast to the sharp mid Victorian distinctions between the deserving and undeserving, the reclaimable and the irreclaimable, the respectable and the residuum, so called. But perhaps we should not exaggerate the differences between these two reformers of different generations, and note also that Octavia Hill was a formative influence on many young women of the 1870s and 1880s, who through working for her were led towards social reforms of different types and of more radical impact.

A final point, and one not hostile to Octavia Hill, concerns matters of scale. Her good practice models in housing design, architecture, cleanliness and behaviour could reach and change the lives of thousands in the 1870s. But the focus of the next generation of Edwardian reformers was on the experience and life-chances of millions. In the 1880s Hill had about £70,000 worth of property under her management, and in the Edwardian period she was managing the dwellings of a few thousand people at most. Compare this with the £1,500,000 set aside for the London County Council's rehousing programme for London's poor in 1901–2. It is a twentieth-century triumph that Britain did manage, eventually, to build municipal homes for millions to live in; it is among the disasters as well that too much of this municipal housing was of poor design and alienating bleakness. The scale of Octavia Hill's projects, as well as their moral underpinnings, must have looked antique to Edwardian Fabians of the Webbian persuasion. But her insistence on good design, pleasant surroundings, community and close interaction between tenants and rent-collecting visitors has had to be rediscovered and reapplied in light of the manifest failings of brutal public developments that have bred crime and isolation. Hill's moralism has been out of favour for many decades but her style and her aesthetic are as crucial today as they were for the mid Victorians.

VI. Hill's legacy

13. 'Some dreadful buildings in Southwark': a tour of nineteenth-century social housing*

William Whyte

> *Miranda and I concocted a letter to the owners of some dreadful buildings in Southwark, which Miss J is ready to undertake, asking to have them put under her care. So we have sent that off; and it may bear fruit now or later. Then we finished the accounts of Gable Cottages, and despatched report of same. They are now complete! Then I settled about the painting of Hereford Buildings. We had an evening's work over Income Tax returns...*
>
> Octavia Hill to her mother, 28 April 1889.[1]

This typically breathless account of Octavia Hill's daily activities is just one of many that could be selected, almost at random, from her correspondence. With its combination of pointillist practicality and earnest enthusiasm, it goes a long way towards explaining her success – and her limitations. Such intensity of focus was often overwhelming, as some of her collaborators found out; but it also contributed to a narrowness of view, an inability – even unwillingness – to see the bigger picture. This short tour of little more than a mile is intended to illustrate some of Hill's work, the fruits of her remarkable energy and extraordinary punctiliousness. It also, however, juxtaposes her achievements with the work of others, including those that she condemned. As a result, we are better able to see what Hill would not, perhaps could not: that she was part of a much wider movement of housing reform which shared many of the same assumptions and much of the same architectural inspiration, even when their methods seemed radically to diverge.

Southwark was not, of course, where Hill's housing work first began. Nor was it the location of the largest projects undertaken by the other philanthropists of the period. Unlike many London councils, too, the Borough of Southwark built no accommodation of its own. Nonetheless,

---

* I am profoundly grateful to Zoë Waxman for her advice and close reading, and to Sue Killoran of Harris Manchester College, Oxford, Jane Ramsay of the Camden History Society, and Christine Wagg of the Peabody Trust for their help with my research.

[1] C. E. Maurice, *The Life of Octavia Hill as Told in her Letters* (1913), p. 501.

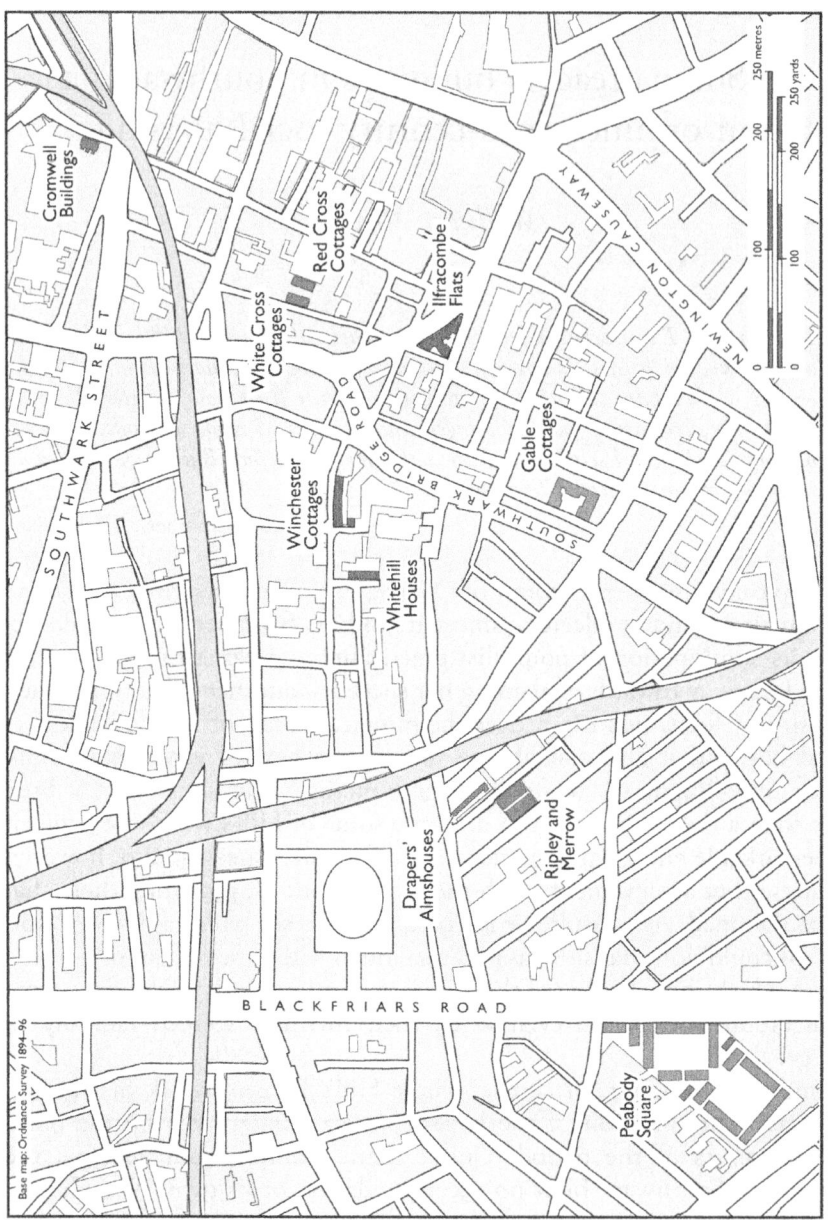

Figure 13.1. Map of Southwark, based on the Ordnance Survey of 1894–96.

A tour of nineteenth-century social housing

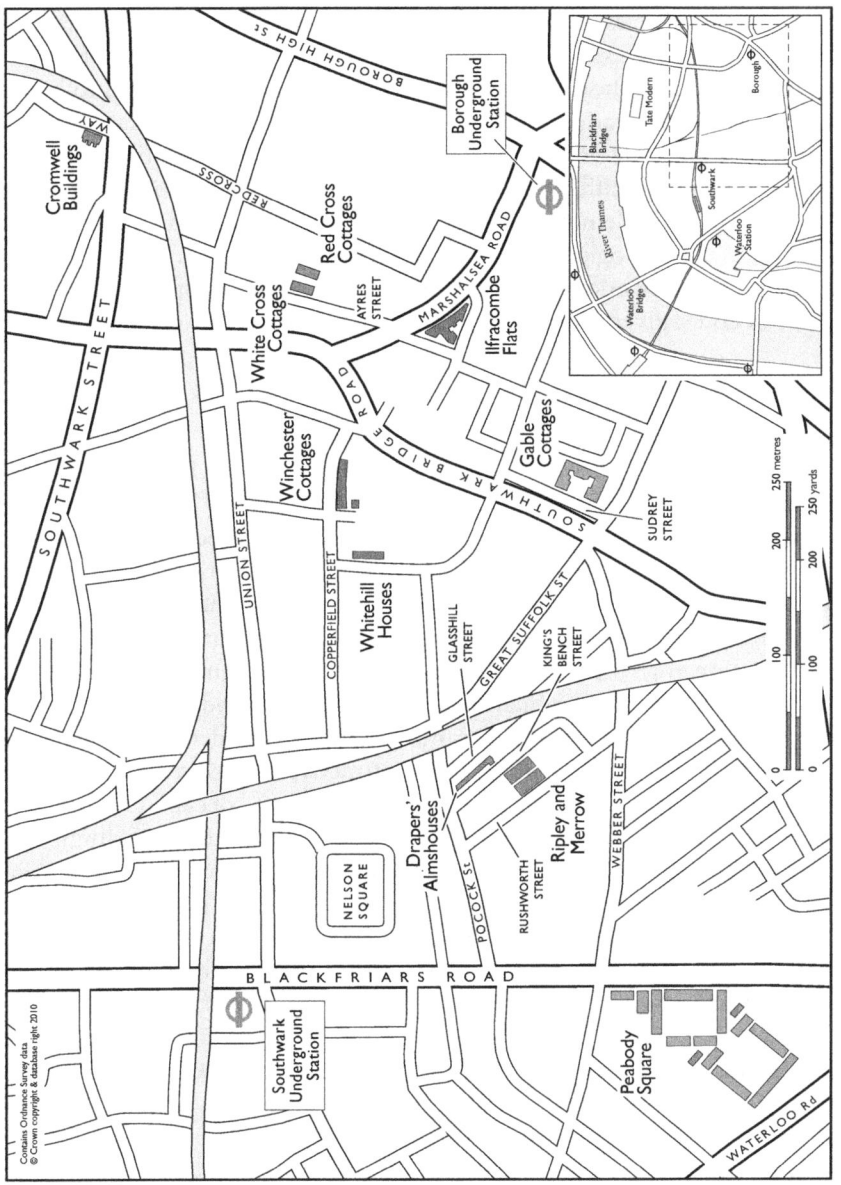

Figure 13.2. Modern-day map of Southwark.

this area provides a useful window into the world of late Victorian social housing, and was the site for several of Hill's most interesting experiments in architecture. This short guide, it should be said, makes no claim to being comprehensive; the variety of projects in the area is huge – and beyond Southwark is yet more diverse. Rather, it seeks to be representative, showing how a spectrum of different solutions was proposed in the search for a solution to the problem of housing 'the poor'.[2] Organized topologically, rather than chronologically or thematically, this chapter also seeks to reproduce the fieldwork done as part of the event which inspired this book. The postal codes given should enable readers to follow our path virtually.

Cromwell Buildings (1864)

Redcross Way, London SE1 9HR

Designed by the philanthropist Sydney Waterlow and the builder Matthew Allen, Cromwell Buildings were among the first erected by the Improved Industrial Dwellings Company (IIDC), which had been founded the previous year, in 1863. The IIDC went on to become the largest housing company in London, providing accommodation for almost 30,000 people in forty-five estates. It was thus the most successful example of Victorian model housing enterprises: a commercial concern, designed to yield profits for its investors; yet also a philanthropic initiative, intended to provide the working classes with superior accommodation. Its founders were especially keen to ensure that the dwellings were attractive as well as practical and reasonably priced. 'Each new building scheme', declared Waterlow, 'represents an oasis of wholesomeness in some dirty desert of dingy and rickety buildings, where toiling millions are presently worse housed than the rich man's horse, ox, or ass'.[3]

To that end, Waterlow and Allen deliberately rejected the types of dwellings erected by many other philanthropists at the time. Visiting Baroness Burdett-Coutts's flats in the East End, for example, Matthew Allen professed himself shocked to find that 'The rooms have only bare whitewashed walls, like the cells of a prison, and the rules prohibit any tenant from knocking in even a nail to hang a picture, or to endeavour to decorate the walls and render the home more cheerful'.[4] Instead, they turned to the model artisans' cottages exhibited by Henry Roberts at the

---

[2] For the wider context, see J. N. Tarn, *Five Per Cent Philanthropy: an Account of Housing in Urban Areas Between 1840 and 1914* (Cambridge, 1973) and A. S. Wohl, *The Eternal Slum: Housing and Social Policy in Victorian London* (1977).

[3] G. Smalley, *The Life of Sir Sydney H. Waterlow Bart* (1909), p. 81.

[4] Smalley, *Waterlow*, p. 61.

Great Exhibition in 1851. This provided them with a template for a self-contained family home which could be duplicated and grouped together with the introduction of external staircases. Cromwell Buildings are a wonderful example of this at work: providing ten four-roomed and twelve three-roomed tenements as well as two shops. There was also a flat roof for laundry to dry and children to play safely. Each tenement had its own kitchen and toilet, all grouped together in projections at the back of the building for convenience and hygiene. Hygienic concerns likewise inspired the balconies and open staircases.

The result is an undeniably attractive building, now grade two listed. Yet there were problems with the IIDC's approach. It was never a wholly successful commercial concern, becoming dependent on the cheap loans the government offered after the 1866 and 1867 Labouring Classes Dwelling Houses Acts. By 1875, it had borrowed £250,000. The plans for Cromwell Buildings were also defective. As John Nelson Tarn observes, 'The advantages of a completely self-contained flat with an assortment of badly-shaped rooms, often under-lit or looking out between cliffs of brickwork were not ... so considerable', especially when compared with the well-lit rectangular spaces offered by other companies.[5]

Above all, the IIDC was criticized by contemporaries for not housing those most in need of accommodation. Rents were initially fixed at 5s to 6s 6d a week, which made the flats cheaper than equivalent commercially-let property. But the company selected its tenants carefully, with a preference for the respectable and those in regular employment. It is an index of its policy that it soon housed more than twice as many policemen as it did labourers. Indeed, with an average income of around 28s a week, the inhabitants of IIDC properties were far better off than those who, on a weekly income of less than 21s, were identified by the social investigator Charles Booth as the 'London poor'.

Further reading: J. S. Curl, *The Life and Work of Henry Roberts, 1803–1876* (Chichester, 1983); R. Dennis, 'The historical geography of Victorian values: philanthropic housing in London, 1840–1900', *Journal of Historical Geography*, xv (1989); G. Smalley, *The Life of Sir Sydney H. Waterlow Bart* (1909); J. N. Tarn, 'The Improved Industrial Dwellings Company', *Transactions of the London and Middlesex Archaeological Society*, xxii (1968); A. S. Wohl, *The Eternal Slum: Housing and Social Policy in Victorian London* (1977).

---

[5] J. N. Tarn, 'The Improved Industrial Dwellings Company', *Transactions of the London and Middlesex Archaeological Society*, xxii (1968), 50.

Red Cross Cottages (1887)
Redcross Way, London SE1 1HA

Together with their garden (restored and reopened by the Bankside Open Spaces Trust in 2006) and with the Red Cross Hall,[6] these cottages represent the realization of Octavia Hill's ideal. They were intended to house six families in separate, self-contained, four-roomed homes, erected at the cost of £220 each. The site was owned by the ecclesiastical commissioners and had fallen into decay, with an abandoned paper factory on one part and a warehouse on the other. In her letters Octavia Hill recorded that it took six full weeks to burn all the rubbish that had accumulated there. The homes were intended for highly-trusted artisans and their families; with a rent of more than 8*s* a week – at least 3*s* above the average – only the well-paid could possibly afford them. But the space as a whole was conceived as an 'open-air summer sitting room' for the wider community – especially the tenants of two large block buildings opposite (now demolished).[7]

Thanks to the generosity of Hill's great supporter, the countess of Ducie, the garden was laid out by the Kyrle Society, with plane trees, a pond, a band-stand, a covered playground and a thousand yellow crocuses. A mosaic of the Good Shepherd by the fashionable artist Antonio Salviati would later be joined by another (still *in situ*) of a man sowing seeds, created by the prominent Arts and Crafts glass-making firm James Powell and Son, after a sketch by the marchioness of Waterford. The Red Cross Hall, intended to be the scene of musical events, lectures and dramatic performances, was to be similarly ornamented inside, with Walter Crane starting – though never completing – a series of murals on the 'Heroic Deeds of the Poor'.

Both the hall and the cottages were designed by Elijah Hoole, who had also built Octavia Hill's own house in Kent (1884). He was a high-minded and socially-aware architect, much in demand for similarly improving projects like the pioneering settlement house Toynbee Hall (1884–5). His cottages here are self-consciously vernacular: tile-hung, bay-windowed, with painted rough-cast ornamentation. Yet the effect is meant to be more than merely pretty. In proper Ruskinian fashion, each house is distinguished from the other – a point made all the more plain by the vertical brick projections between them. Given Octavia Hill's well-known advocacy of the single-family home, this is architecture in the service of an idea. The same is plainly true of the simple pared-down Gothic hall, whose scale and simplicity marks it out as a public rather than a private building. Inside, the hammer-beam roof evokes the hospitality and social harmony of the

---

[6] Since 1934 known as Bishop's Hall.
[7] Hill, *LFW*, 1887, p. 221.

baronial halls depicted in books such as Joseph Nash's *The Mansions of England in the Olden Time* (1839–49).

Further reading: R. Barrington, 'The Red Cross Hall', *English Illustrated Magazine*, cxvii (June 1893); D. E. B. Weiner, *Architecture and Social Reform in Late-Victorian London* (Manchester and New York, 1994); *Octavia Hill and the Social Housing Debate*, ed. R. Whelan (1998).

White Cross Cottages (1890)

Ayres Street (originally Whitecross Street),[8] London SE1 1EX

White Cross Cottages follow the same principles and were designed by the same architect as the neighbouring dwellings in Redcross Way. Each of the six four-roomed cottages cost £200 to erect, although the accommodation was rather larger than the more expensive housing next door. The difference, it is clear, lay in the limited architectural treatment that Hoole was able to provide on a flat façade directly abutting the street. There is no rough-cast here, nor any room for the bay-windows and gables of Red Cross Gardens. The tiles are arranged in a single, horizontal band across all the houses. Nonetheless, Hoole evidently wanted to make the structure as legible as he could: the break between the cottages and the hall is jarring and the distinction between each house is articulated at roof level, with ridges running from the chimneys down to the eaves, terminating in a vestigial gable.

By the end of the century, Octavia Hill's role in this area was not confined to these twelve houses. As agent for the ecclesiastical commissioners, she was responsible for thousands of tenants in a wide variety of properties, including many older buildings in this street and the two large blocks of model dwellings that used to stand in Redcross Way. She was quite clear that, of the two sorts of buildings, the smaller were far preferable, observing to the Royal Commission on the Housing of the Working Classes in 1884 that the working class shared her dread of the 'monotony and ugliness' of large social housing blocks. 'We have one rather pretty group of buildings of old red brick, quite cheaply built and simple', she continued, 'and opposite to it is a perfectly plain one, very ugly, also new; but many of the people will not go near that building'.[9] In White Cross Cottages, she and her architect sought to show that modern, inexpensive model housing could be made more attractive, even on this unpromising site.

---

[8] Ayers Street was renamed after Alice Ayers, subject of Walter Crane's first mural in Red Cross Hall.

[9] *Royal Commission on the Housing of the Working Classes* (Parl. Papers 1884–5 [C. 4402], ii), Q. 9019.

'Nobler imaginings and mightier struggles'

Further reading: G. F. A. Best, *Temporal Pillars: Queen Anne's Bounty, the Ecclesiastical Commissioners, and the Church of England* (Cambridge, 1964); M. FitzGerald, *The Church as Landlord* (1937); I. Ginsberg, 'Octavia Hill and the ecclesiastical commissioners', in *Octavia Hill's Letters to Fellow-Workers*, ed. R. Whelan (2005).

Ilfracombe Flats (1888)

Marshalsea Road, London SE1 1EW

In the 1880s, the Metropolitan Board of Works (MBW) swept through the notorious slum known as the Mint, tearing down houses to create a new thoroughfare, the Marshalsea Road. Part civic improvement, part traffic-alleviation scheme, part slum clearance, it was a development that profoundly changed the topography of the area and also provided opportunities for new and better housing. Indeed, the 1875 Artisans' and Labourers' Dwellings Improvement Act (also known as the Cross Act) specifically required that land cleared in this way be sold to provide accommodation for the working classes, even though the Board of Works accrued enormous losses in the process. The adjacent Douglas Buildings, erected by the IIDC in 1886–7, reveal the potential this indirect state sponsorship presented to housing reformers.

Unfortunately, the Cross Act also stipulated that the number of people rehoused after clearance should be equal to the number who lived there beforehand. In formerly overcrowded areas like the Mint, this created a terrible dilemma for high-minded housing companies which wanted to build improved, lower-density accommodation. It also placed the MBW in an uncomfortable position, unable to sell land which the IIDC and others regarded as unusable, but which the law required them to use for new homes. This inconveniently-shaped triangular island between the Marshalsea Road and Mint Street provides a good example of the problems they faced.

Such an apparently intractable situation created a tremendous opportunity for entrepreneurs and none more so than the remarkable – if somewhat shadowy – property developer, James Hartnoll. He based a brilliant career on buying up land like this at a knock-down price and then building on it at a scale that the housing reformers regarded as improper. The result is a very functional building, lacking the social space and free-flow of air that the IIDC, in particular, regarded as essential. At six storeys, Ilfracombe Flats were also at least one floor higher than the maximum permitted by the model housing companies.

Nonetheless, James Hartnoll's Superior Improved Dwellings were not a new sort of slum. To attract tenants, each flat was well-equipped, with its own kitchen and scullery. The knowledgeable Charles Booth thus thought

Hartnoll's buildings the best of the 'modern' blocks; a 'great advance' on the ugly, older dwellings of the poor.[10] Indeed, the buildings' exterior shows a striving for aesthetic effect far removed from the utilitarianism of much contemporary social housing. With their London stock bricks, painted quoins, string courses and attic storey, Ilfracombe Flats and their twin development – Monarch Flats across Marshalsea Road – form a far from unimpressive façade to frame this new street. True enough, they lack the more strictly classical (and more expensive) details used by the IIDC in the Douglas Buildings, but they do not stand out as significantly substandard. Small wonder that they are still in use, having been taken on by the Peabody Trust 1970. Together with the Douglas Buildings, they now form the Peabody Marshalsea Estate.

Further reading: A. Cox, '"An example to others": public housing in London, 1840–1914', *Transactions of the London and Middlesex Archaeological Society*, xliv (1995); C. Wagg, 'Peabody's past uncovered: Marshalsea', *Peabody News* (summer 2007); I. Watson, 'The buildings of James Hartnoll', *Newsletter of the Camden History Society*, lviii (1980).

Gable Cottages (1889)

Sudrey Street (originally Little Suffolk Street), London SE1 1PF

Built two years after Red Cross Cottages and a year before White Cross Cottages were completed, this development is self-evidently a variation on a common theme. Here are twenty self-contained, four-roomed houses, tile-hung or rendered, with a picturesque variety of roofs and windows, and a small garden at the front. The architect is, of course, Elijah Hoole, who sought to make the place even prettier with what were known as 'diamond lattice windows' (now superseded by a more conventional treatment). As an 1894 report recorded, this building replaced eight two-storey cottages which faced on to the street, together with their large backyards, congested with all manner of detritus. Gable Cottages were consequently a demonstration that housing reformers could achieve a greater density of accommodation and greater beauty at the same time: the garden was not just an attractive addition, and a way of managing a very narrow street; it also 'afforded no waste space for rubbish or lumber'.[11] It is, however, worth noting the differences as well as the similarities between this and the houses Hill

---

[10] Quoted in *The Survey of London*, xlvii: *Northern Clerkenwell and Pentonville*, ed. P. Temple (2008), p. 119.

[11] 'Cottage homes in London under the management of Octavia Hill', *Mansion House Council on the Dwellings of the Poor: Report for the Year Ending December 31st 1894* (1895), p. 12.

'Nobler imaginings and mightier struggles'

herself commissioned. Gable Cottages were cheaper at £175 apiece, and the property was less extensive than the one in Red Cross Way. As a result, Hoole was unable to express the distinction between each home as clearly, while the garden remained a private space.

The client for this project was not Hill herself – which may go some way towards explaining the difference between it and the buildings she controlled directly. Yet she was certainly the inspiration, and (as this chapter's opening epigraph shows) she oversaw the project – which doubtless also accounts for the similarities. In her Letter to fellow-workers for 1888, Hill observed that the demand for places in the Red Cross Cottages 'encouraged me to recommend the repetition of the experiment to a gentleman who consulted me about the best and most remunerative use of a bit of ground in the neighbourhood'.[12]

The gentleman in question was the Revd. T. C. V. Bastow, rector of Little Peatling (now known as Peatling Parva) in Leicestershire. Educated at Harrow and Trinity College, Oxford, Bastow was an antiquary, Alpinist and eccentric, fondly recalled by the occultist Aleister Crowley as 'one of the most original characters I have ever met', not least because he claimed to possess 'a rudimentary tail'.[13] An ebullient figure, who oversaw a parish of no more than 150 souls and sold chrysanthemums on the side, but became a fellow of both the Royal Geographical and Royal Horticultural Societies and a member of the high church Society of the Holy Cross, Bastow wonderfully illustrates how Hill was able to attract and influence the most ostensibly unlikely people.

Further reading: *The Builder*, 9 November 1889; 'Cottage homes in London under the management of Octavia Hill', *Mansion House Council on the Dwellings of the Poor: Report for the Year Ending December 31st 1894* (1895).

Winchester Cottages (1893–5)

Copperfield Street (originally Orange Street), London SE1 0EP
Octavia Hill's remarkable effect on people is also illustrated here with a row of fourteen four-roomed cottages. Again this land was owned by the ecclesiastical commissioners, whose agent she became in 1884. As the standard work on the commissioners records, they 'clearly started by regarding her as a useful and pleasant temporary helper, who would keep the Southwark courts warm pending the completion of their redevelopment plans'. They seem to have imagined this would comprise

[12] Hill, *LFW*, 1888, p. 247.
[13] A. Crowley, *The Confessions of Aleister Crowley*, ed. J. Symonds and K. Grant (1979), pp. 97–8.

the types of large housing blocks erected by the IIDC, together with some more commercially profitable projects.[14] That Hill managed to persuade them otherwise was first revealed at the Red Cross Cottages. In Winchester Cottages, however, something still more significant had happened: for here we see the ecclesiastical commissioners reversing their previous policy by deciding to build and then rent out cottages themselves. As Octavia Hill put it, with quiet triumph, 'Encouraged by the satisfactory result of Red and White Cross cottages and Gable cottages, I suggested … that they should themselves build similar cottages on their own ground in Southwark. They met my suggestion most cordially'.[15]

Erected in two tranches, with the first nine houses opening in 1893, these properties continue in the mode Elijah Hoole established at the Red Cross and White Cross Cottages. There is the same determination to mark out each home, with some given gables and all distinguished with pronounced roof ridges. Working for the cost-conscious ecclesiastical commissioners, however, there was no extra money for significant ornamentation; instead, bands of red brick and attractive vernacular awnings relieved the bareness of the façade. Social space was to be provided by the churchyard opposite, and, instead of having a garden, each home was provided with a diminutive brick-lined plot to the rear: 'We begged the Commissioners', wrote Hill, 'to leave small borders against the walls of the tiny yards, so that tenants may plant creepers, and, at least, a few crocuses and ferns'.[16] No longer social housing, these four-roomed properties now change hands for up to £900,000 each.

Further reading: G .F. A. Best, *Temporal Pillars: Queen Anne's Bounty, the Ecclesiastical Commissioners, and the Church of England* (Cambridge, 1964); M. FitzGerald, *The Church as Landlord* (1937); I. Ginsberg, 'Octavia Hill and the ecclesiastical commissioners', in *Octavia Hill's Letters to Fellow-Workers*, ed. R. Whelan (2005).

Whitehill Houses (1898)

Sawyer Street (originally Lemon Street), London SE1 0EQ

Around the corner is a still less-ornate development erected by another of Octavia Hill's supporters on land belonging to the ecclesiastical commissioners. Whitehill Houses was paid for by the countess of Selborne, daughter of the Conservative prime minister Lord Salisbury and wife of

---

[14] G. F. A. Best, *Temporal Pillars: Queen Anne's Bounty, the Ecclesiastical Commissioners, and the Church of England* (Cambridge, 1964), p. 491.
[15] Hill, *LFW*, 1893, p. 336.
[16] Hill, *LFW*, 1893, p. 336.

the second earl of Selborne, a high-ranking Liberal Unionist politician. She was a considerable force in her own right, with a longstanding interest in housing. Newly engaged in 1883, indeed, she had written to her future husband on 'what I should do if I were a man' to clear the slums and improve sanitation.[17] Her project here comprised twenty-four three-roomed tenements in a four-storey block, and the absence of ornamentation was deliberate. Hill recorded that Lady Selborne proposed 'to spend little in extra appliances, but to make a point of securing the maximum of light, air and space in sound, well-drained buildings, so meeting the needs of the larger families who wish to obtain adequate space in healthy surroundings, and who prefer cheapness to additional appliances'.[18] That this, to all intents and purposes, meant erecting a block not unlike those that Hill herself condemned was something that she chose to overlook.

The contrast between Whitehill Houses and Hill's own cottage properties was exacerbated by Lady Selborne's choice of architect. Instead of employing the experienced and committed Elijah Hoole, she opted for a smarter and somewhat better-connected figure socially: Louis Ambler. Ambler was the author of a paper on 'Artisans' dwellings', but also wrote on the chateaux of the Loire. He would go on to publish a book on *Old Halls and Manor Houses of Yorkshire* as well as one on his own pedigree. Perhaps most importantly of all for his aristocratic client, he became the architect of choice for the duke of Portland, building at least half a dozen churches for him. His Arts and Crafts training does come out in the roughcast top storey, the little dormers, and the way in which the fenestration distinguishes between the staircases' public spaces and the tenements' private spaces, but he seems to have struggled with such an inexpensive project. Nonetheless, as Robert Whelan notes, that a figure as grand as the countess of Selborne should be concerned not just with the provision of housing, but also the specific appliances that it would contain, 'shows how successfully Octavia had made the detailed arrangements for working-class housing the objects of consideration for those of the highest social position'.[19]

Further reading: L. Ambler, *The Ambler Family* (1924); P. Jalland, *Women, Marriage, and Politics, 1860–1914* (1986); *Octavia Hill's Letters to Fellow-Workers*, ed. R. Whelan (2005).

---

[17] P. Jalland, *Women, Marriage, and Politics, 1860–1914* (1986), p. 327.
[18] Hill, *LFW*, 1898, p. 415.
[19] Hill, *LFW*, 1898, p. 415.

Drapers' Almshouses (1820)

Glasshill Street (originally Hill Street), London SE1 0QR.

The Drapers' Almshouses are a relic of an older landscape of social concern in Southwark. Nearby used to stand the Fishmongers' Almshouses (of 1618 and 1719), the Magdalen Hospital for the Reception of Penitent Prostitutes (1772), and the Royal Freemasons' School for Girls (1788). Located elsewhere in the borough are Hoptons' Almshouses (1749), the Edward Edwards Almshouses (1717) and London's largest home for the impoverished, the Licensed Victuallers' Benevolent Institution (opened 1828 and later much extended). It was a sign of the area's declining reputation that from the mid nineteenth century onwards, many respectable charities started to leave, with the Freemasons abandoning Southwark in 1852 and even the Magdalen Hospital vacating in 1869 on the grounds that 'the vice from which it was trying to remove the women was openly taking place in the immediate vicinity'.[20]

This building, the third incarnation of a parochial charity first established in 1642, is more than just a memorial to older patterns of philanthropy, however. It also sheds a revealing light on the architectural typology that Hill and her associates embraced in their own late Victorian projects. Gable Cottages, as we have already seen, followed a similar pattern: a two-storeyed building, with pronounced bays at either end, framing a small garden. Red Cross Cottages were somewhat different, but the large ornamental space in front evoked a similar idea, while Winchester Cottages were gathered around a church in archetypal almshouse fashion. What this exposes is the extent to which Hill's experiments in building ran quite contrary to London housing traditions and instead drew on the charitable architecture of suburban and even rural England. By the end of the eighteenth century, even the simplest London houses tended to be three storeys high. They also typically opened straight on to the street. Moreover, as Peter Guillery has shown, from the late seventeenth century onwards, the subdivision of buildings that Octavia Hill so deprecated was normal – indeed, it was expected, houses being designed with such flexibility in mind from the start. Ironically, for all her claims to be fostering independence among her tenants, by insisting on low-rise, self-contained cottages, Hill was not so much reinstating private domesticity as reinventing the old almshouse pattern.

Further reading: C. Berridge, *The Almshouses of London* (Shedfield, 1987); P. Guillery, *The Small House in Eighteenth-Century London* (New Haven,

---

[20] L. Riley and G. Marshal, *The Story of Bankside: from the River Thames to St. George's Circus* (2001), p. 68.

Conn. and London, 2004); L. Riley and G. Marshal, *The Story of Bankside: From the River Thames to St. George's Circus* (2001).

Ripley and Merrow (1896–7)

Access from Rushworth Street (originally Green Street), London SE1 0QZ[21]

Together with the almost identical Albury and Clandon Buildings on nearby Boyfield Street (originally Gun Street), these two small blocks represent a new development – though not a revolution – in the history of Southwark's social housing. Much against Octavia Hill's wishes, the 1890 Housing of the Working Classes Act finally permitted local authorities to erect their own accommodation. Three years later, in 1893, London County Council (LCC) – dominated by self-professed Progressives – took advantage of this, establishing an office within its architects' department exclusively concerned with the subject. Ripley and Merrow, designed by the architect A. M. Philip in 1896, was one of the first fruits of this new office. Intended to house around 200 people in a mixture of one-roomed, three-roomed and predominantly two-roomed flats, it was far from the largest development planned by the LCC's Housing of the Working Classes Branch even in these early years of its work. But it is noteworthy, not least because its design reveals the ways in which some local authorities shared the idealism and the assumptions that also animated housing reformers like Hill herself.

Indeed, although these three-storey tenement blocks are superficially quite different from the self-contained, two-storey cottages at Red Cross Gardens or Copperfield Street, its architect was equally committed to the Arts and Crafts principles that Elijah Hoole expounded. Philip had trained with the overtly Ruskinian J. J. Stevenson, and in the LCC architects' department was surrounded by like-minded colleagues. The canted corners, the corbelled chimneys, the arched windows and – above all – the delicate iron-work of the railings: all these speak, as Susan Beattie puts it, 'of the unity of craftsmanship and art'. Little wonder that she describes Ripley and Merrow as 'Philip's masterpiece'; nor that they are grade two listed – and have been so since 1977.[22]

Since what the LCC's chief architect described as an improved 'balcony plan' was used, other similarities can be noted between these blocks and the work of the IIDC.[23] And the comparison does not end with this shared belief in the hygienic advantages of open staircases and airy galleries. In the words of Alan Cox, 'The LCC ... inherited from the philanthropic societies

---

[21] The interesting rear elevation can be seen in King's Bench Street, London SE1 0QX.

[22] S. Beattie, *A Revolution in London Housing: LCC Housing Architects and their Work, 1893–1914* (1980), p. 48.

[23] W. E. Riley, 'The architectural work of the London County Council', *Journal of the Royal Institute of British Architects*, xvi (1908–9), 417.

the idea that the main purpose of the buildings should be models of what good working-class housing ought to be, rather than necessarily catering for the more immediate needs of those displaced by slum clearance'.[24] To this idealism was added a more pragmatic need to break even, for the county council had resolved that charges should be fixed in such a way as to ensure that tenants paid the running costs. Rents consequently varied from 4s 6d a week for a single room to 8s 6d for three. This was not cheap – indeed, it was more than a shilling higher than the average local lease – and it inevitably excluded the impoverished.

Ripley and Merrow should not therefore be seen simply as the start of the state's involvement in social housing, much less as a radical break with the past. Indirectly, through loans and the forced sale of slum clearance land, the government had been underwriting the provision of improved working-class accommodation for decades. The architectural idioms and technical specifications were also similar to those used by private housing reformers, as were some of the financial arrangements employed. As this suggests, these blocks are a caution against any teleological story that sees the origin of modern social housing in these state-sponsored developments. Just like much of the philanthropic sector, these were model homes for model tenants; the problematic and the very poor still had to look elsewhere.

Further reading: S. Beattie, *A Revolution in London Housing: LCC Housing Architects and their Work, 1893–1914* (1980); A. Cox, '"An example to others": public housing in London, 1840–1914', *Transactions of the London and Middlesex Archaeological Society*, xliv (1995); *The Housing Question in London* (1900); W. Thomson, *The Housing Handbook Up-to-Date*, ed. C. J. Stewart (1903).

Peabody Square (1871)
Blackfriars' Road, London SE1 8HS
Built on the former Magdalen Hospital site, Peabody Square was the first South London project for the charity which gave its name to the estate. It had been founded less than a decade before by the American philanthropist George Peabody. As the scale of this site suggests, the Peabody Trust was a remarkable phenomenon. 'Of all the agencies erecting model dwellings,' as Anthony Wohl observes, it 'excited the most interest and stimulated most controversy'.[25] This was partly because of its financial strength. Initially set up with a £150,000 capital sum, the trust eventually accrued a £500,000

---

[24] A. Cox, '"An example to others": public housing in London, 1840–1914', *Transactions of the London and Middlesex Archaeological Society*, xliv (1995), 159.
[25] Wohl, *The Eternal Slum*, p. 153.

endowment – an unimaginably large amount for most of its competitors, and one that Octavia Hill feared would enable it to 'paralyse effort on the part of independent builders who would else come forward' to take over slum clearance land.[26] But the Peabody Trust was also attacked, at least initially, for the shocking austerity of its tenement blocks. Employing the architect Henry Darbishire, whose building for Lady Burdett-Coutts had so appalled the founders of the IIDC, the first of the trust's developments still seem, in the words of John Nelson Tarn, 'memorable primarily for their grimness and physical bulk'.[27]

The greater space afforded by cheaper land in South London gave Darbishire a chance to try something new. Instead of large, basic, sprawling and barrack-like buildings, Peabody Square was divided up into blocks, each of which was itself divided into staircases, off which five flats opened on each floor. Bands of white brick and classically-derived cornices broke up the façades, while fancy gables to the street front gestured towards the newly fashionable 'Queen Anne' Revival style. This time, the critics were enthusiastic about the results, with the *Illustrated London News* praising the scheme as 'more homelike and agreeable than the other establishments erected by the trustees'.[28] That the interiors were still Spartan, the services and toilets still shared, and that the block plan resulted in overlapping buildings at the corners of each square, with predictably gloomy consequences for the inhabitants of the affected rooms, did not seem to matter.

In truth, indeed, it probably did not matter all that much. Peabody had been established as a charity – not a company – to provide housing for the poor. Although the courts resolved that in so doing the founder had 'drawn a distinct line between the idle, thriftless and mendicant, and the striving, industrious, and yet unfortunate', the trust's financial clout allowed it to subsidize rents to a significant extent.[29] Indeed, the average it charged in the 1890s was around 4s 9d a week, at least 25 per cent lower than the market rate. Despite the bare walls and absence of luxury, there was thus a two-year waiting list for rooms; on one occasion a man broke his leg in the rush to sign up for a vacancy.

This did not mean, however, that all were welcome. With an average weekly salary of more than 23s, the Peabody tenants were a cut above the inhabitants of the older houses managed by Octavia Hill and her allies

---

[26] *Royal Commission on the Housing of the Working Classes* (Parl. Papers 1884–5 [C. 4402], ii), Q.8874.

[27] Tarn, *Five Per Cent Philanthropy*, p. 47.

[28] Quoted in J. N. Tarn, 'The Peabody Donation Fund: the role of a housing society in the nineteenth century', *Victorian Studies*, x (1966), 22.

[29] Wohl, *The Eternal Slum*, p. 150.

nearby, who might earn as little as 18*s* a week. And for the very poorest, even this most basic accommodation – just like all the other properties we have visited – was an unrealizable dream. They would continue to inhabit the small, over-crowded, often insanitary, 'dreadful buildings in Southwark' that would – eventually – be replaced in the century to come, leaving these somewhat superior dwellings as a memorial to a moment in the history of social housing.

Further reading: E. Bowmaker, *The Housing of the Working Classes* (1895); J. N. Tarn, 'The Peabody Donation Fund: the role of a housing society in the nineteenth century', *Victorian Studies*, x (1966); A. S. Wohl, *The Eternal Slum: Housing and Social Policy in Victorian London* (1977).

14. For the benefit of the nation: politics and the early National Trust

Ben Cowell

From its earliest days right up to the present advocates for the National Trust have emphasized the charity's independence from government.[1] An early fundraising text, entitled 'Its aims and its works' (*c*.1897), opened by observing that the trust operated outside the state's areas of responsibility and was 'the only association that, in the absence of any power under Parliamentary statute to safeguard other than prehistoric remains, can take upon itself to preserve for posterity historic sites and buildings that may be handed to its keeping'.[2] This remained the case forty years later when G. M. Trevelyan noted that 'while we are still waiting for the State to do its duty … the National Trust holds a unique place'.[3]

Even as government intervention in heritage preservation increased after the Second World War, the trust held on to its independence. The Country Houses Scheme of 1937, combined with the creation of the National Land Fund under Attlee's post-war Labour administration, meant that the trust briefly came close to being, as Peter Mandler puts it, 'a semi-nationalised custodian of land and buildings in the public interest'.[4] But the Gowers report on country houses of 1950 helped to reaffirm the principle that government's role was to support private owners. This principle was eventually manifested through a system of grant funding (of which the trust was a significant beneficiary) by the Historic Buildings Councils, established in 1953.[5] Talk of nationalizing the trust subsided.

The long-standing emphasis on independence from government does not mean that the National Trust was not a political organization, but rather

---

[1] 'National Trust is a charity completely independent of Government funding. We rely on the support of the public, through membership and donations' (National Trust website, <http://www.nationaltrust.org.uk/contact-us/frequently-asked-questions/> [accessed 18 March 2015]).

[2] National Trust Archives, 'Its aims and its works', [*c*.1897], copy in Wiltshire and Swindon History Centre, N/600/OM19:03/6208300.

[3] G. M. Trevelyan, 'Foreword', in J. Dixon-Scott, *England Under Trust* (1937), p. xvi.

[4] P. Mandler, *The Fall and Rise of the Stately Home* (New Haven, Conn., 1997), p. 336.

[5] Mandler, *Fall and Rise*, pp. 311–53. *Report of the Gowers Committee on Houses of Outstanding Historic or Architectural Interest* (1950).

that, as David Cannadine has observed, the trust can be viewed as 'the pursuit of politics by other means'.[6] The author of 'Its aims and its works' went on to posit that the trust, as a non-governmental organization, had a duty to influence government policy, helping when necessary to 'stimulate and promote legislation upon matters cognate with its aims and intention'. Not being an organization controlled by or answerable to the state, the trust can, as Melanie Hall argues in this volume, be perceived as sharing domestic virtues personified by its co-founder, Octavia Hill: thrift, self-sufficiency and a certain determination to get a decent job done on the barest of resources. It is a philosophy that the trust continued to observe even as it moved into the territory of rescuing country houses.[7] Not having the benefit of a regular subsidy from public funds focused trust officials' attention on the need to win friends and patrons and to secure philanthropic sources of income through permanent endowments.

Since 1895 the National Trust has grown from a fledgling organization with a handful of staff to the largest conservation charity in Europe, with more than 5,000 employees and an annual turnover of around £450 million. A third of the trust's income derives from its four million members and their annual subscriptions, the rest from investment income, rents, profits from holiday cottages, shops and cafes, and donations and bequests. Considerable in-kind support is provided by the trust's 70,000 volunteers, without whom its activities could not be sustained. Government support is limited to discrete public-sector grants[8] and the fiscal benefits that flow from the trust's charitable status.[9] Financial independence from government means the National Trust can venture comment or even criticism of public policy in those areas relating most closely to its work. Its opposition to government proposals to amend English planning policy in 2011–12, for example, resulted in the unprecedented move in 2011 of inviting visitors to properties that summer to sign a petition calling on the government to 'stop and rethink its planning reforms'. Nearly a quarter of a million did.[10]

---

[6] D. Cannadine, *G. M. Trevelyan: a Life in History* (1992), p. 179.

[7] M. Waterson, *The National Trust: the First Hundred Years* (1994), pp. 109, 266.

[8] Nearly £38 million pounds of income in 2012/13 (from a total income of £457 million) was received in the form of grants from mainly public-sector sources, including £9 million from agricultural subsidies (see National Trust Annual Report for 2012/13 <http://www.nationaltrust.org.uk/about-us/annual-reports/> [accessed 2 Jan. 2014]).

[9] In the UK these include, e.g., exemption from taxes such as income tax and corporation tax, reduced business rates on buildings occupied for charitable purposes, and the ability to reclaim the tax on individual donations under the Gift Aid scheme (see <http://www.hmrc.gov.uk/charities/tax/basics.htm> [accessed 5 July 2014]).

[10] See National Trust Annual Report for 2011/12 <http://www.nationaltrust.org.uk/about-us/annual-reports/> [accessed 28 June 2014].

Figure 14.1. Sir Robert Hunter (undated).

The National Trust remains a private charity operating in the public interest, but enjoying substantial legal powers bestowed on it by statute. Various acts of Parliament have laid the foundations for the charity's work since the first National Trust Act of 1907. This originated as a private member's bill, rather than as a piece of state-sponsored legislation, but such private bills were far more common then than now.[11] Tax arrangements, such as those associated with the acceptance in lieu system (for offsetting death duties or inheritance tax through the gift of land, buildings or objects) or the Country Houses Scheme (which enabled the trust to hold land and investments as endowments, and donor families to reside in houses tax-free), have led at times to the trust's working closely with the treasury and revenue collection agency.[12] Moreover the trust has drawn support and influence from the highest echelons of government throughout its history. Its first chairman, Sir Robert Hunter (see Figure 14.1), was a distinguished civil servant, working at a senior level in one of the biggest and most powerful

[11] 'The National Trust Acts 1907–1971' <http://www.nationaltrust.org.uk/about-us-our-constitution/> [accessed 28 June 2014].
[12] Mandler, *Fall and Rise*, pp. 295–308.

departments of state, the General Post Office; his successor as chairman, Lord Plymouth, was a former cabinet minister.[13] The trust went on to recruit advocates from political leaders of all persuasions, from Conservative Stanley Baldwin to Labour's George Lansbury and Hugh Dalton.[14]

This chapter examines the relationship between the National Trust and government in the trust's earliest decades. It is not based on a paper given at the Octavia Hill conference, but rather draws together some of the themes emerging from other chapters in this volume. Hill is not always the focus, although Hill's relationship with the state and her attitude to the prospect of greater government intervention are summarized, something which Elizabeth Baigent, Gillian Darley and particularly Laurence Goldman, explore in their essays. The chapter invites comparison of Hill with her fellow National Trust founders, especially Sir Robert Hunter, and it concludes that the trust ought not to be seen as wholly independent, but rather as a body that has collaborated closely with public institutions ever since its inception.

National Trust founders' attitudes to state intervention

The National Trust is traditionally viewed as having three founders: Octavia Hill (1838–1912), Sir Robert Hunter (1844–1913) and Canon Hardwicke Rawnsley (1851–1920), though in truth more people were present at the birth of the organization, as Hall and Swenson illustrate in this volume.[15] The influence of these three very different individuals can still be seen in the organization today. Each had his or her own perspective on the role of the state at a time when increasing demands were being placed on national and local government to act in areas such as welfare or the environment.[16]

---

[13] B. Cowell, *Sir Robert Hunter: Co-founder and 'Inventor' of the National Trust* (Andover, 2013).

[14] D. Cannadine, 'Conservation: the National Trust and the national heritage', in D. Cannadine, *In Churchill's Shadow: Confronting the Past in Modern Britain* (2002), pp. 224–43.

[15] Histories of the origins of the National Trust include J. Gaze, *Figures in a Landscape: a History of the National Trust* (Frome, 1988); J. Jenkins and P. James, *From Acorn to Oak Tree: the Growth of the National Trust, 1895–1994* (1994); M. Waterson, *The National Trust*; G. Murphy, *Founders of the National Trust* (2002); M. Hall, 'The politics of collecting: the early aspirations of the National Trust, 1883–1913', *Transactions of the Royal Historical Society*, 6th ser., xiii (2003), 345–57. Gaze suggests a fourth founder in the form of Hugh Lupus Grosvenor, duke of Westminster, p. 12.

[16] J. Winter, *Secure from Rash Assault: Sustaining the Victorian Environment* (1999); and P. Readman, *Land and Nation in England: Patriotism, National Identity, and the Politics of Land, 1880–1914* (Woodbridge, 2008).

Politics and the early National Trust

Figure 14.2. Canon Hardwicke Rawnsley (undated).

Of the three founders Octavia Hill took perhaps the dimmest view of the idea that government had any active part to play in everyday social affairs. As Darley notes, Hill's opinions 'had been formed and set in the strict school of individualism and a distrust of State intervention in any form', thinking that the intrusion of the state or municipality into private lives would corrupt the relationships between individuals and authority and undermine the virtue of the individuals.[17] These may have been commonly held views in the 1850s and 1860s, when Hill's work on housing got under

[17] G. Darley, *Octavia Hill: Social Reformer and Founder of the National Trust* (2010), p. 263.

way, but by the end of her life they were increasingly anachronistic, as Goldman illustrates in this volume.[18]

Hill's opinion about the appropriate size and role of government is sometimes caricatured and taken out of context.[19] Her opposition to female suffrage, for example, was shared by other publicly engaged women of her era and, as Darley shows in this volume, Hill's opposition to party political involvement by women at the national level was combined with support for their involvement at the local level, and her own service on royal commissions.[20] Although, as Darley shows here, Hill turned down the offer of salaried public office, she encouraged other women to accept such roles (her nominee Jane Nassau Senior was appointed to the Poor Law position Hill declined), and she promoted the election of Charity Organization Society (COS) leaders, such as Elizabeth Garrett, to local government posts such as Poor Law guardians.[21] Hill had a strong view of men's and women's respective duties in public life, as explored by Jane Garnett in this volume, although, as Baigent makes clear in her introduction, Hill firmly believed that she and women in general had a clear duty to live a life of public service. During her lifetime she was among those who helped to create a female public sphere of voluntary action.

Similarly Hill's opposition to state welfare provisions such as unemployment benefits or old-age pensions derived from her belief in local support mechanisms organized on family or community lines rather than through large and distant state organizations. Such views lay behind her support for the COS, formed in 1869 to emphasize individual responsibility and to direct charitable help to those who, in the society's view, most deserved it.[22] As Goldman shows in this volume, by the end of Hill's life such views had come to be seen as old-fashioned and unbendingly harsh. Opposing Charles Booth's proposal for universal state pensions, Hill maintained that such a measure would 'do a great deal to destroy what one is of things the most desirous to cultivate – the sense of responsibility of relatives', and moreover that it would do nothing to promote thrift.[23] Likewise Hill was outspoken in her opposition to government housing provision, writing, in *The Nineteenth Century* in 1883, that 'Almost all public bodies do things

---

[18] Darley, *Octavia Hill*, p. 273.

[19] Hill, *LFW*, pp. xxviii–xix.

[20] J. Bush, *Women Against the Vote: Female Anti-Suffragism in Britain* (Oxford, 2007), p. 104.

[21] Darley, *Octavia Hill*, pp. 115, 119–20; S. Oldfield, *Jeanie, an 'Army of One': Mrs Nassau Senior, 1828–1877, the First Woman in Whitehall* (Brighton and Portland, Ore., 2008).

[22] Darley, *Octavia Hill*, pp. 111–26.

[23] Darley, *Octavia Hill*, p. 267.

expensively; neither do they seem fitted to supply the various wants of numbers of people in a perceptive and economical way'.[24] Hill's evidence to the Royal Commission on housing a year later gave her another opportunity to set out her view that building by state or parish authorities would 'paralyse effort on the part of the independent builders' – that is, that public housing provision would deter investment by private individuals who wanted a modest return while seeking to promote the public good – the principle which sustained her own housing schemes.[25] The tensions between Hill's mistrust of government and the realities and scale of social and economic deprivation came to the fore during her service on the Royal Commission on the Poor Laws. Famously, the commission members, unable to reach a consensus, issued two reports: the Majority report in favour of reforms to the Poor Law system and Beatrice Webb's Minority report proposing its abolition and replacement with a local authority-co-ordinated welfare programme. Hill signed the former and added a memorandum in which she repeated her view that 'artificial work provided by State or municipality has never yet been successful, whether financially industrially or in its influence on character'.[26] It was not the provision of work to which she objected – she regularly employed her tenants to clean or maintain her properties when they otherwise lacked paid work and might therefore be unable to pay their rent – rather, it was its large-scale introduction by those who were distant and lacked intimate knowledge of the beneficiaries of such schemes, whose 'character' they might consequently undermine.

As well as becoming increasingly out of kilter with public opinion, Hill's position was not wholly consistent. For all her opposition to public-sector building, she recognized that government intervention through legislation had helped to raise standards generally.[27] On environmental issues, state-led regulatory protections were one response to the desire to preserve landscapes and open spaces, as evidenced in the first faltering steps towards the protection of built heritage after the 1882 Ancient Monuments Act.[28] Baigent suggests in this volume that by the end of her life Hill was reconciled to state and municipal intervention in matters of open space.

In contrast to Hill, who declined public office and thought her influence increased by careful neutrality in party politics, Robert Hunter, her collaborator in founding the National Trust, was a career civil servant whose success owed a great deal to patronage by senior Liberal party

[24] Darley, *Octavia Hill*, p. 211.
[25] Darley, *Octavia Hill*, p. 214.
[26] Darley, *Octavia Hill*, p. 272.
[27] Darley, *Octavia Hill*, p. 263.
[28] B. Cowell, *The Heritage Obsession: the Battle for England's Past* (2008).

figures. Though strikingly different, Hill and Hunter in combination were a powerful force. Hunter was born in Camberwell in south London in 1844, the son of a master mariner and ship owner.[29] He attended Denmark Hill Grammar School before graduating from University College London, with a first-class degree in logic and moral philosophy. As a young lawyer he developed an interest in the law relating to common land, at a time when environmental protection had become a focus of political interest, especially among sections of the Liberal party.[30] Hunter's essay on 'The preservation of commons in the neighbourhood of the metropolis' was highly commended in a public competition sponsored by Henry Peek, whose interest had been prompted by the proposed enclosure of Wimbledon Common in 1864.[31]

Hunter's growing knowledge of the law of commons resulted in his appointment in 1867 to the legal team acting for the Commons Preservation Society (CPS) under Philip Lawrence. Lawrence's appointment as solicitor to the Office of Works the following year led to Hunter's joining Tom Fawcett and Percy Horne as the official solicitors to the CPS. The move recognized Hunter's abilities as a lawyer but also his political connections. Tom Fawcett was the brother of Cambridge academic Henry Fawcett, who was elected Liberal MP for Brighton in 1865 and was subsequently appointed Postmaster General in Gladstone's second administration in 1880. Henry Fawcett married Millicent Garrett in 1867, having previously been turned down by her elder sister Elizabeth (Hill's associate in the COS).[32] Hunter's connection with such a high-ranking Liberal politician is likely to have led to his appointment, in 1882, as solicitor to the General Post Office (GPO). Clearly Hunter's legal battles for the CPS in the defence of such open spaces as Berkhamsted Common and Epping Forest were no bar to his preferment.[33]

There are few published accounts of Hunter's life and most of them skate over his work for the GPO.[34] But this was no small role: as a state department, the GPO was the second-largest employer of civil servants and

---

[29] L. W. Chubb, 'Sir Robert Hunter (1844–1913)', rev. G. Murphy, *ODNB*.

[30] M. J. D. Roberts, 'Gladstonian liberalism and environmental protection, 1865–76', *English Historical Review*, cxxviii (2013), 292–322.

[31] The essay was published, along with the other winning entries, in *Six Essays on Commons Preservation* (1867).

[32] E. Crawford, *Enterprising Women: the Garretts and their Circle* (2002).

[33] G. Shaw Lefevre (Baron Eversley), *Commons, Forests and Footpaths: the Story of the Battle during the Last Forty-five Years for Public Rights over the Commons, Forests and Footpaths of England and Wales* (1910).

[34] Hunter's 30-year career with the GPO warrants just a single short paragraph, e.g., in Murphy, *Founders of the National Trust*, p.47.

by the time he retired Hunter was its second-highest-paid official.[35] Hunter's attention to detail, which served the cause of commons preservation so well, also benefited the postal network. He took the lead over three decades in legal developments that shaped the PO's work into the twentieth century. A warm obituarist noted that he 'instituted the systematic examination of all private bills and provisional orders made by Government departments' in order to gauge their impact on the PO, and claimed that he nearly succeeded to the position of secretary to the GPO since his administrative skills were 'as much appreciated as his legal qualifications'.[36] Hunter prepared the 1893 Conveyance of Mails Act which adjudicated on the remuneration given to railway companies for their part in the postal system. The final years of his career were taken up with the negotiations that followed the 1909 Telegraph Arbitration Act, in which the GPO assumed monopoly control over the nascent telephone network. The importance of his PO work in the eyes of contemporaries can be seen from the fact that Hunter's memorial stone in Haslemere church, Surrey, lists his work for the GPO ahead of his achievements in the preservation movement, which later commentators typically judge to have been more significant.

Hunter was a very gifted public official, presiding over a complex area of state provision with characteristic hard work and diplomacy. It was perhaps his career as a civil servant, rather than his work for open spaces, that may have led to his knighthood in 1894.[37] The contrast with Hill's campaigning career was stark. Hunter's public duties limited his freedom to speak out as Hill typically did (which is perhaps just as well, in a literal sense, since he was said not to have been the most effective public speaker),[38] while his work for the GPO sometimes directly conflicted with his personal enthusiasm for landscape and open spaces, as when the laying out of telegraph posts intruded on country views. In 1912 he joked that his contributions to the open spaces movement had been 'some compensation' for the fact that, as solicitor to the GPO, he had been active in 'forcing unwilling communities to accept overhead wires'.[39]

Canon Hardwicke Rawnsley (see Figure 14.2), the third of the National Trust's founders, was vicar of Crosthwaite and rural dean of Keswick from 1883. Rawnsley, like Hunter but unlike Hill, was actively involved in local

---

[35] M. J. Daunton, *Royal Mail: the Post Office since 1840* (1985), p. 196.

[36] E. Bennett, 'Sir Robert Hunter, KCB', *St. Martin's-le-Grand*, xxiv (1914), 4–9.

[37] Although the *ODNB* entry has it that the honour was conferred in respect of Hunter's work for open spaces conservation. He advanced to CB in 1909 and KCB in 1911.

[38] H. Barnett, *Canon Barnett: his Life, Work, and Friends* (1918), p. 323.

[39] Account of a dinner for the Telephone and Telegraph Branches, given in the GPO staff magazine, *St. Martin's-le-Grand*, xxii (1912), 71.

government. He was elected to Cumberland County Council in 1888, from which position he continued his lifelong mission to preserve the scenery of the Lake District, taking action against mining pollution and road building and favouring footpath signposting. (He lost office in 1895 after objecting to the granting of new liquor licences.)[40] Hall suggests that changes to local government, as much as anything else, provided the spur for establishing the National Trust, as they implied the revived threat of house and road building.[41] Those who cared about the environment could either work with the new arrangements, or maintain their independence. Following the Local Government Act of 1894 Hunter served as first chairman of the parish council in his adopted home of Haslemere. The council took its responsibilities seriously, undertaking activities in relation to sanitation, allotments, lighting, roads and footpaths.[42] By contrast, Hill remained somewhat suspicious of local government, turning down an offer from Kensington Borough Council to manage their stock of municipal housing.[43]

The origins of the National Trust

The prompt for the founding of the National Trust was the case of Sayes Court in Deptford, London. The house had been the home of the seventeenth-century diarist John Evelyn, whose writings on woodlands (*Sylva*, 1664) and smoke pollution (*Fumifugium*, 1661) some have regarded as proto-environmentalist texts.[44] A descendant, William John Evelyn, approached Hill in 1884 for advice on how best to preserve Sayes Court and its grounds for posterity (see Figure 14.3). The house had by this time become a museum dedicated to Evelyn's life, while the garden retained its seventeenth-century character. Hill consulted Hunter, who set out the acts of Parliament that could potentially provide the protection that was required, from the Recreation Grounds Act 1857 to the various provisions for public museums.[45] None, however, enabled the grounds and building to be protected together as a complete landscape. The local authority

---

[40] G. Murphy, 'Hardwicke Drummond Rawnsley (1851–1920)', *ODNB*.

[41] Hall, pp. 349–50.

[42] *Bygone Haslemere: a Short History of the Ancient Borough and its Immediate Neighbourhood from Earliest Times* (1914), ed. E. W. Swanton.

[43] Darley, *Octavia Hill*, p. 264.

[44] Though for a more complex and political reading of Evelyn's texts, see M. Jenner, 'The politics of London air: John Evelyn's *Fumifugium* and the Restoration', *Historical Journal*, xxxviii (1995), 535–51.

[45] Copies of the correspondence are held at the Surrey History Centre, Sir Robert Hunter papers, 1260/4/1–10. A note by Dorothy Hunter on the covering envelope reads 'Valuable Letter, containing Miss Hill's acknowledgement of what was evidently Father's first suggestion for NT'.

Figure 14.3. Sayes Court (undated).

might have been persuaded to take on the grounds, but the museum could not have been taken on as well without a ratepayers' vote. Eventually Hunter concluded that 'an Association for the management of the land and Museum' might be constituted, under either the Charitable Trustees Incorporation Act or the Joint Stock Companies Act, although questions remained as to how such a company could receive the gift of the land and building, how it would be financed, and how future company trustees would be appointed. Hill thanked Hunter for this advice, remarking that 'such a company as you suggest would be valuable', though she did not think there was sufficient time to put arrangements in place to save Sayes Court.[46]

As it turned out, the house at Sayes Court was eventually lost, although the Kyrle Society, established by Octavia Hill's sister Miranda and described by Robert Whelan in this volume, was eventually invited to work on the gardens, which survive as an open space owned by the local authority. But the seed of the National Trust idea had been planted. Hunter developed his thinking further and presented his 'Suggestion for the better preservation of open spaces' at the National Association for the Promotion of Social Science's

[46] Surrey History Centre, Sir Robert Hunter papers, 1260/4/1–10.

annual congress, held in Birmingham in September 1884.[47] In it, Hunter recounted his two decades of legal battles on behalf of the CPS in which he had deployed his expertise to defend places such as Hainault Forest, Epping Forest, Wimbledon Common, Hampstead Heath and Burnham Beeches. Released from his role as its appointed solicitor, however, he also recognized the limits of the CPS's approach. The society had no power to own land and thereby to assume the position of commoner in the eyes of the law. Hunter's role, more often than not, was to act as a legal adviser to a local individual, with an interest in the common land at stake, who was willing to be named as the party bringing a test case for the anti-enclosure action. In the case of Augustus Smith at Berkhamsted and Sir Henry Peek at Burnham Beeches, the approach had worked well.[48] It also had the advantage of thrift: if enclosures could be legally prevented, common land could remain open and accessible without the need for purchase – something which Hill knew demanded unremitting fundraising efforts which sometimes failed when developers' pockets proved too deep. But Hunter also recognized the possible grounds for legal objection to this approach. It would be far easier, he maintained, if 'some association of known public spirit, pledged to oppose inclosure' were in a position to purchase a common, were it suddenly to be available on the open market. Such an association, in the absence of any other provision in statute, would need to be constituted as a corporate company under the Joint Stock Companies' Act for the purpose of holding and managing common land in the interests of the general public. It would not look to make a profit, but would fund its work by careful management of its assets, for example through leasing grazing rights or residential properties, or any of the other methods available to private landlords (including developing estates).[49]

Here, in essence, was the idea for an institution that, just over a decade later, became the National Trust. It was an idea for a private land company 'formed, not for the promotion of thrift or the spread of political principles, and not primarily for profit, but with a view to the protection of the public interests in the open spaces of the country'. Hunter saw the purposes of such a land company as being: to acquire property, especially that over which rights of common existed; to acquire the manorial rights over such

[47] L. Goldman, *Science, Reform, and Politics in Victorian Britain: the Social Science Association 1857–1886* (Cambridge, 2002).

[48] B. Cowell, 'The Commons Preservation Society and the campaign for Berkhamsted Common, 1866–70', *Rural History*, xiii (2002), 145–61.

[49] R. Hunter, 'A suggestion for the better preservation of open spaces', paper read at the Annual Congress of the National Association for the Promotion of Social Science, Birmingham, Sept. 1884 (1884), p. 16.

land, and the open spaces that came with them; and to maintain commons, wastes, moors and other open spaces 'in their natural condition', in such a way as to 'prevent nuisances and preserve order'. In the light of the CPS's early focus on metropolitan commons and of the Sayes Court case, Hunter saw the company as being able to operate in urban as well as rural locations, acquiring open spaces in cities and towns and maintaining and managing gardens and other urban open spaces (and their buildings) 'as places of resort for recreation and instruction'.

Hunter's approach typifies how the perception (and in some cases the legal status) of the commons had changed from their being purely local assets to being 'public' places, managed for the benefit of the region or nation. Hill shared this view, which is elaborated by Readman in this volume. Writing a few years later, for example, Hill asserted that the protection of common land 'should be undertaken by the whole body of the residents in a county, poor and rich', and looked forward to 'the support of the country by south London, of the rural cottager by the suburban districts, and of both by an experienced London executive' being sufficient to arrest the loss of common land.[50] Hunter noted that the main challenge would be in finding the funds to carry out the work. Anticipating this criticism he set out the ways funds might be raised, including leasing the wider estate lands for farming, leasing sporting and other manorial rights, or even charging admission fees for entry into buildings. At first Hunter was equivocal about whether this would necessarily be a single national company. Equally, it could be locally organized along the lines of the Hills' national Kyrle Society, with its provincial branches, as Whelan touches on in his chapter, or in the way that Hill worked for her local CPS committee: 'There might, for example, be such a Company for Birmingham and the neighbourhood, for a county, or for a district like the Potteries'.[51]

Hunter's idea, as set out in his 1884 essay, was a response to a deficiency in the machinery of state provision for open spaces, rather than an idea developed in conscious opposition to government intervention. Nothing in Hunter's essay implies that state-backed solutions were not also possible or desirable. Indeed, a stated ambition for Hunter's proposed company would be, over time, to pass land on to local authorities, for continuing care and maintenance at ratepayers' expense, though this was something which, as Whelan shows, had proved problematic in the past. Local authorities were not often able to acquire whole estates, which is why a private company was

---

[50] Hill, *LFW*, 1891, p. 308.
[51] Hunter, 'Suggestion', p. 16.

needed in order to make the initial purchase on the open market, and then to find strategies for securing the long-term protection of the public interest in the land (which might be by dividing the estate between local authorities and private owners or tenants).[52]

The idea for the National Trust, then, was developed by a public servant and fitted neatly within existing legal and governmental parameters. It presented no threat to state intervention, but rather offered an additional form of protection for commons and other land, without requiring further encroachment on private landowner rights. Moreover, notwithstanding Hunter's view that companies might be local or that a national company might transfer assets to local authorities, the proposed association would be able to take a national perspective rather than a purely local one. Whereas local authorities had powers to hold open spaces on the public's behalf, some places were of national rather than local significance, and private owners 'might not look upon a local body as the fittest repository for possessions which they might be willing to make over to some body constituted on a different basis'.[53] Hill was warm to the idea, though she was insistent that the new enterprise have the word 'trust' in the title in order better to attract private donations. Her initial suggestion of 'Commons and Gardens Trust', however, was not taken up by Hunter who is said to have scribbled a note in the margin of her letter that read '?National Trust'.[54]

Politics and the early National Trust

The idea of a National Trust took a decade to put into effect. The delay was said to be due to the reluctance of George Shaw Lefevre, who correctly anticipated that the trust would compete with his CPS.[55] But the idea proved irresistible. It was taken up first in the USA, with the establishment of the Trustees of Public Reservations in Massachusetts in 1891, as Hall describes in this volume. The spur in Britain was fresh threats to the Lake District, when land at Derwent Water was put up for sale in 1893. Canon Rawnsley's enthusiastic promotion of Hunter's and Hill's idea led to an inaugural meeting in July 1894 at Grosvenor House, home of the duke of Westminster, who agreed to become president. The first meeting of the trust's provisional council took place in January 1895 at 1 Great College

---

[52] Hunter, 'Suggestion', pp. 13, 15.
[53] National Trust Archives, 'Introduction to the first Report of the Provisional Council of the National Trust' (Apr. 1895) (hereafter Annual Reports simply given with date).
[54] Waterson, *The National Trust*, p. 32. Curiously, this letter cannot now be located.
[55] Jenkins and James, *From Acorn to Oak Tree*, p. 21.

Street, London, with Hunter in the chair and Hill, Rawnsley and others in attendance.[56]

The duke of Westminster's presence as president was not the only example of the early trust's drawing on aristocratic or establishment figures for support. At the trust's first general meeting on 9 May 1895, twenty-five council members were appointed. They included, in addition to Hill, Hunter and Rawnsley, the dukes of Westminster and Devonshire, the prime minister (Lord Rosebery), the diplomat and former viceroy of India the marquis of Dufferin and Ava, lords Hobhouse and Thring, the Liberal MP James Bryce, the radical Liberal MP and former miner Thomas Burt, the artists Sir Frederic Leighton and George Frederic Watts, and the architect Alfred Waterhouse.[57] The list is interesting for its mix of social classes (there was a fairly significant social gulf between the duke of Westminster and Thomas Burt, for example), and the combination of open space enthusiasts (such as Bryce) and artists (such as Leighton, Watts and Waterhouse) – the same combination of open space and art was evident in the Hills' Kyrle Society leaders. The overwhelming dominance of the Liberal party among the parliamentarians was also striking. Various professional and artistic bodies, both private and public, nominated members to the early council; they included the National Gallery, the Royal Academy, the Society of Antiquaries and other learned societies, the Royal Institute of British Architects, the CPS and the leading universities.

Cannadine notes that in this early phase the National Trust was 'closer to the left of the political spectrum than to the right'. The Liberal party was the principal source of political support, and early trust priorities were directed towards open spaces and countryside to a degree that implied an anti-landlord stance.[58] By contrast, after the First World War, the trust's supporters shifted rightwards politically. Leading trust figures in the 1920s and 1930s, such as John Bailey, G. M. Trevelyan, R. C. Norman and the marquess of Zetland, were from higher social backgrounds and had more Conservative instincts and affiliations. The trust itself remained apolitical and was able to draw support too from the post-1945 Labour government, in particular Hugh Dalton at the treasury. Indeed, Mandler notes that Hugh Dalton, chancellor of the exchequer under Attlee, was given to describing the trust as 'a typically British example of Practical Socialism in action', something which recalls Hill's often forgotten inspiration of Christian Socialism.[59]

---

[56] National Trust Archives, National Trust Minutes Book 1895–1901 (hereafter 'Minutes Book').
[57] 'Minutes Book', p. 9.
[58] Cannadine, 'Conservation', p. 226.
[59] Mandler, *Fall and Rise*, p. 335.

'Nobler imaginings and mightier struggles'

Neutrality on party political lines, however, did not make the early National Trust unwilling to engage with government or questions of public policy. The early manifesto, 'Its aims and its works', cited the trust's first acquisitions: Dinas Oleu overlooking Barmouth in Wales, Barras Head in Cornwall, and Alfriston Clergy House in Sussex. But the document went on to explain that the trust 'is not only a holder of natural scenery and ancient buildings' but also 'does what it can to promote local interest in the preservation of any worthy historical object or natural beauty'. The trust 'brings its influence to bear in the direction and spirit of its promoters', sometimes alone and sometimes 'in conjunction with kindred societies'. Examples of this influence included the trust founders' advocacy for the preservation of the Trinity Almshouses in Whitechapel, Churchyard Bottom Wood near Highgate, and the Falls of Foyers in Scotland.[60]

The manifesto also made clear that the National Trust was set up to 'stimulate and promote legislation upon matters cognate to its aims and intention'.[61] From its earliest years, in fact, the trust sought to influence government, either to promote its own interests as a charity or to achieve greater protection for places of historic interest or natural beauty. The trust's first meeting in 1894 resulted in a letter to the chancellor of the exchequer, Sir William Harcourt, seeking exemption for the charity from taxes and death duties on any donations of land made to it. Harcourt replied that the letter had arrived too late for consideration in the budget, but that the matter would no doubt be returned to in future years.[62] A bid in 1909 for exemption for the trust from stamp duty met a similarly negative response.[63] However, acceptance in lieu arrangements were eventually introduced as part of Lloyd George's budget in 1910.

Campaigning for enhanced state protection for heritage was another concern that predominates in the early National Trust annual reports. In the first the executive committees lamented the 'impotency of the existing law' adequately to protect such national monuments as Stonehenge and the Antonine Wall. Such was their concern, and the delicacy of the issues at stake, that a special committee was set up, on which sat Hill, Hunter and Rawnsley, as well as the like-minded John Lubbock, James Bryce, General Pitt-Rivers and George Shaw Lefevre.[64] Two years later, in its third annual

---

[60] 'Its aims and its works' (*c*.1897). The trust's geographical remit extended across all of Great Britain and Ireland at this time, although a separate National Trust for Scotland was established in 1931.

[61] 'Its aims and its works' [*c*.1897].

[62] Annual Report (1894/5), p. 8.

[63] Response of Lloyd-George to question by Mr. Horniman, *Hansard*, 5th ser., x (2 Sept. 1909), 751–2.

[64] Annual Report (1894/5), pp. 6–7.

report, the trust was able to report that 'there are many indications that the jealousy or misunderstanding of Government interposition on behalf of the preservation of historic buildings as public monuments is gradually giving way';[65] this is particularly interesting as it shows Hill part of a committee which rejoices in the decline of resistance to state intervention, that is, of a decline in a stance regularly said to be her own unbending one. Nonetheless, the 1882 Ancient Monuments Act remained the only statute and was restricted to prehistoric monuments.[66] A detailed annexe to the third annual report, prepared by Hunter, compared the situation in Great Britain unfavourably with that in other European countries, the USA and Canada, an international comparison which Swenson and Hall continue in this volume. The trust's annual general meeting in July 1897 passed a resolution calling for 'further facilities to be given by legislation to private owners to place historic monuments and places of striking natural beauty beyond reach of destruction or injury'.[67]

Hunter's professional knowledge and personal interest in monument protection led to his being called on to help shape successive acts of parliament. In 1900 Lord Avebury asked him to draft at least one clause in the bill, seemingly because it was better to ask Hunter to do so than to have the drafting 'entrusted to the Office of Works'.[68] The trust's annual report for 1900 went further, and proclaimed Avebury's Ancient Monuments Bill, which became law that year, to have been 'drafted by Sir Robert Hunter'.[69]

The case of Stonehenge, in particular, threw into relief the tensions between the responsibilities of the state and the duties of private landlords for the preservation of sites of national heritage significance. At Stonehenge on the last day of 1900 an upright sarsen and its lintel fell in a storm. The following year the landowner, Sir Edmund Antrobus, ended the long tradition of tourists freely visiting the stones by enclosing Stonehenge behind a fence and charging an admission price of one shilling. This enclosure provoked a huge debate in which the National Trust played a significant role.[70] In 1902 Hunter wrote an article in *Nineteenth Century* about the Stonehenge case, explaining that the trust had 'offered some years ago to use its influence to induce the state to undertake such works as …

---

[65] Annual Report (1896/7), p. 10.
[66] J. Delafons, *Politics and Preservation: a Policy History of the Built Environment* (1997).
[67] 'Minutes Book', p. 24.
[68] Surrey History Centre, 1621/Box 1 /4 (Ancient Monuments Bill), letter dated 5 Apr. 1900.
[69] Annual Report (1899/1900), p. 12.
[70] R. Hill, *Stonehenge* (2008), p. 146.

'Nobler imaginings and mightier struggles'

were expedient to save the stones from falling'.[71] The call had fallen on deaf ears. Nevertheless, enclosure was not one of the options that the trust had proposed for protecting the stones, since according to Hunter there was little 'a barbed wire fence some distance away' could do to prevent a trilithon from falling. Hunter demonstrated that there was undeniably a public right of way to and across the site of Stonehenge and enclosing it would therefore be an affront. His solution was that 'Stonehenge should obviously be in the possession and guardianship of the nation'. Only the state could afford the regular maintenance, upkeep, and research and analysis that the site required. The site could no more be considered strictly private property than could Westminster Abbey, and Antrobus's attempt to repel visitors was doomed to fail, given the site's significance to the nation. 'The recent inclosure will prove to be a blessing in disguise if it leads to the formal transfer of Stonehenge to the care of the nation', wrote Hunter; 'but the barbed wires must be removed, and the harmony of the monument and its surroundings restored'. Hunter was here agitating for more state control over Stonehenge, in the interest of both conservation and access, which two could be reconciled but only with financial support from the government.

The scandal that broke when the Tattershall Castle fireplaces were removed in 1911 provoked the National Trust into a fresh round of agitation for new monuments legislation. The castle had been put up for sale a year earlier, and the removal of its fireplaces and their intended export was one consequence. Lord Curzon intervened to reunite the fireplaces with the castle and eventually donated the whole to the National Trust. Once more Hunter was in the lead, writing to *The Times* to argue that the Tattershall disaster could again prove a 'blessing in disguise' for heritage if it meant that the event supplied 'the motive power necessary to carry a measure through Parliament'.[72] The trust, under Hunter, drafted a fresh Monuments Bill creating an advisory board to the commissioners of works and conferring new suspensory powers on the commissioners to protect monuments. Although other bills of a similar nature were also in circulation, including one that Noel Buxton MP prepared for the Society for the Preservation of Ancient Buildings (SPAB), the National Trust claimed in its annual report the year following that the 1913 Ancient Monuments Act was 'largely as a result of their efforts'.[73]

The most significant illustration of the early trust's political influence, however, is the National Trust Act of 1907. Such was the volume of property coming to the trust in its first decade of operation that there were moves

---

[71] Sir Robert Hunter, 'The inclosure of Stonehenge', *Nineteenth Century*, lii (1902), 430–8.
[72] *The Times*, 23 Sept. 1911, p. 8.
[73] Annual Report (1913/14). A somewhat different version of events is presented in S. Thurley, *The Men From the Ministry: How Britain Saved its Heritage* (2013).

by 1905 to 'reconstitute the Trust on a more authoritative basis'.[74] By this time it held 1,700 acres of land and twenty-four properties; its founders clearly anticipated that more was on its way. The hope was that the trust could secure a royal charter and various statutory powers of 'preserving order and preventing nuisances upon its properties'.[75] The following year the argument for putting the trust on a surer footing became even more pressing after it acquired the Hindhead Commons, including the Devil's Punch Bowl, near Haslemere, as a direct result of Hunter's interventions. Perhaps, too, the trust founders wanted to limit their successors' ability to alter the organization's charitable purposes, or to deviate too far from the cause of open spaces and historic landscapes. A private member's bill, in the name of the National Trust for Places of Historic Interest and Natural Beauty, was introduced in the House of Lords in February 1907. It was heard in the Commons in June and, following amendments, received royal assent on 21 August 1907.[76] The act provided for the establishment in statute of a National Trust for the purposes of 'promoting the permanent preservation for the benefit of the nation of lands and tenements (including buildings) of beauty or historic interest and as regards lands for the preservation (so far as practicable) of their natural aspect features and animal and plant life'.[77] The wording closely matched the trust's original founding documents when it was set up as a limited company, yet the ingenuity of the act's drafting was in its general, open-ended nature. The trust was established not solely for preservation, but rather for 'promoting' preservation – a formulation that the trust can still fall back on to justify activities that go beyond the formal ownership or management of property, such as its opposition to English planning reform mentioned at the start of this chapter, or its social engagement activity in cities such as London – this latter a return to the field of action which characterized Hill's own work. The words also ensured that the trust's focus was on whole landscapes, made up of buildings, nature, and animal and plant life, rather than any one element of these. Section 21 meanwhile gave the trust the power to hold property inalienably. This powerful concept denied the trust the right to dispose of any of its inalienable property except where parliament allowed a derogation from the act. A schedule to the act listed the twenty-six freehold properties initially declared inalienable. Only a few other organizations (including the National Trust for Scotland) share the power to hold property inalienably in this way. It

[74] Annual Report (1905/6), p. 13.
[75] Annual Report (1905/6), p. 13.
[76] *Hansard*, 4th ser., clxxxi (21 Aug. 1907), 758.
[77] National Trust Act 1907, 4 (1).

is the greatest legacy of the trust founders' foresight and influence, and in particular of Robert Hunter's legal and political acumen. It must also have been something with which Hill sympathized, not least as she had proved utterly vulnerable to a sudden change of heart on a landowner's part, when Ruskin decided to sell houses long under her management, as Darley illustrates in this volume.

Conclusion

This brief survey has attempted to illustrate the many links between the National Trust and the state in its earliest decades. Whereas the trust was, and remains, an independent and apolitical charity, it was arguably just as much a creation of the state as the government's official guardians of historic sites in the Ministry of Works. Essentially, the trust was formed to fill the gap left by government non-intervention in environmental protection. While the 'men from the Ministry' took on increasing responsibilities for historic sites after the 1913 Ancient Monuments Act,[78] the National Trust Act six years earlier was in many ways an even more powerful piece of legislation. It charged the trust to act on the nation's behalf to protect land and buildings, and gave it a distinctive range of powers to hold property inalienably, powers which justify the present trust's claim that it acts 'for ever and for everyone'. Moreover, with Hill such an important figure in its activities and figurehead for its cause, the trust also provided a more domestic and feminized complement to those 'men from the Ministry', as Swenson explores in her chapter.

The distinction between the National Trust's work as a private charity and the state's public responsibilities continued to be drawn through the trust's earliest decades, the state most often being depicted as delinquent in its duties. In a volume published in 1945 to mark the trust's first fifty years, G. M. Trevelyan reflected on how

> a place of natural beauty may be destroyed, and is often so taxed by the State that it must be sold to the jerry-builder. Meanwhile, the State pours forth the money of ratepayer and taxpayer for the perpetration all over the island of outrages on the beauty of the country ... Destruction walks by noonday. Unless the State reverses the engines and instead of speeding up destruction, plans the development of the country so that the minimum of harm can be done to beauty, the future of our race, whatever its social, economic and political structure may be, will be brutish and shorn of spiritual value.[79]

---

[78] Thurley, *The Men From the Ministry*.
[79] Trevelyan, 'Introduction', in *The National Trust: a Record of Fifty Years' Achievement*, ed. J. Lees Milne (1945), p. xii.

This was written at a time when the state had grown substantially during the second world war, but it is noticeable that the call was for the state to reach even further and to adopt some of the responsibilities that the trust had taken on in protecting places of beauty (such as in the call for national parks, which were eventually established in 1949).[80] This is despite the fact that Octavia Hill, a trust founder, spent much of her career speaking out against the extension of the state. Hill took an independent view of the world, insisting that state largesse would undermine the feeling of responsibility that Christian citizens ought to have for one another and their surroundings. The National Trust was created at a time when there was little government intervention in matters of landscape or heritage protection in the UK, in contrast to the situation in continental European states and the USA, as Swenson describes in this volume.[81]

The founding of the National Trust was a shared endeavour. Much can be traced back to the correspondence between Hill and Hunter over Sayes Court in 1884. Hunter's essay of the same year fleshed out the idea in more detail. The concept of a property-owning trust had the merit of being entirely independent of government, and of shouldering responsibilities that, a few decades later, the government itself would adopt. The passing of the 1907 private member's bill putting the trust on a statutory footing indicated parliamentary approval of its work and longer-term goals. Subsequent acts have extended the trust's powers, for example in 1937 and 1939 when its Country Houses Scheme was made possible by legislation changes to enable the organization to acquire entailed estates.[82]

Although the National Trust continues today to emphasize its independence from government, the truth is more complicated. If one of its founders, Octavia Hill, was at times strident in her opposition to state intervention, another, Sir Robert Hunter, worked at the heart of government as solicitor to the GPO. If Hill provided the spiritual fire and motivation behind the trust's establishment, Hunter used his legal expertise to integrate the trust into the machinery of late nineteenth- and early twentieth-century governance. He did so by giving it a generously wide scope of powers (to 'promote' the preservation of land and buildings), and by ensuring that the organization remained politically neutral, despite the clear Liberal party affiliations of many of its earliest proponents. In December 2013, in the 1913 Ancient Monuments Act's centenary year, and despite the opposition to its earlier proposal to dispose of state-held woods and forests, the UK

---

[80] Mandler, *Fall and Rise*, pp. 311–53.
[81] A. Swenson, *The Rise of Heritage: Preserving the Past in France, Germany, and England, 1789–1914* (Cambridge, 2013).
[82] Mandler, *Fall and Rise*, 1997.

government proposed passing the day-to-day management of its heritage estate in England to an independent charity.[83] In this way it might be observed that the post-war consensus on the state requirement to intervene in matters of environment protection has been replaced by an explicit recognition, at least from Conservative quarters, of the charity model's value, working hand-in-hand with the state. Whether the new charity vehicle for heritage, the English Heritage Trust, proves as successful as the National Trust in garnering public support for its work remains to be seen. It might be argued that the change owes much to political expediency and is philosophically grounded, desiring to limit state expenditure rather than recognize the value of charitable endeavour that Octavia Hill gave to the National Trust in its earliest years.

This embrace of charitable endeavour is just one of the ways in which Hill left her mark on the National Trust. If this chapter has argued for Hunter's importance in the trust and for the perception to be modified that it always saw itself as independent of and sometimes in contradistinction to the state, it certainly does not in consequence suggest that Hill's role in the trust was unimportant, or that she was a mere figurehead. Indeed, with its recent efforts to extend its reach into cities and among their considerably more diverse populations, the trust in many ways now more closely reflects Hill's values than it did in some other periods, most obviously that between the world wars. A good example of its inner city work is the new playground at Sutton House, Hackney, the trust's house where the conference which gave rise to this book was hosted. Moreover, the trust continues to seek to act, as Darley describes in this volume, along the same lines advocated by Hill, that is, attempting to notice need and respond flexibly to it, rather than to codify and follow through a rigid system. Though its founders gave it a complex legacy, the National Trust continues to bear the mark of each of them – not least Octavia Hill.

---

[83] Department for Culture, Media and Sport, 'English Heritage New Model: Consultation' (7 Dec. 2013) <https://www.gov.uk/government/consultations/english-heritage-new-model-consultation> [accessed 2 Jan. 2014].

Index

Adams, Charles Kingsley, 134
Aira Force (Lake District), 236
Alden, Percy, MP, 269–70, 272
Alford, Revd. B.,124, 267
Alfriston Clergy House (E. Sussex),40, 41, 165, 225, 226–31, 310
All Saints' Mission Hall (Grays), 99
All Saints' (Mile End) church, 105
Allen, Matthew, 280
Ambler, Louis, 288
Ancient Monuments Act (1882), 301, 311
Ancient Monuments Act (1900), 311
Ancient Monuments Consolidation and Amendment Act (1913), 23, 312, 315
Anderson, Anne Hoole, 61
Anderson, Elizabeth Garrett, *see* Garrett, Elizabeth
Antonine Wall, 310
Antrobus, Sir Edmund, 311
Argyll, duke of, 235
Army Cadet Force, 3, 21, 24
Arnold, Matthew, 67, 92, 141, 248, 252, 253
Artisans' and Labourers' Dwellings Act (1875), 41, 160, 284
arts, 24–5, 36, 47, Chapter 3 passim, 89, 91–2, 129, 130–1, 194–5
Arts and Crafts Exhibition Society, 72
Arts and Humanities Research Council, 23
Ashbee, Charles R., 196, 199, 205, 218, 230–5, 236
Ashbee, Janet, 230–1, 232–6
Ashdown Forest (E. Sussex), 237
Asquith, Herbert, 137

Association for Protected Nature Parks (Germany), 198
Association of Women House Property Managers, *see* Society of Women Housing Managers
Attlee, Clement, 295, 309
Ayres, Alice, 69, 72, 73–6, 86, 87–9

Bailey, John, 309
Baldwin, Stanley, 298
Balfour, Max, 230
Bankside Open Spaces Trust, 282
Barnardo, Thomas, 115
Barnett, Henrietta, 6, 7, 116, 125, 128, 137, 138, 259
Barnett, Samuel, 59, 92, 93, 125, 137, 244, 259, 262–3
Barras Head (Cornwall), 180, 310
Barrett's Court (Marylebone), 49
Barrington, Emilie, 65, 68, 70, 78, 82, 84, 85, 89, 120, 131
Barton family, 131–3
Barton, Anne, 132
Barton, Lieutenant-General Charles, 132, 133
Barton, Lieutenant-Colonel Hugh William, 133
Barton, Colonel Nathaniel Dunbar, 133
Bastow, Revd. T. C. V., 286
Beaufoy, Mark, MP, 106–9
Bedford, duke of, 107
Bell, Enid Moberly, 7, 48, 59, 122, 148
Benyon, Revd F. W., 227
Berkhamsted Common (Herts.), 306
Bermondsey Boys' Club, 100
Besant, Walter, 68, 213

Beveridge, William, 262, 270
Black, Clementina, 88
Bodichon, Barbara, *see* Smith, Barbara Leigh
Bond, Nigel, 219, 222
Booth, Charles, 281, 284, 300
Booth, Mary, 123, 127
Booth, William, 115
Borzello, Frances, 111
Bosanquet, Helen, 7, 14, 260–1
Bowditch, Henry, 200
Boyd, Nancy, 16
Brabazon, Lord Reginald, 166–7
Brabrook, Sir Edward, 268
Brace, Catherine, 151
Bragg, Melvyn, 13
Brandelhow (Lake District), 235
Bremner, Robert, 13
Brion, Marion, 18 n. 51, 20, 57, 60
Bristol Civic Society, 3
British Museum, 219
Bronte, Charlotte, 136
Brown, Ford Madox, 71, 82, 85
Brown, Frederick, 76
Brown, Gerald Baldwin, 204, 205
Bryce, James, 167, 174, 212, 216, 220, 309, 310
Burdett-Coutts, Baroness, 280, 292
Burne-Jones, Edward, 65, 130
Burnham Beeches (Bucks.), 115, 306
Burt, Thomas, 309
Butler, Henry Montagu, 213
Butler, Josephine, 16, 17, 126
Buxton, Noel, MP, 312

Cadbury, George, 12
Cannadine, David, 182, 296
Carlisle, Lord, 222
Carlyle, Thomas, 82, 100, 218, 225, 309
Castle Yard, Institute (Blackfriars), 98
Chance, Sir William, 267
Chandler, Elizabeth, 78

Charitable Trustees Incorporation Act (1872), 305
Charity Organization Society, 3, 7, 11, 14, 30, 149, 176, 251, 260–3, 300
Chartism, 258
Chase, Ellen, 59, 145–6, 148, 157, 200, 206, 214–15, 229
Christian Socialism, 34–5, 40, 164, 172, 181, 309
Church Army, 134–5
Churches, *see* All Saints', Holy Trinity, Leytonstone Baptist Church, St. Clements, St. George the Martyr, St. George's, St. John's, St. Jude's, St. Mary's, St. Nicholas, St. Peter's, St Saviour's
Churchyard Bottom Wood (Highgate), 168–9, 310
City Parochial Charities, 108–9
Clarion Cycling Clubs, 175–6
Clayton, Peter, 20
Clemen, Professor Paul, 204
Clifford, Edward, 134, 249
Club for Factory Girls (Aldersgate), 100
Cobbledick, John, 106–7
Cockerell, Sydney, 51, 121, 124, 125, 170, 181
Coleridge, Samuel Taylor, 213
Collingwood, W.G., 39
Collins, Ellen, 200, 216
'Colour, space and music for the people' (1884), *see* Hill, Octavia
Commons Preservation Society, 3, 40, 95, 107, 115, 117, 159, 163, 165, 170, 178, 184, 187, 193, 195, 212, 219, 221, 302, 306–9
Cons, Emma, 59, 107
Contagious Diseases Acts (1864, 1866, 1869), 256
Conveyance of Mails Act (1893), 303
Cooper, Anthony Ashley, MP, 221
Corn Laws, 258
Corporation of City of London, 115

Index

'Cottage Property in London' (1866), see Hill, Octavia
Countrywide Holiday Association, 176
Cowper, Henry, MP, 66
Craik, Georgina, 100
Crane, Walter, 48, 49, 56, 65, 69, 70–89, 98–9, 112, 120, 131, 158, 282
  Ideals in Art, 70–1
  Aesop's Fables, 116
Creighton, Beatrice, 233
Crockham Hill (Kent), 7, 8, 9, 14, 15, 143, 167, 172, 190
Cromwell Buildings (Southwark), 280–1
Cross Act, see Artisans' and Labourers' Dwellings Act
Crowley, Aleister, 286
Cruikshank, Frederick, 129
Cumberland County Council, 304
Curtis, Lionel, 226, 230
Curzon, Lord, 312

Dalton, Hugh, 298, 309
Darbishire, Henry, 292
de Morgan, William, 69, 121
Demos (think-tank), 22
Denmark Hill (Camberwell), 36
Denmark Hill Grammar School, 302
Deptford (London), 59, 99, 105, 141, 144, 146, 156–7, 160, 200, 214, 221, 304
  and see St. Luke's parish hall, St. Nicholas, Sayes Court
Derby, Lord, 173, 181
Derham, Walter, 107
Derry Street (Camden), 42, 43
Derwentwater (Lake District), 111, 235–6, 308
Devil's Punch Bowl (Surrey), *see* Hindhead Common
Devonshire, duke of, 309
Dickens, Charles, 126

Dictionary of National Biography (Oxford), 7, 24
Dilke, Sir Charles, 42
Dinas Oleu (Barmouth), 213, 310
Disused Burial Grounds Act (1884), 160
Dodd, John Theodore, 266–7, 270, 272
Douglas Buildings (Southwark), 284–285
Doulton, Sir Henry, 109
Dowling, Linda, 111
Drapers' Almshouses (Southwark), 289–90
Driscoll, Samantha G., 17–18
Drury Lane burial ground (Camden), 103–4
Ducie, countess of, *see* Moreton, Julia Reynolds
Duff, Lady Grant, 120
Dufferin, Lady, 217
Dufferin, Lord, 213, 217, 235, 309
Dulwich College (Southwark), 158
Dundas, Lady Jane, 66

Eales, George, 82
Ecclesiastical commissioners, 65, 66, 221, 227, 231, 282, 283, 286, 287
Edward Edwards Almshouses (Southwark), 289
Egmont, dowager countess of, 224
Eliot, Charles, 216
Eliot, George, 30
English Heritage, 21, 23, 316
Epistle to Bathhurst, 95
Epping Forest (Essex), 141, 147, 176–7, 184, 306
Evelyn, John, 304
Evelyn, William John, 304

Falls of Foyers (Inverness-shire), 310
Falls of Lodore (Cumbria), 213
Father Damien, 134–5

Fawcett, Henry, MP, 105, 113, 302
Fawcett, Millicent, 105, 107
Fawcett, Tom, 302
Fedden, Robin, 210
female suffrage, 4, 11, 178
Fighting Téméraire, 52
Fishmongers' Almshouses (Southwark), 289
Flight, Mathilda, 43, 44
Flight, Thomas, 42, 43, 44
Fors Clavigera, see Ruskin
Forster, W. E., MP, 179
Fortnightly Review, 37, 39
Fox, Hannah, 216
Freshwater Place (Marylebone), 39, 49, 70, 148, 154

Gable Cottages (Southwark), 285–6, 289
Garbutt Place (Marylebone), 19, 21, 36, 37, 39, 57
Garibaldi, Giuseppe, 100
Garrett, Elizabeth (Anderson), 34, 300
Gaskell, Elizabeth, 174–5
Gates, Barbara, 16
Geddes, Patrick, 234
General Board of Health, 30
General Post Office, 302–3
Gillies, Margaret, 31, 129
Gladstone, W. E., 302
Gomme, Austen, 234
Gomme, Sir Laurence, 234
Gordon, General Charles George, 100–1
Governesses' Benevolent Institution, 34–5
Gowbarrow (Lake District), 164, 236
Gowers Report (1950), 295
Grasmere (Lake District), 213
Greenaway, Kate, 52
Gregg, Miss, 105
Grimston, Edward, 130, 136
Grimston, James, 130

Guild of Handicraft, 230–1, 233
Guild of St George, see Ruskin
Guillery, Peter, 289

Habitual Criminals Act (1869), 256
Hainault Forest (Essex), 306
Hammersmith Socialist Society, 86
Hampstead Garden Suburb (Barnet), 137
Hampstead Heath (Camden), 170, 193, 306
  see also Parliament Hill Fields
Harcourt, Sir William, 42, 310
Harris, Mary, 50, 131, 249
Hartnoll, James, 284–5
Haslemere (Surrey), 303, 304
Henry Place (Southwark), 60
Herbert, George, 56, 100, 102, 113
heritage, 182–4, Chapter 8 passim, 207–8, 310–11
Herkomer, Hubert von, 137
Hewison, Robert, 48
Hibbert, Sir John, 220
Higham, Florence, 133
Highgate (London), 31
Hill, Emily (Maurice), 7, 29, 35, 125, 133, 134
Hill, Florence, 29, 93, 200
Hill, Gertrude, 29, 30, 50, 247
Hill, James, 27, 28, 29, 30
Hill, Miranda, 38, 121, 123, 134, 135, 163, 277, 305
  birth, 29
  and Kyrle Society, 36, 40, 65, Chapter 5 passim, 193
  buried at Crockham Hill, 7, 8
Hill, Octavia
  birth, 27, 29
  education, 34–5
  influence of early life on character, 29–30, 33, 194
  personality, 6, 121–2, 138, 277
  religious beliefs, 7, 11, 16–17, 25,

35, 85, 105, 131, 150, 152–3, 167, 224–6, 238, 247, 249–50, 315
work as a teacher, 35, 141
work for Ladies' Cooperative Guild, 33–4
architectural preferences, 56–7, 61, 66–7, 228, 234, 239, 273
cadet force, 3, 11, 21, 24, 147–8
as campaigner, 40–1, 44, 303
as public speaker, 35, 303
as fundraiser, 39, 223
relationship with Ruskin, 36–9, Chapter 3 passim, 194–5, 229, 239, Chapter 11 passim
nervous breakdown, 39
view of women's public roles, 4–5, 25, 39–40, 41–2, 247, 300
opposition to female suffrage, 4, 11, 178
social philosophy, 41, 89, 152–61, 164, 168, 178–9, 197, 266, 270–1, 315
opposition to state pension, 268, 300
home at Larksfield, Crockham Hill, Kent, 7, 160, 167, 190, 282
founding of National Trust, 111, 163, 187, 192, Chapters 10 and 14 passim
portrait by John Singer Sargent (1898), 5–6, 7
influence in Europe, 24, 200–6
influence in USA, 12–13, 17, 18, 20, 24, 123, 200, 214–18
professional reputation, 14–20, 23
later reputation, 5, 6, 11–26
obituaries, 6
memorialization and commemorations, 7–10, 25, Chapter 6 passim, 143, 190
biographies, 6–7, 13
centenary of death (2012), 21–3, 191

publications, 37, 39, 42
Letters to fellow-workers, 13, 38–9, 67, 87, 93, 109, 111, 112 ,142, 164, 165, 169, 180, 194, 204, 223, 248, 252–3, 286
'Cottage Property in London' (1866), 37
The Homes of the London Poor (1875), 4, 39, 41, 200, 203
Our Common Land (1877), 4, 180, 194, 195, 200
'Colour, space and music for the people' (1884), 203
and see arts, heritage, housing, Kyrle Society, National Trust, open spaces Red Cross Cottages, Sayes Court, Swiss Cottage Fields, welfare
Hill, Thomas, 28, 29
Hill, William Thomson, 7, 127, 128
Hilton, Boyd, 258
Hindhead Common (Surrey), 313
Historic Buildings Council, 295
Hobhouse, Lord, 309
Hodson, William, 29
Holland, Sydney, 267
Holme Court Industrial School (Isleworth), 99
Holmes, Charles, 128
Holy Trinity (Lambeth) church, 99
Homerton Parish Hall (Hackney), 100
Homes of the London Poor (1875), *see* Hill, Octavia
Hoole, Elijah, 48, 58, 61, 66, 71, 282, 285, 287, 288
Hoptons' Almshouses (Southwark), 289
Hornby, James, 213
Horne, Percy, 302
Horne, Richard Henry, 31, 129
housing, 5, 12, 16, 18, 36–9, 42, 47, 49, 160–1, 178, 193, 194, 200, 265
Housing of the Working Classes Act (1885), 42

Housing of the Working Classes Act (1890), 290
Howitt, Anna Mary, 33, 129
Howitt, William, 31, 129, 178
Hughes, Jeanie, *see* Nassau Senior, Jeanie
Hughes, Thomas, 34, 40
Hunt, Tristram, MP, 22
Hunter, Sir Robert, 6, 23, 40, 107, 111, 155, 160, 163, 164, 166, 173, 184, 187, 190, 205, 207, 209, 214, 216, 220, 223, 224, 227, 234, 297, 301–3, 304, 305–6, 310, 311
  attends Denmark Hill Grammar School, 302
  attends University College London, 302
  work for Commons Preservation Society, 193, 302
  chair of Open Spaces Branch of Kyrle Society, 103
  appointed Solicitor to the General Post Office, 302–3
  as public speaker, 303
  develops idea of National Trust, 194, 212, 305–6
  involvement in Ancient Monuments legislation, 311
  views on Stonehenge, 311–12
  centenary of death (1913), 23, 192n.
Huxley, Professor, 213
Hydon Heath (Surrey), 187
Hyndman, Henry, 86

Ide Hill (Kent), 8, 237
Ilfracombe Flats (Southwark), 284–5
Imitation of Christ (Thomas à Kempis), 248–9
Improved Industrial Dwellings Company, 280–1, 284, 287, 290
Institute for Economic Affairs, 17

Jackson, T. G., 61
James, Henry, 197
Jamieson, Alex, 72, 81–2
Janes, Emily, 217
Jewish Girls' Club (Bayswater), 99
Jex-Blake, Sophia, 34, 35
Johns, Catherine, 224
Johnston, Susanna, 132
Jones, Samuel, 22
Judge, Betty, 20–1

Kanturk Castle (County Cork), 224
Keatinge, Lieut.-Gen., 107
Keats, John, 224
Kennington Working Mens' Club, 100
Kensington Borough Council, 304
King's College (Cambridge), 158
King's College (London), 35
Kingsley, Charles, 34, 35, 47, 49, 100
Kinloss, Lady, 231
Kipling, Rudyard, 237
Kirby-Turner, Karel, 37
Knole Park (Kent), 177
Knutsford, Viscount, *see* Holland, Sydney
Kyrle Society, 3, 25, 36, 40, 48, 53, 65, 66, 68, 71, 84, 85, Chapter 5 passim, 120, 153, 163, 166, 184, 193, 198, 222, 282
  Decorative Branch, 96, 98–101, 103, 116
  Literature Distribution Branch, 96, 97, 98, 103, 113
  Musical Branch, 96, 97, 98, 103, 113, 116
  Open Spaces Branch, 96, 97, 98, 101–5, 113, 115, 116
Kyrle, John, 95

La Thangue, Henry Herbert, 76
Labouring Classes Dwelling Houses Acts (1866, 1867), 281

Index

Ladies' Cooperative Guild, 33–4, 36, 131
Ladies' Sanitary Association, 4, 47, 147
Lake District, *see* Aira Force, Brandelhow, Derwentwater, Gowbarrow, Grasmere, Latrigg, Monk Coniston, Thirlmere, Ullswater
Lake District Defence Society, 177
Lake Louise (Canada), 217
Lambeth Guardians' School, 100
Lane, Laura, 88
Lansbury, George, 260, 298
Latrigg (Lake District), 177, 178
Lawrence, Philip, 302
Lees-Milne, James, 190
Leigh Hunt, James, 31
Leighton, Lord Frederick, 53, 65, 68–9, 84, 112, 116, 213, 309
Leonard, T. Arthur, 176
Letters to fellow-workers, *see* Hill, Octavia
Lewes, Charles, 30
Lewes, George Henry, 30
Lewis, G.R., 50
Lewis, Jane, 14, 57
Leytonstone Baptist Church, 116
Liberal party, 28, 180, 212, 213, 214, 219–20, 262, 302, 309, 315
Licensed Victuallers' Benevolent Institution (Southwark), 289
Liebmann, George, 17
Lincoln, Alice, 200, 216
Lincoln's Inn (Camden), 35
Linton, William James, 86
Livesay, Ruth, 14, 62
Lloyd George, David, 310
Local Government Act (1894), 304
Local Government Board, 40, 41
Loch, Charles Stewart, 123, 126, 260
London County Council, 5, 290
London Fever Hospital, 30

London, open spaces, *see* Churchyard Bottom Wood, Parliament Hill Fields, Poor's Land, Postman's Park, Purley Beeches, Swiss Cottage Fields, Vauxhall Park, West Wickham Common
Long Crendon Court House (Buckinghamshire), 196–7, 231–5
Lowell, James Russell, 215, 237
Lubbock, James, 310
Lumsden, Mary, 209, 225
Lynch, Miss, 105

Macmillan's Magazine, 39
Madox Brown, Ford, 59
Magdalen Hospital for the Reception of Penitent Prostitutes (Southwark), 289, 291
Malpass, Peter, 12
Maltz, Diana, 14–16, 57, 87, 156
Malvern College Mission (Canning Town), 100
Manchester Town Hall, 71
Mandler, Peter, 295, 309
Manea Fen (Cambs.), 29
Mann, Peter H., 18
Mansfield House (Canning Town), 269
Mansion House (London), 98
Mariners Hill (Kent), 169, 172, 237, 238
Married Women's Property Act (1870), 33, 258
Marsh, Jan, 227
Marylebone (London), *see* Barrett's Court, Freshwater Place, Garbutt Place, Nottingham Place, St. Christopher's Buildings, St. Francis Home for Working Boys
Maurice, Charles Edmund, 7, 129, 133, 227
Maurice, Emily Southwood, *see* Hill, Emily

Maurice, Frederick Denison, 7, 25, 34, 35, 44, 48, 124, 131–3, 152, 167, 224, 243, 246, 249–50, 253
Mead, Edwin, 82
Meath, Countess of, 96
Meath, earl of, *see* Brabazon, Reginald
Memorial to Heroic Self-Sacrifice, *see* Postman's Park
Metropolitan Association for Befriending Young Servants, 267
Metropolitan Board of Works, 107–8, 284
Metropolitan Industrial Dwellings Association, 65
Metropolitan Open Spaces Act (1881), 104
Metropolitan Provident Medical Association, 268
Metropolitan Public Gardens Association, 101, 166, 217, 219, 221
Michelangelo, 50
Mill, John Stuart, 255
Miller, Hugh, 196
Mines and Collieries Act (1842), 31
Minet, Miss, 105
Ministry of Works, 314
Mr. Straw's House (Notts.), 183
Mocatta, F. D., 107
Modern Painters, *see* Ruskin
Mole, David, 156
Money, J. H., 131–134
Monk Coniston estate (Lake District), 224
Moreton, Julia Reynolds, Lady Ducie, 66, 215, 282
Morgan, Victoria N., 16
Morris, Ernest William, 267
Morris, William, 40, 70, 86, 92, 106, 112, 180, 192, 194, 196, 199, 204, 205, 219, 225, 230
Muchelney Priest's House (Somerset), 225
Muthesius, Herman, 204

Nash, Joseph, 283
National Committee for the Promotion of the Break-Up of the Poor Law, 262
National Gallery, 309
National Health Society, 93, 147
National Land Fund, 295
National parks, 218, 235–6
National Portrait Gallery, 7, 22, 23, 24, 124–5, 218
National Trust, 3, 8, 9, 14, 21, 22, 23, 25, 40, 48, 111, 117, 120, 163–5, 167, 173, 178, 180, 187–90, 194, 195, 208, Chapters 10 and 14 passim
National Trust Act (1907), 297 312–313
Council, 219
influencing government, 296, 310
Country Houses Scheme, 190, 295, 297, 315
Neptune Coastline Campaign, 182
and see Alfriston Clergy House, Barras Head, Berkhamsted Common, Brandelhow, Dinas Oleu, Hindhead Common, Ide Hill, Kanturk Castle, Long Crendon Court House, Mariners Hill, Monk Coniston estate, Mr. Straw's House, Muchelney Priest's House, Rainham Hall, Sutton House, Tattershall Castle, Tintagel Old Post Office, Toys Hill, Wallington Hall, Winster Market House
National Union of Women Workers, 217
Nattali, M. A., 95
Naumburg, Paul Schulze, 204
Nene, river, 27
New Poor Law Act (1834), 28, 40, 41, Chapter 12 passim
Newall, Christopher, 119, 136, 137
Niagara Falls, 217

Index

Nightingale, Florence, 16, 100, 244
Nineteenth Century, 39
Norman, R. C., 309
Norton, Charles Eliot, 216
Nottingham Place (Marylebone), 113 n. 89, 141

O'Neill, Morna, 71, 76
Octavia Hill Association, Philadelphia, 12, 17–18, 200, 216
Octavia Hill Birthplace Trust, Wisbech, 21
Octavia Hill Housing Trust, 14
Octavia Hill Society, 20
Octavia Housing, 21, 23
Old Age Pension Act (1908), 5
Oliver, Francis, 187
open spaces, 16, 24, 40, 65, 101–6, Chapter 7 passim, 160, 163, 164, 165, 171, 173, 181, 184, 194, 307
Ormond, Richard and Leonée, 126
Our Common Land (1877), *see* Hill, Octavia
Owen, Robert, 28, 29

Paradise Place (Marylebone), *see* Garbutt Place
Parkes, Hilma Molyneux, 88
Parliament Hill Fields (Camden), 190
Parrish, Helen, 216
Passmore Edwards, John, 126
Pater, Walter, 25
Payne, James, 17
Peabody Square (Southwark), 291–3
Peabody Trust, 291–2
Peabody, George, 11, 291
Peek, Henry, 302, 306
People's Palace (Mile End Road), 68
Pestalozzi, Johann Heinrich, 29
Philip, A. M., 290
Photography, development of, 119
Pitt-Rivers, Augustus, 310
Plymouth, Lord, 298

Pollock, Lady Frederick, 123, 126
Poor's Land (Bethnal Green), 105
Pope, Alexander, 95
Portland, duke of, 288
Postman's Park (London), 69, 121
Potter, Beatrix (Heelis), 224
Powell, James, 105, 282
Princess Alice, 200 205
Princess Louise, 106, 109, 217, 222, 235
Prochaska, Frank, 16
Public sphere, feminine, 4, 18
Purley Beeches (Croydon), 108, 165

Queen Victoria, 92, 112, 121, 222
Queen's College (Harley Street), 34–5
Quelch, Harry, 265, 272

Rackham, Arthur, 99
Ragged School, 24, 33
Rainham Hall (Essex), 183
Raphael, 50
Rathbone, Eleanor, 269, 272
Rawnsley, Canon Hardwicke, 6, 40, 70, 173, 177, 187, 190, 199, 204, 205, 207, 209–10, 214, 215, 217, 220, 224 228, 235, 298, 303–4, 310
Recreation Grounds Act (1857), 304
Red Cross Cottages, Hall and Gardens (Southwark), 21, 25, 48, 49, 53, 56, 61, 62, Chapter 4 passim, 98, 105, 113, 120–1, 131, 149, 157–9, 229, 282–3, 289, 290
Reform Acts (1867, 1884), 179
Regent's Park (Camden), 141
Report of an Inquiry into the Conditions of Dock Labour at the Liverpool Docks (1904), 269
Reynolds, Dame Fiona, 21, 191
Richmond, George, 136
Ripley and Merrow buildings (Southwark), 290–1
Rooke, Thomas Matthews, 188

Rosebery, Lord, 213, 309
Rossetti, Dante Gabriel, 68
Rousseau, Jean-Jacques, 226
Rowe Housing Trust, 14
Royal Academy, 119, 219, 309
Royal Commission on Housing of the Working Classes (1884), 42, 221, 260, 283, 301
Royal Commission on the Aged Poor (1893), 260
Royal Commission on the Employment of Children (Mines) (1842), 30–2
Royal Commission on the Poor Laws (1905–9), 24, Chapter 12 passim, 301
  Minority and Majority Reports, 260–2, 301
Royal Freemasons' School for Girls (Southwark), 289
Royal Geographical Society, 286
Royal Horticultural Society, 286
Royal Institute of British Architects, 309
Rudorff, Ernst, 204
Ruskin, John, 25, 36–9, Chapter 3 passim, 84, 92, 124, 126, 129, 131, 136, 141, 150, 156, 192, 194–6, 197, 204, 205, 225–6, 229, 230, 235, 239, Chapter 11 passim
  Guild of St George, 39, 252
  Modern Painters, 36
  Fors Clavigera, 39, 252
  Sesame and Lilies, 244
  Unto This Last, 245

St. Christopher's Buildings (Marylebone), 113–14
St. Clements, Fulham Palace Road (Hammersmith and Fulham) church, 100
St. Francis Home for Working Boys (Marylebone), 98
St. George the Martyr (Bloomsbury) church, 105
St. George's Guild, *see* Ruskin
St. George's, Hanover Square (Westminster) church, 105
St. John's, Waterloo (Lambeth) church, 56, 100, 113
St. Jude's, Whitechapel (Tower Hamlets) church, 92, 125, 259
St. Luke's parish hall (Deptford), 99
St. Mary's, Bryanston Square (Westminster) church, 38
St. Nicholas (Deptford) church, 105
St. Patrick's Benevolent Society (Southwark), 99
St. Peter's, Bethnal Green (Tower Hamlets) church, 105
St. Saviour's (Southwark) church, 88
Sala, George, 65
Salisbury, Lord, 221, 287
Salt, Titus, 12
Saltaire, 61–2
Salviati, Antonio, 105, 282
Samuel, Raphael, 192
Sanitary Laws Enforcement Society, 147
Sargent, Charles, 218
Sargent, Charles Sprague, 219
Sargent, John Singer, 5–6, 7, 22, 23, 122, 123–8, 134, 136, 137, 138, 217–18
Sayes Court (Deptford), 304–5, 307, 315
Scharf, George, 130
Schulyer, Georgina, 223
Schuyler, Louisa Lee, 200
Schuster, Paula, 222, 231, 235
Scott, William Bell, 71
Selborne, countess of, 287–8
Selborne, earl of, 288
Select Committee on Artisans' and Labourers' Dwellings Improvement (1882), 260

Index

Senior, Jeanie Nassau, 34, 42, 300
Sevenoaks (Kent), 61
Sexton, James, 270, 272
Shaen, William, 39
Sharples, James, 82
Sharrow Cross, Ripon, 225
Shaw-Lefevre, George,107, 155, 187, 211–12, 220, 308, 310
Sheffield Clarion Ramblers, 176
Smith, Barbara Leigh (Bodichon), 33
Smith, Greg, 85
Smith. Augustus, 306
Snowdon, mountain, 213
Social Democratic Federation, 86, 265
Social Science Association, 251, 305
Socialist League, 86
Society for Improving the Condition of the Labouring Classes, 164
Society for Promoting Women as County Councillors, 220
Society for the Diffusion of Christian Knowledge, 93
Society for the Protection of Ancient Buildings, 40, 194, 195, 204, 205, 219, 227, 235, 312
Society of Antiquaries of London, 23, 130, 136, 194, 205, 219, 309
Society of Friends (Quakers), 17, 131
Society of Women Housing Managers, 18
South Africa, 200
South London Working Men's College, 92
Southey, Robert, 213
Southwark Cadet Company, 3
Southwark Cathedral, 21
Southwark, London Borough of, 21, 25, 158
and see Cromwell Buildings, Douglas Buildings, Drapers' Almshouses, Dulwich College, Fishmongers' Almshouses, Gable Cottages, Henry Place, Peabody Square, Red Cross Cottages, Ripley and Merrow buildings, St. Saviour's, Union Steet, White Cross cottages, Winchester Cottages
Southwood Smith (Hill), Caroline, 28, 29, 31, 33, 34, 223, 238
Southwood Smith, Thomas, 30, 33, 129, 221
Spain, Daphne, 18
Spencer, Isobel, 85
Spicker, Paul, 12
Springhill, John, 11
Spuybroek, Lars, 54
Stanley, Arthur, dean of Westminster, 35
Stansfield, James, 41
Stansky, Peter, 211
State Charities Aid Association of New York, 200
Stedman Jones, Gareth, 11, 17, 62
Stephens, Leslie, 175
Sterling, John, 133
Stetz, Margaret, 119
Stocks, Mary, 128
Stonehenge (Wilts.), 310, 311–12
Strachey, John St. Loe, 227
Sunday Society, 92
Sutherland, John F., 12–13
Sutton House (Hackney), 183, 316
Swaffham (Norfolk), 177
Swift, Jonathan, 179
Swiss Cottage Fields (Camden), 40, 163, 193
Symonds, Richard, 17

Tabor, Margaret E., 7
Talbot, Fanny, 213
Tanner, Slingsby, 106
Tarn, John Nelson, 281, 292
Tate, Henry, 107
Tattershall Castle (Lincolnshire), 312
Tawney, R. H., 270–2
Telegraph Arbitration Act (1909), 303

Tennyson, Alfred Lord, 87
The Spectator, 65, 68
The Star in the East, 28
Thirlmere (Lake District), 40
Thompson, F. M. L., 174
Thompson, Mrs Childers, 224
Thring, Edward, 49
Thring, Lord, 309
Tintagel Old Post Office (Cornwall), 224
Tinworth, George, 109
Tooke, Thomas, 31, 32
Townsend, Charles Harrison, 109, 112
Toynbee Hall (Whitechapel), 137, 230, 259, 270, 282
Toys Hill (Kent), 19, 237
Trevelyan, C. P., 174
Trevelyan, G. M., 295, 309, 314
Trevelyan, Sir Walter and Lady, 71
Trinity Almshouses (Whitechapel), 310
Trinity College Mission (Camberwell), 99
Trustees of Public Reservations (Boston, USA), 214–16, 219, 308
Turner, J. M. W., 36, 47, 51, 52, 213

Ullswater (Lake District), 111, 164, 167
Union Steet, Borough (Southwark), 76
Upcott, Janet M., 18

Vachall, Ada, 150
Vauxhall Park (Lambeth), 105–11, 113
Verulam, Lord, *see* Grimston, James
Victoria Hospital (Chelsea), 100
Victoria Women's Settlement, 269
Victorian Dwellings Association, 65
Voysey, C. F., 99, 112

Waldo, Fullerton Leonard, 12
Walker, Stephen, 18
Wallington Hall (Northumberland), 71

Walmer Street Industrial Experiment, 38
Walton, John, 173, 177
Wandle, river, 9
Waterford, Lady, 105, 282
Waterhouse, Alfred, 309
Waterlow, Sydney, 280
Waterson, Merlin, 125
Watts, George Frederic, 65, 68–9, 84, 89, 98, 112, 120–1, 125–6, 131, 173, 309
Watts, Mrs G. F., 99
Webb, Beatrice (Potter), 14, 59, 257, 260–2, 263–5, 272, 301
Webb, Sidney, 260–2
welfare, 5, 11, 21, 24, 36, 153–4, 221–2, 235, Chapter 12 passim, 299–300, 315
Wentworth, Lady, 69
West Wickham Common (Bromley), 171
Westbury College Gatehouse (Bristol), 225
Westminster abbey, 19, 23, 215, 312
Westminster Union Workhouse, 99
Westminster, duke of, 193, 212–14, 220, 308–9
Whistler, James McNeill, 52
White Cross cottages (Southwark), 48, 283–4, 285
White, Elizabeth E. M., 7
Whitechapel Art Gallery, 92
Whitehall Houses, Southwark, 287–8
Whitney, Henry, 233
Wiener, Martin, 180
Wilcock, Ann A., 18
Wilkinson, Fanny Rollo, 105, 108–9
Williams, Clare, 16
Willsdon, Clare, 71
Wilson, Eliza, 120
Wimbledon, 29, 306
Winchester Cottages (Southwark), 286–7, 289

Index

Winster Market House (Derbyshire), 224
Winter Hill (near Bolton), 177
Winter, James H., 16
Wisbech Society and Preservation Trust, 20
Wisbech (Cambs.), 20, 21, 27, 28, 29
Witt, Sir Robert, 230
Wohl, Anthony, 11, 23, 291
Women's Liberal League of New South Wales, 88
Women's University Settlement, 4, 21

Wordsworth, William, 226, 236
Workhouse Girls' Aid Society, 267
Working Men's College (Bloomsbury), 35, 131
Working Women's College (Bloomsbury), 35
Wyclif, John, 225

Yonge, Charlotte, 100
Yorke, Harriet, 7, 222, 226, 227

Zetland, marquess of, 309

Lightning Source UK Ltd.
Milton Keynes UK
UKOW06n1300200316

270512UK00001B/8/P

9 781909 646001